WORDS OF PRAISE FOR
out of this world:
THE STORY OF ZOLAR X®
***

"I first found out about Zolar X when I was in high school. I found a copy of Rock Scene magazine that Lenny Kay put out. It had a photo of Zolar X in it and I thought *boy this is the most ridiculous looking band I've ever seen!* I didn't really relate to Glam rock at all. I had hippie hair like Black Sabbath.

I wondered if I would ever hear these guys, then years later I did hear them when I found a semi-bootleg album at Aquarius Records in San Francisco. I put it on and I'm like 'My God this is really good! It's like the missing link between Chrome and the Stooges'. So I bought a whole bunch of copies and gave them to my friends all over the world.

Then later on, I found out, through Chuck Nolan, that we could find Ygarr who had all the tapes and maybe somebody ought to resurrect this stuff and put it out and do it justice. So that's what we tried to do."

Jello Biafra, Alternative Tentacles Records and the infamous, former singer of the punk rock band, Dead Kennedys

WORDS OF PRAISE FOR
out of this world:
THE STORY OF ZOLAR X

***

"All the bands that came up when my first band Silverhead was arriving on the planet seemed to be inspired by the usual iconic artists like the Rolling Stones and the New York Dolls. Zolar X was literally from another planet. Their commitment to the Alien nation they became was absolute. I had and have enormous respect for them. Sustaining what they believed in and making great music is a tremendous equation in the world of Rock 'n' roll. X is for excellence."

The astonishing Marquis Michael Des Barres

***

"I was spellbound into the Outer Limits by Zolar X when I first saw them with Jello Biafra. Since that night I have been lost in space."

Ginger Coyote White Trash Debutantes / Punk Globe Magazine

***

"A lot of Punks moved into this building called the Canterbury which was near the Masque which was the hub of the Punk thing in L.A. Everyone moved there including me. I had just moved from Phoenix, early '78 and met this weird guy on the 4th floor who had a Les Paul who always played it really loud. He had these giant amps in his room. And that was Ygarr. I remembered him from Zolar X who was this weird, kitschy legend. I thought he was really cool and weirdly a hero to me. He was a great, fucking guitar player and so we got to be friends."

Don Bolles, American drummer involved in the 1970s and 1980s punk scene in Los Angeles, DJ, writer, punk rock historian

***

"After Zolar X played, I sat in the balcony, nervous as hell as the band members showed up one by one to hang out with their friends. Ygarr caught me staring at his beautiful space suit, alien hairdo, and antennae. It wasn't like a costume, it looked like he LIVED the part! So I was rather intimidated by his larger-than-life persona. But for some inexplicable reason, he walked right over to me, put out his hand, and said "Hi, I'm Ygarr—did you see our set?" I was so star struck I could barely blurt out: "Yeah, that was a mind-boggling show! How do you do all that? I'm a musician too, my name is Geza X."

Geza X, American producer and Punk pioneer during the Los Angeles scene of the 1970s and 1980s

***

"Long ago, I saw flashing lights and laser beams arc across the musical sky. When I got closer to the source, I ventured inside their mysterious craft. I experienced a Whole New World that no Earthling had ever seen before!"

Brian Kehew, Los Angeles-based musician, record producer and co-author of the Recording The Beatles

***

"Out of This World, the Story of Zolar X, is a compelling, first-hand tale sharing the history of the extremely unique, talented, and visually engaging musical group, Zolar X.

The first-hand recounting of their exploits is recalled in vivid and entertaining detail, which immediately draws you in, and makes it difficult to stop reading. I strongly recommend this book and encourage you to check out their music as well. It will be time well spent."

Bill Billard, PNX News

***

"I finished the book last night, an absolutely fantastic read! I couldn't put it down, and it was great that Ygarr included his punk days in the Spys.

I was transported back to the 70s. I could really feel the atmosphere and vibe of Hollywood – it was like watching a movie. Top stuff!"

Wes Tough, Punk Rock Fanatic / Collector

***

"Zolar X are back from the future to refuel our imagination and fill our hearts with "Space Age Love"! I'm so glad I had a role in their return. Sonic and visual pioneers, they influenced many from Van Halen to Kiss.

As a musician, costume designer and music historian, I have seen their look pop up in many unexpected places. Stay tuned and let's see what kind of adventures visionary Ygarr Ygarrist and Zolar X lead us on in the future!"

Onwards, upwards and beyond… Tony Mann, New York City

***

"Zolar X: Glam Rock's Forgotten Pioneers

Rock 'n' roll failures are often more interesting than the successes, and it's clear that Zolar X have unfinished business."

Ben Myers, an English writer and journalist

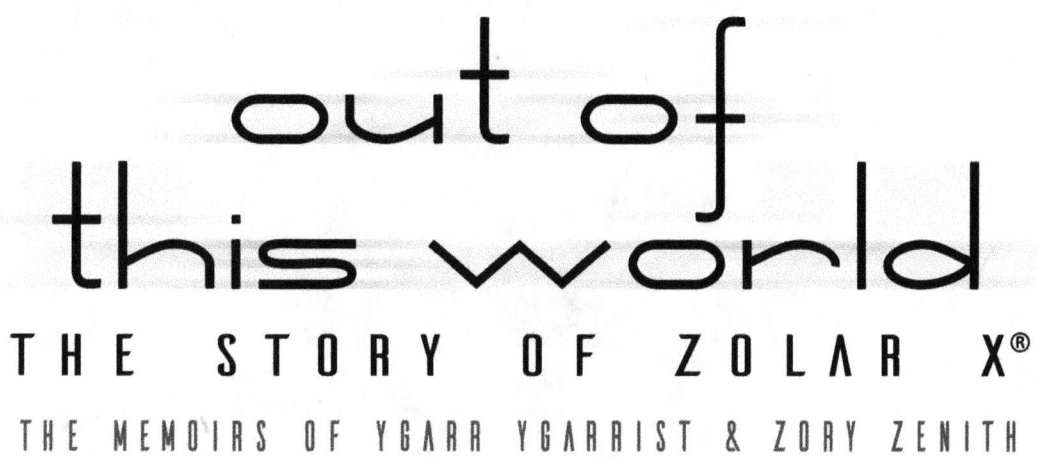

out of this world
THE STORY OF ZOLAR X®
THE MEMOIRS OF YGARR YGARRIST & ZORY ZENITH

ISBN Print/Softcover: 978-1-7353676-8-2

Copyright ©2016, ©2020, ©2022 by Ygarr Ygarrist, aka Stephen Della Bosca; Zory Zenith, aka George William Myers; Raidii X, aka Rhaine Della Bosca.

All rights reserved. No part of this book may be used or reproduced in any manner whatsoever without written permission except in the case of brief quotations embodied in critical articles or reviews.

FIRST EDITION

For my sister Zoann Abel
Artist ... Angel ... Zolar X's biggest fan

Your star burns brightly in the universe.

For Charlie Patton
Visionary ... Dot-connecter... Life Support

You were more than a friend, and kept us afloat. You believed!

ABOUT THE AUTHORS

Raidii X and Ygarr Ygarrist

Ygarr Ygarrist and Zory Zenith are lyricists, poets, writers in a world of sound, crafting fresh meaning with words and notes. Raidii X, a modern-day Renaissance woman has an extensive background in the arts, from creative writing and music to the visual arts.

The husband-wife team, Ygarr and Raidii, have a knack for creative projects and finishing them. This is a group of multi-talented individuals that chose to go forward in a world of art and music throwing out convention and rules, making it their universe. After all, this is the anthem and mantra of all things Zolar X.

Through memory, audio recordings and putting pen to paper, they have crafted a glimpse inside another space and time, a place where the experience of life outweighs the idea of life and where otherworldly visions become a real thing.

Get ready to blast off.

Zory Zenith

out of this world
THE STORY OF ZOLAR X

Told by Ygarr Ygarrist, Zory Zenith, & Raidii X

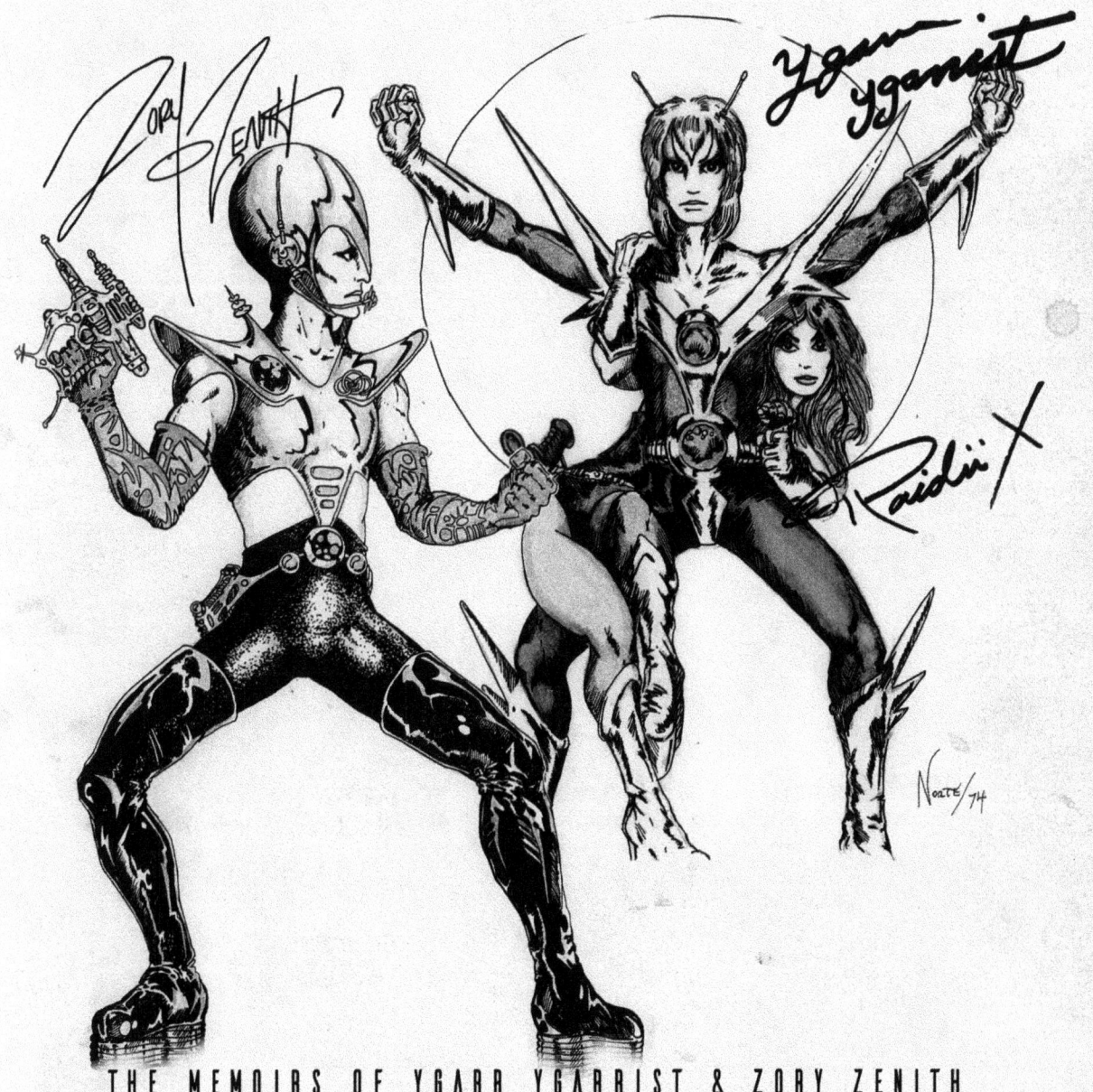

THE MEMOIRS OF YGARR YGARRIST & ZORY ZENITH

ACKNOWLEDGEMENTS

The idea of writing a Zolar X book was easy, the steps in creating it were something else. We thank all the generous humans who contributed their time, efforts and expertise to make the vapors of the idea become a concrete, physical reality.

Chris Walter - Editor *Ou*

Michael Essington - Editor *Tay*

Bill Billard - Dot Connector *Komata*

Brian Kehew - Pathfinder *Oogma*

Photo credits:

- Jim Williams - front cover

- Buddy Rosenberg - Part 1 photo of Zolar X

- John Tremblay - Part 2 photo of Zolar X

- Jerry DeWilde - back cover

Art credit-drawing of Zolar X: X-Etron, aka Armando Norte

Layout and design: Raidii X

Table of Contents

ABOUT THE AUTHORS	viii
ACKNOWLEDGEMENTS	xi
INTRODUCTION	xvii
DON'T FUCK WITH MY ANTENNAS	1
STRIP CLUB NIGHTS	5
HAIRCUTS & ATTITUDES	9
PAUL McCARTNEY'S COUSIN	15
THE BIG MOVE	19
PREDESTINATION AT THE DISCO	23
HOTSHOTS	27
LOOKOUT MOUNTAIN	29
THE RAINBOW	31
THANKS, MR. SPOCK	35
ZOLARIZED	39
THE ASSIGNMENT	43
LOS ANGELES	45
INSIDE THE "X"	49
LIGHTS CAMERA ACTION	53
WORK AND LOTS OF PLAY	57
THE BOOMERANG INCIDENT	61
CUTE SHORT AND SKINNY	65
X MARKS THE SPOT	67
HOLLYWOOD QUACK	69
PARTY AT DRESS REVIEW	71
LITTLE GREEN PILLS	75
GARY "DALLAS" FONTENOT	77
400 LIGHT-YEARS FROM HOME	81
STAR GIRLS	83
RODNEY'S ENGLISH DISCO	85
ALIEN VISIONS	89
THE VISIT	93
WINDS OF CHANGE	97
HOUDINI	101
ALIENS IN SUBURBIA	103
TICKLED PINK	107
CALM BEFORE THE STORM	109
LET THEM EAT CAKE	113

PICKLED HERRING, CAPERS, AND BEETS	117
ZOLAR DIY	123
HAPPY BIRTHDAY YGARR	127
STRIKE TWO	131
ZOLAR X LANDS	139
PRESENCE OF AUTHORITY	147
ZOLAR'S WORKSHOP	155
DIDN'T SEE IT COMING.	157
THE VILLAGE GIG	161
HIGHLAND BUNGALOW	165
KISS MY…	171
ASTRO TOTS	175
LIES OF THE WOOD	179
CHARLIE PATTON	185
MY FAVORITE MARTIAN	187
TIGHTS, CAMERA, ACTION!	189
TO BE OR NOT TO BE!	191
CRYSTAL STUDIOS	193
PARTY POISON	199
TOM SNYDER	203
DEAD TIME	205
STEVE BINDER	209
JAMMING WITH THUNDER	211
THE TROUBADOUR SHOW	215
SWAN SONG	219
SIXTH FINGER	223
FILLING THE VOID	229
BILL AUCOIN	231
BULLET WITH NO NAME	233
REFLECTIONS.	235
HUNG OUT TO DRY	237
NEW YORK NEW YORK	247
BROKEN.	251
THE SPACERZ	255
SOMETHING'S MISSING	259
FREEDOM	261
MEMPHIS – ROUND TWO	265
ARDENT STUDIOS	269

REDEMPTION	273
BACK IN HOLLYWOOD	277
RHINESTONES FOR SAFETY PINS	279
SMILE AND SAY MOON CHEESE	281
SPACE SOAP	283
MABUHAY GARDENS	287
HIATUS	291
ROCK BOTTOM	293
THE AURORA PUSHUPS	299
ROOFTOP POETRY	301
INITIATION	303
FORTRESS	307
WHAT'S IN A NAME?	309
THE EARTHLINGS	311
THE WRITING'S ON THE WALL	313
THE CANTERBURY	317
THE SPYS RECORD	323
QUICKSAND	325
JET STAR 19	327
THE CADILLAC IS BUCKLING	331
PREAMBLE TO A NIGHTMARE	333
27 DAYS	337
CLIMBING OUT OF THE SHITHOLE	341
BUYER'S REMORSE	345
PONG	347
THE POWER OF THREE	351
SERMON AT THE FAB MAB	353
DESERTION	355
COMMITMENT	359
LEAP OF CONVICTION	365
DESTINATIONS	367
LEAKING SECRETS	371
LEGACY	373
CONTINUING MISSION: 1983 - ?	379
CONVERSATIONAL ZOLARIAN FOR COSMIC TRAVELERS	393

INTRODUCTION

It was 2012 on a Sunday and Raidii and I were having zakoo (coffee). Looking back, it's strange how something so small and benign could have so much power but there it was - yet another post by a well-meaning fan about Zolar X that was a diluted, half-truth. That small, 20-something smattering of words was what slid the scale. It was the tipping point. Until that moment we had been holding back the yarns, the nuggets, the pictures that not only showed but told the first-hand accounts of what it was really like to have lived the Zolar X lifestyle 24/7 in the 1970s.

Zory was en route from Oregon and would be staying for a week so besides catching up, recording music, and doing some photography, we decided we could also set up the microphone and record audio. We would capture the stories, the accounts, and histories of Ygarr Ygarrist and Zory Zenith and write a book. It would be the full, complete story to the best of our ability and we would tell it with the all the quirks and craziness found on another world, and with the gut-wrenching honesty that would make a human gasp, groan and exclaim, "Holy shit! Who"d-have-thunk-it?"

Since that fateful Sunday, ten years later, we ended up with over 12 hours of audio recordings of the three of us, hashing out dates, timelines, comparisons, and yarns. Much of the audio was transcribed and would become gold as we dove deeper into the unraveling of how it went down so many decades ago using Ygarr and Zory's actual words in the telling.

There's only one 'Bot, Zory Zenith, one Plutonian Elf, Ygarr Ygarrist, and one Raidii X. And through all its incarnations and ups and downs, there is only one Zolar X.

Strap in and prepare human, for warp speed.

We look forward in communications.

Ygarr Ygarrist

Zory Zenith

Raidii X

PART 1

supernova

1972 TO 1975

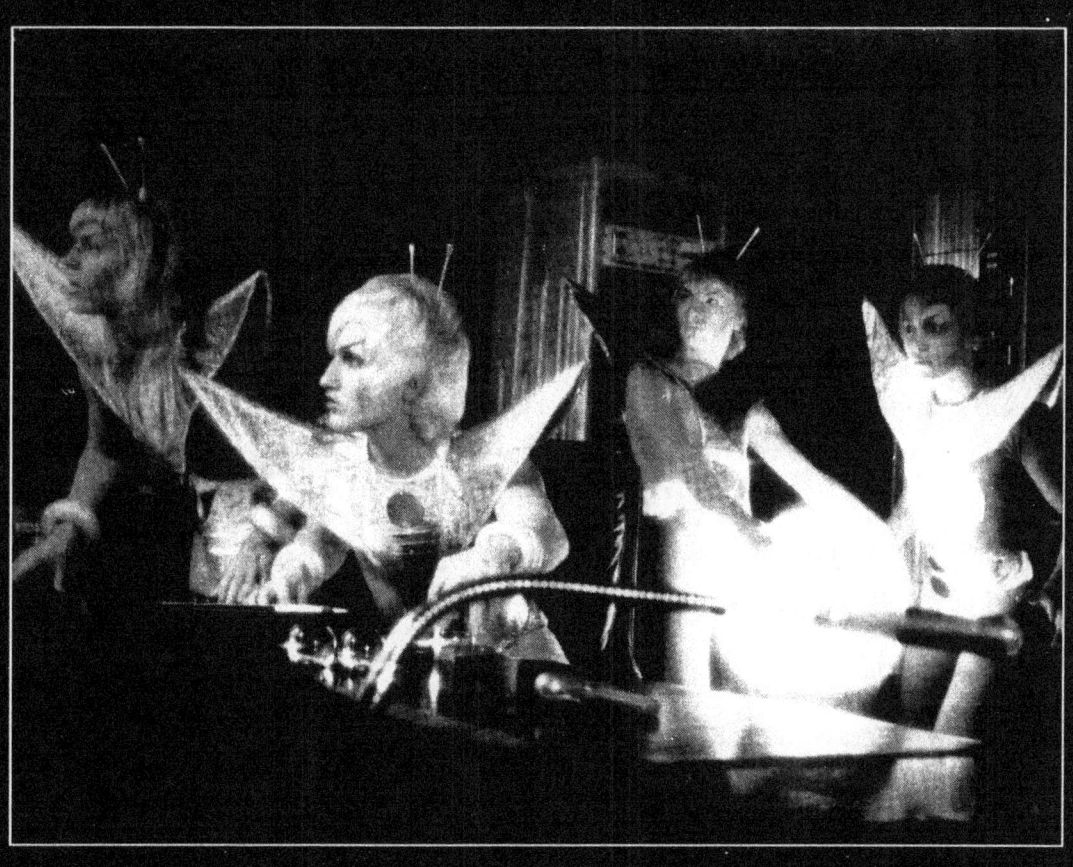

1

DON'T FUCK WITH MY ANTENNAS
HOLLYWOOD - JULY 1974

The band was all dressed up and ready for the Rainbow. Eager to represent, we were looking sharp in our colored tights, silver donuts, space boots, the regular stuff. For this occasion, we were even wearing our antennas. Everyone was feeling good, and the band was in a mood to celebrate because we'd just been given a week-long engagement at the Troubadour supporting Jobriath. Things were finally moving along for Zolar X.

Before the show, we'd decided to grab some dinner and drinks with two girlfriends, Syndee and Veonity. We parked near the 9000 Sunset Building and made our way towards the 'Bo on foot. Two attractive young girls, dressed to kill and swinging their hips like Marilyn Monroe, started chatting with us. I didn't see the harm in flirting back, but I can see now how that might have been a mistake.

I felt a sharp thump on my back and heard a screaming, hysterical voice. "Stop it, Ygarr! You bitches leave him alone! He's mine!"

"Fuck, Syndee! Calm down!" I said, even though that has never worked in the history of time.

But Syndee was on a roll, plus she was high as fuck. Still screaming, she flailed her arms and stomped her feet. "You think I don't know about all your fucking around? I have connections! Do you think any of these sluts are going to take you to dinner and foot the bill?"

"Shit, I told you I didn't want you to come with us tonight, but here you are!" I shouted, suspecting the worst was yet to come.

"I'll fix you!" she yelled, grabbing at my antennae.

"Fuck, don't mess with my antennas, bitch!"

Syndee's eyes blazed furiously. She went for me again and somehow managed to get her hands on them. In a flash, she yanked my antennas off my head and threw them to the ground.

My feelers lay mangled on the sidewalk. I'd had enough. "You can mess with my tights, and you can break my guitar strings, but don't fuck with my damn antennas!" I said, royally pissed. "Get fucking lost. I don't wanna see you tonight. Go home to your rich daddy!"

Amazingly, Syndee did as she was told and stomped away, still hurling angry swear words as she stormed down the sidewalk. She could be a real handful.

"Sorry you guys had to witness that," I said, turning to the band apologetically. In truth, they'd seen many similar scenes. Syndee had a flair for drama.

"Fuck, Ygarr," said Zory, our singer. "That was so entertaining it was like watching a movie! I wonder what the onlookers thought of your show? We have a bit of a crowd!"

I looked over and saw about 20 people watching from across the street. Scooping my silver antenna from the sidewalk, I was amazed to see they weren't seriously damaged. I walked over to the reflective windows of the 9000 Building and angrily straightened a few minor kinks before putting them back on my head. We went for dinner and then to the Rainbow for a wonderful evening without Syndee.

I didn't feel too bad the next day considering we didn't get home until the sun was coming up. The phone rang and I glanced at the clock. "Hello?" I said, picking up the receiver. It was nearly 2:00 p.m. already.

"Hi, Ygarr. Sorry about last night. I was stoned. Do you forgive me? Did I break your antennas?"

"Syndee? What the fuck do you want?"

In one long frantic breath, she said, "You've got to come down to SIR Studios right away. I've been partying with the New York Dolls all night. If you hurry, you can meet them. I think you'd like this band. They wear makeup too! They've even heard of Zolar X. Just forget about last night. They're going to be playing at the Whisky and the Roxy. I'll pay for everything, but you've got to get down here right now! Grab a cab and I'll meet you out front. Love you!"

I was pissed off and a little jealous that she'd been partying with another rock band all night. What the fuck had she been up to?

Like lightning, I got Zolarized and started walking down Santa Monica Boulevard East, looking for a taxi or a bus. Within fifteen minutes I was at SIR, where I found the Dolls puttering around their studio room. Unfortunately, I'd just missed their rehearsal. Syndee introduced us, and they looked more British than American. Their clothes were definitely from London, and they were better-looking men without makeup than KISS were without theirs by far. Their platform shoes had to be at least four inches high, so there was a bit of glitter/glam in them. That wasn't surprising since glam was the glue holding the new music together. My first impression of the Dolls was that they were Zolar X contemporaries in the time zone of now. They seemed friendly, but there was an ego, an arrogance about them. I didn't like it, but I understood because I knew my ego could be fairly thick. Any musician in another band was the competition.

I felt a slight but distinct animosity when I shook hands with the Dolls. Sylvain Sylvain and David Johansen were like, "How ya doing?" Jerry Nolan was a little friendlier, and I could see he had a good buzz happening. Johnny Thunders was cool, possibly because we were both guitarists. But Arthur Kane? It was hard to tell what he was thinking, but he seemed to be intrigued by our outfits.

These guys were hardcore rockers from the streets of New York—signed with an album out. Yeah, I was pissed. I'd heard their album. There was nothing progressive about it, just simple bar chords, yet I liked it. They had attitude and I was fucking jealous.

All in all, it was nice meeting them, but I was ready to get out of there before long. I didn't need to be reminded that Zolar X still hadn't found a record deal.

As we were getting in her car, Syndee said, "Don't you just love 'em? Aren't they cool? They gave me tickets to their show."

OUT OF THIS WORLD: THE STORY OF ZOLAR X

2
STRIP CLUB NIGHTS
SAN FRANCISCO - 1972

Richard Nixon was president, and everyone was yapping about the Watergate scandal. The ridiculous Vietnam War was still going on, but I'd been lucky enough to escape the draft. Apollo 17 was the next planned moon mission, and gasoline was fifty-five cents a gallon. Led Zeppelin was the number one band on the planet, and the Rolling Stones were touring again. The Beatles, on the other hand, had broken up over a year ago. Protesters, hippies, and pot smokers were everywhere, all of them wearing bell-bottoms and miniskirts.

My name is Stephen Della Bosca. I was twenty years old and living in my third apartment, located at 2112 Green Street in San Francisco. My job was playing music at the Garden of Eden strip club with my band Bosca, but we'd changed our name to Gilded Flesh for the club gig. Although I'd grown a mustache to look older, Bob the owner said he didn't give a shit if I was twenty-one or not, but I'd have to look the part when the cops dropped in. We played behind curtains five hours a night, five nights a week, providing backing music for the strippers. We'd been doing the gig for six months. It was by far the best job I'd ever had.

The club was so successful that Bob closed the place one weekend and told the entire staff—including the band and the strippers—that he was taking us to Las Vegas for a two-day vacation, all expenses paid. We flew to LAX for a connecting flight to Vegas but learned upon arrival that we'd missed the flight. Not to be deterred, crazy Bob negotiated with the owner of an eleven-seat Lear jet to fly all seventeen of us to our destination. We were crammed in there like sand in a shoe, but it wasn't so bad because a stripper sat on my lap with her big tits in my face. There were worse ways to travel.

That was all fine and everything, but then the pilot let Bob take the controls, which scared the shit out of everyone and destroyed the buzz I'd been trying to build. "We're all gonna die!" piped the terrified stripper on my lap, clutching my arm tightly. Luckily, the pilot took over after several tense minutes and we landed safely in Vegas.

At the hotel, Bob booked six rooms and told us to make our sleeping arrangements, which meant we'd have to bunk up. We ate at a fine Italian restaurant and a limousine picked us up afterwards and took us to the casino. Since I couldn't drink or gamble legally, I spent a good chunk of time back at the hotel fucking strippers and ordering room service. Again, things could have been worse.

Back in San Francisco, everything was business as usual. Our world was the strip club, and we smoked pot on a rear fire escape we called the "balcony". The Garden of Eden was the only strip club in the City with a live rock band. Customers told us we were really good. One night a man wondered why we didn't open the curtains so they could see the band. I told him, "You're here to see the pussy, not us."

The glow of the lights behind the curtains was barely bright enough for us to see our instruments. I was at the left, on the narrowest part of the stage. The strippers had to pass me to enter the stage, so I came to know them all. They'd request the song they wanted, then slip through the slit in the curtain onto the stage. The curtain was thin enough so we could see them dance. Night after night, the girls brushed past me, their bare flesh teasing mine. I even created an instrumental piece "The Naked Dance of Seduction" for the finale, in which husband-and-wife team, Billy and Sasha, fucked onstage.

As good as it was, as great as it sounds, the gig eventually became tedious. I found myself getting bored playing cover tunes. The band didn't seem to be getting anywhere. Our drummer Gary and bass player Kevin managed to fall in love with two strippers. My little brother Kevin began shooting heroin, which didn't impress anyone. Gary's stripper/girlfriend became pregnant. It was a bit of a shit show.

Ed Dorn (vocals/organ) and I were getting fed up. To break away from the club periodically, we took in a movie or went antiquing at La Salle's gallery on Union Street. We must have seen *Clockwork Orange* and *Slaughterhouse Five* at least three times on acid, but we always returned to the reality of our world. We weren't playing the new, original music I'd been writing like "Moonbeam" or "Nativity". Those melodies were so much more than just simple Rock 'n' roll. We weren't recording either, and for me, the end of the band was in sight. I wanted more from my musical career than meaningless gigs at strip clubs. I'd also been dealing with chronic pain in my right side for more than a decade. The doctors were confounded.

Inevitably, the band fell apart. I moved back to Newark in the East Bay with my mom, and Ed went back to his mom's in Fremont. We weren't quite responsible enough to hold things together in the big city. Gary and his pregnant, ex-stripper girlfriend also relocated to Fremont. I didn't miss the Garden of Eden and the boatloads of free booze, but the steady paycheck and the stream of carefree sex was harder to let go. I was young, remember?

The Garden of Eden - L to R: Ed Dorn, Assorted humans and strippers
San Francisco, CA, 1971
Photographer unknown, photo courtesy of Ed Dorn

The band, Bosca - L to R: Gary McDaris, Ed Dorn, Stephen Della Bosca, Kevin Bodenhammer
Golden Gate Park, San Francisco, CA, 1971
Photo credit: Jeff Austin

3

HAIRCUTS & ATTITUDES
SAN FRANCISCO - 1972

My time in San Francisco was an extreme experience. Kevin elected to stay and got so strung out that he had to quit the band. I missed my little brother, but the show had to go on. To address my problems, I had exploratory surgery and they eventually removed my appendix. No more pain.

Secondly, I began searching for a new bass player. Then my friend, Jeff Austin, told me about a bassist from Hayward who was in-between bands. Jeff said the guy would be at a party on the weekend, so we set off to see him when Friday rolled around. At the party, the muffled but unmistakable sounds of live music emanated from the garage.

Inside the house, Diane the hostess pointed to the garage entrance and said, "Booty's in there if you want to meet him."

"Who's Booty?" I asked.

"He's the one you're here to meet. He's the best bass player in the Bay Area."

We walked into the garage where a four-piece band was rocking out. They weren't the best band I'd ever heard, but they had some talent, especially the bass player. I could see he was a typical longhair, but the fucker could play. His style combined arpeggio fragments with classical bottom signatures. Very progressive.

During a break, Jeff motioned him over. "Stephen, this is Bruce, but everyone calls him Booty."

We discussed our influences and I immediately felt a bond – a shared vision. Booty was influenced by Pink Floyd and Chris Squire of Yes, whereas I preferred Hendrix and Led Zeppelin. I countered his Beatles with my Stones, and his Yes to my Yardbirds. We both liked Beethoven and Mozart, and we shared a mutual admiration for Picasso, Van Gogh, da Vinci, Stanley Kubrick, Ray Bradbury, and comic maven Stan Lee.

Booty and I began spending time together, sharing musical ideas, and formulating them into songs, either at his parents' apartment or at my mom's house. We both felt the next evolution in music would be very futuristic. It got us thinking when we realized that *Star Trek* was our favorite television show.

Meeting Booty, everything began to change: visually, musically, but mainly our attitude. The identity of the new band was evolving into something totally unique, and there was no way Bosca could have continued, even though we kept Gary on drums and Ed on keyboards. A new chapter was about to begin.

One of the challenges was to present the new band in a new and exciting way. I didn't think it would be too tough because I'd always been ahead of the curve in suburbia, and I was the first kid in my school to have long hair. I was a cool dresser and considered myself a fashion trendsetter with an English Mod style. Sporting velvet shirts with ruffles, knee-high boots, sexy see-through women's tops, and bitchin' pants my sister had modeled after Mick Jagger's trousers, I was the coolest kid around. Now, at this place in life, I found myself ahead of the curve again. I was thinking no mustaches, no Pendleton shirts, no ripped Levi's or bell-bottoms, and no more damned San Francisco hippie long-hair look. I wanted something bold and new.

With those thoughts, I called upon my sister Zoann, a professional hairstylist, and asked her to give me a futuristic style. In traditional English rock style, my shoulder-length hair was light brown with no bangs, but she gave me a shagged, layered cut before giving me three jagged points for bangs—two small ones on each side of a larger one in the middle. It was…different.

I looked in the mirror and said, "Get rid of the two points on the sides but leave the big point in the middle."

Zoann did as I asked before adding some intense blond streaks. "This is really futuristic!" I said happily. "I have to call Booty!" I got on the phone. "Booty, you've gotta see my new haircut and color! You're not going to believe it! I have pointed bangs and blond streaks all over. It looks really spacey. You have to do it too!"

The space-age haircuts sparked something extraordinary—they changed us. Our new hairstyles allowed us to discard old-fashioned ideas and constraints. The floodgates were open and a new dawn had begun.

Now, all we had to do was write some music that was totally different from anything that had been done before. Booty and I got started and the songs began to flow. We wrote original music and left the covers for other bands. When I was studying guitar and beginning to write my own songs, the first few ideas had been based mostly on British Rock 'n' roll influences. Clapton, Beck, and Page were a big part of that, and so was my favorite songwriter, John Lennon. Now Booty and I were influencing each other. Although our music was brand new, we were becoming individual composers with separate identities.

At one of our first rehearsals, we began working on a song with a very ballsy rhythm and a bitching melody I called "Space Age Love". Ed was the main lyricist and lead vocalist in Bosca, so I decided to give him a shot. "Hey Ed, do you wanna write some lyrics for this puppy, or do you want me to do the honors?"

Ed said, "I'll take a crack at it. 'Space Age Love', huh?"

A few days later he said, "Hey Steve, do you wanna hear what I came up with for the first verse?"

"Hell yeah, I want to hear it!"

We don't give a damn what your parents say
Cause we're out in space, light years away
Far from the earth and its moon above
Ready to ignite space age love

I was impressed. "I love it! Are you going to finish the song?"

"Yeah, I'm gonna try."

"Cool! I'm really loving the direction of these new songs."

"Me too."

It was like spontaneous combustion, and the melodies continued to flow. Booty wrote a progressive musical arrangement that was very cool. The classical bass patterns that sounded like cellos were phenomenal. I added an intro by taking a section he'd written, slowing it down, and inverting the singular notes into a drone with chords. With the new intro, the song became majestic. I thought, *Wow! This is really cool!* We called it "Parallel Galaxy". This was the birth of space symphony.

Ed and Gary loved the progressive melodies Booty and I were writing, but they wouldn't hop on the haircut bandwagon. They both had dark hair and still looked like English mods. And that was okay because we were concentrating on the music. For the time being.

With two new haircuts and two new songs, it was time to name the band. It was

October 1972, Booty had just turned 20 and in a month, I'd be 21. Ed was the only one of us with a car: a dull gray '54 Cadillac. The massive boat was a great place for the three of us to turn on our imaginations and get away from the chaos of normal life. We cruised the East Bay area with no destination in mind, talking about planets in the solar system, the names of stars, and solar constellations. I rode in the front passenger seat, Booty sat in the back, and Ed was driving. Quiet and stoic, Ed didn't add much to the conversation, but we knew he'd speak up if he heard something. We were on a mission.

Out of nowhere, Booty said, "I like the Uninhibited."

We ignored him. Not spacey enough. I'd always loved the letters X, Y, and Z, and gazing into the starry sky was like turning on a light bulb. "What about Zolar X?" I said. "It has a celestial ring to it." I can still see and smell that memory.

Booty leaned forward through Ed's cigarette smoke and said, "How about Zolar X and the Uninhibited?"

"Let's just go with Zolar X and fuck that Uninhibited shit!" I said, making everyone laugh.

Ed smiled and nodded "That's it!"

It was time to upgrade our equipment, so I traded my '62 Fender Brownface Pro amplifier and Gibson Echo plus some cash for a new 100-watt Hiwatt stack and Echoplex. I already had four fine guitars, so I didn't need more. Booty swapped his Fender Precision bass and amp for a Danelectro Longhorn bass and an Ampeg head with two 8 x 10 cabinets. Gary declined. He kept his double set of hand-painted Ludwigs. He was kind of like a member, but I didn't see him being there at the finish line. Then there was Ed with his Hammond organ and Leslie speaker. I knew I'd have to talk to him about that. Synthesizers were the future, and Hammonds were the past.

I decided not to hold off any longer. I looked Ed square in the eye and said, "In my brain, I'm hearing French horns, flying saucers, violins, and photon torpedoes to go with our new songs, and your Hammond organ just ain't cutting it! You love this music and you want to make it great, so why not go all the way? Maybe you don't want to streak your hair blond and get it cut spacey, but surely you want us to sound good, right?"

"Shit Steve, I'd love to get a Minimoog, but I don't have a thousand bucks!"

Money was always a consideration. "Can't you get it on credit or trade in the organ?

That Hammond is such a monstrosity!"

"I don't have any credit."

"What about your mom?"

"Shit, my dad won't let her help me!"

Ed kept the Hammond.

I received a call from my friend Karen on the afternoon of October 27, 1972. She was yapping about some weird spaceman and was a bit hard to follow. She finally told me, "There's a band coming to Winterland – a spacey band like you guys want to be. His name is David Bowie."

I said, "Shit! That doesn't sound very spacey!"

"But his new album is called *Ziggy Stardust and the Spiders from Mars*."

"You gotta be kidding! We have to see this!"

On the night of the show, Booty, Gary, and I piled into Ed's big gray Cadillac. The first show was only half-full, so we were able to walk right up to the stage. Mick Ronson was superb, and his ballsy Marshall rhythms and one-note sustained leads were out of this world. For a moment, I wondered if maybe I should have bought a Marshall instead of a Hiwatt, but then I realized I had to be unique. Mick had his sound and I had my own.

The show was so great. Stage lights illuminated the top of Woody Woodmansey's platinum blond head, and I could see this was the direction we needed to go with our hair. What can I say about David Bowie? His songs, his voice, and his makeup were outrageous and so inspiring. For me, everything up to this point had been about learning. I'd been paying my dues with school, my high school bands, and the strip club band. Now it was time to take our band into the world and see what we could do. After watching David Bowie at Winterland, I knew Zolar X was definitely on the right track. We went back the next night to make sure.

The band spent the rest of '72 rehearsing at my mom's house, working on musical ideas and making plans for the future. We could hardly wait for the world to get a load of us.

L to R: Stephen Della Bosca, Zoann
San Francisco Bay Area, CA, 1972
Photo credit: Bobbie Minor

L to R: Bruce Allen Courtois (Booty), Stephen Della Bosca
San Francisco Bay Area, CA, 1972
Photo credit: Jeff Austin

L to R: Ed Dorn, Stephen Della Bosca, Bruce Allen Courtois (Booty) and friends at a party,
San Francisco Bay Area, CA, 1972
Photo credit: Jeff Austin

Stephen Della Bosca
San Francisco Bay Area, CA, 1973
Photo credit: Jeff Austin

4

PAUL McCARTNEY'S COUSIN
LOS ANGELES - 1972

ZORY GLORY

Ethics have never existed in Hollywood, and the idea of changing one's persona is nothing new. In fact, Hollywood is still the place to re-invent yourself. With that firmly in mind, I adopted an English accent, legally changed my name from Billy Myers to Billy McCartney, and began promoting myself as Paul McCartney's cousin. I even used my graphic and artistic skills to create a side-by-side picture of me and my "Cousin Paul". It was easy.

I quickly landed a sponsorship deal with Jordon Electronics, the same company that sponsored the Doors. They gave me roughly $10,000 worth of equipment with no questions asked. I was still living with my mom and dad, and there was so much stuff it wouldn't fit into my bedroom. Sadly, however, Jordon's soon got wise. A representative dropped by to see how the band was doing, but there was no band. It was just me in my little Beatles haircut and fake British accent. They made me give all the equipment back. I was bummed, but life went on.

A few months later, I auditioned for the drummer spot in a rock band Shady Lady. I tried to pull the "Paul's cousin" act on them, but they weren't buying. The singer looked at me doubtfully and said, "Oh, come on, man. Talk normal and quit this crap." He didn't need the Internet to know I was full of shit.

"Fuck you!" I said, embarrassed to have been found out. These guys were a bunch of scammers and thieves from New York City, and you'd have to be really good to pull anything over on them. We all laughed and then I was in the band. I guess they appreciated my effort.

The Los Angeles scene was all torn-up jeans, bell-bottoms, suede vests with fringes, handlebar mustaches, long straggly hair, and round granny glasses. John Denver's "Rocky Mountain High" had continuous play on the airwaves, and Carole King had nabbed every damn Grammy in sight. The hippie thing was fucking boring.

As you can guess, I wasn't on that train. I was into the Rolling Stones, having seen them at the Forum in '69. I'd also seen the Beatles in '66 at Dodger's Stadium, and my fashion sense was heavily influenced by the first wave of British rock music. As far as I knew, the only other people wearing "fem" stuff like eyeliner, velvet suits, and high-heeled boots were Alice Cooper, T Rex, and my new band Shady Lady. I loved the style of the Who and Elvis Presley with his bejeweled jumpsuits. This whole new way of dressing was just starting to happen, but at the time there were only a few people in the underground who had the balls to adopt the look on a full-time basis. It helped to be fleet of foot.

We began recording our debut album at the Record Plant West in Los Angeles. Our engineer Malcolm Cecil had programmed Stevie Wonder's synthesizer, so it felt like the big time to me. After a session, I saw Steven Stills finishing up in another vocal booth. I thought, *this guy is huge and I'm in the same studio!* How cool was that?

Then I saw they were setting up the banquet room for a big party. They had twelve-foot tables loaded with shrimp cocktail, meats, cheeses, champagne, and caviar. Silver goblets at the end of each table contained neatly rolled joints. Rock star life.

On the other side of the room, I saw a cute bleached-blonde chick with a China doll haircut. She wore the rich satins and velvets I'd seen at the Rainbow and definitely had a look going on. I'd seen her before, but we'd never really talked because she was always with a guy, and I have radar for that sort of thing. I never went out of my way to pick up chicks. I'd just stand there and try to look approachable. Isn't it more captivating and mysterious if you're not one of the run-of-the-mill dumbbells hitting on all the girls? It's better to stand in the corner and let your clothes do the talking.

Having partaken generously of the champagne, I was munching a pastrami sandwich with spicy mustard when the pretty girl grabbed four joints from one of the goblets and walked over to me. Looking all mysterious and sexy, she lit one and passed it over. Twenty minutes later, I was so baked that I passed out in a drum booth. I remembered her name was Kitty but the rest of the night was a total blank. I'd like to tell you that never happened again, but apprentice rock stars live crazy lives.

Everything was great, and our manager Robert Fitzpatrick set us up in a rambling mansion in the star-studded Hollywood Hills. Teenage groupies in tiny bikinis hung out every day and the sun shone brightly. With all the alcohol and dope around, they clearly thought we were the next big thing. When the girls weren't in the pool you could find them in one of the many bedrooms. Just about anything can happen in Hollywood.

My best friend in Shady Lady, bassist Gerhard Helmut, was banging some chick that lived at Wolfman Jack's house. Gerhard came home one day and said in his thick

Austrian accent, "I have tickets to a David Bowie concert at the Santa Monica Civic. He's from England. Do you want to come?"

I didn't have anything else to do so I said, "Concert? Yeah, sure. Why not."

A few weeks ago, I'd seen a small black-and-white photo of some guy with spiky hair, satin pants, and white lace-up boots in *Rolling Stone*. I thought he was a ballet star. The caption identified him as David Bowie.

Shady Lady were never out of costume, so naturally, I looked my frilly best at the Bowie concert. I wore a three-piece Lurex suit with just my vest and no shirt, and a silver cord strung with miniature plastic eight balls adorned my bare chest. I also boasted full makeup and an almost identical copy of the floppy red velvet newsboy cap Mick Jagger wore in *Gimme Shelter*. I rounded out this stunning ensemble with high-heeled silver boots trimmed in black velvet. It was my duty to represent the band, and I took the job seriously.

I had no idea what was about to happen. I still had that black-and-white image of Bowie from *Rolling Stone* floating around in my mind, and there he was in full color and sound. His persona completely stunned and blew me away. Not only was Bowie the lead vocalist, but he also played an acoustic twelve-string guitar. With his shocking orange pompadour, he did a great job of channeling Elvis from another planet. Mick Ronson was awesome too, and the stage show was fantastic.

To top it off, Gerhard and I got invited to a party at Wolfman Jack's house in Bel Air after the show. He was throwing a party he for Bowie. I met up with Kitty again, and this time I didn't pass out anywhere. We began seeing each other on a casual basis.

I was so knocked out after seeing Bowie. A key went into the ignition switch in my head and opened a child's tickle trunk. The lid flipped open, and out came Gort from *The Day the Earth Stood Still* and Robbie the Robot from *Forbidden Planet*. A whole host of childhood memories of outer space, astronauts, and superheroes tumbled through my head. Caught up in a huge rush of futurism, I dyed my hair and styled it to look like Bowie's. I loved the romance and mysticism of the colors. Very glittery, silver, bright blue, bright purple, and bright lime green, my hair was completely against the grain of what was going on.

At the same time, it was becoming clear to me that I didn't belong behind a drum kit, so I made a commitment to go out on my own. I was sick of being a backing musician. Local lead singers looked like spastics to me, and I was sure I could do a better job. I had to find my road. My destiny had yet to be decided.

the Hollywood groupies. We talked a bit and they sucked down a couple of our beers. Their eyes swelled with anticipation when I pulled the Quaaludes from my pocket, and I immediately knew two things: Booty and I would get lucky tonight, and these girls were like puppies. They'd follow us anywhere.

Hollywood Sign
Wikimedia Commons https://commons.wikimedia.org/wiki/File:HollywoodSign.jpg

Hollywood Freeway
Wikimedia Commons https://commons.wikimedia.org/wiki/File:HollywoodSign.jpg

near Hollywood and Vine was $100 a month, utilities included. With two of us on Unemployment at seventy-five bucks a week, we felt rich. Cramming our equipment into the semi-furnished studio apartment with a single pull-out bed took the four of us an hour, tops. The place was too small for the four of us, but we didn't care. With our rock-star attitudes and kick-ass haircuts. We were ready to conquer the world.

After settling in a bit, Booty and I scoped the area for the best place to meet people and be seen. To the casual observer, we probably looked more glam than spacey. My new wardrobe included two custom made Italian jackets: a mid-thigh brown leather, and a full-length white canvas coat with cape. The jackets were special to me because they looked very futuristic and you couldn't get them anywhere. I loved the way the cuffs rolled back on the sleeves of the canvas coat. They reminded me of something elves might wear, and I began thinking of the jackets as my "space-elven" look. A black derby hat and cane completed my new wardrobe. Decked out in our faux *Clockwork Orange* attire and pointy haircuts, Booty and I were dressed to kill.

We were only in Hollywood for a few days when Booty and I heard about Rodney's English Disco from some rockers down the hall. The place was spinning vinyl seven nights a week, and not your usual Top Forty shit. One Tuesday, we hopped on a bus and headed down to check out the scene and get the hell out of the one room apartment. I was twenty-one now so I could drink legally. I got us a couple of drafts and we nursed them carefully. Between the two of us, we had maybe six bucks in our pockets. Although our rent was low, money somehow never seemed to last.

Then two chicks walked in. We could tell they were groupies by their attire, which included very short skirts, fishnet stockings, and heavy makeup. My mind flashed back for a couple of seconds to the strip club days. Many of the girls who worked there weren't twenty-one but wore makeup to look older and usually got hired. From experience, I guessed the two girls couldn't have been older than eighteen. The little darlings stopped directly in front of us, snapping me out of my trance. They looked at us like we were fresh meat. Before we knew it they were sitting in our laps. Outrageous.

The taller blonde said, "You two are new in town, huh? Let's go party in the back."

We followed them through a maze of tables, across the dance floor, and past the washrooms to an exit that led to the parking lot. It was a full-on party out there, crowded with underage kids and their quarts of beer from the liquor mart across the street. We grabbed a six-pack and joined the teenage scene of sex, drugs, and Rock 'n' roll. Our new friends turned out to be Sable Starr and Laurie Maddox, the queens of

5

THE BIG MOVE
LOS ANGELES - JANUARY 1973

After a few rehearsals in Northern California we made a band decision to move Zolar X to Southern California, where we had a better shot at being signed. Gary, still our drummer at the time, was the first to head south. He found an apartment and arranged with the manager to let him know when another unit opened up. We didn't need a lot of preparation for the move. I mean, we were young and didn't have a lot of stuff other than our musical equipment. One thing I wanted, however, was something to help me sleep. I scored 200 Quaaludes at a local park for a dime each. Not only would they help me sleep, but they'd also get me laid.

Within a month, Booty, Ed, and Mike, an old friend of mine, were on our way. We loaded our amplifiers, guitars, Ed's organ, my leopard mattress, and our suitcases into a trailer and hitched it to Ed's old Cadillac.

I rode with Mike in his 1960 Mercury station wagon with the fake, wood paneled sides, and Booty rode with Ed. We made good time but had to stop every hundred miles or so to fill up. Both cars were gas pigs, and they burned holes in our pockets, even at fifty-five cents a gallon. The frequent stops gave Mike and I chance to recover from the stress of watching the wind knock Ed's Caddy and heavy trailer back and forth across the highway. Although it wasn't much, everything we owned was in that trailer, including my '59 Les Paul Sunburst.

Many roadside piss stops and greasy burgers later, we reached the Grape Vine, that magical mountain range separating Los Angeles from the rest of the world. Ed's ancient Cadillac wasn't faring well, and we cringed at every puff of black smoke and loud pop of backfire. You didn't have to be a mechanic to know the Caddy could crap out at any moment.

After more than eight grueling hours on the road, our two-car caravan stopped in front of Gary's two-story, white stucco crash pad. Ed pulled in first, and Mike and I parked directly behind him. Against all odds, the Caddy had survived the trip. We locked up and knocked breathlessly on Gary's door. Zolar X had landed in Los Angeles.

The LA weather was unbelievable and rent at the old brick apartment complex

OUT OF THIS WORLD: THE STORY OF ZOLAR X

I soon had my first experience with psychedelics. Your life changes when you read Captain Marvel on a quarter tab of good windowpane LSD. Sitting there, I had an image in my mind I wanted to capture. With a pencil and tracing paper, I drew my face. I couldn't form a pompadour very well, so I sketched jagged bangs with pointy spikes on top. As I continued, the bangs started to look more futuristic, with a longer point in the middle. After my tenth sketch or so, I had Kitty cut my hair into the new style.

My character needed a name so I put my mind to finding one. Maybe it was because of a childhood affection for the swashbuckling hero Zorro, but I'd always been attracted to the letter Z. I liked the way he carved the letter Z into everything with his sword. Or maybe it was just because Z is the last letter of the alphabet.

I doodled many variations and finally came up with a graphically futuristic Z. Next, I drew three pictures: the first was Zory Glory, a space-born superhero, kind of like Captain Marvel meets *Star Trek*. The second drawing was a stage with space-age amps and a drum set on a sci-fi riser with silver beams of light behind it. Then I sketched four faces on the UFO-shaped stage. My hand moved wildly. I conjured surreal imagery of my future bandmates with the same pointy, platinum hair as the *Children of the Damned*. I sat back to look at my work. The one in the center looked like me.

Shady Lady: L to R – Leonard "Bones" Denault, Stefen Shady, Zory Glory, Gerhard Helmut, John Christian, circa 1973
Photo credit: Norman Seeff

Billy McCartney, 1972
Photo credit: Stefen Shady

L to R: Zoann, Stephen Della Bosca, 1973
Photo credit: Dave Abel

Rodney Bingenheimer, Rodney's English Disco, circa 1973
Photo by Richard Creamer/ Michael Ochs Archives/Getty Images

6

PREDESTINATION AT THE DISCO
HOLLYWOOD - JANUARY 1973

Booty and I were impressed with Rodney's. We got lucky our first night there, and it was a weekday. What would it be like on the weekend? We invited the other guys to come with us when we returned the next Friday, but they declined.

This time there was a lineup out front, and Sable and Laurie were posing for pictures. Inside, it was elbow to elbow. Decked out in tiny skirts, tons of glitter, and outrageous platform boots, the kids were dancing to "Suffragette City". A buzz rippled through the crowd that Bianca Jagger was up in the VIP booth. Shit, I didn't even know they had a VIP booth. I glanced over to a slightly elevated area and saw an entourage surrounding someone. I ordered two beers and we grabbed a table. Although I was hoping for an experience to match or exceed our visit earlier in the week, that might have been asking too much. Last time was beyond cool, so how could tonight be better? I sensed everybody glancing our way, taking in our pointed haircuts, eyeliner, and *Clockwork Orange* threads.

I'd just taken off the derby to adjust my point when Booty elbowed me and nodded towards the door. Looking over, I saw a distinctive looking character strut into the room. His bright red hair came to a point in front just like ours. Coolness radiated from him in waves and groupies shouted, "Shady Lady!" as he walked by and sat down to order a beer.

A bolt of lightning zapped me from head to toes. How could this guy have hair just like ours? Buzzed and a little pissed as well, I picked up my cane and headed to the bar. I wasn't a violent person, but I needed answers and I needed them immediately.

The redheaded stranger took a long drink of draft as I walked up and I tapped my cane on the bar. "Who the fuck are you, stealing our haircut idea?" I said, still in shock.

The stranger looked up, and I saw him looking at my pointed haircut. "I don't explain myself to cocksuckers," he said, grinning just a little. "Can't a man get a beer without a million questions?"

"That was only one question. Are you a musician?" I asked, angry and curious.

The stranger sighed and took another swig of beer. "If you must know, I'm Billy McCartney, but you can call me Zory. For now, I'm the drummer in the rock band Shady Lady, but I have other plans."

The adrenaline in my veins began to subside, but I wasn't ready to shake hands yet. Then I felt Booty by my side. "I'm guitarist Stephen Della Bosca, and this is bassist Bruce Allen Courtois, who goes by Booty," I said, wondering how much to tell the stranger. "Our band is Zolar X and we play space symphony. We're not ready to play yet, but we soon will be."

Zory looked slightly dazed, and I didn't know he was thinking about the sketches he'd done just a few weeks earlier. His futuristic spacemen with pointed haircuts and the band name that started with the letter Z had stepped off the page and come to life. We were all in a state of shock.

The awkwardness eventually passed and things started to get interesting. We decided to take our conversation outside, away from the noise. There was an immediate, magnetic pull that made it seem like we'd known each other forever. Parallel forces had pushed us together to create a new future for Rock 'n' roll. It was all preordained.

"Hey, Zory," I said during a pause in the conversation. "We booked a rehearsal at Studio Instrument Rentals for tomorrow at 1:00 p.m. Would you be interested in checking us out?"

"Yeah, I'll come and check you out as long as you know I'm not going to audition as a drummer!"

We stood around talking about the future of music, comic books, and outer space as the night sang its low song into dawn. Although we didn't get laid, our expectations had been exceeded. Things happened at Rodney's.

I didn't sleep much that night, but I was excited just thinking about rehearsal later that day. In the meantime, I needed to eat. "Hey Booty, I'm going to Denny's to grab some breakfast. Do you and Ed wanna join me?"

Booty's head was still inside his sleeping bag. "Uhhhhh!" he grunted, unwilling to move.

Denny's was a few blocks away, and the walk gave me time to think about the band. We needed a new drummer, and Ed should at least paint his organ silver if he planned to keep it. Silver paint might help it look a bit like a spaceship. We also wanted him to bleach his hair. My mind drifted to the music. "Space Age Love" needed more lyrics. Then there were all the other new melodies I had in my mind. I knew Booty had a lot of ideas too.

A woman in a brown and orange jumpsuit said, "How many in your party, sweetie?"

"One, but there might be two more if they wake up in time."

I followed the hostess to a table in the back. She called me "sweetie," and it didn't matter that I looked like an alien. Hollywood was awesome.

The waitress arrived and she was just as pleasant. "You look like you could use a cup of Joe!" If she thought I looked like a weirdo, I couldn't see it in her eyes. She was good.

"Yes, please! And keep it coming!"

I stared into my coffee as I added cream and sugar. Stirring, swirling, my brain was whirring. I was 400 miles from home in a new city, and we'd stumbled onto a guy with a hair cut just like us? As far as I could tell, Zory had the same ideas about haircuts, futuristic space music, and sci-fi costumes as we did. As if that weren't enough, his name started with a Z. It was all very cosmic.

Ed and Booty arrived. "Ha! No way!" Ed said to Booty as they slid into the booth. Booty, who looked somewhat the worse for wear, was telling Ed about our encounter at Rodney's the previous evening.

"He's just like us!" said Booty, trying to straighten his crooked point with his hands.

"I don't believe it! He has hair like you guys? Where's he from?"

"Zory is from Hollywood and he looks cool! He's a drummer but he wants to be a lead vocalist," I said. The coffee was already helping my head.

"But *I'm* the lead vocalist!" said Ed, nervously tapping his ashes.

"We've invited him to our rehearsal today," I continued. "Maybe we could talk him into taking Gary's spot since Gary doesn't want to be a drummer anymore. Fucking crazy—he wants to open a karate school instead of doing music! Besides Ed, you'd have plenty to do, even if you didn't sing. You have the keyboards and you could move on to synthesizers."

Ed was quiet while he took a long drag and exhaled slowly.

SIR was the big time, and we were very excited to have time booked. Our room was

OUT OF THIS WORLD: THE STORY OF ZOLAR X

a fair size with a two-foot elevated stage and drum riser. Everybody from the Stones to Zeppelin had been there. I was on the right and Booty and Ed were stage left. Gary, with his '60s double bass psychedelic-painted Ludwigs, was in the middle. The only songs we could play from start to finish were instrumental forms of "Energize Me" and "Parallel Galaxy." We also had the first verse of "Space Age Love", which Ed sang. After running through the songs a few times, Zory walked in looking more like a member of Zolar X than Ed and Gary combined. His red hair and point were perfect, and he was wearing a space-age Lurex top that looked like something Marvel comics had invented. I don't know where he got them, but he had silver space boots that zipped. Shit, he looks like our frontman.

I winked at Booty surreptitiously and he gave me a positive nod. After a quick round of introductions, the band played "Space Age Love". Zory parked himself directly in front of me, so he could hear the guitar. I watched his face as I used the Echoplex to mimic the sound of a UFO landing. Zory was stoic and hard to read, but I knew he had to be feeling something because the music was just so damn good. Then we played "Parallel Galaxy", and I knew he'd never heard a song like that before. In between tunes, I cranked out a few leads to impress him even more. I'd already made up my mind that I wanted him in the band, but I needed to know if he could sing. Could he write lyrics?

L to R: Billy McCartney, aka Zory, Stephen Della Bosca, 1973
Photo credit: Suzan Carson

7

HOTSHOTS
LOS ANGELES - JANUARY 1973

ZORY GLORY

I thought the band was as impressed with me as I was with them. It wasn't every day you'd meet two weird-looking space dudes in a Hollywood disco. I knew I had to pull off something special to impress them, but I thought maybe I already had. This time, I'd be representing Zory Glory, not Billy McCartney, so I took my futurist look to the max when I got ready to see them at SIR. On the way, I wondered if their music would be as exciting as their fashion sense. I was greatly relieved when I heard them playing Beethoven and Bach mixed with science fiction and horror to create wild futuristic rock from outer space. I looked at my sketches and couldn't believe the characters I'd drawn looked exactly like Stephen and Booty. I wanted this.

My desire to join the band happened organically. Instead of picking up speed, things started slowing down for Shady Lady. We weren't getting any shows. Then rumors started to spread that John, our lead guitarist, was hanging out with Iggy Pop and had become a junkie.

Not just that, but our manager Robert Fitzpatrick was claiming he had no cash. The situation was looking bleak and we all knew it.

With all that shit going on, we still had our photo session for the Shady Lady album cover with photographer Norman Seeff. The shoot was wild, with the guys wearing masks and me with my red-pointed hair. I felt like the future, looking at the past.

About a week later, Norman made an appointment with me for some outtake shots. His book *Hot Shots* was coming out soon, and I would be in it. He asked, "How do you want your photos billed?"

Although it was kind of strange, I blurted without thinking, "Zolar X."

Zory at Kitty's apartment-outtake photoshoot, 1973
Photo credit: Norman Seef

8

LOOKOUT MOUNTAIN
FEBRUARY 1973

The studio apartment got smaller with each passing day. We had Booty's amps, my amps, Ed's organ and speaker, and eight guitar cases – even Mike had amplifiers. Then there was the bedding. I think Booty slept on his speakers. Thank God Gary's apartment was just down the hall, where we stored other stuff. We needed more space to spread out. I was tired of sleeping in the kitchen.

To escape, we hopped in the Cadillac from time to time and cruised the boulevards. We were still acclimating ourselves to Southern California and it was fun. Sometimes, we headed to the beach to see the ocean, or we'd head up Mulholland Drive for the spectacular view. On one occasion, we drove down Laurel Canyon Boulevard towards the Valley to see if Warner Brothers Studios would give us work as extras. They didn't even let us in.

But we did meet two girls leaving the studios who gave us some valuable insight on how to find that sort of work. They turned out to be mother and daughter, Stacey and Tracey. They were both mildly sexy, and I couldn't tell them apart. They were also very nice. The women commented on our hair and asked where we were from. I jokingly pointed to the sky. Stacey put her hand on my arm and leaned into me. I felt her boobs hot against my arm as she whispered, "Take me to your leader." My hormones kicked into high gear. How can I maneuver my way into their pants? Oh well, maybe next time. And there *will* be a next time.

One day near the end of January, Booty and I were jamming and the door banged open. Ed was so excited he almost fell into the room. We stopped playing and waited to see what would come out of his mouth.

Ed shouted, "I was cruising Laurel Canyon and pulled into the Country Store to check out the bulletin board and there is a house for rent on Lookout Mountain! I called the number and it's still available. $300 a month!"

"Did you take it?" I ask quickly. It sounded too good to be true.

"I put down a fifty-dollar deposit and told him we'd pay the rest today. It's a four-bedroom house, and one of the rooms is underground. That could be our studio! Let's go pick up the keys! Am I the man?"

"Shit! You're the man! When do we move?"

Ed grins. "Now!"

Between the four of us, we quickly scraped together the rest of the rent. I sold some Quaaludes and we pawned a couple of guitars. In one afternoon, we went from living in a dump on a backstreet of East Hollywood to a house in Laurel Canyon that felt like a mansion. It was a miracle, and Ed *was* the man.

The first evening at Lookout Mountain I sat down on the wooden porch with my acoustic guitar. My feet touched the earth and I looked across the hills and up to the twinkling stars. The view was very inspiring. I saw palms and green plants. I heard the sounds of a little stream a hundred feet away. A warm, easy breeze caressed my skin. Yesterday I was in a tiny apartment where the only view was an asphalt parking lot. There was nothing emotional or inspiring about the smell of rancid beer piss rising from the sidewalk. I strummed a few chords, happy to be on Lookout Mountain. We were closer to the stars.

Because we were up in the hills, we didn't go out as much. Instead, we concentrated on our music. Booty and I soon finished the arrangements of "Parallel Galaxy", "Energize Me", and "Space Age Love". We also made our first stab at writing lyrics for "Parallel Galaxy", which was shaping up to be a very cool song. We also worked hard to teach Ed the songs. In our downstairs studio, we composed a fair repertoire of original space music for the live Zolar X show. We were working on nine different ideas at once. Not having titles and lyrics to those ideas didn't seem as important as finishing the melodies.

Gary's drums sat largely unused. He'd drop by now and then to play chess on Quaaludes and smoke a little pot. He pounded the drums during some of our rehearsals, but he still lived in the dumpy little Hollywood apartment with his heavily pregnant girlfriend. He talked a lot about giving up the drums. He talked about getting married and opening up a karate school with his brother. We couldn't relate.

9

THE RAINBOW
FEBRUARY 1973

Our roommate Mike came home after partying one night with some big news. "Okay, my favorite spacemen, gather 'round. There's a new club on Sunset Boulevard called the Rainbow Bar and Grill, and if you want to be seen then this is the place for you! All the rock stars from Alice Cooper to Zappa hang out there, and it's the place where anything can happen. There's a VIP room upstairs where they get crazy!"

"How do you know so much about the upstairs? Did you go up?" I asked,

"I sure did. I was with Terry Moore, the actress!"

"Didn't you get my jackets from her?"

"Yep. That's Terry. She's still a good piece of ass, even though she's older than me. And she has money and connections."

"You're such a gigolo!"

"Here's my point: anyone can go to the Rainbow and order food, and anyone can sit at the bar, but you need a $100 pass if you wanna go upstairs."

"If we get the money together, will one pass work for all of us?"

"It should. That's what the doorman told me. His name's Tony."

I was thinking this would be an investment—a way to be seen and to meet people in the record industry. Maybe we'd even get some publicity.

The next Saturday we stood inside the door at the Rainbow. The smell of pizza and cigarette smoke hung in the air and drunken laughter swirled around the crowded bar. A man came towards us. Ed pulled out our pass and said, "We're Zolar X".

"Zolar X, huh?" said the doorman. "You guys have some crazy haircuts. Show your pass to Bruno over by the stairs when you're ready to go up. I'm Tony, by the way. Do you wanna eat first?"

Ed and I glanced at each other, and I said in a low tone, "Shit, we've got to act the part—let's eat and we'll worry about the money later."

We quickly decided on escargot with avocado vinaigrette, stuffed mushrooms, and pizza with the works. For drinks, we splurged on a pitcher of Heineken. Until now, we'd been subsisting on a steady diet of cheap beer, bologna sandwiches, chips, and beans. No wonder we were rock-star skinny.

At the top of the stairs, the dimly lit space opened into a good-sized room. Clouds of smoke stung the eyes and there was a musky smell of sex and drugs. I scanned the sea of faces and saw June Lockhart from *Lost in Space* drinking sangria with somebody who looked important. At another table, Keith Moon waved a half-empty quart of 151 and said something to Jeff Beck, who was sitting across from him. I stood there feeling like I'd walked into a different dimension. The Rainbow was everything Mike had claimed and more.

From across the room, I saw Zory with a sharp looking blonde. He motioned me over and introduced me to his girlfriend Kitty.

"Kitty gave me my haircut," Zory explained.

"Great to meet you, Kitty!" I said, just a little dazed. "These haircuts are so wild! It kind of feels like destiny." Then I looked at Zory. "So what have you been up to, man? It's been a few weeks. You still drumming for Shady Lady?"

"Shit no. I dumped those coke-snorting Ouija board rockers a long time ago," said Zory, looking just a bit sheepish. "I mean, take Alice Cooper and the Stones and throw them in a blender, hit frappe, and that's Shady Lady. A whole bunch of shit went down in a short amount of time, and almost all our equipment was gone. Fucking John, the lead guitarist, sold our shit to support his heroin habit. To cap it off, Scepter Records didn't pay the $35,000 bill at the Record Plant and our management dropped us. The music was too fucking dark anyway. The lead vocalist Stefen is cool but the music sucks."

I paused for a second and said, "I don't know what to say here. Am I happy for you or sad?" The news sounded good to me, even though I was bummed that Zory's shot at stardom had gone down with all hands on deck.

"Well, that depends on you guys. Know what I mean? I wanna be your new vocalist!" For a guy whose life had been upended he seemed fairly chipper.

"You've got to come up to our apartment and see his sketches!" said Kitty, batting her pretty eyes. She was something.

THE RAINBOW

"Sounds cool. I'll have to get your address and phone number. We just moved to a house on Lookout Mountain in Laurel Canyon. You should come to visit. We have a downstairs studio and tons of room!"

"Wow! A house in Laurel Canyon? I can't wait to see it!" said Zory, mouth agape. "That's where all the big rock stars live!" He was too young to play it cool.

The world stopped moving as we talked about music and the direction we wanted to take our band. Booty and I were even thinking about changing our earth names into space names. Shit was cosmic.

Then we heard, "Last call!"

Ed was suddenly at my elbow. "Come on guys, let's go!"

"Where you been all night, I forgot you were here!" I said, feeling a bit guilty because I was courting his replacement. Then I turned to Zory and his girlfriend. "Booty and I are going up north to score some money. When we get back, I'll come to see your apartment and you can come and see our house. Nice to meet you, Kitty," I said, still buzzing with excitement. Our fates seemed to be unavoidably intertwined.

Kitty, aka Ve Neill, 1973
Photo credit: Zoann

The Rainbow Bar and Grill, Hollywood, CA
Photographer unknown

Sunset Strip, Hollywood, CA
Photographer unknown

10

THANKS, MR. SPOCK
SAN FRANCISCO - MARCH 1973

Seeing my family again was cool. Nothing much had changed with the house, except now my grandma was living with my mom. But it all felt so different from what I was doing and where I was now. At least Mom had prepared my favorite, Swiss steak.

"Are you getting enough to eat? You look pretty thin," said my grandma.

"I'm getting plenty to eat. I like being skinny." I said, quickly changing the subject. "Hollywood is big, Gram. You can run into all kinds of celebrities there. I saw Marshall Dillon—I mean James Arness—when we were driving past CBS Studios. Then I saw Pat Boone in his Rolls-Royce pulling into a Winchell's Donuts. Last but not least, I saw Lawrence Welk over by ABC Studios."

Her eyes lit up but she still looked doubtful. "I still say you look too thin."

I spent the rest of the evening catching up with my sister, Zoann.

Zoann looked at me. She'd always been cool. "Mom told me you guys are only going to be here for a couple of days. I'm off work tomorrow, so I could give you a trim. Your point is getting a bit long."

"That would be great! I could use it."

"The blond streaks still look good."

"Yeah, I'll probably need a touch up when you and Mom come down next month. By the way, did Mom tell you we moved to a house in Laurel Canyon?"

"Yeah, she told me, but the news about your new band is even more interesting! Are you guys playing yet?"

"No, Zolar X isn't complete yet. We need a drummer, but we met a guy, Zory Glory, whose hair is just like ours. Unbelievable! Adding him to the band will take us over the top. We're going to be huge – space-age Beatles!"

"Wow! Are you kidding me?" said Zoann, eyes sparkling. "That's amazing! Let me put my sewing talents to work! Do you need stage clothes?"

"Yeah, I have some ideas I want to go over with you."

Zoann was a talented hairstylist and seamstress – a true artist by any definition of the word. We talked about my ideas and wondered which colors might work best. She took my measurements and said she'd have my new clothes when she came to visit.

"It's been a long day," I said, yawning. "I'm gonna hit the sack." My brain was overloaded, just like always.

I'd been awake for a while listening to the steady pulse of the coffee percolator in the kitchen. Those coffee commercials were cheesy as shit but they stuck in your head. Lying there, I slowly realized that the percolator was in the key of D. The noise was almost like music. I heard notes and a mathematical tempo. Something clicked in my brain.

I jumped out of bed and searched the closet for my old guitar. Amazingly, the battered instrument was still in tune, and I quickly laid the foundation for a new song before the notes in my head faded away. It seemed worthy, so I grabbed my cassette player and recorded the new melody. I was ready for a cup of shitty Maxwell House coffee.

The phone rang. It was one of those old rotary style deals, fire engine red and built to last a million years. It'd been hanging on the wall since I was in grade school, waiting for modern technology to render it obsolete. My mom picked up the receiver. "It's for you, Stephen."

"Who is it?"

"It's Booty, your bass player."

I grabbed the receiver. "Hey, what's going on? Did you get some money?"

"Yeah, yeah – I'm cool."

"Me too. So, we're set there."

Booty almost cut me off and I could hear the excitement in his voice. "Hey Stephen, I have something wild that you just have to see! You've got to come over right away!"

Booty didn't live too far away, so I was knocking on his door in no time.

"Come in," came his muffled yell through the door.

The sounds of *Star Trek* radiated across the room as I stepped inside. Booty stood chuckling with his back to me. As he turned, I saw that he'd drawn a single Spock eyebrow on his face with an eyebrow pencil. He pointed to it and said, "What do you think of this?"

"Damn! As Spock would say, it's logical! With our pointed haircuts, this is a great new look! Where's the razor and eyebrow pencil? I'll do mine right now!"

We thought it was hilariously funny and cool. Soon our eyebrows were done and we stood back to admire ourselves in the mirror. Two alien images stared back at us. We laughed with amazement at first and then gazed at ourselves in pure silence. "Wow!" we both uttered.

"This is really a neat sci-fi, Rocket roll look."

"Rocket roll. Cool."

"Yeah, no more Rock 'n' roll. It's Rocket roll from now on."

Stephen Della Bosca, 1973
Photo credit: Jim Williams

L to R: Bruce Allen Courtois (Booty), Girl, Kitty aka Ve Neill, 1973
Photo credit: Jim Williams

11

ZOLARIZED
LOS ANGELES 1973

Ed's old gray Cadillac rumbled toward us and pulled over to the curb at Burbank Airport. Booty and I threw our luggage into the huge back seat and off we went. At first, Ed seemed happy to see us, but then he did a double-take and shook his head. "First, you guys have to do your hair all crazy with the blond streaks and pointed bangs, and now the eyebrows too? The music is great, but don't you think you're going overboard with this gimmick?"

"It's not a gimmick, man—it's a way of life! We're becoming Zolarized! You should try it, Ed. It's really fun. Oh, by the way, we got the money, and with our Unemployment coming in, we should be good for the next six months."

"Good," said Ed. "You know Gary's leaving the band, so I hope we can find a new drummer."

"Don't worry. We'll find a drummer. Let's go to the Rainbow tonight. I'm ready to party and eat some pizza. We have to show off these new eyebrows! Come on Ed, my treat!"

Booty and I styled our points to perfection and dressed in our spacey clothes: synthetic fur jackets and "punk" pants, which were actually boys' size fourteen Levi's. For the pièce de résistance, we drew on our eyebrows with great care. We pulled out all the stops that night. The crowd at the Rainbow wouldn't know what hit them.

The Sunset Strip was bumper to bumper with fancy cars and limos on Friday night—the glitz of Hollywood in all its dirty glory. We should have been traveling by spaceship, but there we were in Ed's old Cadillac. Horns honked and girls standing up in convertibles shouted addresses for parties. The sidewalks buzzed with foot traffic up and down the street. As we passed the Whisky A Go-Go, we saw a lineup that snaked around the corner. The marquis overhead announced the band Silverhead. "Hey, Booty," I said. "That's the guy we met at Rodney's – Michael Des Barres. That's his band. They're from England."

We elected to park the car around the corner and save the valet money for pizza.

We were slightly embarrassed to be seen in the Caddy, even though it's a classic now. Something I'd learned in the short time we'd been in Hollywood is that making an entrance was important. First impressions and standing out from the crowd went hand in hand. Booty and I looked great, but Ed's resistance was a bit of a drag. We looked at each other, then we looked at Ed and shook our heads. "When are you going to join the band *visually*, Ed?" I asked.

He ignored me.

Tony, a fixture of the Rainbow, stood at his post by the front door. He smiled as he saw us approach and shouted, "Hey, Zolar X! Come on in! Your other bandmate is here already. He's upstairs." He swung the door open with a great flourish.

Other bandmate? It had to be Zory Glory. I was hoping he'd be here. "Let's get pizza later and see who Tony's talking about," I said to Ed and Booty.

Upstairs, Ed reached for his wallet to get the VIP pass, but Bruno, the upstairs bouncer, waved us in before he had a chance to pull it out. "Don't worry about it, Ed. You won't need that anymore."

The place was elbow-to-elbow but we found Zory without much trouble. I tilted my head to show off my eyebrows as I walked up to him. "Notice anything different?"

"I wanna get mine done!" said Zory. "Talk about representing! Let's get a table and order a round."

I had a few bucks in my pocket so I ordered a carafe of wine for a change. It felt like a celebration. "Hey, Booty," I said, sipping my wine, "We have to come up with space names like Zory's."

"By the way, I've changed my name again!" said Zory. "I'm now Zory Zenith, Mechanical Mediator! You know Booty, you're a zany character with a great sense of humor. Let your name define you!"

"That's it!" Booty chuckled. "Zany will be my first name, and my last name will be Zatovian because I love Beethoven. I'm Zany Zatovian."

"I love it," I said. "You guys have the Z's covered."

As they talked, I had an idea about using the letter Y. The word guitar had to be part of my name, but I also wanted to get the letter Y in there somewhere. Then it came to me. "Ygarr Ygarrist – that's it!" I exclaimed. "That's my name! So now we've had X, Y, and Z covered! What about you Ed? Are you going to come up with a space name?"

"I'll start thinking about it, but it isn't one of my priorities," said Ed, looking annoyed. "I want to find a drummer and get out there and start playing! Stop worrying so much about our appearance. The music is more important than the look."

"In today's world, you need both!"

We changed the subject and, as usual, spent the rest of the night talking about Marvel Comics, sci-fi theater, and the future of rock music. Just before the kitchen closed, we went downstairs to get pizza. As we were eating, I made plans to visit Zory and Kitty's apartment the next day. We still hadn't heard him sing, but I was sure it was meant to be.

L to R: Ygarr Ygarrist, aka Stephen Della Bosca, Zany Zatovian, aka Bruce Allen Courtois, 1973
Photo credit: Jim Williams

12

THE ASSIGNMENT
LOS ANGELES 1973

I walked down the hill from our house to meet Zory and Kitty at the Country Store on Laurel Canyon Boulevard. Zory had told me that Kitty drove a silver Volkswagen Bug, and I saw it parked in front. I was pumped up and excited to see them. The couple got out of the car and the first words out of Zory's mouth were, "Notice anything different? I did them as soon as I got home last night!" His blue eyes twinkled, and I saw that his Spock eyebrows were drawn on perfectly. We laughed.

Kitty's old Hollywood apartment had style. It hit me that this was the first apartment I'd seen that felt like people lived there. There were arched doorways, French windows, art deco light fixtures, and bright orange pillows to accent the couch. Curtains with geometric patterns draped from the ceiling created separate living spaces. It was visually appealing, homey, and comfortable.

After knocking down a couple of beers and watching an episode of *Star Trek*, Zory pulled his sketch pad from a shelf and plopped it onto my lap. The first sketch was his Zory Glory flyer. I was amazed. Turning the page, I saw a sketch of a band. Not just any band, but four members with matching pointed haircuts. "When did you draw these?" I asked.

"You might not believe this, but I sketched that a couple of weeks before I even met you guys! Some might call it time travel, and some might call it psychic. All I know is that I drew the future!"

"That makes it even more outrageous! Talk about supersonic, precognitive powers!"

"I escaped the degradation of drumming for Shady Lady after seeing Bowie at the Civic Center. Then I found myself transitioning from a street-level glam rock star into an alien creature from another world! I don't believe in coincidences, Ygarr. I'm meant to be in Zolar X!"

I couldn't have said it better myself. Zory had passed the first audition from the moment I saw him walk into SIR. Now, I needed to know that he could sing, and it would be a bonus if he could write as well. I pulled a piece of paper from my pocket, where I'd scribbled the first verse of "Space Age Love". As I handed it to him, I said in a *Mission Impossible* style voice, "Good afternoon, Zory Zenith. Your mission, should you choose to accept, is to write the rest of the lyrics for "Space Age Love." As always, should any member of your force be zapped or cloned, we will disavow all knowledge of this transmission. Report to the Laurel Canyon headquarters when you've finished the assignment. This offer comes from ZX Command. Good luck."

"Wow, Ygarr. I wanna do it, but I'm not sure about the song's arrangement."

I reached into my boot and pulled out a cassette tape. "This will help."

Zory Flyer, 1973
Art credit: Billy McCartney, aka Zory Glory, aka Zory Zenith

13

LOS ANGELES
SPACE AGE LIFE 1973

ZORY ZENITH

Ygarr had beamed out, Kitty was counting sheep, and I was ready to work on my assignment. I had all sorts of ideas – some of them kind of nebulous – just drifting around in my head. I'd dropped a quarter tab of windowpane acid to assist my psychedelic visionary mindset, and it was starting to kick in. Settling into my altered state, I gazed out at the night sky. The universe was so big that it was impossible to grasp the scale of it. How many galaxies were in the universe? How many stars with orbiting planets were out there? Surely, some were capable of supporting life. What sort of life could it be? How did those beings govern themselves? The possibilities were endless. What would Captain Marvel do?

I looked at the first verse their keyboard player, Ed, had written. "We don't give a damn what your parents say." It wasn't alien in any way, shape, or form, so I changed it to: "Well, we don't give a zam what your TVs say." Television and movies influenced the unread masses more than books did, so from an alien perspective, it was like saying we don't give a zam what your media tells you, because you might be brainwashed. By changing just a few words, "Space Age Love" establishes the first contact. "We're far from your earth and its moon above, but we're ready to ignite Space Age Love."

I felt an awesome responsibility to craft the song to my utmost ability. Our band was there for a purpose, and maybe there was a master plan behind it all. Amidst the fun, it was also starting to feel very serious. It was one thing to represent the suits, but it was a whole other thing to represent beings from another world. I picked up my pen and went to work.

YGARR YGARRIST

The sun streamed through the hills and into my bedroom window on a glorious spring morning. Grabbing my acoustic guitar, I headed to the kitchen to brew some coffee. I had to capture the music from my dream last night before it vanished. Strumming away, I heard Ed practicing on the Hammond. Heavy footsteps sounded like Zany's pounded up from the studio. I could always tell it was him because he sounded like a clown with big shoes clopping along. He was funny even when he wasn't trying to be.

Sure enough, the bass player opened the door and walked into the kitchen. "Zany, come here for a second," I said. "Wow, it feels weird but natural to call you Zany instead of Booty."

"I know what you mean, YGARR!"

"You should have come with me to Zory's apartment. I gave him the assignment to finish the lyrics to "Space Age Love," and I don't know if he'll be able to do it or not – we'll see. He had sketches of a band that he claims he drew weeks before he met us, and they looked just like us! I couldn't believe it!"

"The guy is super cool. I hope he can sing."

"I hope so too. I just have a feeling. It's hard to put into words."

Someone knocked on the front door and rang the doorbell impatiently. "Open up, it's me!" said Zory through the closed door.

Zory walked in decked out in silver boots, tight pants, and a matching silver space top. In contrast to the whiteness of his skin, Zory's red hair formed a perfect V between his eyes. His stylized eyebrows were a sci-fi treat.

In a monotone voice, he said, "Greetings Ygarr Ygarrist and Zany Zatovian. I have completed the mission. I did not know I had it in me. I have been consumed for 11-hours, avoiding all Earthling thoughts. I am meant to be in this club. See for yourself."

His movements seemed robot-like and choreographed. We watched in amazement as he took a large artist's pad from under his arm and presented it to us. He then took three stiff, robotic steps backward as Zany and I held the newly written lyrics in our hands.

I looked at the handwritten lyrics on the 18" x 24" sheet of paper. It was impressive. When I got to the line "with kinetic powered thoughts from our satellite," I thought, *Oh shit, he's not just a poet, he's a sci-fi, comic book genius. Exactly what Zolar X needs.*

Well, we don't give a zam what your TVs say
We're out in space light-years away
Far from your earth and its moon above
Ready to ignite Space Age love

LOS ANGELES

With kinetic powered thoughts from our satellites
We're the faces that you see in your dreams at night
You'll love the zip zap zam of our Zolar guns
And the star stellar thrills of our space-age fun

We can take you on an orbit of our pink playground
You'll love the sputnik spin of our Zolar Go-Round
We can stop on Zic-Con Zoo for a soda fizz
And beam you home by 9:00 before your parent's quiz

Well, you may not like our powered hills or pointed hair
So we'll steal you out in secret leaving them a spare

"I can't believe you've finished these already," I said, amazed. "I just gave you the assignment last night! Hey Ed, come check this out!"

"These are good!" murmured Ed as he scanned the lyrics.

I grabbed the acoustic guitar and we spent the rest of the morning going over the lyrics, making sure the syllable mathematics fit inside the melody. The lyrics were Zory's written assignment, but now he was singing and this was the real audition. Although he didn't have a lot of power at first, he became more comfortable each time we went through the song. He had the attitude—he just needed practice and the repetitive nature of memory, melody, and lyric to find his true voice.

We stopped for a break. Zory put his hands on his hips and said, "Are we going to do this merger or what?" His penetrating stare held the three of us frozen in time. I was searching for another way to say "I always knew you'd be in the band" when Zory piped in again.

"Well? Am I in? Did I pass the audition?"

"Yes!" I said quickly. "You're a ZX man now! Zory Glory, the space-born superhero! I mean Zory Zenith!" In my private thoughts, I knew this was much more than a random fluke. This was nothing less than divine intervention.

In an endearing robotic tone, Zory said, "Thank you for this opportunity. It has brought a lightness to my program." We celebrated by breaking out a round of Strawberry Crush, my favorite soda pop.

Having Zory in Zolar X gave us a rush of energy, and what I was hearing was pure magic. This was fresh and strong and nothing could stop us. But "Space Age Love" still had a few loose ends. "Hey Zory, we need two more stanzas to finish off the fourth verse," I said.

"Yeah, I wasn't sure how many we needed."

The four of us started shouting out phrases. The weirder the better.

"Don't be a clone."

"It's not in the past."

"Why act so human?"

"Come on guys, we're getting close."

Then Zany shouted out, "Why act prehistoric?" We all started busting up. It was perfect.

Ed chimed in with, "Don't be so square!"

"Through teleport," I offered.

"You'll be with us and still be there," said Zory, finishing the song.

We played "Space Age Love" at least twenty times and cracked up every time "Why act prehistoric? Don't be so square?" This was the first comic book set to music, no doubt about it.

"Okay Zory, now that you're in the band, you might want to think about moving in," I said. "There's a bunch of songs we need to work on. You can crash in Mike's room when he's not here."

"Shit guys, I've always wanted to live in Laurel Canyon!" said Zory. "It'll be great not having to crash at Kitty's pad all the time, especially when I want to hook up with another chick. Know what I mean? All my shit is still at my mom and dad's place, but I can get a mattress." He took a swig of Strawberry Crush and said, "I feel like I've joined a club—not just the drummer in somebody else's band. Damn, I've been promoted!"

14

INSIDE THE "X"
LOS ANGELES - APRIL 1973

Zory Zenith cemented himself into Zolar X on April 11, the day he came to the house with the lyrics to "Space Age Love" handwritten on his artist's pad. On that day, he not only became a member, but he became the vocal leader as well. The next day he brought his mattress, a sleeping bag, and of all things, an artist's easel and it felt like I'd known him my entire life.

At twenty-one years old, my life was about music, Zolar X, and chasing skirts in that order. Every day I could feel us growing as a band, and maybe more importantly, as brothers. Zory and I were early risers, and it became our routine to grab a soda or make some coffee and head outside to the porch to work on lyrics to finish songs. It was always the greatest weather; not too hot, not too cold—just sunny blue skies with an occasional breeze. Zory had his small yellow notepad and I had my acoustic guitar. What fun we had. The days turned into weeks as we worked our way through the music. It was hard to say when spring ended and summer began.

One morning we were talking about *Star Trek* and how Captain Kirk always ended up with the babes, and I said to Zory, "I have a song called 'Energize Me' that needs lyrics. It's kind of a ballad – a love song. I hummed the vocal melody and strummed the chords as Zory began doodling lyrical content.

"Hey Ygarr, how's this for the first verse?"

Feeling weak from my endless patrol
I felt sensations to dream

"Let's try it. If it doesn't work, we'll write something else."

We went back and forth like that, searching for the line, searching for the rhyme, and we just knew it when the magic happened.

"Damn, Ygarr, this is good shit! I'm going to transfer it to the large note pad."

"I'll get Ed and Zany, and we'll bang this sucker out in the studio."

Zory propped the lyrics on the easel.

Even though we didn't have a drummer, we still had a great wall of sound: imagine a '59 'Paul echoing out of a Hiwatt, and Zany's bass booming through his massive rig. Even Ed's Hammond didn't sound too bad. Zory had all the attitude a great frontman could ever want, but he also needed vocal practice – all he could get, especially with a microphone.

Counting off: "One, two, three, four…"

"It sounds great guys, and it will sound even better once we get a drummer."

"Hey, let's try Space Age Love," said Zory. We went long into the night, adjusting lyrics and running through the songs again and again. About midnight, we were ready to close it down.

While unwinding, we began to contemplate the meaning of our name. I said, "So what does the 'X' stand for?"

"Extreme Butt!" Zory shouted.

Zany followed with, "Uma goomba, uma bay!"

"Come on guys. I'm serious. It has to have some sort of triumphant meaning."

Zory glanced at me. "You mean like good versus evil?"

"Like light versus dark, right?" asked Ed.

"Yeah, like a silver beam from heaven cutting through a black beam from hell!" I said, warming to the subject.

"Shit Ygarr, you're serious," said Zany.

"Sure I am, and we need a logo to match. Somebody get the sketch pad and let's get this down on paper."

"What about using those new spacey, futuristic letters for Zolar?" asked Zany.

"It has to be original, and I like what Ygarr said about the beam from heaven and the beam from hell," said Zory, sketching. The lines and angular shapes began to take form. After a few minutes, we stood back and looked on in amazement. There was our band name chiseled in graphite: ZOLAR X.

"Can you imagine the X being twelve feet tall on stage behind us?" said Zory.

INSIDE THE "X"

"Wow!" we all said at the same time.

The Canyon was very inspirational for what we wanted to portray in the songs – a glimmer of hope and vision, the superhero, and the dream of a new and better Earth.

15

LIGHTS CAMERA ACTION
LOS ANGELES - MAY 1973

Band talk was ongoing. Even though we lived together, there was still a lot of work to do to get Zolar X ready to play live. The three of us were crammed in front of the big bathroom mirror admiring our pointed haircuts and the subject of having some pictures taken came up.

"I know someone!" exclaimed Zory. "Her name's Suzan Carson, and she goes back to the Shady Lady days. She was intimately involved with several members. She always has a Pentax strapped to her back, and she did an 8mm film of Shady Lady at Dress Review. I could call her?"

"Sounds terrific! Does she have any friends?"

"I'll ask her if she can bring Anne Moore along, who I know even better!" said Zory. She's a Rock 'n' roll journalist that writes for *Teen Screen*, *Sixteen*, and *Fave*. Back in the Doors' heyday, she was one of Jim Morrison's local lays. I'd tried getting intimate with Ann once but was so drunk that it didn't get past the heavy petting stage. That didn't bother her. Morrison wasn't able to perform on command either, not with the cornucopia of pills he took and all the booze he drank.

The women stopped by later in the week to socialize, and it ended up being the first of many visits. We went down to the studio to play some of our music for them. Susan brought a portfolio of her work, and we scheduled a shoot for a week later. Another time, they brought a test pressing of Queen's first album, which didn't impress me. On one of those nights, Susan stayed over and we gave my leopard mattress a workout.

Like the Beatles with their matching haircuts and suits, our aspirations were gigantic. Zolar X was a unique entity, and we fell in love with looking like and pretending to be aliens. This wasn't just a band—it was an entirely new way to live.

We had a few spacey tops and jackets but desperately needed more; stage wear, streetwear, and life wear. The three of us knew we couldn't just wear polyester suits with white loafers, no matter what. The normal dress was so archaic. The futuristic, sci-fi, space theater trip consumed us. Now it was up to us to look the part.

"Ed, now that three of us have pointed haircuts and arched eyebrows, when are you going to join up?" I asked. It was a legitimate question.

"What the hell Steve, will you get off my back?" He still called me Steve just to be a dick.

"You're being stubborn about being human! You could at least do your eyebrows!" The argument felt like it was going nowhere and I was becoming more pissed by the second. I'd hold my tongue for now on the hope that he'd come around. Strike one.

Zory came into the room and my thoughts turned to a question. "Hey Zory, where'd you get those metallic-red high-topped sneakers?"

"You mean my sequined tennis shoes? Oh yeah, and I have a matching jacket too – a sweet little ensemble! I'll show you guys around. I've gotta take you to all my underground Hollywood haunts. Let's go shopping!"

When we weren't rehearsing, writing songs, or partying, we were shopping. One of our stops was Granny Takes a Trip, where Zany found silver metallic high tops and a matching jacket. I ended up with nothing because they didn't have my size.

My luck changed at the next shop where, using transfers, they printed black T-shirts for us with our space names spelled horizontally. That was all the rage in those days. Along with my band T-shirt, I also had them make me an orange T-shirt with "Space Age Luv" ironed onto it, and a black shirt emblazoned with "Rockett Roll". For a few cents more, we had the letters pressed in metallic silver. Ed didn't have a space name so he got a blue shirt. I don't know why he was even hanging out with us.

Zory had his footwear covered. Not only did he have the metallic high tops, but he also had silver boots with wedge soles that I highly coveted. When I asked where he bought them, he told me he had them made at a cobbler's in Hollywood. The next day we found ourselves standing in the doorway of L'Artisan's. I showed the owner my brown lace up boots and asked, "Can you make these into space boots?" The one-room shop on Fairfax was hot as hell, so we did our negotiating just outside the front door. The short, little foreign man said in a heavy accent, "Seventy-five American dollars, four-inch platforms, make them silver. Ready in two weeks. Good?"

"Very cool!" We smiled and shook hands.

Next door to L'Artisan's, we found ourselves looking into a display window. Silver mannequins wearing outrageously colorful outfits and high collars with zippers peered back at us. Some of the leotards were sleeveless or even one-sleeved. We looked at each other and said, "Yeah baby! We've got to go in!"

Two women greeted us as we entered Karabel's Men and Women's Dancewear. We introduced ourselves as Zolar X, and they showed us around the store. We ended up staying a while and I bought some black foot-in tights to go underneath the new knickers my sister was making.

The following morning, Zory and I were on the porch working on another song when a blue Ford Cougar hot rod pulled up to the curb. I didn't know who the hell it was, but then my sister Zoann got out. My mom was driving. The last I knew, she had a green Ford Galaxy. I introduced them to Zory and showed them around the place. It was cool to have a mother that accepted the outer space thing I was doing with my band and a sister who cut my hair and made clothes for me.

I noticed they were both looking across the room at the chessboard and the empty glasses on the floor next to a pile of albums. "There isn't much to sit on, but this is our living room."

With no table and chairs, the band played chess on the floor, but we spent most of our time in the studio or on the porch.

"I finished your space knickers in white satin," Zoann said. "Wait till you see them!"

"Are you going to go out to dinner with us?" asked Mom.

Zory said, "Go to the Rainbow. Maybe you'll run into Elvis! Thank you. Thank you very much!"

"Yeah, that will be fun. You guys will like the place. It's full of famous people."

Zoann said, "That sounds groovy. I'm dying to see how your pants fit. They're at the hotel. Why don't we go there afterward, and I'll do your hair too?"

"Sounds great, and this is perfect timing. We have a photoshoot coming up this week!"

It was great to see my family and get the new white, satin knickers. They had elf cuffs that matched my jacket. Zoann added rhinestones along the zipper, and the sparkle gave them a spacey feel. They will look great over my new black tights. Now the three of us are set!

It was very windy on the day of our first photoshoot. Instead of pointing down, our v-shaped haircuts pointed up. It felt like a catastrophe, but Susan kept clicking.

Zany shouted, "Let's go inside the house to get out of this wind!"

"Let's go to the Hollywood Toy Store and take pictures there!" suggested Zory.

It was unanimous! Hollywood Toy Store was the coolest toy store I had ever been in. They had everything from Walt Disney costumes to superhero suits. They had ray guns, and Frankenstein and Dracula outfits. If you wanted a toy they didn't have, they could order it from any place in the galaxy. The place was a collectibles extravaganza. Zory posed with a miniature UFO. Click! I tried on a space helmet. Click! We posed by the toy robots. Click! We had so much fun that they kicked us out.

L to R: Ygarr Ygarrist, Zory Zenith, 1973
Photo credit: Suzan Carson

16

WORK AND LOTS OF PLAY
HOLLYWOOD - JUNE 1973

By June, Zory had already been in the band for two months, and we'd made the most of it. Twice a week we rehearsed at Dress Review. Dress Review was a lot cheaper and smaller than SIR. The Blue Room had a stage, which gave us room to work on choreography. The Orange Room had no stage, but the PA system was better. Both rooms were fine for our purposes.

We also placed an ad at Dress Review that read, "DRUMMER WANTED". The responses were frightful and auditions were a joke. We'd tell the candidate when to show up and meet him in front of the studio. He'd pull up in an old clunker, usually dressed like a casual hippie. Most of the time his drums wouldn't even be in cases, and they were usually red or turquoise metal-flake Ludwigs. We'd help him carry them in. When his drums were set up, we'd run through our easiest song, "Space Age Love" while he listened. Then we'd let him try to add his drums to the song. Without fail, four bars into the song, Zory would throw his arms in the air and yell, "Halt!" Then he'd storm over to the guy and say, "Look, it's basically a simple straight-a-way in the beginning. It'll have some tom fills later but forget about that for now. You have to get the slap-a-dap-pa part together, so let me show you." Zory was forceful and intimidating, but his knowledge of percussion was spot on.

After every audition Ed would ask, "Why are we looking for a drummer when we already have one?"

"Ed, are you ever going to realize the vision?" I'd say.

Using our imaginations, and with purchases from thrift shops and T-shirt shops, our street identity was taking shape. We'd take a regular brown belt, and with some silver spray paint, turn it into a cosmic holster for a ray gun. With a trip to Pier One Imports, we'd take a clear planter and chrome caps from a deodorant can to make a space helmet. We even used stuff from the local hardware store. We'd buy clear plastic tubing, fill the tubes with food-colored water, and cap them to make space bracelets and necklaces.

Zory made space tops with shoulder wings from metallic Lurex. Talk about cool.

There was an orange one, a green one, and a purple one. We could wear them with nothing underneath, or they would look great over black, sleeveless leotards. Worn with black tights and space boots, we'd be ready for some superhero action down at the local Fatburger.

Speaking the words Ygarr Ygarrist, Zory Zenith, or Zany Zatovian was damn cool, but it was even more terrific to see those names on T-shirts. It was sci-riffic. XYZ seemed very different from ABC in the eyes of a Zolarian. The band was starting to feel like a unit.

After several days away servicing one of his girlfriends, Zory returned to the house toting a red portable Panasonic cassette recorder.

"Very cool! Where'd you get it?" I asked.

"Macy's. Where else?"

"We have to get one too!" Zany and I said at the same time.

The only other colors in stock at Macy's were blue and white. We never dreamed we'd end up promoting the "old red, white and blue," but that's how it went. Without delay, I recorded some sci-fi, Echoplex sound effects, and followed them up with an instrumental version of a new song called "Void of the Pointed People." I made two copies, giving one to Zory and one to Zany. Our new tape recorders gave us superpowers.

Armed with the patriotic Panasonics, we headed to Hollywood Boulevard to mess with the tourists. "This is gonna be great!" said Zory, watching innocent citizens on the sidewalk. Dressed in our spacey T-shirts, we pressed "Play" and the fun began. What sounded like a UFO invasion soon transitioned into the theme song "Void of the Pointed People". Our goal was not to entertain the citizens but to shock them. We sang, "Zero minus zero equals nothing but space. Very similar to your whole human race."

I don't know what inspired us, but we also made funny little sound effects with our throats. It sounded like we were receiving alien transmissions. The average person must have thought we were from another country. But we knew we were from another world.

We learned to ignore the honking horns and people yelling obscenities, but karma struck the humans one night as we walked down Sunset to Rodney Bingenheimer's English Disco. Some assholes shouted, "Get off the street, you weirdos! Go back to

WORK AND LOTS OF PLAY

Mars!" Then they lost control of their vehicle and plowed into the car in front of them. BOOM! CRASH! SCREAM! Nobody was seriously injured, but we had a good laugh. Our look was more powerful than I'd first realized. What else could we accomplish simply by looking like freaks?

We were digging the Hollywood nights. Going out was also about being seen. Sable Star told Zory about a party—not just any party, but a party at John Phillip's mansion in Bel Air. Yes, John Phillips of the Mamas and the Papas. Rumor had it that Mick Jagger stayed there when the Stones were in town. The party was more like a wild orgy and we had a great time. We even banged a couple of chicks on the thirty-foot cherry wood dining room table. I'm not sure if we were seen doing that, but it wouldn't have hurt us any if we were.

Looking back, these were the best times of our lives. We were like over-sexed spacemen trying to fuck every Earth girl we could. We enjoyed the beer and pizza, and the experiences provided us with enough stimuli to amplify our creative imaginations. Every day was something different and we never knew what would happen next.

L to R: Zory Zenith, Zany Zatovian, Ed Dorn, Ygarr Ygarrist, 1973
Photo credit: Suzan Carson

Vintage Panasonic Portable Recorder, 1973

L to R: Zany Zatovian,
Ed Dorn,
Ygarr Ygarrist,
Zory Zenith, 1973
Photo credit: Suzan Carson

L to R: Zory Zenith,
Zany Zatovian,
Ed Dorn,
Ygarr Ygarrist, 1973
Photo credit: Suzan Carson

17

THE BOOMERANG INCIDENT
LOS ANGELES - JUNE 1973

Zory and I were off to the Rainbow. As usual, Zany and Ed declined. I understood Ed not wanting to come—he was in love with Patty, his girlfriend from San Francisco. Unlike the rest of us, Ed wasn't interested in fooling around. But I didn't know why Zany wanted to stay behind. I guess he just didn't like the nightlife like Zory and I did. We were two peas in a space pod.

We finished up the last few strokes on our eyebrows and tucked a few Earther dollars into our space boots before walking down the mountain to Sunset Boulevard. We could take a bus or a taxi or hitchhike, but none of those options resembled space travel. Getting out of a vehicle was so mundane—we wanted to appear on the scene as if we'd beamed in.

Zory liked to get a buzz before we arrived at the club, and as cheaply as possible because we couldn't afford big bar tabs. On this occasion, we bought a couple of sixteen-ounce malts from the liquor mart down the street. We headed to an elevated parking structure next to the 'Bow, where we talked about anything and everything.

"Here's to being on our way!" said Zory, clinking cans with me. "Our biggest dilemma is deciding whether to cross-breed the alcohol or stick with beer all night,"

We laughed and I said, "I don't think it matters as long as somebody else is buying. Between the two of us, I'm sure we have enough for a couple of rounds. Maybe even a small pizza."

"I'm digging the lyrics to 'Energize Me'!" said Zory. "It's sounding great. The chorus has such potential for harmony."

"Yeah, I know what you mean."

"So what do you want me to do, Mr producer? Should I be using my robot voice or my melodic voice?"

"This one is a ballad. It's all melodic, and I'll harmonize with you."

In an English accent, Zory said, "You mean like John and Paul?"

Laughing, we paused to sip our malts. In that brief moment, we both happened to look up at the same time. There was an object in the sky that couldn't be explained. Without a word, we looked at each other. It was impossible to talk. Looking up again, we could still see the boomerang shape hovering about a half-mile up in the starry night sky. There was no need to say anything—we were communicating telepathically. We glanced up a third time and the object was still in the very same spot. My lips moved, and finally, the words came out. "Are you seeing what I'm seeing?"

"I don't believe it," Zory uttered. "Or maybe I *do* believe it."

We looked up a fourth time and the object was gone. Sitting quietly, we tried to process what we'd just seen.

"Okay, what do you think that was?" asked Zory.

"That was a UFO!"

"Did you see the moving mist surrounding it?"

"Yeah, and the green lights along the wing looked like portals."

"The silence is what got me. Totally silent."

"That was a fucking UFO!"

We tipped our cans to get the last drops, but we were so awestruck that the thought of going to the Rainbow seemed anticlimactic. I said, "What do you say we grab a six-pack and head home?"

"Sounds good. Damn, this experience was definitely from beyond the Earthling realm!"

We'd gone out to be amongst the humans – to observe and to be seen – but we'd never dreamed of being seen *this* way. Walking up Lookout Mountain, our minds were still in the stars. The black stillness was the perfect place to reflect on what we'd just witnessed. Colors were brighter and sounds were crisper. Even the smoggy Los Angeles air felt cleaner.

Back home, our creativity surged. Melodies that stretched sound waves and bent time took our songwriting to a new dimension. Mysterious alien words tumbled from our mouths.

"Nok voo – thank you. Artia – love. Wooteeta – cool."

THE BOOMERANG INCIDENT

"Hey Ygarr, what do you think of this for the new one… E-LEE-VOW, KAR-DOM VOO?"

"Shit, yeah! I love it! What does it mean?"

"Whatever we want!"

"Hell, we're creating our alien language!"

"From a supernatural standpoint, that's perfect!"

"Zory, let's call this song 'Silver Shapes'. The melody goes like this. It has a 4/4 beat with a warp jump and a sci-fi-military pulse."

"I think we have something here. This is brilliant, like Klaatu talking to the scientist in *Day the Earth Stood Still*. Hidden cities floating in a skyway. Silver Shapes approaching."

"Figures of emblazed imagination taking on human form!" said Zory.

It felt like we were writing from a place, not of this earth. Had we become subliminal transceivers? Were these signals guiding us somewhere? Were we talking through our mouths and transferring messages to paper? Or was this something else?

"Let's call this the Boomerang Incident," said Zory.

"What?"

"The fucking UFO! That's what that was. And I think it stays between us."

"Yeah, Ed and Zany would have been with us if they were meant to see it. I think the Boomerang Incident was meant for just the two of us."

"It was almost like a stamp of approval from out there," said Zory. "I'm sure they could tell we're the 'friendlies'. They must've gotten a kick out it, or at least they did if they have any sense of humor and aren't 100% logical. I just wish they were our managers."

Talking, writing, erasing, rhyming – it was like we were on a space high unbeholden to gravity. Oxygen with a helium kicker. And then "Silver Shapes" was finished.

Hidden cities floating in a skyway
Landing in the deserts late at night
Silver shapes, approaching from the shadows

Multi-brains from planets far and bright

Figures of emblazed imagination taking on human form

Slightly different from the population

bringing on a change of mind reform

Golden cosmos seekers of eternity

Technologist from time and space

Cybornauts programmed for recovery

Challenging invaders of faith

Keepers of a parallel dimension

Messengers with a clue, selecting chosen few who believe

to beware of those who deceive

Look up look high, look-up to the sky

Silver shapes in the sky

Silver shapes in the sky

ELEE VOW KARDOMVOU, ELEE OKK NEBBULOR

18

CUTE SHORT AND SKINNY
HOLLYWOOD - JULY 1973

Los Angeles – movie capital of the world – a haven for the starstruck. You'd find the eccentrics, the kooks, the mega-talented steeped in booze and cocaine. Studios, clubs, bars, and grills – anywhere and everywhere aspirants hang out and wait to be discovered. But somehow, even with all the thousands of musicians floating around Hollywood, we were unable to find a suitable drummer for Zolar X. It did not compute.

"Hey guys, it's been a month since we had our ad up at Dress Review, but what the fuck has it got us?" I asked, strumming my acoustic.

"Uma goomba, uma bay!" said Zany. "Yeah, a bunch of cavemen!"

Zory laughed. "Yeah, when that last guy showed up I asked myself, what the hell is this the *Beverly Hillbillies*?"

"I didn't think the last guy was that bad!" said Ed.

"You mean Jethro?"

Zory spoke with an exaggerated southern accent. "If I'd known the Clampetts was gonna show up, I woulda asked Ellie Mae to come an' sit on my lap."

We laughed.

Jokes aside, I returned to the matter at hand. "I revised our ad to weed out unsuitable applicants. None of the drummers we tried have the talent, visuality, and attitude we need." I coughed for emphasis. "Here's what we have so far."

WANTED: ALIEN DRUMMER!
Must be cute.
5'5" – 5'8"
Skinny
Loves music and science fiction.
Willing to be groomed into a character.

Must be a hard hitter. Keith Moon, Carl Palmer "whack-a-whacka!"

"I'll say it again," said Ed, almost shouting. "Why are we looking for a drummer when we already have one?" He resented being bumped from his role as lead vocalist.

"If you think this drum spot is hard to fill, try finding a frontman who can do what I do", Zory said irritably. "Okay, maybe I don't have the best voice yet, but I have some range that can be developed, and I'm also an original robot character doing mime! Where would you find a lead singer who can do that? As hard as it might seem, drummers are a hell of a lot easier to find than theatrical singers who can design clothing, write songs, and sing. Are you serious, Ed?"

"Let's broaden the search," said Zany, eager to get back on track. "I know a band from Hayward called Legs Diamond. Their drummer, Jeff might be interested. I could invite him down for an audition."

"What does he look like?" Zory and I asked simultaneously.

"Uma goomba, uma bay!" said Zany. "He's a caveman, but maybe we could get him to cut his hair."

"We haven't had any luck yet, so give him a call. And let's put up the revised ad too. We're not messing around here."

19
X MARKS THE SPOT
LOS ANGELES - JULY 1973

The view from Lookout Mountain was a panoramic, kaleidoscope of Hollywood. We climbed the trail to the top at least once a week. Sometimes, all four of us hiked, but mostly it was Zory and me. When it was just the two of us, we talked about our shared vision and it strengthened the bond between us. There was something very cosmic about the way we wrote songs and identified with each other —the way our minds connected on that dusty mountain overlooking the planet. Things were out there for the taking. We could almost touch them.

During the day, we could see down the mountain to the beach—all the way to the ocean, the horizon, and the vast enormity of time and space. Moving beams of headlights and electricity illuminated the darkness at night. The glow and energy of the city was hypnotic. Gazing down at the streetlights, we could see the intersection of San Vicente and La Cienega. From our lofty spot high in the sky, the intersection appeared as a bold "X". The visual affirmation warmed us from inside. Our destiny was at hand.

"I wish they'd come back," I said wistfully.

"The visitors? The Boomerang Incident?" asked Zory. "Do you think we'll ever see anything like that again?"

"Hard to say. We saw it but the rest of Los Angeles didn't."

"Why were we the only ones who saw that in a city of millions? Nothing about it on TV or in the newspaper. What does it mean?"

"Maybe we were chosen!" I said, looking out over the glittering globule of jewels. "Maybe it was a freak thing because we're the only sci-fi band on the planet!"

"Who gives a shit?" Zory scowled. "Maybe we don't have proof, but I know what we saw and that's good enough for me!"

Armando Norte Drawing

20
HOLLYWOOD QUACK
LOS ANGELES - JULY 1973

ZORY ZENITH

All of my family is fat, and I followed suit. I've always had a tough time controlling my weight. So right around the time I met Ygarr and the guys, I went to my dad's doctor, who was kind of a quack but had been in Hollywood for years. He was used to just about anything coming in the door. I showed him a page from *Vogue* magazine about models getting injections for quick weight loss and he didn't even flinch. The ad featured a skinny woman and a big syringe filled with green shit. Getting straight to the point, I said, "Look, I have a part in an upcoming movie, and I have to lose twenty-five, maybe even thirty pounds within fourteen to eighteen days. Is that possible?"

"I don't know if you'll lose the weight that fast, but we can get you started!" the doctor said helpfully. He gave me the whole speech about being careful and all that bullshit before injecting the green shit into my hip. Then he gave me these little green, candy-coated pills and told me to take two a day. After the first day, I pretty much lost my appetite, so the weight dropped off quickly. The only time I got hungry was at Laurel Canyon, or Kitty's apartment when I might smoke a joint. I was eating every other day, and even then, it wasn't a full meal—just a hamburger, no fries, or even a soda. Kitty made me eat at least every couple of days and fed me Shepard's pie or huge meatballs with garlic bread. She kept me alive.

Within a few days after treatment, I started peeing turquoise. The first time was at the house in Laurel Canyon. I went up there in the afternoon and we were hanging out. When I went to the toilet, I saw that my piss was a beautiful shade of aquamarine. I said, 'Hey you guys come here and look at this!'" I was all excited, like a little kid with an enormous turd.

I told Ygarr, "I know you have no problem staying skinny, but I thought you might like the rush from my little green diet pills."

"Hell, yeah! I've always liked speed!" he said.

"I've got a packet full of this shit. I'm on a mission!"

"I'll join you on that mission! And peeing green? That's an alien bonus!"

"After all, even an ounce of fat will show in our new space gear when we're wearing tights! Supersonic dress review tonight!" We were very weight conscious, or at least I was.

Fifteen minutes later Ygarr was feeling alright. "I'm flying at light speed, baby!" he said. "Mike's bringing some party girls and supplies!"

"Eep Opp Ork Ah-Ah Jet Screamer!"

"Since this will be our first rehearsal with an audience, I'm wearing my orange space top with my silver boots."

"I'll wear the green top you gave me and my new space boots!" said Ygarr

"Zany, are you gonna wear your silver lame jacket and matching tennies?"

"Beep-a-dee-deep! Let's get some space-age fun tonight!"

"Where's Ed?"

"He's loading up. Let's help him and get going."

21

PARTY AT DRESS REVIEW
HOLLYWOOD - JULY 1973

Rehearsing at Dress Review was a treat. It was a great place to stroke our egos, to be seen, and to spread the word about Zolar X. We assembled our songs at the Lookout Mountain studio, but we put the act together at Dress Review.

Between Dress Review rehearsals, we were always working. I honed my skills on lead guitar, Zany was designing a Space Age Luv sticker, Zory was making a Zolar X stencil and, we continued to add to our alien wardrobe. And Ed? He was still trying to gather the nerve to cut his hair into a point.

We were flying high, but the circuitry of the band was still a mishmash of schematics, components, and techniques. The ideas and fragments continued to pour in from our Panasonic walks, porch sessions with Zory, and sit-down talks, where we discussed our dreams and desires. None of it ever felt like work but rehearsing at Dress Review was more like a vacation. Being in a Rock 'n' roll studio was much different than creating music in your little hovel. The spacious Orange Room had bright orange shag carpet, professional lights, a decent PA system, and plenty of microphones. We walked into the hall where the hippie band from the other room was drinking beer and partying. After they got over the shock of our look, they offered us a toke of their joint. Hollywood Boulevard was a lot of fun in 1973.

I flipped a switch and heard my Hiwatt hum. Zany had dialed in his Danelectro bass to give it a spacey, cello-like boom. Over in the corner, Ed was fooling around with the stops on his Hammond, trying to find a cosmic-sounding French horn. Lately, I'd been Echoplexing power chords to give our sound a double-thick tone. We wanted to be as good as possible when we finally found a drummer. I hoped that happened soon.

Zory tested the mic with his finger in his ear, making sure he could hear himself. It's one thing to want success, and it's another to think it, but it's the ultimate task to find a successful sound. I could see that desire in Zory's face and his approach. He was very comfortable being the center of attention, but his confidence needed stroking from time to time. I knew he wanted to be the best singer out there, and he knew there was work to be done. If he sounded as good as he looked, he'd be the best rock singer on the planet. He was original.

We tuned up and finished the mic checks. We could hear the sounds of the other bands in the hallway and even the distant ring of a payphone outside the door. All those minor noises fell away in a wall of sound when we dropped into "Space Age Love". After the first run through, Zory waved his arms to get our attention and said, "I have an idea I want to try! Play the song again!"

The band kicked into "Space Age Love" again, and using his arms, Zory created exclamation marks at the interludes between the verses—robotic phrases masterfully executed from a theatrical standpoint. The flares were dramatically on tempo. The song was part talk, part rhythmic mime, and very "Broadway".

"Our retro is hot!"

"Supersonic!"

"Fly us, cosmic lovers."

"Up we go!"

"Humans are fun!"

"You know, some people think we look kind of crazy. That's ridiculous because, I mean, we think all of you look astronomical!"

"Zap! You're Zolarized!"

At the end of the song, I turned the knob on my Echoplex to make it sound like a flying saucer was taking off, turning it up again to replicate the saucer shutting off its engines. Zany and I strolled towards each other pounding the final B chord as the song came to a close. In a final climactic gesture, we formed an "X" with the necks of our guitars.

"Shit, Zory! That's outrageous. When did you come up with that?"

"I was on autopilot last night. You know – the little green pills? I put myself in a strange dimensional space and asked, is there a message here?" Zory paused to make sure we were all listening, and then he yelled, "It's fucking *Earth vs. the Flying Saucers!*"

I cracked up and shouted, "Invasion!"

Zany said, "Yeah, that's cool Zory – what you added to the song!"

Ed agreed, "Yeah! Killer!"

"Let's work on 'Energize Me' after this break," I said, "Ed, did you find that French horn yet?"

"Funny, Steve," Ed said, unsmilingly.

"My name's Ygarr, and we need some liquid! Are you guys thirsty?"

"Did I hear someone say thirsty?" We turned to see Mike stumble through the door with a case of beer and three hot chicks.

"You saved the day, Mike. Now we don't have to make a run to the store!"

Zory nodded his head toward the girls and asked, "Which one's yours, Mike?"

Mike lit a joint and said, "It's a party. I don't care."

I took a few tokes and downed half my beer. "I'm ready to run through 'Space Age Love' again," I said, eager to play. "We have an audience!"

Mike raised his beer and said, "Show us what you've got, Zory!"

I looked across the room and saw Zory flirting with the three chicks. Two of the girls were huddled at the coffee table snorting thin white lines of powder with a straw. The other girl was sitting on Zory's lap and they were laughing hysterically. Sex, drugs, and Rock 'n' roll.

"When you're done with your fooling around, do you want to play a song for the girls?"

"Come on, Y. You're just jealous!" said Zory, still laughing. He waved to his harem. "I'll be back, my space-age chickadees!"

"What should we do, guys? 'Space Age Love', 'Parallel Galaxy', or 'Energize Me'?"

"Let's play 'Space Age Love'," said Zory. "I know it best."

"Okay, I'll start the flying saucer."

We tore through the song and didn't mess it up too badly. Afterward, the girls applauded with great enthusiasm. "You sound great – kind of like David Bowie!" Mike said to Zory.

I knew Zory had been wondering if he was trying too hard to sound like Bowie. He opened his mouth to say something negative but closed it again. He'd decided to accept the comment as the compliment it was meant to be.

"More! Play some more!" screamed the chicks. "You guys are great!"

We played "Energize Me" and "At Home in my Dome", causing the girls to cheer even louder. Then I introduced a new, untitled song to our small audience. Starting with a heavy machine-gun riff, it was a jaw-dropper.

22

LITTLE GREEN PILLS
LOS ANGELES - JULY 1973

Zory and I had been popping the little green pills for days on end. Until today, we'd been working on lyrics for the untitled new song, which we decided to name "Spacers". As much as I liked speed, it made sleep difficult and I became agitated at the smallest annoyances.

"Ed, do you want to come out with us tonight?" I asked, a bit irritably.

"No, I don't have money to waste on partying."

"Shit, Ed. It's fun to go out and spread the word about Zolar X."

"We only have one more month of Unemployment and rent for August is coming."

"You're so damn conservative, just like an old man! It'll be fine. We'll have a yard sale or something!"

"You and Zory party too much. Don't you think I've noticed you popping those pills?"

"Stop acting like you're my father. You have no authority over me!"

"And your leads have been sounding sloppy lately!"

"Fuck you, Ed! Sloppy guitar huh? You fuckin' asshole!" I left the living room, slamming the door behind me. He could be a dick.

Back in my bedroom, I practiced every scale over and over, faster and faster, free-forming leads from classical to blues. I was feeling crazy from the diet pills and knew I had to stop. Tomorrow maybe. Hours later, I glanced up and saw the long shadows outside. Shit, it was dusk already. How long had I been here? I saw the deep grooves on my fingers but I kept going. More leads. More notes. My hand began to cramp and my fingers were bleeding. But that son of a bitch Ed. Sloppy guitar? I'd show him.

Ed had always been able to push my buttons. Seven years with the guy in the same band. We went to rock shows together, partied together, played chess, and went to movies together but bickered when it came to music. Why did I put up with him? Well, because he was one of my best friends, and there were more good times than bad. He also had a car.

I heard laughter and music coming from the living room. It sounded like Bowie's new album, *Aladdin Sane*. Putting my guitar down, I went out to join my roommates.

"Hey, Ygarr? What were you doing in your room all this time?" asked Zory.

Knowing Ed was within earshot I said, "Playing guitar because of what *Ed* said. See my fingers? No more sloppy leads!"

"So that's what the argument was about?"

"Comments like that get to me, but what are you guys doing – having a party?"

"Play 'Watch That Man'!" yelled Zany, ignoring me.

"Yeah, sing it with Zory," Mike added. "He reminds me of Bowie!"

Next thing I knew, Zory was face to face with Mike. "Fuck Mike, I'm sick of hearing that! I'm Zory Zenith, a one of a kind, android vocalist. Stop comparing me to Bowie! It's NOT a compliment! Here's what I think of Bowie!"

I couldn't believe it when Zory grabbed all six of his Bowie albums and smashed them to bits. Then he took the vinyl shards and torn album covers and tossed them into the fireplace. The melting vinyl hissed and popped as the cardboard covers burnt merrily.

"Shit, Zory. He was just complimenting you!"

"It gets under my crawl!" snapped Zory.

An odd silence followed. It was the first time I'd seen him this way. At first, I thought it was kind of funny. He'd never been a mild-mannered Clark Kent, but this explosion was over the top. Then I wondered if maybe it was the little green pills.

23

GARY "DALLAS" FONTENOT
LOS ANGELES - AUGUST 1973

I heard chatter coming from the kitchen. As I shuffled past the living room, I couldn't help but look over at the remnants of Zory's Bowie collection in the fireplace. I was sure he'd regret smashing his albums, but this was a new day and it was better just to forget.

I walked into the kitchen to hear Zory explain, "Okay, we all know last night was kind of crazy, but it's time to get on with today's agenda. First, we need to get Zany's Space Age Luv stickers from the printer. I also brought the silver and black spray paint for my Zolar X stencils. Soon we can plaster Zolar X all over fucking Hollywood! And finally, let's check out that club Stefan Shady was telling us about, the Starwood! Maybe we can get a gig."

The phone rang and Zany picked it up. "Hello? Yeah, we're looking for a drummer. Why?" We saw him smile as he listened to the caller on the other end. "Yeah sure, that would work. Hang on and I'll ask." He held the phone away from his ear and said, "It's Jeff, the drummer from Legs Diamond. He wants to come down from the Bay area to audition!"

We looked at each other and I shrugged. "When?"

"He says he'll be here this weekend," said Zany.

"That's perfect. Give him the address. Looking forward to checking him out."

Zany hung up and I said, "I hope this guy works out. Are you sure about him, Zany? We can't afford to waste time on another caveman."

"I can't make any promises," said Zany. "All I know is he's a damn good drummer.

"Beggars can't be choosers," says Ed.

"Shucks, Uncle Ed. Why can't beggars be choosers?" said Zory, mimicking Jethro Clampett. Everyone laughed as he turned his head mechanically from side to side and said in a monotone voice, "As Roger McGuinn of the Byrds would say, 'Now spacemen, it is time to transport to the Earther print shop. We must advertise from within our space bubble.' I'm the mediator for Zolar X, am I not?" He turned his head robotically, looking at each of us.

"You're too much!" said Zany, laughing.

We busted up laughing as we went out the door.

The Space Age Luv stickers were beautiful. The black and white sticker portrayed an alien being with a massive brain and pointed ears. "Zolar X" was at the top and "Space Age Luv" was crafted in futuristic calligraphy in the white space beside it.

"Let's slap these on every pole around Rodney's and the Rainbow. Then we'll go check out the Starwood!" said Zory. We used almost a full tank of gas that afternoon, but we stickered just about every block on Sunset from La Brea to Doheny.

Eventually, we stopped in front of the Starwood. As we got out of the car and walked towards the door I said to Zory, "We should come back and do the stenciling here and at Rodney's when there's less traffic and humans. I really don't think this is legal on planet Earth."

"Okay, Y. Let's start at Rodney's and work our way back after the humans are gone."

We looked up at the Starwood marque, which read "Buckingham Nicks and Stray Dog." We tried the door but it was locked. We rattled and pounded, hoping someone would hear us. A woman finally came to the door and shouted through the glass, "Are you guys Stray Dog?"

"We have an appointment with the booking manager," Zory yelled back.

"You mean Gary?"

"Yeah, he's expecting us."

"You'll want to go through the back lot and up the stairs."

"What are you doing?" Ed said under his breath. "We don't have an appointment!"

"I'm getting us a gig!"

"Come on Ed, you should be happy," I said. "Now we'll *have* to get a drummer!"

We rang a buzzer at the top of the stairs. I heard footsteps and the door slowly opened. I could only imagine how we must have looked. Four guys with Zolar X T-shirts, pointed hair, and (except for Ed) Spock eyebrows. The staff member squinted in confusion and looked us over carefully before breaking into a wide smile. "What can

I do for you, boys?" he asked in an effeminate manner.

"We're here to see the boss," Zory said quickly.

"You mean Mr. Nash?"

"No, his name's Gary."

"Oh, you mean Mr. Fontenot! He's in a meeting, but I can give him a message."

"That would be great! Hey Zany, hand me one of our stickers. Yeah, if you could give him this – you got a pen? Hey Ed, what's our number?"

Zory scribbled our number on the sticker and handed it to the guy. "Darlin', tell him we're Zolar X—the next big thing in science fiction rock music."

Space Age Luv Sticker, 1973
Art credit: Zany Zatovian

OUT OF THIS WORLD: THE STORY OF ZOLAR X

24

400 LIGHT-YEARS FROM HOME
LOS ANGELES - AUGUST 1973

"Zany, what time is that drummer coming today?"

"Jeff just called and said he'll be here within the hour."

"We really shouldn't worry about his looks – only that he can drum," said Ed.

"Don't kid yourself, Ed," said Zory. "Looks are just as important! I mean, we're a theatrical band and looks count. This is the same sort of thing as casting for a motion picture. We can't settle for a deadbeat!"

"You guys and this image. We're musicians, not actors!"

"Speak for yourself, Ed. This is show biz!"

Zany went to the door and yelled, "Jeff's here."

We stood at the window and watched.

"First impressions can be spot on. Check out his Aerosmith T-shirt."

"Damn!" said Zory. "His hair is long!"

I looked at Zory. He looked at me and we both shook our heads negatively.

"Yeah, for Zolar X, adaptability and willingness to become something more is key." Watching this guy, I couldn't help but think he'd never cut his hair. He kept tossing it and brushing it back from his face like a girl. "Old school Rock'n'roll," I muttered.

After brief introductions, we helped the stoner bring in the drum kit. As usual, we started with "Space Age Love". Zory told him, "it's 4/4. Simple – try to keep up!"

There might have been a glimmer of hope in the beginning, but as the afternoon wore on, it became clear that Jeff's style wasn't going to fit with the progressive beats of Zolar X. He argued about everything we said, and it was obvious–there was a stubborn streak to the guy.

"You'll need to cut your hair," said Zory, after a particularly irritating exchange.

"And draw your eyebrows up," I said, upping the ante.

"Fuck, I don't know about that!" said Jeff. "Cut my hair? Shit, I don't really think I could be a spaceman."

He didn't make the cut. Even excluding the way he looked and how he played, there was simply no magical attraction. With Zory, there was a destiny factor at play, and I couldn't help but think that surely the stars would align again when we found the right drummer. After traveling 400 light-years to find Zory, we weren't about to accept a lemon.

Jeff packed up his stuff and drove away, never to be seen again. Zory looked at us. "Well, that guy wasn't very friendly. Just another hippie generation burnout!"

"I liked him," said Ed. "I thought he played good!"

"He was alright only because he's my friend," admitted Zany. "I don't think he'd fit our band, but I kind of feel sorry that he came all this way."

"He was throwing up all kinds of red flags: 'I don't want to cut my hair. I won't change my name.' Our image scared the shit out of him. You guys know it!"

"I agree," said Zory. "Especially when you consider what we would expect him to become. He was a waste of time."

"Well, I could call Legs Diamond's' guitar player. I went to high school with Craig. He's short, cute, and a great musician," said Zany.

"But he's a guitar player," Ed objected.

"Yeah but he's jammed on drums at lots of parties. He could learn this music and he definitely looks the part."

"I remember him. He's really cute and short. Yeah, he's a damn good guitar player. If you think he'd give it up to play drums, let's contact him."

25

STAR GIRLS
LOS ANGELES - 1973

Everywhere we went, eyes were always on us. Zory had a knack for spotting the hottest chicks with his actinic radar. One day we were walking down the boulevard and two really cute chicks were coming towards us. Breaking into one of his *Three Stooges* routines, Zory sounded exactly like Curly. "Wait a minute! Wait a minute! Incoming! Argf! Argf! Argf!" he yelled, in a high-pitched nasal voice. There was a fifty percent chance they'd turn around and run – which was also funny – or they'd start talking with us. You never knew, but there was nothing to lose.

Since we started wearing tights, it seemed that every girl we met wanted to find out what was under them. Talk about oversexed little aliens. If we went to Rodney's 100 times, we'd ended up getting laid ninety-eight of those times. We never asked their ages and never wore rubbers. We just did what we did. Zory often brought girls back to the house in Laurel Canyon. We'd entertain them musically, drink a little wine, and take them to bed. We referred to the older women who picked us up at the Rainbow as the "older chick buffet". Any girl more than eighteen was "older". On other occasions, we'd meet girls at the market or a clothing store. You could never tell when they were going to pop up.

Stacy and Tracey, the mother and daughter duet, picked us up a couple of times at the Rainbow. They became our chauffeurs for an underground nightlife we didn't know existed until now. One night, they took us to a gay comedy club where Paul Lynde was performing. We didn't want any misunderstandings, so we quickly told the girls we weren't gay. Later, after proving to them we weren't, they started taking us to X-rated movies and orgies in the Valley.

Each time they took us back to Hollywood, they'd always ask where we lived. We'd say, "Just drop us off at the same alley as last time." We'd hide, then peek around the corner and wait for them to leave. Then we'd walk to wherever we were going. When we'd see them the next time, they'd ask, "Where did you guys go?" And we'd always answer, "We beamed back to our ship." I truly believe they thought we were aliens.

Zory had been in long-term relationships most of his life but fucked every skirt available when he was in Shady Lady. These days, he had Kitty but maintained a roving eye. To be honest, I think he liked the attention more than the actual conquest. The guy could get laid at Rodney's every night if he tried, so I guess he was still looking for his special star girl. "Hey, Ygarr," he said to me, smiling his familiar smile. "How about we hang out at Rodney's tonight?"

26

RODNEY'S ENGLISH DISCO
LOS ANGELES - 1973

ZORY ZENITH

Rodney's was comfortable. It always felt like my place because I had a history there. If anybody fucking deserved to be at the club and hang out like it was their place then it was me. People accused Rodney of being a male groupie, which was bullshit, and a lot of people laughed at him behind his back, but I liked him. Not only was he always respectful and friendly to me, but he'd carved out a cool niche for himself in Hollywood. Anyone who hassled Rodney in my presence risked a punch in the face. I felt that close to him.

YGARR YGARRIST

Rodney Bingenheimer's English Disco was the first club Zany and I visited when we moved to Hollywood. Most importantly, that's where I met Zory. I'd seen Rodney around the club and had said hello a few times, but nothing more than that. He didn't seem like he was famous enough to have a club named after him, but he always had a cute teeny bopper on each arm. One night, Zory formally introduced me to him. Rodney was a very soft-spoken little guy. We talked about music and the scene. He asked Zory about Shady Lady, and Zory said, "That band's dead. My new band is Zolar X, and I'm the lead singer. I don't play drums anymore."

Rodney smiled meekly and said, "Zolar X? Far out name."

"Do you know any drummers?" I asked.

"I know a lot of drummers, but they're already in bands."

"Are you going to have live bands here?" Zory asked.

"Yeah, I'd like to."

"We'll let you know when we're ready! We want to be one of your first acts!"

"Cool. I'm gonna spin some records now. I'll put Bowie on in honor of you guys."

I watched Rodney walk away and said to Zory, "He must have an aggressive side to be able to connect with so many famous people in the rock world." There was more to the little man than met the eye. Bear in mind that Zory and I weren't very large either.

"Yeah, he's a mover and a shaker in this world. It would be cool to see how many autographed, framed pictures dating back to the mid-'60s he must have hanging on his walls. He knows the Beatles, David Bowie, Sonny and Cher, Led Zeppelin, and Rolling Stones personally."

"He seems kind of shy."

"I like him because he's a geek and he's little like us."

We looked around the packed dance floor. "Hey, Ygarr!" said Zory. "Get a load of the platforms on that guy! That's Chuck E Starr, one of Hollywood's most famous male groupies. And that's Kim Fowley over there. He's a small-time record producer. The chick in the black leather jacket beside him is Joan Jett. Pretty tough, huh?"

"She looks mean. Is she a rocker?"

"Yeah, I think she wants to be."

My mind had already wandered. "So Rodney's name is out front, but does he actually own this place?"

"No, Rodney is just the front. It's owned by Tom Ayres."

"This is the wildest, loosest club I've ever been in!"

"It's very decadent. The easiest place to pick up chicks and get laid!"

"Well, that's one of the things we're here for. Hey, look! There's Suzan Carson. Of course, she has her camera."

Susan saw us and walked over. "You guys are really getting the looks tonight. What's going on?"

"We came here tonight on an after-hours mission," Zory said mysteriously. "After closing, we're going to stencil the sidewalk out front with Zolar X. I have our stencil and spray paint stashed out back."

Susan agreed to give us a ride home later, and we spent the rest of the night drinking beer and listening to English rock. Towards closing, I got a blowjob in the bathroom. Not from Susan.

"Last call!" shouted the bartender. We finished our beers slowly and went to hang out at Susan's car while the crowd thinned. Zory walked over to a bush and lightly kicked at something underneath. He walked back to us, his thumb up in the air. "Still there," he said, smiling.

Eventually, Susan's car was the only one left, and the hum of the streetlight was the only noise. Even Sunset was empty. It was time to get to work.

A true artist, Zory moved like he'd done this a hundred times before. He quickly placed the stencil on the sidewalk, shot it with black, moved the stencil slightly, and shot it with silver to create a 3D, drop-shadow effect. Then he moved across the street to repeat the process. When he was done, there were ten Zolar X stencils in the shape of a fingernail moon. We stood back to admire his art. "This is so fucking cool!" I said "It's not a star on Hollywood Boulevard, but it's our logo on Sunset! People won't be able to miss it!"

L to R: Zory Zenith, Ygarr Ygarrist
Rodney's English Disco, circa1973
Photo courtesy: Chuck E Starr
Photographer unknown

OUT OF THIS WORLD: THE STORY OF ZOLAR X

27

ALIEN VISIONS
LOS ANGELES - 1973

Zory and I envisioned a thematic story based on a series of events about alien life. We'd been working hard these last few months to create a theatrical show for Zolar X—one that would incorporate flying saucers, lasers, robots, holograms, and alien habitats onstage with us as we performed. We also developed characters for a story that took place in another galaxy. One race of characters was called the Zoomen, who captured specimens for their homeworld of planet Zoo. We added the Pointed People and the Galaxy Girls, and the story grew into a full-blown sci-fi adventure. The first song to come from the concept was "Void of the Pointed Creatures", which became our favorite song to play on the Panasonic players when we pandered to the citizens on Hollywood Boulevard.

We'd been working the better part of the afternoon on lyrics for the song "Zoomen", and felt good about what we'd done. We were almost ready to move on to the other new song "Spacers", but decided to go through "Zoomen" again. "Okay, once more from the top," I said, strumming the rhythm. Zory sang the lyrics from his huge note pad.

Our human life is over
Saved were just a few
We were taken as samples
by the programmed men of Zoo
Here in a cube the size of a thri-thernal vacuum
we were kidnapped from afar
Refaced, replaced and cataloged
for a circus on a star

"I can see it now, Zory! You're singing from inside the cube cage, surrounded by a troupe of snarling Zoomen!"

"Yeah, nothing has ever been done like this on a rock stage before. We'll be the first!"

Pleased with our progress, Zory thought we should move on. "Let's work on Spacers. I love the opening machine-gun guitar riff!"

"It kicks ass, doesn't it? But let's call it a laser-lead riff. Do you have lyrics for it yet?"

"I have the concept for it. The Spacers are messengers telling planet Earth that there are others above. It goes something like this."

Million-lon cruise as we pivot along
Progression bends our mind
Faster than you and further than he
the Spacers race against time

The lyrics came together quickly. In no time, we were harmonizing the chorus.

In '72, we pointed our hair
Giving birth to our space-age love
The credit is God's
Since he put us here
To tell you
There are others above

After a short break, we heard Zany downstairs, who was also working on "Zoomen". But his tone didn't sound like the SVT. In fact, his bass sounded like it was coming from a very small speaker. We went downstairs to check it out and found him playing through my reel to reel. I shouted for him to stop, but he'd already blown the left channel. Great.

"What the hell are you doing playing out of the tape recorder when you have a perfectly good amplifier?" I asked angrily.

"I was trying to record a double track but wasn't sure how to operate your machine."

I was really pissed but what could I do? He was a great bass player. "Shit, Zany! You're supposed to monitor music through the headphones, not those little two-inch speakers. You wrecked the reel to reel for all of us! Oh well, at least the song sounds great, and we have some lyrics." I was already starting to forgive him.

The three of us spent the rest of the afternoon working on "Zoomen" and fantasizing about what a circus on a star would look like.

"How big is a thri-thernal vacuum?" I asked Zory.

"Big enough for a lion or a few humanoids. Maybe it has a force field or laser beams to keep the living samples pinned inside."

"Maybe this joint can take us where no Zolarian has gone before," said Zany, holding up a big fat joint. "This is some crazy shit, Zory. Have you ever tried it?"

"No, but I'll try anything once."

"Hey Ed, so you want to join us?" I shouted.

Ed walked into the room. "It's been a while since I smoked angel dust, Steve. Light it up!" Yes, he *still* called me Steve.

"Okay, Zory," I said. "This is your first time, so be prepared for a far-out trip! Just remember, you're safe at home with your brothers in Laurel Canyon."

After the first toke, an odd taste hit my tongue. I wasn't sure if it was PCP or the parsley Zany rolled it in. There was an electric fog and a sensation of floating—I guess one could say weightlessness. Unlike LSD, the hallucinations from PCP are more like real objects dissolving and reforming. Sounds became heavily amplified.

A voice split the air. "FUCK!" shouted Zory. "This is the most putrid smelling shit I've ever smoked! It's like a dead body!"

We all cracked up.

"Aside from this awful odor, it is kind of a funny high! Shit, I hear little pops and crackles inside my head!"

Ed started laughing. "Oh, that's just your brain cells frying."

"What? Fuck!"

We all laughed again. Ed had more experience with PCP, so he was having fun with Zory. He offered Zory another toke. "Oh my God, Ed!" said Zory, taking the joint. "What are you trying to do to me?"

"Hey guys, come check this out!" said Zany, calling us from the next room.

ZORY ZENITH

When we got there, Zany was standing in front of a full-length mirror. Suddenly the mirror melted like liquid metal, but I could still see our reflections. Ygarr and I both slowly reached toward the mirror. My hand looked like it was going *through* the glass like the glass was no longer a mirror but a portal to another world. I felt as if I could step into the unknown dimension beyond. I started to panic as Zany egged us on and Ed giggled devilishly in the background. Then Ygarr slapped my back and said, "It's just a mirror!"

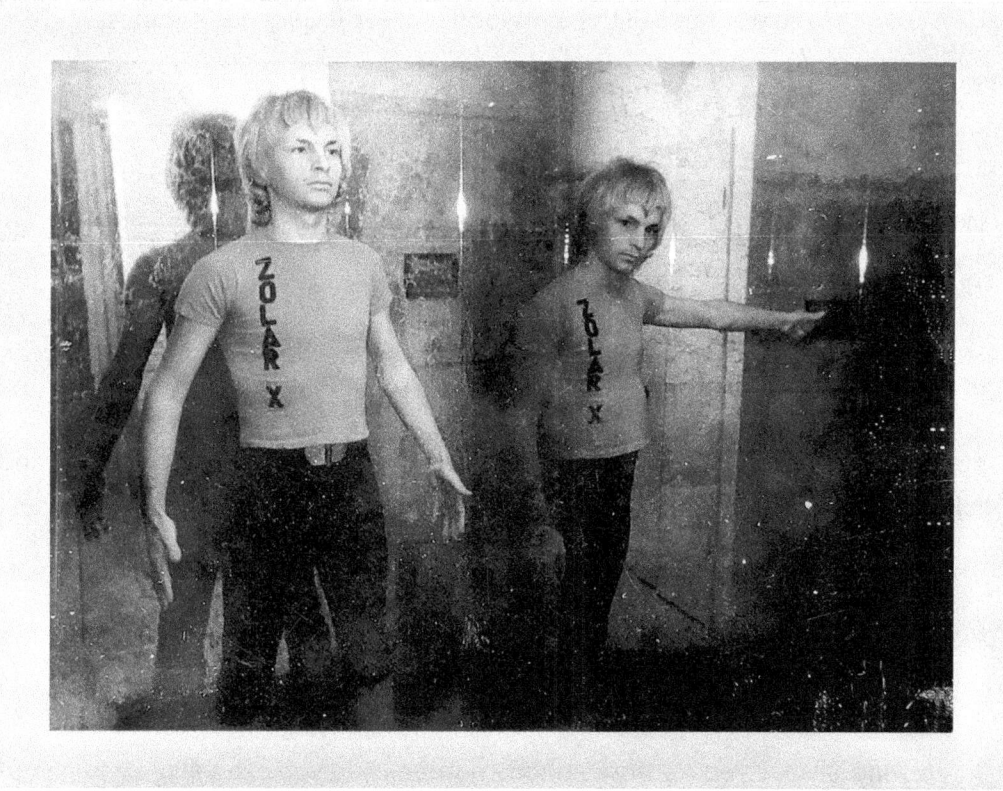

Ygarr Ygarrist, 1973
Photo credit: Zoann

28

THE VISIT
LOS ANGELES - 1973

After a crazy evening of chemically-induced multi-dimensional travel, we settled into our normal routine of styling our pointed haircuts and eyebrows and dressing in our tights and gravity boots. We liked to get Zolarized.

"Hey, Zory. Do you want to call the Starwood and see if Gary got our message?"

"Yeah, I'll call him."

The phone rang as he was reaching for it.

"Hello?"

"Hi, this is Gary Fontenot, manager of the Starwood."

Zory cupped his hand over the receiver. "Hey, Ygarr! It's the Starwood! This is freaky shit!"

"I book the acts," Gary continued. "I'm intrigued by your Space Age Luv sticker and what Peter told me about you dudes."

"That's supersonic! We're going to have the best show on this or any other planet!"

"Do you guys have a manager?"

"No manager and we're still looking for a drummer."

"Interesting. I'll give you my home phone number, and you can tell me when you guys are ready to play out. I have some open dates toward the end of the year."

Zory hurriedly jotted down the information. "That's great, Gary. Thanks a lot. We'll be in touch!" He pumped the air with his fist as he hung up the phone. "We're gonna get a gig at the Starwood!"

"But we still need a drummer," said Ed, always the wet blanket.

"And you still need to get Zolarized!" Zory and I said in unison.

"Hey, Zany. Did you hear that?" I called.

Zany ran up the stairs. "Yeah, that sounds cool! The Starwood looks like a great club to play!"

There was a knock at the door, and Zany yelled, "I'll get it!"

I heard talking and laughter. Whoever it is, he's calling Zany by his old name Booty.

Zany walked into the room and said, "Look who's here! It's Craig Rinehart, the other guy I called about being our drummer. We went to high school together. Craig is a great musician, and I know he can play drums because I've heard him at jams."

"Yeah, I've seen him around playing his Les Paul Jr. through a Marshall stack," I said, shaking hands. "Nice to see you again. Do you remember Ed? This is Zory, our new frontman."

"We met at that little hall in Hayward," said Ed.

"Shit, Zany. You were right. He *is* cute and short! Exactly what we're looking for!" said Zory. Then he broke into his robot voice: "Nice to meet you, Earthling. With the right amount of reconditioning, you can probably come on board and be a part of this crew. Please submit yourself to the laboratory. We promise you will no longer be the same after being discharged from indoctrination within the ship. Be prepared."

"Hold on!" said Craig. "I'm here on my way to Disneyland, but I thought I'd stop and check you guys out. You're the talk of the Bay area. Jeff snuck off behind our backs and came down here to audition. When he got back, he said he didn't want to join a crazy space band where he had to cut his hair. He said the music wasn't very good, but I knew it had to be something special if Booty and Steve were both in it."

"So, are your original songs for Legs Diamond any good?" asked Zory, somewhat cheekily.

"They're alright. It's just hard rock."

"Let's go downstairs to the studio and we'll play a song called 'Parallel Galaxy.' You have to check out my 100-watt Hiwatt, Craig. This sucker has balls!"

Down we went, and soon we were ready to play.

Zory counted off. "One, two, three, four!"

Craig's eyes opened wide and his jaw dropped as we thundered through the song.

THE VISIT

He shook his head when we crashed to the conclusion. "That's fantastic!" he said. "I've never heard a song like that before! You guys have something going on here, but what you need is a Keith Moon style drummer. I've only fooled around on drums and this is a serious project."

"I have a double set of clear Fibes!" offered Zory. "You'd just need the hardware."

"This is very tempting; a professional band. It's a lot to think about, but the main problem is that I'm in the Bay area and you guys are here in LA."

"I know giving up your guitar for the drums and moving to LA would be a lot to ask," I said. "We just want you to know that we have plenty of room here. You'd look great in a Zolar outfit!"

Craig just stood there looking a bit dumbfounded. "I'll be in touch," he finally said, walking to his car.

We looked at each other as he drove off. "I think we planted a seed," I said.

L to R: Zany Zatovian, Craig Rinehart, Zory Zenith, Ygarr Ygarrist, 1973
Photo credit: Zoann

OUT OF THIS WORLD: THE STORY OF ZOLAR X

29

WINDS OF CHANGE
LOS ANGELES - 1973

As always, we woke up, showered, styled our points, drew on our eyebrows, put on our space suits, and got ready for the day. Inevitably, one of us would say something like "Let's go to the market" or "Let's work on the new song." This is how we lived.

On this day, I beat them to the punch. "Hey guys, let's head down Sunset to check out Earther chicks and go to the music store."

"After that, maybe we could go to the West Coast Hollywood Theater and see two movies for a buck," said Zory. "They're playing *Silent Running* and *Slaughterhouse 5*! And Rodney's is just down the street."

"I've already seen *Slaughterhouse 5* three times but I haven't seen *Silent Running,* so I guess I'll go," said Zany.

"When we get back unless we get lucky, we can work on music."

"For five bucks we can get two movies, popcorn, and Cokes."

"That's pretty damn good!" I said.

We headed out, not knowing where we'd end up eventually. Walking down Sunset, we always got strange looks and honking horns, but we were used to it. The world was our stage.

Much later, we were back at home working on music in the living room. I played the new song on my acoustic guitar.

Zory looked at a Marvel comic book on the floor and said, "I have an idea. I want to write a song called 'Thru Comic Doors', and the Zory character could be a superhero." He grabbed his notepad as I plucked out a few notes and sang the title.

At the speed of light, Zory started scribbling lyrics:

Stepping into twilight
Beyond the after

Crossing thresholds
Known to no one
Superhero knowing more

When we got to the break where the vocals came back in, I suggested to Zory that he could use his mechanical Zorbot voice. He wrote:

In my altitude of brilliance
I feel super to behold
Through space, through time, through nothing
Challenging a wicked foe

We continued to write while Ed and Mike played chess and Zany heated a can of soup. There was a pounding at the door. Not knocking. Pounding.

"Shit!" said Ed. "I wonder who the fuck is thumping at our door?"

I looked over and caught a glimpse of a man in a three-piece suit. I couldn't hear what he was saying to Ed, but it sounded serious. I heard Ed say, "You gotta be kidding me!"

Soon the man left, and Ed walked back to the living room holding a business card. "You guys aren't going to believe this, but that was the owner of the house! He was abroad for four months on business, but when he got back, he found that rent hadn't been collected on this property. He thought we were squatters until I explained how we came to live here. He claims we've been paying rent to some fake landlord who was the last tenant! He said we can stay here and pay the same rent, but we'll have to make our checks payable to his company. Get this: he's not even going to charge us back rent. He said we were scammed too!"

My jaw fell open. "You mean we've been paying rent to some con artist when we could have been living here for free?"

"I guess, but if we want to stay here, we're gonna have to come up with some money because our Unemployment is running out."

"Let's have a yard sale on Sunday and break out that box of collectibles we brought with us for an emergency. I'll even sell my '59 Les Paul Junior if we need it."

"That will take care of August if we sell all that stuff, but what are we gonna do next month?" asked Ed, quite reasonably.

"This is a lot to process," I said. "We could stay here, or we could move back up north. Rent is cheaper, and that cute guitarist/drummer Craig Rinehart lives there. Zory, would you be willing to relocate to northern California?"

Zory stroked his chin thoughtfully. "We can't afford to live in Laurel Canyon without income, so let's just do what we have to do. Let's get this band up and running."

"Okay, I'll talk to my mom. Zany, your parents are in an apartment, and I know your dad, Ed. He's too smart to let any of us stay there. Maybe Zory and I could stay with my mom, and we could rent a rehearsal studio with the money we save. Shit, I better call her and see what she thinks about the idea."

I called my mom, Bobbie, and explained what happened. I told her we were thinking about moving back and asked if Zory and I could stay with her. Ed and Zany could stay with their parents as well. It wasn't the best plan but it was all we had.

Mom said, "I have a better idea. I'm tired of living in this house. It reminds me too much of your father, and I'm ready for a change with my new husband. The band can stay here if you pay the mortgage, which is 75 dollars a month. But there's one condition: Zoann gets to stay."

I couldn't believe what I was hearing. Seventy-five dollars a month? The whole band? A back yard, front yard, studio room, and a garage. It was almost too good to be true.

"Okay, guys," I said after hanging up. "This isn't science fiction—this is science fact. Sit down and hold onto your seats."

I told them the news, and the decision to move back was unanimous. Except for Mike, who elected to stay behind. We'd be minus his vehicle for the return trip.

Ygarr Ygarrist, 1973
Photo credit: Jeff Austin

Zory Zenith, 1973
Photo courtesy of Ed Dorn

30

HOUDINI
LAUREL CANYON - 1973

The yard sale was a success, and we were able to unload the collectibles. I also sold the Les Paul Jr. to a music store for $250. We'd have the money we needed to rent a trailer for the trip north. The money also covered our mortgage for the next three months. It was sad to leave Los Angeles and Laurel Canyon, but I looked forward to the promise of a house together, where we could build the stage show we'd always envisioned. At my mom's, we'd have access to tools, a garage, and two vehicles, which included Zoann's El Camino, the next best thing to a pickup truck.

"Okay amigos, we leave in five days," said Zory, "so I thought we could go on a walking tour of LA today. I want to show you where some of the rock stars live. I've been meaning to do that for a long time."

"Yeah, I wanna go to X Marks the Spot again!"

"I wanna get another Fatburger!"

"We should go to Pioneer Chicken, across from Rodney's. Maybe we'll see Eric Burdon of the Animals again," added Zory.

"Yeah, I wanna do that too, and maybe hit the Rainbow for a pepperoni pizza?" said Ed.

"And what about Rodney's? We have to go there before we leave."

As we headed out the door, Zory said, "It's always such an adventure walking around with you guys. I feel like a tour guide. When we go up the hill towards X Marks the Spot, that's where John Densmore of the Doors lives. And down the hill is Frank Zappa's old place. See that log cabin? This neighborhood is dotted with historical houses from rock figures to movie stars, where all the big-money people live. Over there on the right is where Mickey Dolenz lived. I heard when two of the Beatles were in town in '66, they stayed there and jammed with Roger McGuinn and the Byrds. Mickey supposedly recorded that jam on reel to reel. I think Denny Doherty and John Phillips from the Mamas and the Papas were there too."

"Shit! Wouldn't you like to hear that Beatles jam?" I said.

On Laurel Canyon Boulevard, we came to the Country Store. Zory pointed above the shop and said, "That's where Jim Morrison lived. There's something really special I want to show you guys. Follow me."

He took us to a vacant lot. It was a dried up, weeded area. The only thing left of the house that had occupied the land was rubble and broken bricks scattered about.

"This is a real fire hazard," Ed said, looking at a pile of old dry lumber.

Zory led us to a cement, rectangular structure roughly the size of a small swimming pool. "The most famous escape artist and magician of all time lived here!" he said, gesturing around.

"You mean Harry Houdini?" said Zany.

"Yeah. This cement pool is where he rehearsed his underwater escape tricks," said Zory, pointing to the hole in the ground. "Creepy, huh?"

It felt supernatural to me. We were standing on the very spot where Harry Houdini had lived—a man who tried his best to contact the other side. I wonder if he'd succeeded?

31

ALIENS IN SUBURBIA
BAY AREA - SEPTEMBER 1973

ZORY ZENITH

I was a little surprised that Kitty wanted to come with us. My first thought was why? So we're apart for six weeks or six months – whatever – I'd be back. But I decided not to make a fuss or question it because Kitty loved me and wanted to be a part of Zolar X. She was also a great hairstylist and seamstress.

At first, I was apprehensive about leaving Hollywood. I'd already done Shady Lady and was plugged into the rock community by the time I met Ygarr. Now I was trying to focus on getting Zolar X up and running, but how long would that take? At least we'd have a decent rehearsal space and time to hammer out the kinks.

YGARR YGARRIST

We returned to the Bay area with far more than we'd left with eight months ago. Now we had Zory and all his clothes, Zany and his stuff, a double set of drums, Kitty, and some furnishings from her apartment, including her blow dryers, makeup, and everything else a girl needed. Choosing our bedrooms, we settled in. Zoann already had a room, Zory and Kitty grabbed the third bedroom, I took the master bedroom because I could, and Zany got the couch. We set up our amps, drums, and the organ in the back room. Ed decided to stay with his parents, which took some of the pressure off and gave us more living space.

After a brief party to celebrate our move, we focused our attention on convincing Craig Rinehart to drum for our band. Zany gave him a call and told him we'd moved back to the Bay area, asking if we could come for a visit. Because we didn't take no for an answer, Zory, Zany, and I got fully Zolarized for the important meeting and drove out to Hayward in Zoann's El Camino. Craig was impressed with our look and took us to the garage, where he had a bunch of musical equipment set up. After running through "Space Age Love" on drums several times, he jumped at the opportunity to become a member of Zolar X. He moved in the next day, and we finally had our drummer.

Craig put his mattress on the floor next to the gear in the rehearsal room. He could roll out of bed and take two steps to his drums. Talk about living the Rock 'n' roll life. Over the next few days, he came up with cymbals, stands, and sticks —everything he needed to complete the kit Zory had brought from LA. Zolar X was complete.

We rehearsed every night and Craig quickly started to sound like a real drummer. The transition was relatively easy because he was already a musician. Dynamics, tempo, and melody were part of his soul. Meanwhile, Ed took a job at his dad's shop to make some extra cash, so he usually showed up around 5:00–missing all the fun.

During a break one day, we were watching the *Jetsons*, and an episode came on featuring the character Jet Screamer. He sang "Eep Opp Ork Ah Ah", which meant "I love you" in alien. We all busted up. It was such a cool episode. Zory said, "Instead of counting in normally on 'Parallel Galaxy', let's use Eep Opp Ork Ah Ah instead!"

I said, "Yeah, let's do that when Ed gets here and see what he does. It'll be funny!"

"He'll freak!" Zory agreed.

Ed rolled around as soon as he got off work. After some small talk, we headed to the studio to play "Parallel Galaxy." Zory took the mic and whispered in a surreal tone. "Eeeep Opppp Orkkkk Ahh Ahhhhhhhh." Ed didn't know what to do, but the rest of us jumped in and didn't miss a beat. Never mind that the new count was five beats not four.

"What the hell was that!" asked Ed, bewildered.

"That's the new count in," I told him.

"Well, somebody could have told me before we started the song!" he said crossly.

"It's not like we spend the day waiting for you, Ed. We're busy using our imaginations. For example, I'd like you to meet Eon Flash." I gestured towards our new drummer.

"You guys are getting too far out!"

"Thank you! Thank you very much!" said Zory in his best Elvis voice.

We all chuckled, and I could feel the tension dissolving.

Ed was resistant to change, but his keyboard melodies, and vocals fattened our sound. If only he had a synthesizer instead of that damned Hammond organ.

"How did you come up with that name for me?" Craig asked between songs.

"I always liked the *Flash* comic book character and you just look like an Eon, so I simply put the two together. Do you like it?"

"I love it! Just call me Eon."

There were six of us under the same roof, and we were very busy with rehearsals and formulating ideas on how to build Zolar X into a global phenomenon. We spent some of the time getting to know each other better. Zory and Kitty were getting along great, even though they'd already lived together. They came up with pet names for each other, and they sounded hilarious when they said "Bitsy" and "Babers" in high-pitched whines. It might sound annoying but it wasn't. We all loved Kitty partly because she immediately got a job at Red Barn and brought food home most every night.

Zany and my sister Zoe formed an atomic attraction to each other. They had so much in common that their neutrons and protons bonded as one.

The girls were incredibly important and helpful with their abilities to take simple thoughts or ideas from a sheet of paper and turn them into costumes. Thanks to them, our hair was always perfect. My band was my family, and I felt like I had two sisters.

"Hey, Kitty," I said. "Most of us have space names. Do you want one too"

"Sure! I'm digging it!"

"V isn't an X, Y, or Z, but it's close to the end of the alphabet. How about Veonity? You can call yourself Ve for short. What do you think?"

"I love it! Now I feel like I'm a member of the crew!" said Ve.

We talked every night, and there was so much to cover: space, life, religion, *The Three Stooges*, and Elvis. The talks went on and on, sometimes till dawn.

"When we get our record deal, I want to buy some land and build a dome house."

"Yeah, domes!"

"Why don't we all have one?"

"Yeah, one big, central dome for rehearsals and each member could have his own dome and they'd all be connected to the main one."

"Wouldn't it be cool if we could build them on the moon?"

"Hell, this is 1973. Surely by 1980, there will be a colony on the moon!"

"We've got to take this thing to the precipice – the absolute top!"

The Beatles were our main inspiration, and we hoped to duplicate what they did to achieve mainstream popularity. Zolar X would be the next huge thing in music, and everyone who lived in the house had devoted themselves to the cause. With our minds, hearts, and souls, we focused entirely on that goal.

32
TICKLED PINK
BAY AREA - SEPTEMBER 1973

Our hair went back to a combination of Woody Woodmansey, *Children of the Damned*, and the colored wigs in *Clockwork Orange*. Two plus two equaled five. Living with Zoann, I noticed party colors in her arsenal of hair supplies. I held up a bottle of Tickled Pink and asked, "Will this make my hair pink?"

"Your hair would have to be a light shade of blond to absorb that color."

"You mean like platinum?"

"Yeah, that would work but these aren't very intense colors. They're kind of pale."

"Could we add food color to them?"

"We could. But it might take a long time to wash out."

"Great! Let's start by cutting my hair shorter and bleaching it out. I need something a little more alien."

"With four of us being blond, it will set a precedent," said Zory.

We set up an assembly line in the kitchen and soon all four of us were blond. The acidic smell of peroxide hung in the air as we cracked jokes and wondered if blonds had more fun. Three of us got pixie cuts, but Eon chose to leave his hair a little longer. Zoann and Veonity slashed Eon's bangs to a point and re-did his eyebrows. Ed kept his normal, boring hair. He was always the freak of the group.

A week later, we were ready to step into the world of color. Nobody except maybe the Moon Maids on the British sci-fi TV show *UFO* had colored hair, and those were wigs. Even colored hair rinses were considered outrageous. Zoann's colors included Tickled Pink, Mauve Decade, Green Fields, and Peacock Blue, but they were deadly dull. Like scientific aliens in the laboratory, and aided by our imaginations, we mixed hair dye with food color to get what we wanted. We added red food color to Tickled Pink to punch it up a little. We mixed Mauve Decade with blue to make it deep purple. Zory mixed up a batch of turquoise to match his wild blue eyes. Zany opted for Martian Green to match his personality. New to the club, Eon sprinkled a little blue here and there. For myself, I chose Tickled Planetoid Pink. I loved the color and didn't give a shit what was manly or not manly. Don't forget, pink is the color of passion.

33

CALM BEFORE THE STORM
BAY AREA - SEPTEMBER 1973

Zolar X lyrics reflected peace, good over evil, creation, and optimism for a better world. We believed that if aliens landed on Earth, they would not be monsters or abnormal creatures. They would look upon us simple humanoids with empathy and understanding. Their advanced civilization and progressive technology would offer humanity a glimmer of hope. We sat around discussing these weighty topics on many nights, aided by the occasional beer or joint.

Passing a joint, Zory said, "There must be a multi-system of galaxies where interstellar flight is normal—dimensional travelers so technologically advanced they can reach planets light-years away. War and weaponry are not the answer. Earthers need to stop thinking they're the only creatures in the universe. Like Klaatu said just before he took off, 'We're not putting up with this, so get it together. We'll be watching and waiting to hear from you.'"

I agreed and added, "Yeah, Zolar X is lasers versus cave-man fire, ray guns versus bullets – basically the future versus the past."

Now that we were a complete band, we talked constantly about building the stage show we wanted to present to an audience. Unfortunately, we knew our imaginations were much larger than our pocketbooks. Our wish list grew immensely when we watched sci-fi movies such as The *Day the Earth Stood Still*. Seeing the inside of Klaatu's spaceship with the Plexiglas rings, the flickering lights, and pulsing diodes inspired us to dream beyond Earth. Too bad we didn't have Hollywood carpenters to build them for us.

We rehearsed every day, fine-tuning every note. Musically, we were very close. Zory and I had finished all the lyrics down to the last exclamation mark. We now had a set.

Parallel Galaxy
Space Age Love
Energize Me

Thru Comic Doors

At Home in My Dome

Spacers

In Command

We were never idle. When we weren't rehearsing, we were designing space suits, helmets, and ray guns. Zory was working on a Zolar X logo stencil for the drumheads. We spray painted our amplifiers silver and cut out a large plywood X for our backdrop. Zany even bought a batch of mother-of-pearl rhinestones and cemented them to the front of his Danelectro bass guitar. Just to keep up, I refinished my Stratocaster in pink and lavender to match the lyrics for "At Home in My Dome". The guitar also matched my hair.

"We have to start thinking about some 8 X 10 glossies for promotions," said Zory.

"My friend, Jeff Austin, is a photographer," I said. "Let's arrange something."

"I also have a friend, Jim Williams, who's a photographer!" said Eon. Photographers were not in short supply.

"Let's give them a call and get cracking!" said Zory. "The sooner we have photos to promote us, the sooner we'll be able to book shows."

"Or find a manager. You know we'll be needing one," I added.

Zory grinned. "Yeah, like a Brian Epstein or a Colonel Parker!"

"Maybe we can book the first show ourselves. Let's rent a hall," I suggested.

"We know a lot of people around here that could help," said Zany.

"Everybody will show up if we do!" said Eon. "You guys are famous around here!"

"That's funny, Eon," I said. "You're part of the band too, you know."

"Oh, yeah," said Eon. He smiled and laughed.

For our second photoshoot—the first with a complete band—we set up lights and draped a sheet across the wall of the backroom for a backdrop. The main object was to obtain photos for our first show flyer. For the occasion, we wore the most spacey clothes we had, and Zoann and Ve paid extra attention to our hair and makeup. The room was too small to capture full-length shots of the five of us, so we settled for individual shots and some closeups of the band. Jim the photographer asked if we wanted him to shoot in color or black-and-white. We choose black-and-white to give it a more '50s sci-fi look. This was the first time Ed had both his hair in a point and his eyebrows drawn up. Unbelievable.

"Hey, I've got an idea. I'll be right back!" said Zory. He ran from the room and returned with a book by Isaac Asimov titled *The Martian Way*. Chrome domes peeked through his hair where his ears should have been. They looked like caps from spray paint cans. Walking in a stiff, mechanical way, Zory stood against the backdrop with the book and read a line in his robotic voice. "Get out of your rut. Open your mind! The whole universe is waiting for people who aren't afraid to think in new ways – of doing new things." He paused, looked at the photographer and said, "Still thinking like an Earthling?"

CLICK CLICK CLICK.

I could tell the shot would be a classic.

Zory Zenith, 1973
Photo credit: Jim Williams

Zany Zatovian, 1973
Photo credit: Jim Williams

Ygarr Ygarrist, 1973
Photo credit: Jim Williams

34

LET THEM EAT CAKE
BAY AREA - SEPTEMBER 1973

ZORY ZENITH

After I met Ygarr and became a part of Zolar X, science fiction came to dominate the inner workings of my mind. I began watching anything and everything sci-fi on television: *UFO*, *Star Trek*, and *Outer Limits* were on every week. After seeing *The Day the Earth Stood Still* and *Forbidden Planet* at a dollar theater on acid, I knew how I wanted to decorate our stage. Nothing less than an entire alien world would do.

"You guys know I designed a whole stage set, right?" I told them one day.

"Yeah, Zory. We've seen your sketches. They're great, but they will cost money!"

"Hell, Ygarr! You never know what we might find just looking around. We can fabricate almost anything with silver spray paint and duct tape! We'll just apply the same principles we used to make our Zolar X clothes, only we'll be applying them to props."

"Where do you think we should start? You have the eye of a scavenger."

"Let's check the local mall. We might get lucky in some of the dumpsters, but we should go at night."

"So we're looking for any type of blinking lights, orbs, or other electronic stuff?"

"Yeah. We're also looking for anything we can turn into a drum riser."

"Zoann said we can take the El Camino any time we need it for Zolar X. Let's go see what we can find."

We waited until dark, and our expedition to the mall was a success. When we returned, the El Camino was loaded with cool stuff. We had six large Formica slabs and a huge window display that had been leaning against a dumpster.

"We'll be able to use these slabs for the stage! I don't mind hauling heavy shit around in the dead of the night. It's heavy, back-breaking work, but totally worth it!" I said.

"You bet it is!" said Ygarr. "Zolar X needs a science-fiction atmosphere!"

Zany walked into the garage and asked, "What the hell is that big brown thing over there? It looks like a dirty wall!"

"I'm going to turn that into a futuristic comic book rack and seat. When we're playing 'Comic Doors'. I'll sit down and read a comic. This is theater, you know!"

"I get it. That's funny and cool! But it looks like you have your work cut out."

"We'll need some roadies to help haul all this stuff."

"I have a friend with a milk truck who wants to roadie," said Eon. "He'll haul this stuff!"

"A milk truck? Did you say a fucking milk truck boy?" crooned Zory in a southern-hillbilly accent. "Dang boys, I just slopped the hogs and milked the cows!" He bent over laughing so hard he could barely talk. "Why can't it be a beer truck?" he gasped finally. "At least we could have a few brewskies on the way!"

"Shit, you should have your own television show! You have so many characters inside of you!" I said, shaking my head.

Everyone was excited about Zany's upcoming birthday. We checked the TV guide and saw that *Forbidden Planet* was on at 10:00 p.m., perfect for our surprise party. Zoann and Ve had already baked a UFO-shaped birthday cake with silver frosting. They used green M&Ms for portholes, and two red-hots at the back for thrusters. It looked like it could fly.

Zory dipped his finger in the frosting and said, "Supersonic! This is a space age treat!"

Ve slapped his hand and Zoe whisked the cake from the table. "I'm going to hide this until they get back," Zoann said reproachfully.

"I hope Eon remembers to go to the music store for the Rotosounds," said Zory, "Surely little E won't forget. We all pitched in to buy them."

All of a sudden, we heard horns honking from the driveway. I looked out the window and saw Eon and Zany parked in front of a crazy milk truck. "Hey Zory, come here," I said excitedly. "You have to see this!"

Zory joined me at the window and yelled in his hillbilly voice, "Well, I'll be! If it ain't the fucking milk truck! I guess that'll be the new Zolar mobile. Yee-ha!"

Zany walked in with several bags of groceries and made the introductions. "Hey everyone, this is our new roadie, Slim."

"Hi!" said Slim! "I'm small but strong, and my truck has a new engine. It might look weird, but it runs great!"

"Can I paint it like a spaceship?" asked Zory.

"Shit, yeah!"

We all laughed.

Zoann gave Zany a big hug and said, "Happy, birthday, Zany! You're 21 today, huh? You're finally old enough to drink legally!"

A party atmosphere was developing already; and there was something sneaky about Eon that I couldn't quite put my finger on. He was a smiley kid, but he'd been smiling non-stop since he arrived. I walked over and whispered, "Did you get them?"

Eon whispered back, "Yeah, I got 'em. They're under my seat in the van."

"Cool. You seem a little happier than usual. What's going on?"

Before Eon could answer, Zory handed us each a beer. Holding up his can he yelled, "To Zany Zatovian, the best damn space bass player on this planet or any other!"

We all cheered as Zoann and Ve carried the UFO cake into the room singing "Happy Birthday." We all joined in, but when the last notes faded Eon raced to the back room and crashed his cymbals. The rest of us followed to see what was going on.

"Okay, now that I have your attention," Eon said happily. "One of my promoter friends, Mark, booked a hall for us in San Lorenzo. We have a show! Happy birthday, Zany!"

"We have a show? That's fantastic!"

Zory picked Eon up in a bear hug. "When is it?" he shouted.

Eon waited for Zory to set him down before pulling a business card from his pocket. "December 22! Saturday night!" he said, reading the back of the card.

"That's a great birthday present!" said Ygarr.

"That gives us three months to promote the show and make final changes on our stage clothes and props."

"That's plenty of time. I have an idea for the promo poster, and we already have a good start on the props. Wait till Ed hears about this!"

"He'll be here at 5:00. We'll tell him then."

We set up the back room with blinking Christmas lights and a fog machine to create a spacey atmosphere. Not only were we celebrating Zany's birthday, but we were also celebrating the arrival of our first show. This was the first step in our journey towards the stars.

Later, the Zolar X family enjoyed *Forbidden Planet* for the umpteenth time. Robby the Robot was our favorite character. The party turned out great, the cake was a big hit, and Ed was finally happy.

Vintage Milk Truck
Photographer unknown

35

PICKLED HERRING, CAPERS, AND BEETS
LOS ANGELES - SEPTEMBER 1973

Even though Zory thought we had plenty of time, I knew three months would fly by at warp speed. The music was written, the songs were arranged, the set was ready, and we'd seen the hall and met Mark, the promoter. Then, at the last minute, we decided to change our stage clothing. After all, first impressions are important. No detail was too small.

"I just got off the phone with Hollywood Toys and they don't even know what space suit I'm talking about," I grumbled. "Shit, I even know exactly where it is in their store!"

"Hmm…. Hey Moe, what suit ya talking about?" cackled Zory in his Curly of *The Three Stooges* voice.

I laughed. "You know the child's size 14 cadet space suit I bought at Hollywood Toys for the photoshoot with Suzan Carson? I thought the suit would stretch more than it did, but it's too small. My mom needs more material to alter it, so I want to buy another suit. Anybody wanna go to LA?"

"Hell, yeah!" said Zory. "There are a few things I'd like to pick up. I wanna get my weights from my mom's house, and the iron fabricators on Western must have finished the base for my mic stand as well."

"Yeah! I wanna go too. Remember, we ordered those Plexiglas fins for our space helmets?" said Zany.

"I'd like to go, but I can't get away from work. My dad would kill me," mumbled Ed.

"Hey, Eon, do you wanna go?" asked Zory. "We could swing by Karabel's and get you some Zolar X life wear. They have the coolest colors, and you'd look great in tights! We need to get you out of those Levis!"

"Sure, I'll be brave! Who's driving?"

"You are!" we said in unison.

Eon didn't even blink. "Maybe we'll be able to get a hold of the manager of the

Starwood. Wasn't his name Gary?"

"Yeah, Gary Fontenot, and I have his number right here in my briefcase," I said, way ahead of him. A thing like that wasn't about to slip my mind.

"Cool. Let's make this a priority," he said, ready for adventure.

Seven hours went by quickly—almost at light speed. Zory was non-stop entertainment. When he wasn't doing one of his many impersonations, we blasted our Panasonics to fill the void. In between all of that, of course, we talked about the band. We made our preparations and got ready to leave. Highway 5 was a wormhole that would take us all the way to Hollywood.

Zory made arrangements to stay with his parents, and we arrived after supper on Friday night. We were delighted to meet his mother Anna Lee and father George for the first time. These were the people who made "the Bot," as we lovingly referred to our singer at times. Anna Lee, a plump southern Baptist Jewish woman, set out a smorgasbord of West Virginian treats. I was unfamiliar with offbeat delicacies such as pickled herring, capers, and beets, but they were interesting to my palate. George struck me as being a quiet man, sitting calmly in his easy chair drinking beer. The conversation livened up when they began talking about the hardships of coal mining in West Virginia, and about how they'd made the difficult move to Southern California to find a better life for their only son. Zory's folks were behind him 100%, no matter what he wanted to do with his life. Music wasn't a safe bet, but neither was coal mining.

By 10:00, we were ready to go out and his parents were ready to turn in.

"Hey, Eon," I said. "You've never been to Rodney Bingenheimer's English Disco? As fellow Zolarians, we have a solemn duty to take you there."

"I'm game. I've heard the stories!"

"Did I say we were giving you a choice?."

"Do you still have your key, Billy?" asked Anna Lee, trying not to intrude. "We'll leave the porch light on for you boys."

"Yeah, thanks Mom," said Zory, ashamed yet proud at the same time.

We awoke to the clanging of pans, the smell and hiss of frying bacon, and the clinking of dishes in the sink. There was something very special about the sounds of a mother in the kitchen, but I sure could have slept for a few more hours. Four hours ago we'd been walking down Sunset, a little tipsy and high on excitement.

Anna Lee yelled from her post in the kitchen, "I heard you boys talking last night about all the things you have to do while you're here, but you'll eat before you go and I won't take no for an answer!" Dishes clattered and delicious smells filled the air.

We gathered for a hearty meal of bacon, eggs, and buckwheat pancakes. "It's so good to have my son back!" Anna Lee said happily as if her son had been on Pluto rather than the Bay area these last few weeks. "Don't forget the toast!"

Zory picked up a plate and whispered in my ear, "See, Ygarr? This is what I have to put up with! You gotta love her, but damn, this is why my family is so fat!"

"Don't worry about it," I whispered back, failing to see the problem. "You're not fat, and besides, this is really sweet." I turned to his mother and smiled with appreciation. "This spread is delicious, Mrs. Myers. Thank you!" We were polite aliens.

Eon and Zany both said, "Yeah, thanks so much for having us." We were all lucky to have such cool, supportive parents.

Eventually, we finished eating the huge breakfast. "I love you Ma, but you're still trying to get me fat," said Zory, rising to peck his mom on the cheek. He didn't know how to act around her in front of his peers.

Anna Lee pretended she hadn't heard Zory's comment, "I hope you space boys want showers. We have clean towels for you in the linen closet down the hall."

"You guys go ahead," said Zory. "I'm gonna call the Starwood."

By noon, we were ready to hit the city. I was looking forward to everything we had to do. The Toy Store, the iron fabricators, and Cadillac Plastics were almost within walking distance from each other. Hollywood was so cool.

Eon seemed a bit worried as he headed the van down Sunset. "So you spoke with the manager, Zory?" he asked.

"Yes, I did. He sounded really interested to meet us. Our appointment's at 3:00 pm. Just follow our lead and act like an alien."

"This is crazy! He doesn't even know what we sound like!" Eon wasn't convinced.

"So that gives us time to go to Karabel's and the T-shirt shop too," added Zany changing the subject. "Let's head there now and pick up some streetwear for Eon. He needs an Eon Flash T-shirt."

"This is Hollywood," I quickly added reassuring Eon. "We must have stirred up a bit of interest by now. We blitzed Hollywood with our brand and we've never played a single show! It's impossible to look like this and not draw attention. They know that." No more running around in your old Levis, Craig! You're officially Eon Flash!"

He laughed nervously. "Okay, I'll wear my new T-shirt and tights for the meeting."

"Shit yeah, and we'll make sure our hair and makeup are perfect for this. Zory, are you ready?"

"I've been ready my whole life," said Zory.

We parked by the Starwood and paused to catch our breath. Eon changed into his new shirt and we checked each other's points to make sure we looked our alien best. Zory whipped out an eyebrow pencil from his boot and touched up Eon's brows. "There! Now you're ready, little brother!"

"Does any of this feel like déjà vu to you?" Zory asked Zany as we walked up the stairs. Before either of us could answer, Eon rang the buzzer. A husky man with straight brown hair styled like a surfer opened the door. His demeanor was businesslike, but he also looked cool in his cowboy boots. With a slight southern accent, he said, "Come on in. Welcome to the Starwood. I'm Gary Fontenot, the manager. My friends call me Dallas. I've heard a great deal about you guys already."

Zory introduced us in his robotic voice. "Greetings. I am Zory Zenith, mechanical mediator and vocalist extraordinaire. This is Ygarr Ygarrist, laser lead guitar. On space bass is Zany Zatovian. Next, we have Eon Flash, pattern timeist. Missing in action is Ed, our humanoid keyboard player."

Dallas stopped laughing long enough to say, "That's awesome, but I'll get right to the point. I'm willing to take a chance on you guys because I dig your look. I'm offering you a show on New Year's Eve. I'll even give you the best time slot from 11:00 – 12:00. You want it?"

All of us said in unison, "Shit yeah!"

"You won't regret it, Earthling," Zory promised.

"We have a show on December 22 in the Bay area if you want to check us out. We're looking for management, and we'd love to see you. Here's our phone number," I said, passing Dallas a slip of paper. You can reach us any time."

With business concluded, we shook hands and left the building. Everyone started talking at once as we climbed into the van. I let the gravity of the event sink in. "Shit, that took all of seven minutes!" I said, still in shock.

"Did that really happen?" asked Zany.

"That was fucking surreal!" said Zory.

"I can't believe he gave us the New Year's Eve show!" said Zany.

Eon said, "And that time slot! Can you believe it?"

"And we haven't played a note!" I added.

"Zolar X has landed on New Year's Eve! Hollywood here we come!" said Zory. "It's not *The Ed Sullivan Show* but damn, we're on our way!"

"Let's celebrate tonight," I said. "It's a Rainbow kind of night! Maybe we'll run into Eon's favorite rock star, Keith Moon."

"Hey Eon, pull into Thrifty's parking lot," said Zory. "They have a payphone around the back. I want to let my mom know we'll be out late tonight, but that we'll see them before we leave tomorrow."

I wondered if Mrs. Meyers would serve more capers, beets, and pickled herring.

The Starwood
Photographer unknown

OUT OF THIS WORLD: THE STORY OF ZOLAR X

36

ZOLAR DIY
BAY AREA - OCTOBER 1973

We got back late from Hollywood, but I was already putting new strings on my Sunburst Les Paul, bending and stretching them to stay in tune. I was still a little overwhelmed that we had a show on New Year's Eve in Hollywood.

Zory was bent over the kitchen table looking like a space age scientist. Spread out in front of him, he had an assortment of *Popular Mechanics*, *National Geographic*, and *Life* magazines, Zolar X photos, scissors, Elmer's Glue, pens, magic markers, and a large poster board. Looking up from the cut out pages he said, "This is called Do-It-Yourself. You know, when you want something done right, do it yourself? This will be our promo poster for the shows. My idea is to have some sort of a spacescape to show the alien world we inhabit. These stills from *Destination Moon* look pretty good. How's that for off the beaten path?"

"I like it," I said. "Looks as good as the pictures from NASA."

"I think we'll need more band photos though. I can't find a tight enough shot of us."

I looked at the glossy 8 x 10s on the table. "I see what you mean. We're too spread out."

"Yeah. It would be sweet if we had a shot of the band where we're even closer together so I could fit it into the bottom of the poster."

"Let's try Jeff this time for photos. He has his own darkroom."

"Okay, Y. Sounds good. We'll need blow-ups of the band because the poster is going to be 24 x 36. You see this area here above the lunar scape? I'll black out all the advertisement text with a magic marker and leave a few white dots for stars."

"It looks like a jig-saw puzzle. Lots of pieces to make one poster."

"Whatever it takes," said Zory. "I'll move these lunar mountains around this crater and paste the Zolar X logo right here." He pointed to the middle area where Earth was suspended amongst the stars.

"This is going to be so cool! I can't wait to get a copy. How many are we going to print?"

"Enough to saturate the whole Bay area! We'll need a shop that can do oversized prints."

"I'll look in the Yellow Pages for a print shop and call Jeff to set up a shoot," I told Zory. "Then I'll call Ed and give him the news about our Starwood show."

Back home in the Bay area, we were always on the prowl for anything and everything that looked even slightly futuristic. We went to Mission Boulevard one day, and we found plenty of thrift shops along the way. We hunted for rings, belts, planet-shaped necklaces, anything spacey for our next photoshoot. Men's shoes were always hideous: Hush Puppies, wingtips, work boots, and penny loafers—there was no way to find anything that looked even halfway Rock 'n' roll by shopping in the men's shoe department. For that reason, we went to the women's section. Lucky for us, we had small feet.

Zory mused about makeup. "Petty human intolerance makes people forget that actors have used makeup in one form or another for centuries. Makeup enhances both male and female features. Why do females use it every day? Because it works! Eyes look better, and cheekbones come out. The jawline sharpens. But Zolar X needs theatrical makeup, not the ordinary stuff models use. Theatrical makeup is necessary onstage, where spotlights can erase normal features. Growing up in Hollywood, I had friends whose parents were actors, light technicians, and makeup artists. Those things were everyday topics of conversation."

"We scored today!" I said excitedly, cutting him off. We had bags of stuff, including bubble clogs and other cool accessories. I bought a Martian Green orb ring, and we'd also found several pairs of black fishnet fingerless gloves that came way past the elbow. Very sexy.

Before heading home we stopped at a 7-Eleven for some beer. No sooner had we climbed out of the van when we heard, "Fags! Crazies! Go back to Mars!" Whether we were in LA or in East Bay suburbia, we always had to put up with assholes screaming at us. My first instinct was always to pull them from their cars and slap the shit out of them. How dare these fucking Earthers judge our book by the cover? Then the fear would settle in. What if they had baseball bats, crowbars, knives, or guns? You never knew if they'd jump out of their cars and chase us. I hated the feeling of being vulnerable and unprotected. It was the yin and yang of Earthers looking into the unknown. On this occasion, nothing happened and we drove off with the beer. Maybe next time they'd try to bash in our heads. We never knew.

To add a little more on this subject, Halloween is the one holiday in America where people can dress up and not be ridiculed. Everyone wears some outrageous costume; it's a celebration where the imagination can go way outside the box. It's the one day to be anybody or anything, and it's perfectly acceptable. On Halloween, people might look at us and say, "Cool costume!" From somebody else you might get, "Groovy!" But when we wore the same outfit another day, they might throw bottles and try to smash our faces, yelling "Weirdos!" Just to be different, Zory and I thought about dressing up in suits and ties for Halloween.

The photoshoot with Jeff was marvelous. Our friendship dated back to high school, and I bought him his first camera at a San Jose swap meet in the '60s. Outside of my Zolar X bandmates, Jeff was my best friend in the world. We set up in the back room again, but we didn't need a backdrop because Zory planned to cut us out like paper dolls and discard the background. Then he'd glue us onto the lunar scape to finish the poster. I was positive that Jeff had captured the shot Zory was looking for.

We pulled into Hayward Printers one beautiful Saturday afternoon. We were all semi-decked out, and Ed was even with us. I was so damn proud of the band. We were doing it. The man behind the counter smiled. "So here you are in the living flesh! I've been staring at your faces all week." He put the large tube on the counter and pulled out one of our posters. "What do you think?"

The poster looked terrific. It was one thing to see it in bits and pieces on the kitchen table, but the finished item was truly impressive. We left with 100 24 x 36 posters, 500 legal-size flyers, and even a roll of printed tickets.

"The stuff looks fabulous!" said Ed, surprisingly cheerful.

I said, "Yeah, it came out well."

"You know we have to give half of these to the promoter, right?" said Zany.

"Yeah, and I'll take Mark his share this week," Eon promised.

"Never too early to start promoting!" said Zory. "We have two months to get the word out."

"We'll be handing these out everywhere we go, slapping them on telephone poles, and putting them in music and record store windows," I said.

"From San Jose to San Francisco!" added Zory. Then, in his high-pitched Curly voice, he said, "Hey wait a second! Knuk! Knuk! Knuk! This sounds like a job for the goils. How about we all hit the street, but the goils can hand out flyers while we pose and smile for 'em? Knuk! Knuk! Knuk!"

We all busted up, and then I said, "So let's get the girls and do Southland Mall!"

"Soy-tanly!" said Curly-bot. "Knuk! Knuck! Knuck!"

Zolar X "First Show" Poster
Art credit. Zory Zenith

37

HAPPY BIRTHDAY YGARR
BAY AREA - NOVEMBER 1973

I was turning 22 on the 2nd of November, and we were in San Francisco looking for shows. By the time I was 23, I wanted to be rich and famous and living in a mansion somewhere exotic with large bodyguards and a harem of sexy girls. I wanted a dome on the moon, and I wanted to be the first band to play on the moon. Was that too much to ask?

Zory intruded on my thoughts. "What do you wanna do on your birthday?"

"I wanna go to San Francisco and be treated to some Italian pasta at Little Joe's. Many a time, I've sat at the counter staring at the fire watching the guy with the skillet flipping food. The place is so small it feels like the guys with white hats outnumber the customers, and there's always a line out the door. Then I'd like to check out a few clubs, find a chick, and get laid."

"Oh, that's all, huh," said Zory. "I can help with the first two."

"North Beach rock clubs like Bimbos and the Village have shows," Eon said.

"Yeah, let's check them out and see if we can get a gig," said Zany.

"It would be cosmic to get Ygarr a gig for his birthday!" said Zory.

"It's not a dome on the moon, but I'm feeling lucky," I said.

The rock band Doobie Brothers was playing at Bimbo's. The crowd had a Haight Ashbury '60s hippie vibe to it. To us, these Neanderthals were very much yesterday's news. I'd been to this same club many times when I lived here during the Garden of Eden strip club days. This is where parties began, loose women roamed, and cheap drinks flowed. On this night I ran into bartender Jerry from my old job. He introduced us to a promoter at the Village, a venue down on Broadway. Again, without playing a note, we had our third show. January 19, 1974, in San Francisco.

Autumn in San Francisco seemed even warmer than the summer. There were lots of shops, many street vendors, and a multitude of street acts. Ah, the City.

"Hey Zory," I said. "We've been talking about checking out North Beach for a while. You wanna go? It's such a beautiful day!"

"Sure!" said Zory. "I've been wanting to visit a fabric boutique called Britex near Union Square to see if we can get some Lurex for the new outfits we designed."

"Union Square is near North beach. New outfits? I don't know about you, but I'm ready to take our look to the next level."

"After we get our space jumpsuits made and the guys see how cool they are, I hope they'll get them too."

"Shit, yeah! In a variety of colors!"

"We can't be the space-age Beatles without matching suits!" enthused Zory. "If we want to encompass that, then we have to raise the stakes considerably. As writers and composers, we must look into the future for direction. Then, and only then, will we get our star on the Hollywood Walk of Fame. We have to prove we're from a whole other galaxy."

"That's some heavy shit! Why not us? All we need is a Brian Epstein and the space-age suits."

"I have this idea of tufted rings. Very spacey like Klaatu's collar on his spacesuit."

"You mean things that aren't attached to the suit?"

"Yeah! These rings will wrap around our arms and legs on any outfit. Like bracelets, they'll sit at the top of the boot or on the bicep to give us a real sci-fi look. I've seen them in comic books, but not on the street."

"We should hang down at Union Square and check out the shops. Maybe pick up a hot dog and an Orange Julius?"

"The mime artist Robert Shields will be doing his act at Union Square today. I'd like to check that out. Saw him a few years back on Hollywood Boulevard outside the Wax Museum."

"Mime has always been your forte, not mine. Performance art is interesting I guess, but I have no real love for it."

I was wrong though, and the show was fun. Seeing Robert Shields was something else. I'd heard about him a little over a year ago, and he was a big up-and-comer in the world of mime. He reminded me of the things I saw Zory do every day, like coming out of the bathroom or walking across a room. Zory studied his every move, and I knew he was taking mental notes. They were two different things though: Robert was performing in the street, but Zory was about to bring robotic mime to a rock stage.

ZORY ZENITH

Robert Shields was more original and much better than a lot of dancers on TV or in the movies. He had two basic looks: one was his white face with several different costume changes, but his most impressive act, in my mind, was his tribute to the stage and screen actors of Hollywood's Golden Era. For those performances, he utilized flesh-tone makeup with a thinly penciled-on mustache and a classic tux with tails. I was impressed that a performer of his caliber could be doing this on the street. There was something very ancient about it. I wondered how Robert would look performing in brightly colored Lurex? His fluid, robotic moves seemed to precisely fit my android character Zory Zenith, intergalactic rock star. I could separate myself from run-of-the-mill and often spastic lead singers if I used some of his moves in my act.

We left Union Square and went to Britex. I was shocked by the size of the store and the massive amount of fabric. There were rows and rows of cloth in the most incredible colors. Walking through the doors of Britex was like entering a world of possibilities. I looked at Ygarr in amazement. "Damn, this store has everything we'll ever need!"

YGARR YGARRIST

I'm sure the store would have been heaven to a professional costume designer or seamstress, but it was cool even to a guitarist. I could see the suit I designed in my mind, and I'd picked the colors pink and green. I hoped that they'd have those colors in stock and that I could get the material that day. I looked up and saw big rolls of stretch Lurex in Martian Green and Planetoid Pink staring back at me. It looked like amphibian skin. "Hey Zory, they have my colors!" I said happily. "Did you find yours?" I looked over and saw him holding up a roll of turquoise Lurex that looked almost fluorescent.

"This place is an acid trip!" said Zory, amazed. "I've been wanting to visit this San Francisco landmark for ages! Not just that, but the original Macy's is just down the street!"

We found a sales associate and asked about prices. She didn't say anything at first and just looked at us. Smiling, she said, "The stretch Lurex is $11 a yard. Are you two working on a picture? You look like you just stepped off a movie set."

Zory answered in his robotic voice, "You're close, but not quite. We just stepped off our spacecraft from Planet Zolar."

"We're the sci-fi band Zolar X," I explained.

She didn't know if we were serious or not, but the total was $150 plus change. We left with enough material for two space suits and enough silver Lurex to make Zory's tufted rings and then some.

"This is kick-ass!"

38

STRIKE TWO
BAY AREA - DECEMBER 1973

Ed was still singing lead vocals with Zory at rehearsal, which wasn't giving Zory the leeway to develop. "Give me a little space here, Ed!" said Zory, annoyed.

"I was the lead singer in Bosca and I've always been the lead singer!" Ed protested.

"Look, I don't wanna be an asshole, but this ain't Bosca! This is ZOLAR X and I'm the lead singer!"

"Calm down boys. We have a show coming up in a month!" said Zany. We hadn't fought much in the past, so this was out of place.

Ed was always coming into conflict with the rest of the band. He showed up late almost every day and was never Zolarized. He complained about our drinking or our makeup. His shit was getting old real fast.

"I see you guys are drinking wine and watching that damn *Star Trek* again! Shit, isn't this the same episode you watched a couple of weeks ago?" Ed asked.

Zory laughed and said, "Yeah, but I was just a little buzzed at that time. Today I'm coming off a quarter tab of Orange Sunshine. I could watch the same episode twenty times and still get something different out of it. Last week we smoked a finger-sized joint of Panama Red. You weren't here, and we had the best time ever watching the "Parallel Universe" episode of *Star Trek*!"

I yelled, "Shit, Ed, you just show up and play that fucking Hammond! You don't wear anything spacey. You don't do your hair spacey or your eyebrows. You need to get here on time and start living this with us!"

"Well, I have to work. I need to make money."

"What are you spending your money on?"

"I'm saving for a rainy day."

"That rainy day is here! Buy a fucking Moog!"

"You guys have known each other for years," said Eon. "Stop bickering. Tomorrow is Thanksgiving."

"Good thing. I think we all need a break. A day off won't kill us," said Zany.

December was only days away, and it was good to get back to the world of Zolar X. We were thinking about renting a rehearsal studio with a stage and a PA—someplace large enough for us to work on our stage show. With Zory talking about doing costume changes mid-show, he had to get his timing down to see how long it would take to dress and undress. We also had to figure out the set order and pick a song for an encore – just in case.

"What are you going to wear at the first show?" I asked our singer.

"One of my mom's dresses."

"Okay. What does it look like?"

"It's a viper-red Rudy Gernreich original – I found in my mom's closet. She looked at me kind of funny when I asked for it, but then I told her it was for a spacesuit and she laughed. Ve worked her magic and turned it into a futuristic jumpsuit."

Zany bounced into the room and said, "I'll be wearing silver bubble clogs, purple hair, and a leotard top."

"I'm wearing my astro-cadet suit and silver lace-up cosmic boots," I said, picturing it in my head.

"We'll have the girls do Eon's makeup, and he can jump into a pair of black tights," mused Zory.

"He'll be sitting down in the back, but he's so damn cute that we'll have to get a drum riser soon so the teeny-boppers can see him."

Zory leaned in and whispered, "Did you see that gaudy gold thing Ed thinks is spacey? He's going to wear *that* for the show? God, he's such a fucking buzz kill! I hate it!"

Zany nodded in agreement and said, "Uma goomba uma bay!"

I busted up laughing. Poor Ed.

I'd never thought of myself as a designer. At best, I might have been able to draw Fred Flintstone or use a ruler to form an X, but I was somehow able to convey my ideas to a professional seamstress and explain exactly how I wanted my spacesuit to look. She wrote down my instructions, gave me a quote, and told me when I could pick up the garment. Done deal.

I turned to Zory. "I found a little shop in Fremont that will make my pink and green suit, so tell Veonity not to worry about it. It'll cost me 75 bucks, but it'll be worth every dime! I'll take the material to her tomorrow. It will have a tall collar, kind of like your design, with a pink inlay of the letter Y on the back. I asked for pink elf cuffs with green sleeves, like my leather jacket. It will also have stirrups, so it will fit sleek and stay down inside my boots."

"Sounds very similar to mine! But mine is going to have huge shoulder pads. And of course, it will be silver and turquoise to match my eyes. Nah, not really," Zory laughed bashfully. "Too bad it's not going to be ready in time. I've been thinking about what it'll take to get it done right, so I'm not gonna put pressure on her to get it done next week."

"My seamstress told me mine will take at least a month, because she has other clients ahead of me."

"So our suits will be done at the same time. This is the real comic book stuff. I think it's going to beat everything of Bowie's except maybe that black vinyl Ronald McDonald suit by that guy Kansai in Japan."

"How many costume changes are you thinking? I'm okay with whatever you have in mind, just so long as you don't come out in some skimpy Frederick's of Hollywood getup." We had to draw the line somewhere.

"How many times do I have to tell everyone, I'm not David Bowie!" said Zory with feeling. "I'm just thinking about how many different getups I have in total. Out of that bunch, how many will fit under other getups? I'm getting a bit panicky. How much time will I have to change? I might have time during one of your solos, but will it be enough? And where can I change at this first show?"

"Well, that's what dress rehearsals are for. Just try different things and keep what works."

"Besides, I don't think there will be a place for you to change at the first show, so don't worry about it. We'll look great anyway. I'll be there to hold your hand," I added sarcastically.

"Oh, fuck you."

Zory wasn't the only member suffering from anxiety. He'd be singing lead vocals for the first time, so we were nervous too. For all our outward confidence, we wondered how the band would be perceived. No band had ever attempted to do what we were doing. Would the kids love us or hate us? We certainly weren't the Doobie Brothers.

We barely had enough room to rehearse, yet excitement grew with every passing hour. With Eon's bed, our equipment, the props, and our gigantic plywood X, the backroom got smaller each day. To get away from our tiny space just for a while, we booked a rehearsal studio in Oakland for three days. Gameday was almost upon us.

"Hey, Ygarr, do you realize this will be my first public performance ever!"

"No, not ever. You played drums and sang in your '60s rock band Butterscotch, plus you played drums for Shady Lady, so how can you say this is your first public performance? Come on now, Bot!"

"Well, I just mean this will be way different than just standing in front of the mirror with a hairbrush pretending to be Mick Jagger, okay?"

"Yeah, but our girl visitors liked the way you sang. Besides, you're not just a lead singer of a rock band—you're an android from another planet! If you feel nervous up there, just hide behind the android. Make him do the work. It will be like wearing full body armor! You'll do fine. Get over it – you're gonna be great!"

A thick fog rolled across the bay as we approached our turnoff to the studio in Oakland. Festooned with millions of tiny lights and decorations, the Bay Bridge twinkled brightly, reminding us that the holiday season was upon us. "I'm dreaming of a Green Christmas!" I sang, channeling my best Bing Crosby.

"Corn-nee!" Zory and Zany exploded in unison.

"You little green elf!" continued Zory. "Shouldn't you be busy in Santa's workshop about now? What are you doing here?" Then, in his best Curly voice, he said, "Oh yeah! I fergot! You're down here to play lead guitahr! MMMMMMHMM!"

"Santa Claus is coming to town, and I want a record deal!"

We were riding in Eon's van, and he turned to interrupt our jovial antics. "Hey, which way do I go? Right or left? The caravan behind us also needs to know."

Ed struggled with a huge map that took up most of the cab. He was trying to read the map with a flashlight, but the rustling made more noise than all the chatter in the van.

STRIKE TWO

"Shit Ed, get that map out of my face!" said Eon. "I remember now that it's Foothill! I'll pull over at the next right to make sure we didn't lose the milk truck."

We eventually found our way to the studio and parked outside. Phil, the soundman, and manager showed us where to load in. "Did you have any trouble finding the place?" he asked.

"No problem at all!" I lied. Then I looked around. "Shit, this isn't a rehearsal studio—this is a fucking auditorium! If we could transplant this joint to suburbia, we could pack it every night! Look at this stage!"

"Check out that *Star Trek* light panel on the back wall," said Zory. "I want one for my bedroom!"

The room was great and the band was on fire. We arranged and played our set at least three times, getting it tighter and tighter each time. Finally, we were happy with the final arrangement.

Parallel Galaxy
Space Age Love
Energize Me
Thru Comic Doors
At Home in My Dome
Spacers
Encore: In Command

I popped three strings off my Stratocaster during "At Home in My Dome" but somehow managed to finish the song. Zory sounded great, and there was so much echo in the room that we didn't even need the second Echoplex. Ve and Zoe snapped shot after shot with the Kodak. Thunder filled the big room as we played, and the ten friends we'd invited wandered around clapping and shouting.

"Woo hoo!"

"Party on!"

"We love Zolar X!"

CHECKLIST – TWO DAYS BEFORE THE SHOW

Bring spray paint

Get together with roadies

Final wardrobe plans

Makeup case and mirror

Hairspray

Make sure Zory has his tea and lemon

Remind Zory not to stick his finger in his ear and yell "test"

Bring X stencil for touch-ups

Extra strings and picks

Extra drumsticks

Verify guest list

Stock refrigerator with beer, wine, and soft drinks for after-party

Talk with promoter about PA system and microphones

Check lighting for show

Call Starwood to see if any of them are coming to the show

Arrange for pictures to be taken before, during, and after the show

Try to find somebody to record the show. Reel to reel, four-track, or anything decent

Look at the contract again to confirm that we get 50% of ticket sales

I stumbled through the day, but all I could think about was our show the next night. The house was eerily quiet, and everyone seemed deeply reflective. I found myself pacing the floor and contemplating the upcoming event. My brain stayed sharply focused on the music. I played the set in my head like a recording. We were ready.

We had to make sure our roadies Slim and Jim would be around to load up the next day. We weren't playing until 11:00 p.m., but our gear had to be set up and sound checked by 6:00 p.m., so we had to make sure they'd be there for that. The large Formica slabs for Zory's runway had to go into the milk truck first. Then we'd put the X in sideways because it wouldn't fit any other way. Although the milk truck was eight feet high, the X barely fit inside. Finally, we would cram Ed's organ and the amps in the back. The drums and the rest of the gear would ride with Eon.

We spent the rest of the day answering the telephone. People were calling us asking, "Where's it at?" "Is Craig Rinehart there?" "Hey Steve, remember me?" "Tell Booty

I'll see him there!" We took shifts in answering calls, which was a unique experience. I was beginning to think we'd need a secretary.

FINAL REHEARSALS BEFORE OUR FIRST SHOW
Oakland CA 1973

L to R: Zory Zenith, Ygarr Ygarrist
Photo credit: Zoann

Ygarr Ygarrist
Photo credit: Zoann

L to R: Ed Dorn, Zany Zatovian, Zory Zenith
Photo credit: Zoann

OUT OF THIS WORLD: THE STORY OF ZOLAR X

L to R: Zany Zatovian, Zoann
Photo credit: Jim Williams

L to R: Ed Dorn, Zory Zenith
Photo credit: Zoann

L to R: Ed Dorn, Zany Zatovian
Photo credit: Zoann

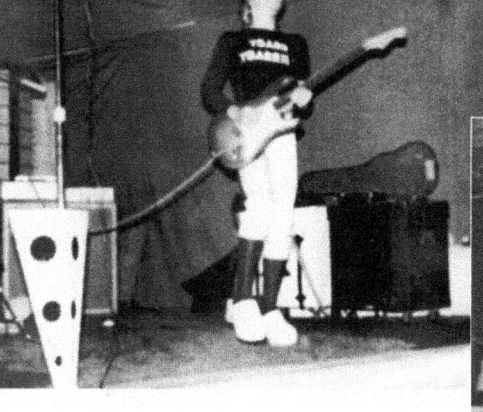

Ygarr Ygarrist
Photo credit: Zoann

L to R: Ed Dorn, Zany Zatovian, Eon Flash
Photo credit: Zoann

39

ZOLAR X LANDS
BAY AREA
DECEMBER 22, 1973

After a year of rehearsal, our first live show was staring us in the face. Writing the songs had been an artistic marathon — sometimes spiritual, and sometimes cosmic. Hell, sometimes the process had even been comic. A melody might jump up to bite us, and other times it would seem like an accident. The mind thinks one thing and then something magic changes everything. Powerful things had been happening since the beginning, and the band would never have happened if it weren't for a supernatural mix of coincidences and accidents. Meeting Zory at Rodney's was no fluke. He was exactly where he was supposed to be at exactly the right time. There was no other way to explain it. What an odd little bunch of renegade aliens we were.

ZORY ZENITH

The hall was bigger than I imagined. It was packed! Roughly the size of a small supermarket but with a lower ceiling, the place probably held about 300 comfortably, and we had maybe 500 guests in attendance. The kitchen had a roll-up window with a stainless-steel serving counter, where the organizers sold plastic cups of beer for 50 cents apiece. We got a cut of the booze sales too, but we had to change in the kitchen, which was no easy feat. Ve somehow teased my hair into a beautiful Rod Stewart-ish peacock, and my clothes were perfect. I could tell that costume changes would be difficult, but I didn't have time to worry about that.

My nerves had subsided somewhat. Perhaps it had something to do with the fifth of bourbon in Ve's bag, which by then, was only half a fifth. Ve lit a joint and said, "Just take one deep toke. That's all you'll need!" I did as instructed.

Slim led us through the crowd with a flashlight and said, "I think this is the opener's last song. This is the only clear passage, so just stay close to the wall." Halfway to the front, the pot started to come on. I was a bit anxious at first, but then I became interdimensional and the tension melted away as I walked. For a minute I was sad that I was doing my first performance synthetically, but then I remembered that androids are synthetic anyway. All I had to do was make a graceful entrance onto the stage.

OUT OF THIS WORLD: THE STORY OF ZOLAR X

YGARR YGARRIST

We made our way through the crowd as we caught Octavius's last song. The big double doors at the back of the auditorium were open, and more guests were outside than inside. A cloud of cigarette smoke hung in the air, and every kid had a beer in one hand and a smoke in the other. The air was full of tension, smoke, and excitement. The day was finally here. I was nervous.

"Would you look at the crowd!" said Eon.

Two teenyboppers turned to us and said, "Oh my God! You're Zolar X!"

The girls started pointing to us, tapping people in front of them saying, "There's Zolar X!" I tried to keep chatter to a minimum as I moved through the crowd, avoiding the guests as much as possible. I had to stay focused and didn't have time for long dialogues. Unless pretty girls were asking—then we made arrangements to meet them at the after-party later.

By now, the opener Octavius had finished their set and our roadies were moving our gear onto the stage. I stopped what I was doing to watch them hang our enormous, eight-foot black and silver X on the wall. Eon was particular about his drums so he helped the roadies set up the acrylic Fibes kit to his exact specifications. Zory's monstrosity comic book chair sat majestically on the side of the stage, with our three space helmets draped across the top like jewels on a crown. Ed's brown organ stood out like a sore thumb next to the silver Ampeg and Hiwatt amplifiers. We should have covered it with tinfoil.

I studied my bandmates. Zany looked very cool in his pink socks, silver bubble clogs, purple top, and purple hair. Eon seemed a bit nervous, but I could understand that. He'd switched his primary instrument and this was his hometown crowd. Ed, of course, was his usual stubborn self, but his Hammond would give us a fuller sound, even if it looked crummy. Zory Zenith was stunning in his flaming-red designer jumpsuit, turquoise hair, and silver bubble clogs. He'd have everyone's attention the second he stepped on stage.

I'd always been able to play guitar with the best of them, but I also had a hard time singing in front of an audience. To overcome that shyness, I often relied on a glass of wine or a shot of whiskey. Alcohol helped to ease my nerves, so I had a 7-Up bottle full of gin and tonic sitting by my Echoplex. The trick was to drink just enough to take the edge off.

We took our places on stage and I gazed out past the bright lights into the packed auditorium. Every folding chair was full, and even more people were standing. The long-haired teenagers looked like your typical Grateful Dead clones in old Levis and T-shirts, but they were going wild. I could feel the excitement in the air and nothing like this had ever happened on planet Earth. They were blown away by our pointed haircuts, the Spock eyebrows, and the turquoise, pink, and purple hair. They couldn't believe what they were seeing.

"BEAM ME UP!" screamed the audience. Fans yelled our Earth names: "Go Booty!" "Yeah, Steve!" "Zolar X rules!" Flashbulbs exploded, Polaroids and Nikons were everywhere.

A sudden hush blanketed the crowd as Zory moved to the mic. He counted off with "Eeeep Opppp Orrrrk Ah Ahhhhh," and the band fell in behind him perfectly. All eyes were on Zory as we moved through the intro of "Parallel Galaxy" into the first verse. I'd never felt that way on stage before, and I loved having the audience in the palm of my hand. The band sounded great. This was all I'd ever wanted.

Five minutes into the song, the classical influences of Beethoven merged with heavy rock for Zory's fourth verse.

On comes the scream of the contact machine
The message: will you live or die?
Imprisoned by colors molecular structured
We're trapped with no reply
The musical computer has rung its bell
All life support systems have failed

Zory's theatrical scream resonated authoritatively across the hall, leading the audience into the climactic false finale. They started to applaud and *boom*—we ripped back to the intro and led the crowd into an elfin jig with counterpoint melodies followed by vocal harmonies.

Come this way follow thus
Come this way follow us

We built up an enormous crescendo for the final climax. *WOMP!*

The crowd screamed and applauded wildly as I created the sound of a flying saucer landing with the feedback loop of my Echoplex. The fast-paced tempo and power chord structure of "Space Age Love" brought the audience to its feet and pulled them closer to the stage. Zany's bass was heavy thunder, like Entwistle but better. Eon looked like he was at the controls of a massive space cruiser, his limbs moving fluidly in perfect synchronization. I wailed on the lead – playing every note in a precise sequence, structured like a star chart in my memory. Zory Zenith hypnotized the front row with his robotic command. Part singer, part talker, and part robot, he delivered the last lines like an alien Macbeth:

Humans are fun
You know some people think we look kind of crazy
That's ridiculous
Because I mean, after all, we think you all look astronomical.
Zap! You're Zolarized!

I moved the Echoplex from thirty-five to zero to mimic the sound of a UFO flying off. Zany and I walked towards the center stage and stopped in front of Eon, crossing the necks of our guitar necks to form an X. The song ended and the crowd went crazy. During the applause, I took a big gulp of 7-Up and gin.

We bounced directly into "Energize Me", our ballad with balls. I sang the first verse and then Zory took over the lead vocals, thank God. The Lennon/McCartney harmonies melted the girls in the front row and the boys didn't hate it either. The whole band sang the chorus, repeating the song title over and over like an alien chant before the build up grew to emphasize a classical melody designed for French horns. Layer upon layer, three dynamic chords surged until the guitar took over with continuous trills. Eon twirled his sticks between each pulse as Zany's bass chords synced with my guitar. The classical ending had everyone on their feet again.

The roadies slid the gigantic chair into place for "Thru Comic Doors" but we didn't realize it would block Eon completely. Would the fans even be able to hear the drums? Oh well, there was nothing we could have done about it. Luckily, the drums were audible, and the heavy percussion boomed through the auditorium before colliding with my heroic guitar and Ed's keys. Zory sat in the chair with his comic book open as I approached the microphone. The haunting melody fortified the dynamic nature of the lyrics:

Stepping into twilight beyond the after

Crossing thresholds known to no one
Superhero knowing more

Zory joined me at the mic with a comic book in hand to harmonize.

Having powers disappearing
Identity, a secret for dreams explored, thru comic doors
Turning pages find me flying
Streaking inner space with gold

The fans clapped and shouted. We were classical and progressive, with an exciting Rock 'n' roll twist. Zolar X was a space symphony: heavy guitars, heavy bass, monstrous drums, and melodies galore. Like Tchaikovsky meets Hendrix, there was nothing ordinary about our music.

"Thru Comic Doors" took rock to its simplest form. Just two chords, with Zory, the ultimate superhero, miming every word robotically. He was brilliant.

In my altitude of brilliance
I feel super to behold
Through space through time through nothing
Challenging a wicked foe
Honesty for my weapon
The stars give me strength
Eliminate opposing forces
The hero stops the show
The hero stops the show
Hero!

Eon owned the room with his double bass drum fills as Zory sat down to read his comic book again. The song ended in layers of alternate melodies, creating a vision of the superhero conquering the villain. Wild applause echoed throughout the room.

Zory, Zany, and I grabbed our helmets from the mammoth chair as the roadies slid it over to the side of the stage.

"Nok voo, thank you, San Lorenzo," said Zory, addressing the noisy crowd. "This little song is about our home planet, where the sky is pink and lavender." He put on his helmet with no faceplate, making it possible to sing.

"Our planet is a very special place," I bragged. "No hate, no greed, and no wars."

"This one is called 'At Home in My Dome'!" Zory shouted.

The number was a slower-paced, dreamy affair, with vocal harmonies that painted a romantic picture of life on Plutonia. I heard people in the crowd yelling, "I wanna go there!" "I wanna dome of my own!" I remember thinking *me too*. The song was also a perfect bridge for our next tune, "Spacers".

I could only hear Ed through the monitors, so I looked over to see if I could find him. His gold lamé top was visible in the corner, and so was his black hair, but he was mostly hidden behind the right PA speaker. His keys added flavor to the songs, so I hoped the audience could hear him. Too bad he still had that old Hammond instead of a Moog.

The song ended with a muffled boom and Zory shouted, "All right, humans! Are you ready for some real Rocket roll? This one's called 'Spacers'! Hold onto your helmets because we're about to lift off!

I pulled my jumpsuit open to proudly display my sweaty Rocket Roll T-shirt underneath. The audience cheered loudly. Most of them probably couldn't even read it, but they had a good buzz going by now and didn't care anyway.

Zory introduced me with a grand flourish and said, "Take it, Ygarr!"

I ripped into the song with what Zory called my "machine-gun riff". My fingers flew on the fretboard as the band crashed into the song with the weight of a falling piano. I was there to inspire the young guitarists, show 'em how it's done. Shock and amazement radiated from their stoned, hypnotized faces. I felt an almost otherworldly sense of time and space—as if I was from another planet. With the music in my head and the crowd screaming their love, I soared to a place beyond our sad little planet. I looked out at the ecstatic fans and knew we were bringing them home with us. Sweat rolled down my back and adrenaline sang in my veins as we finished the song.

The encore was glorious. We fled the stage with thunderous applause ringing in our ears. The crowd looked stunned. They'd never seen or heard anything like us before. The response was like something from *Beatlemania*. If we weren't local, the girls might have been afraid to approach us. That was something we might have to deal with later, but not that night.

FIRST SHOW
San Lorenzo CA 1973

L to R: Ed Dorn, Zany Zatovian, Zory Zenith, Ygarr Ygarrist & Eon Flash is behind the prop
Photo credit: Zoann

L to R: Zany Zatovian, Zory Zenith, Kitty
Photo, courtesy Clay Babb,
Photographer unknown

L to R: Zany Zatovian, Ygarr Ygarrist
Photo credit: Zoann

L to R: Zany Zatovian, Zory Zenith
Photo credit: Zoann

L to R: Eon Flash, Zory Zenith
Photo credit: Zoann

L to R: Ed Dorn, Eon Flash, Ygarr Ygarrist
Photo credit: Zoann

40

PRESENCE OF AUTHORITY
BAY AREA
DECEMBER 27, 1973

"New Year's Eve in Hollywood?" said Zory. "I gotta warn you, there are so many frickin' parties this time of year that we wouldn't be able to make them all if we had twenty-four-hour limo service! If anybody approaches you with an invitation, just lemme look at it before you decide to go. Some are too far away!"

I stroked my chin thoughtfully. "First we have to get to Hollywood with five band members, all our equipment, the roadies, and the girls. Zory, have you talked to your parents yet? We'll need a place to stay."

"They have a partially furnished suite for us at the Carlton Towers—an apartment complex they manage. It only has one bed, so bring sleeping bags and pillows."

"Let's book a rehearsal at Dress Review just before we leave so we can get ready for the big night."

"Are we bringing all the big props?" Slim the roadie asked nervously.

"Hell, yeah!" said Zory. "We're bringing everything!"

"Does the Starwood have a drum riser?" Eon asked.

"No, it doesn't, so you'll be setting up on the floor. Down the road, we'll need to get you elevated."

"Now's the time if anyone wants their hair touched up or trimmed," said Zoann.

"I have your makeup covered," added Veonity.

"I'm gonna invite Stefan Shady to Dress Review and the show since he helped us get the gig," said Zory.

"This is so outrageous!" I said, pleased. "We just played our first show and now we're heading to Hollywood!"

We arrived for rehearsal at Dress Review on December 30, 1973. The roadies carried the gear inside and began to set up. We weren't famous yet, but at least we had roadies.

"It's good to be back here," I said, looking around at the familiar orange walls. "This is your first time here, Eon. Do you feel like a rock star yet?"

Eon chuckled. "I love it! It's so *orange*! This is the life!"

As usual, Ed was all business. "Let's get started," he said, looking sober and old.

"Relax, Ed!" I said. "Try to have some fun tonight!"

"Fuck, maybe we'll get a record deal tomorrow night!" said Zany.

"Nah," said Zory, shaking his head. "Nobody does business on New Year's."

"Hey, Eon," I said. "Since we're the only solo guys here, do you wanna go to Rodney's later and have some fun? Being the week of New Year's, everybody will be on holiday and there will be tons of chicks! We'll be able to promote our show!"

"Definitely!" said Eon. "I have to check it out!"

We ran through the set and we were still damn tight.

During a short break, Stefan Shady, lead singer of Shady Lady, walked in with a cute redhead.

"Hey! Come on in, guys!" said Zory. "Stefan, I think you know just about everyone except our new drummer, Eon, and Zoann, Ygarr's sister."

"Hi, everybody," said Stefan. "How ya doing? We thought we'd stop by and see what's happening. This is Syndee, by the way."

I kissed Syndee's hand like a gentleman. She was very foxy, but I was thinking about Rodney's later. There was never a shortage of sweet young things at the disco. Plus she was with Stefan.

"I love your hair. Is that pink?" Syndee chattered gaily. "I just got back from Led Zeppelin's castle. Do you like my jacket? I bought it in London. My dad the judge, blah blah blah…" She kept talking and wouldn't stop. We decided to start playing just to drown her out, which was more than fine with Ed, of course.

I made eye contact with Zory and rolled my eyes at Stefan and his date.

Zory smiled. "Okay, everybody. This one's called 'Space Age Love'!"

PRESENCE OF AUTHORITY

Hours later, Rodney's was buzzing. The place was jammed with cuties, we were playing the next night, and I was on my third beer. I had money in my sock just in case, and I was feeling alright. The planets seemed to be aligning in our favor.

I'd lost Eon in the crowd when I zoomed in on three blondes approaching. If everything went the way I hoped it would, I'd get the bed because it was first come, first serve. I was standing there about to pick which of the three I'd like to take back to the apartment when I felt a hand on my shoulder. Turning around, I saw the redheaded girl who loved the sound of her voice. I looked over at the blonde teenyboppers and back to the redhead. I had to admit, the redhead was much better looking.

"Ever hear of love at first sight?" said the redhead, smiling brightly. "When I saw you, I just knew I had to have you!"

I thought to myself, *this girl is nuts*. I said, "Well, I'm not looking for a girlfriend!"

"I'm so attracted to you that I can't control myself," she continued.

I shrugged. The matter seemed to be out of my hands. "If you insist."

We bought a pint of Southern Comfort and drank half the bottle on the way to the apartment. I think she ran every red light and it was a miracle the cops didn't pull us over. In a drunken haze, we stumbled into the apartment. We proceeded to fuck, drink, drink some more, do crazy shit, fall out of bed–repeating this cycle again and again. The sun was coming up when I realized I had to shuffle her out of there before everyone woke up. The place was like a battlefield, with bodies strewn about everywhere.

Syndee was a nice lay and it was fun, but I wasn't in LA to find a girlfriend. I was there to play a show.

Zory opened our door around noon. "Just making sure you're all up," he said, smiling. "The Starwood called, and they want us there at six for load-in. With so much going on tonight, no one will be getting a soundcheck, so we'll just do a quick line check onstage. The stage manager Dutch will do his best to get everything set up to our specifications. We might have to share our dressing room, but we can order anything we want from the menu."

"We'll be dressed already, but at least we'll be able to touch up our makeup," said Zany.

"This is the best New Year's I could ever imagine!" I said, feeling the usual butterflies.

"I'm flying high!" said Eon.

"Oww! I feel good!" sang Ed in his James Brown voice.

"Oh, by the way, guys, Dallas would like us to stay on stage after our set and lead the audience in the ten-second count down for the New Year," said Zory.

"I'll drink to that!"

"Make mine a double!"

"Right on!"

"Well, it's 5:00. Are you guys ready to head down there?" I asked. Tonight the Starwood, and tomorrow the rest of the world. There was no doubt in my mind that we'd have a record deal and be recording within the next three months.

We got a look at the interior of the club and the stage for the first time. I was excited. Our first show was great but it didn't have an elevated stage and proper lights. This time, the place would be packed with revelers celebrating the incoming New Year.

The rest of the band and crew hovered around the restaurant area ordering food. I didn't like to eat before going on stage, even hours before set time. But a few drinks? I was more than okay with that.

Hanging out in the dressing room, we went over the set arrangement. I tuned my guitars and watched Zoann spray some kind of gold shit in Ed's hair because he refused to dye it. He just didn't get it. Zory sipped hot tea and honey, which he claimed helped his pipes. He looked up at me and said in a perfect Elvis impersonation, "Well, if it's good enough for the King, it's good enough for me. Know what I mean?"

"So, you're doing three outfit changes tonight? Do any of them have rhinestones?" I asked, laughing.

"Nothing that elaborate. I just want to get a feel for costume changes."

"Myself, I'm just gonna do a striptease on stage. That's why I'm wearing my jazz slippers."

"What? Strip?" asked Eon, alarmed.

I was still laughing. The booze might have had something to do with that. "No, little E. I'm simply going to slip out of my satin overalls to show off my tights."

PRESENCE OF AUTHORITY

"That's a relief!"

"Where'd Zany go?" I asked.

"He went outside with a can of silver spray paint. Said he'd be right back."

Zany walked into the room and held up a silver left hand. "Hey guys, check this out!"

"Hey, you painted your hand silver. Looks cool! Like a glove!"

"Hey, Moe!" quizzed Zory in a high-pitched Curly voice. "Where'd ya get dem big ears?"

The room filled with laughter. It was a great tension breaker.

I held up a pair of large pink elf ears. "We're so close to the Toy Store that I walked over yesterday and found these in the bargain bin. I think it will be hilarious to wear them during the first song and then throw them into the audience," I said, looking around for approval, but everyone was too busy to pay much attention.

Slim came into the room accompanied by a couple of nerdy characters. "These guys are giving out badges for some comet or something."

One of the guys, wearing a sweater and thick glasses said, "It's no ordinary comet—its Comet Kohoutek, and it won't be back for 75,000 years! It's going to be so bright that you'll be able to see it in the daytime!"

"You guys want some badges?" grinned his sidekick. He was a skinny little fellow with a prominent Adam's apple and acne.

Dutch walked in and said, "Ten minutes to showtime!"

Zory turned to us. "Everyone out except the band! Okay, boys let's raise our drinks to 1974! This is going to be our year! Let's make it happen."

Dutch led us from the backstage area to the stage. Overlooking the room at the top of the landing, I felt a powerful presence of authority. We weren't going to play on that stage—we were going to fucking own it. The emcee announced us as we walked down the stairs. "Now, to usher in the New Year we have a very special treat for you. From a wild planet far, far away, we bring you, ZOLAR X!" The crowd roared.

And what a crowd. The balcony was stuffed with people, and drunken party-goers packed the floor. Even the sound booth was stuffed with guests. Time slowed to a crawl and everything around me stood out in extra high definition. Eon settled behind his kit and rumbled the kick drums. Ed and Zany gave me a nod of approval. I checked the settings on my Echoplex and signaled my readiness. Zory appeared out of the darkness as a thin beam of blue light grew wider, illuminating him to the audience. "OHHHHHH!" gasped the crowd.

Then we blasted into "Space Age Love" and people went apeshit. They rushed forward, pushing to get to the front of the stage. You could feel the energy. Between "At Home in My Dome" and "Thru Comic Doors", I spotted Stefan Shady and Dallas at the top of the stairs zooming in on our performance. The night was flying past so fast it felt like a blur.

Zory's retrorockets fired on all circuits. He lunged forward with the microphone and yelled, "Okay, Earthers. Ready to leave this planet? This one will blast your socks off! SPACERS!" The crowd made another massive surge towards the stage.

It was time to get serious, so I slipped the two little straps off my shoulders and let my satin overalls fall to the stage. I kicked them into the crowd and watched two girls fight for ownership. My laser lead solo was coming up, so Zory ducked behind the comic book chair for his last costume change. He emerged moments later as if he'd just beamed in from a spaceship—part rock god and part mechanical man. I was still soloing when he did a robotic glide to center stage to finish the song. The audience seemed a bit baffled as we sang "Nic-Koo Nah Ze Ott-Ree Abh Bly Darr," but they were digging it anyway. Horns and whistles filled the air. I was having too much fun to be nervous.

During our anthem "In Command," Zory tossed a bucket of space glitter into the crowd. That set off a wild chain reaction as guests hurled confetti they'd been saving for midnight, followed by a wild cacophony of horns and noisemakers. The craziness segued into "Parallel Galaxy" as the crowd went mental. They were well oiled by now.

Then it was two minutes till midnight. The house lights glowed warmly as the staff passed out hundreds of paper hats emblazoned with "New Year's 1974". Zory started the countdown and everyone else joined in. "10… 9… 8… 7… 6… 5… 4… 3… 2…1… HAPPY NEW YEAR!"

The dressing room was hot, crowded, and noisy. "That was a great show guys!" I said, face flushed, hair soaking wet. "I'm dripping pink sweat!"

"I love you all! We kicked ass!" said Zory.

"You think anyone important in the music business was out there?"

"You never know."

"Drinks for everyone!"

Slim walked over. "Dallas and Arthur are waiting outside."

"Cool. Thanks. Slim. Let 'em in."

Dallas walked in with another man. "Hey guys, I want to congratulate you on a great show. This is my second in command, Arthur."

Arthur's assertive handshake told me he was all business. He was short and Jewish, with curly black hair and a full black beard. Could he be our Brian Epstein?

"You guys could be the next big thing," said Arthur. "You just need the right management team."

"We know this isn't the time to talk business but let's talk soon," said Dallas. "In the meantime, here's some money to put in your pocket, or should I say tights." He took a white envelope from the inside pocket of his brown corduroy sports jacket and handed it to Zory. "When's your next show?"

"January 19 at The Village in San Francisco," said Zory.

"Great! I'll be there!" said Arthur. "I have all your contact information so I'll be in touch."

"You guys go ahead and enjoy the rest of your evening. Happy New Year and the drinks are on us!" said Dallas.

More people piled into the dressing room. Everyone wanted to congratulate us: groupies, wannabe girlfriends, even guys from the other acts. It was one big party in there, wall to wall and elbow to elbow. The drinks flowed and the joints went around.

A stranger called out, "Hey guy!!" and I turned to see a thirty-something-year-old man sipping on a pint of whiskey. Smiling ear to ear, he walked over to introduce himself as Charlie Patton from Memphis, Tennessee. "You guys are space-age Mozarts! This is going to be the biggest act on the planet!" he said in a thick Southern drawl. "We gotta get you to New York to meet Andy Warhol! I could get Lloyd Cross to make a hologram of you guys. I know all about lasers too—Kryptonite green with an inch-wide beam." He took another sip from the pint and slipped it into his pocket. Then he handed Zory a gold chain with a hologram medallion on it. I'd never seen a hologram before, but it was one of the coolest things I'd ever seen. Maybe this drunken

Southerner knew what he was talking about.

A grizzly man about fifty years old walked over to Charlie. The man stuck out among the young groupies and fans. I tried not to stare but couldn't help notice that one of his eyes didn't point in the same direction as the other.

Charlie pulled out the pint again and took another belt. "This here is my friend, John Desko," he slurred drunkenly. "John manages rock bands. Did I tell ya, I played football with Elvis? I really wanna work with you guys. Call me if you ever need any help or wanna borrow my laser, or if you ever need a place to stay. Hey John, what's my phone number?"

Desko gave us Charlie's number and we talked a bit. The man was personable, but he also had a demonic quality that I found a bit unnerving. Maybe it was his wonky eye.

"We wanna see that laser sometime," Zory said to Charlie as the conversation wound down. "We're gonna cruise the club now, but we'll be in touch."

"He may be drunk but he gets it!" I said to Zory as we walked away.

"I'm flabbergasted by this Charlie character," said Zory. "He's a big, drunken Southern teddy bear, and I wasn't sure whether to hug him, hit him, or dismiss him — but I rarely hit anyone I don't know."

I looked around. The excitement was high on the main floor of the club. It was time to get out there and represent. Skirts were waiting.

L to R: Ygarr Ygarrist, Stefen Shady, (Balcony)

Starwood New Years Eve Show, Los Angeles, CA December 31, 1973. Photo credit: Zoann

41

ZOLAR'S WORKSHOP
BAY AREA - JANUARY 1974

I was on cloud nine. Managed by the Starwood? Meeting Charlie Patton who knew about laser beams? Andy Warhol? New York City? This was only the beginning.

I walked into the living room and saw Ve fitting Zory for his Lurex space suit. Zoann sat at the kitchen table sewing small rectangular pieces of silver Lurex. Just beyond the machine, I saw stacks of Lurex she had cut into a variety of sizes. A box at the end of the coffee table contained four tufted, silver Lurex bracelets.

I picked up a bracelet and pretended to take a bite. "I want coffee with my donut!"

Everyone laughed and Zory said, "We were wondering what to call them!"

"Yeah, donuts. Cool!" I slid the bracelet onto my arm. It fit perfectly.

"We're making them for the arms and legs—all sorts of sizes," said Zoann.

Zory took one of the bigger donuts and pushed it up his arm to his shoulder. "Gimme another one!" He admired himself in the mirror and said, "This is the ticket, Ve! Take out the shoulder pads on my suit, and let's go with two donuts on each shoulder instead!"

"We'll have to attach them so they don't slide down your arm," said Veonity.

"I'm going to take one of these to the shop and have some pink ones made to go with my spacesuit," I said. "Zany! Eon! Come check these out!"

"I'll need some help if the whole band is going to wear these. I'll handle the sewing machine, but you guys can be my little helpers and stuff the tubes," said Zoann.

"I'll close the donuts after they stuff them," added Veonity.

Eon, Zany, and I sat on the couch while Zoann showed us how to pin the tubes and stuff them. We were like alien elves helping Santa at the North Pole on some distant planet. "These donuts are an extreme fashion statement!" I said excitedly. "Add these to our new spacesuits, the new tights, our space tops, and boots, and we'll be the talk of the planet!"

Our routine these last two weeks was something like this: wake up, clown around, experiment with makeup and hair color, try on combinations of tights, rehearse, watch *Star Trek*, paint new boots, stuff donuts, drink wine, smoke joints, and deal with Ed. Repeat.

42

DIDN'T SEE IT COMING
BAY AREA - JANUARY 1974

I set the red receiver back onto the wall and let the caller's words soak into my brain. "That was Arthur!" I said to my bandmates. "He's flying up for our show, and he'll be here tomorrow. He wants to come over and talk business on behalf of Dallas and the Starwood."

"I dunno about that. They're going to want us to move back to LA. I think we should stay here in the East Bay," cautioned Ed.

"Why?" snapped Zory. "Why in the fuck would we want to stay in suburbia instead of moving to Hollywood? Especially if the Starwood is paying!"

"We could keep working on our stage show here and be comfortable. We don't have to be in the public eye all the time. You guys are always in your space suits just going to the market. Heck, save it for the stage! I'd rather be incognito."

"Damn it, Ed! I can't understand why you don't get it. Why are you stuck in the dark ages while we're trying to move into the stars," I said, frustratedly.

"Hell, these guys have as much money as Robert Fitzpatrick, and he set Shady Lady up in the Hollywood Hills. We can at least get that much out of them," added Zory.

"We'll get them to buy some new equipment. Maybe they'll buy you one of those new synthesizers! Don't stick your fucking head in the sand when the dream is so close!"

"All I'm saying is why go to LA again when we just got back?"

"Ed, it's gonna be different," I argued. "We could be the house band—like the Beatles at the Cavern in Liverpool."

Zory threw his arms open dramatically. "I love you Ed, but you're either with us or you're not. This is getting down to the serious fucking shit now. You guys know how it works in Hollywood—when things happen they happen quickly, and they don't happen at all in shit hole Newark, USA! We have to go where the money is. This is not New York or Los Angeles! We're moving in a new direction: this is music, image, theater, and a progressive vision for the culture. And I don't want to hear any more fucking whining!" He lit a cigarette and stomped away, his anger still lingering in the air.

Ed turned towards me as Zory left the room. "Like your outer space look makes you a better musician than me!"

"We're into this image and this lifestyle, but you're not, Ed!" I said angrily. "All you wanna do is stay here and play dress up every once in a while."

"What's wrong with that?" Ed growled.

Eon was eager to change the subject. "Are we gonna rehearse tonight?"

Zory walked back into the room and yelled, "Let's rehearse! Ygarr, you want another glass of wine?"

"You guys are drinking way too much!" said Ed, frowning in disapproval.

"So what if I'm drinking wine? I'll drink all the fucking wine I want. You're not my dad. Fuck you!" I shouted.

"Fuck you, Steve. I'll show you!"

BOOM WHAM BANG. The next thing I knew I was pinned to the ground. I heard Eon say, "Come on you guys, you've been friends for years!"

The guys pulled Ed off. "Just fucking leave," I told Ed. "Get outta here!"

We were standing around in the rehearsal studio the next day and Arthur said, "You guys sound great! You have great songs and you look fantastic! You're the most original rock band we've ever seen, and we want to give you the right environment to succeed! We're talking about recording opportunities, new equipment, a place to live and rehearse, and a showcase for the LA record companies."

Everything sounded fantastic. This was an opportunity of a lifetime. Trading Newark for Hollywood was a no-brainer.

"Sounds good!" said Zory. "We have a dream of creating a stage set where the audience is transported to, let's say, the bridge of a spaceship."

"Our carpenters at the Starwood can build anything."

"Excellent! What about a drum riser? Can they build one of those? Oops, sorry!" said

Eon, afraid he'd overstepped his boundaries.

Arthur laughed. "Sure, you've got it! Tell me about the other guy, the one with dark hair. Why isn't he here?"

"Oh, you mean Ed? We had a fight last night, and I don't think he's cut out to be a member of Zolar X anymore. He's just not into it like we are."

"Well, do you want me to take care of it? Nothing should hinder you on your journey."

I looked at the brown organ, the hole in the back with the wires sticking out. It looked like it belonged in a church, not on the stage with Zolar X. The last thing you need when you meet other minds on the same pathway is an old flat tire. "What do you think?" I asked the guys. "Do we move on without him?"

"He's never going to change. He's prehistoric," said Zory.

"Ed is a party pooper, and he's no Keith Emerson," added Zany. "The image is one thing, but he's not even willing to get the right equipment. He has a job, so where is all that money going? He won't even have to pay rent if we're on the road! We need a proper synthesizer and someone with the right attitude!"

"Whatever you guys want," said Eon, compliantly. He was very easygoing.

"What time is Ed coming over?" asked Arthur.

"He'll be here at 5:00 for rehearsal."

"I'll take care of it."

Ed showed up on time, but he must have felt something in the air. I found it hard to look him in the eye as he lit a fresh smoke with the butt of the old one. Arthur pulled him aside and they talked quietly. I heard Ed say, "How can you do this to me?"

I felt like I was about to tear up, but Ed had to go. I walked over to Ed and Arthur. "You can find another band, Ed. You're a good musician, but Zolar X isn't your cup of tea. You have to admit, it's not your thing."

Ed wouldn't agree or disagree. He looked glumly around the room at us. "Well, I guess this is it. Good luck, guys." A tear rolled down his cheek as he walked out the door and out of Zolar X. He must have felt like Pete Best.

"Shit! I wish it hadn't happened like this, I really do!" said Zory. "But we can't turn back now. We have everything invested in this, and as much as I hate to say so, I won't let anyone or anything hold up the bandwagon! We have to make this happen if it kills us, and it just might!"

"I'm relieved you were here to do that for us, Arthur. Thank you," I said.

"All four of us are in agreement about the management," said Zory. "Let's do it."

"Great! I'll call Dallas with the good news when I get back to the hotel, and I'll see you all tomorrow night at the show."

"He's quite the salesman!" I said after Arthur left. "This is definitely a step in the right direction."

The guys could only nod in agreement. We were on our way.

43

THE VILLAGE GIG
SAN FRANCISCO - JANUARY 1974

This show would be the first time we played San Francisco, the first time without Ed and the first time with management. I looked at the boys as we walked onstage. Everyone was Zolarized and I didn't have to twist any arms to do it. I felt good.

The Village held about 400 people, and the place was half full. The Tubes, who were playing down the street at Bimbos, had probably pulled some of our crowd away. Not that we were bummed. Our new space suits were awesome. They looked great and they felt great too. Shiny and tight fitting, we were definitely onto something. Eon looked fantastic in my cadet space suit and Zany was terrific in silver spandex. Of our first three shows, we looked the best that night.

We played our same set, but with extra, added energy. Zory had his Zolar X weights, which he pumped onstage during my solos. Nobody did that. The band sounded more powerful without Ed's church organ – a power trio with a robotic-mime lead vocalist.

Zory stood alone at the mic bathed in spotlights. There were only two downsides that night. First, was load-in, when the roadies broke the tip off our X backdrop. The second was seeing the girl who loved her own voice, Syndee. She glared at me from the dance floor. I had to admit she looked great, but I wasn't looking for a girlfriend. As usual, the crowd loved us. Three shows and the response was exactly the same. They ate it up.

Fans swarmed around us as we fled the stage to the dressing room. They all had questions.

"When's your album coming out?"

"Can I take a picture with you?"

"You guys are far out!"

"Those are some wild hair colors!"

I had to get away. "I'm heading to the dressing room to dry my sweaty pink hair and slip into some casual tights."

A variety of refreshments awaited us backstage. Zory looked around and asked, "Let's have a vote. Did we miss Ed?"

"Ed? Ed who?" said Zany.

"It felt cleaner like it's supposed to – like the Who!" said Eon. "Pure raw power!"

Zory said, "We're a hot, space-age rock band with a Rocket roll twist! Hey E, you did some incredible work tonight. And remember, that's coming from a former drummer. I think, if anything, maybe some more bass fills? But it was still great!"

"You guys were fantastic again!" said Arthur. "I talked to Dallas last night, and we'd like to get you down to LA for a showcase next week. He's also scheduled a number of shows for February."

"Wow! That soon huh? How many?"

"A total of seven shows in two weeks."

That was all Zory needed to hear. "I'll call my Mom and see if my parents have an apartment available," he said eagerly.

"You don't need to do that. You can stay at Dallas's bungalow until we find a better place for you. Are you guys good with that?"

I scanned the guys' faces for their reactions – a faint nod, anything.

"I'm half packed already!" said Zory. "I never wanted to leave Hollywood in the first place."

"You bet! I've never lived in LA before. Swimming pools, movie stars!" said Eon.

"Will there be room for Zoe and Ve?" I asked.

"We'll make room for everyone, including your road crew."

"Then we'll see you soon!" said Zory.

The house in Newark was jammed later. I looked around at all the chicks and saw some I'd fucked and some I wanted to fuck. I even saw some strippers from the Bosca days. Then, like déjà vu, I felt a tap on my shoulder. I didn't even have to turn around to know who it was.

"I just had to see you again," said Syndee. "When are you coming back to LA? Do you want some cocaine?"

THE VILLAGE GIG

I didn't know how to get rid of her. She was pretty and fun in bed, but I wanted to be single. What should have been a kick-ass time with a couple of strippers turned into a game of hide and seek. At that point, I just wanted to hide.

ZORY ZENITH

Aftershow parties were fun, but they could also be a bit annoying. Outside of Ve, Zoann, the boys, and the road crew, I didn't know many of the people. San Franciscans consider Angelenos slimy and we think of them as snobs, so I wasn't sure if I wanted to interact with anyone outside the Zolar X family. But I did meet a couple of very attractive young ladies, Kristen and Karen. Kristen was there with Rich, her musician boyfriend, but Karen was loose.

Rich broke out some coke, which I wasn't big on at all. But there was a joint, so I smoked some of that. Pot made me paranoid sometimes, but it also helped with my insomnia, because once I emptied the refrigerator, I was down for the night. Tonight I had enough beer in me to keep the paranoia at bay, so everything was alright.

Karen kept staring at me and then coyly would look away. Besides her beautiful face that I hadn't really noticed before, she also had beautiful hands. This was imperative for me. I enjoyed breasts of any size, but I've never really needed more than a mouthful of champagne glass titties anyway. I was more of a leg man, and she couldn't have two big hams with high heels on them. She couldn't have man hands either. A woman could look like Raquel Welch, but the night was over before it started if she had hands like a man.

Zolar X, The Village, San Francisco, 1974
Photo credit: Syndee

OUT OF THIS WORLD: THE STORY OF ZOLAR X

L to R: Zory Zenith, Ygarr Ygarrist, The Village, San Francisco, 1974
Photo credit: Jeff Austin

L to R: Zory Zenith, Ygarr Ygarrist, The Village, San Francisco, 1974
Photo credit: Jeff Austin

44

HIGHLAND BUNGALOW
HOLLYWOOD - FEBRUARY 1974

We were happy to be back in Los Angeles and excited that the Starwood was managing us. Hopefully, this would be the trip that turned us into actual recording artists. It would be great to have money in our pockets and nice places to live. We were tired of being broke.

The first stop was the Starwood to store our equipment and connect with Dallas. After we unloaded the milk truck, we still had the suitcases, guitars, and trunks of stage outfits that would come with us to the new pad. We pulled up to the Hollywood Hills Highland Bungalows overlooking the Hollywood Bowl and climbed out of the truck. Dallas, leading the way, parked his car and showed us where to unload. The first thing we saw was a giant cement staircase that reminded me of a *Three Stooges* movie, where they comically hauled a huge block of ice up a mile-long staircase. We weren't laughing.

"Oh shit! Looks like a thousand steps up!" Eon shouted.

"You want us to walk up this shit every day?" Zory asked Dallas.

"You're young! It's great exercise!"

"I'm going to need my gravity boots!" said Zany.

We climbed the stairs to the bungalow landing. Hollywood lay below us like a crazy carpet. "Wow! Talk about a great view!" I said, impressed.

"You can hear shows at the Hollywood Bowl from here," said Dallas.

"I wish I would have been here when the Beatles played!" said Zory

Dallas opened the door and said, "Come on in. Let me show you around."

It was then that we realized that Dallas had not rented us our own pad and that we would be staying with him.

"This isn't what I expected!" I whispered to Zory. "I didn't know he was going to move us into his place. I thought we were getting a place of our own! Hell, there are only two bedrooms – one for him and one for his male nurse roommate. The location is great, but we just left a three-bedroom house where everyone had their own room. Now seven of us will be claiming spots on the living room floor and sleeping on foam pads!" It took me two seconds to follow with, "Oh well, it's still the Starwood. Pretty damn cool!"

"I still feel sort of euphoric," said Zory. "I figure the worst-case scenario is that this situation will last maybe a week or two until the Starwood finds us a house. Besides, Ve and I can always stay with my parents to give you more room."

The place had a lot of history and I thought it would be fun. We were a quarter-mile above the Hollywood Hills, and the last row of seats of the legendary Hollywood Bowl was just beyond an ivy-covered chain link fence. I could imagine Zolar X rocking out onstage as green laser beams shot up to the stars. How absolutely perfect.

The next day we hit Guitar Center on Sunset for some new equipment. It was quite the place.

"Go ahead – grab anything you want!" said Dallas and Arthur.

I shrugged. "I don't really need that much. But I guess I could use a guitar cord, a couple of sets of strings, and a few picks." For guitars, I already had a Flying V and my Sunburst Les Paul. My Hiwatt amplifier still worked perfectly and so did my Echoplex. What more could I want?

"Buy something you want, not something you need!" insisted Dallas.

"I might if they had a synthesizer for guitar," I said.

A salesman hovering nearby moved in for the kill. "We do! We have the EMS Synthi from England!" He rushed off and returned with a shiny instrument.

I toyed with the thing for a while, but it didn't blow my mind.

"Do you want it?" asked Dallas.

"It's alright, but it doesn't have any classical instrument sounds like a Moog, and with our showcase only two weeks away, I don't have the time to learn."

"Well, get something! We have tons of money!"

"Okay, I'll take this Maestro Phaser pedal. I think it'll add a nice, soft acoustic sound to 'Energize Me.'"

HIGHLAND BUNGALOW

Zany grabbed a set of bass strings and picks. Eon chose new drumheads, sticks, and an expensive Zildjian ride cymbal.

"If you guys are open to the idea," said Zory, stroking his chin thoughtfully, "I could probably use some sort of foot-operated special effects pedal for the vocal mic—not just for singing, but something that would give me a creepy robot voice when I'm addressing the crowd between songs. Something that sounds like an intercom system from a flying saucer."

"Excuse me!" said Arthur. "We need a salesman over here!"

Another salesman with dollar signs in his eyes rushed over. "Hey, guys! What can I do for you?"

"I need an effect to amplify my android vocal tones. Can you assist, human?" said Zory, in a robotic, monotone voice.

The salesman was happy to oblige. "Maestro makes the top-rated analog effects, and I think the Ring Modulator would serve you well. Heck, that thing has articulate pitch shifting, preset tuning, selectable waveforms, and external controls. It'll give you all the robot sounds you want – like you'd see on TV or the movies."

"You guys really know your shit," said Zory. "I don't know what you just said, but color me sold! I'll take one of those *and* an Echoplex!" Now our show would be totally interstellar.

We eventually wound up in the keyboard/synthesizer room. Needless to say, we all fell in love with the sounds coming from the various keyboards: photon torpedoes, spaceships, laser blasts, violins, horn sections – they were amazing.

"Can we really have anything we want?" asked Eon.

"Check out this fucking Moog! It's $1,200. Do you think they'd go for that much?" said Zany, excitedly.

"I don't know, but I can't play the damn thing!" said Zory.

"We could hold off and be mannerly about it…" I said.

"But you never know what's going to happen in this town," countered Zory.

"If this all goes the way we hope it will, we could probably come back and pick it up later," I added.

"But it might be now or never," said Zory.

"Let's make sure we get a place to live instead of spending money on this Moog. Let's just get what we need right now," I said.

Back at the Starwood, carpenters were building a semi-circular drum riser for Eon. They also constructed individual risers for each bandmember topped with matching black carpet that we called "discs." A ten-foot tall X was also in the works but this one would be hinged, making it easier to move. Along with a new comic book rack, new vinyl stage costumes, and a shit load of theatrical makeup, we'd also have twelve Plexiglas rings for our mic stands and five Plutonian green rings for my Flying V. The designs in our brains were coming to life.

Zory also asked the builder to cover the discs with chrome Mylar. The drum riser already looked like the edge of a flying saucer, but Zory would probably ask them to cut portholes in front and light the whole thing up from inside.

Before the construction was finished, Zory and Zany called a band meeting with Dallas and Arthur. "As you know," said Zory, "we've been formulating an idea to make our stage look like the bridge of a spaceship."

"I think we can cut Styrofoam slabs to hide our amps and create a futuristic atmosphere!" said Zany, almost bursting at the thought.

"Won't it absorb the sound?" I asked. "Wouldn't the Styrofoam need to be treated with a sealant?"

"We'll cut openings for the speakers!"

Arthur looked at Dallas, who nodded in approval. "Where do we get Styrofoam slabs?"

"There's a place in the Valley called Everything Styrofoam," said Zory.

Dallas smiled. "This is going to be a hell of a show!"

Arthur, Zory, Zany, and the lead carpenter picked up twenty slabs of foam and other materials needed to construct the set. They began the next day, cutting and arranging each piece to specification until Zory and Zany agreed on the exact placement. Unsurprisingly, that took a considerable amount of time.

"Are you guys done yet? I thought it looked pretty cool a couple of hours ago!" said Dallas. "Tonight's acts will be loading in soon, so you'll have to shut it down for today."

The Styrofoam worried me a bit. "Shouldn't we do a soundcheck with this stuff?"

Zory agreed. "Yeah, let's run through a song or two. Hey Dutch, make sure the sound guy bumps the vocals up as high as he can through the monitors."

"Yeah, let's make sure this crap doesn't suck up our sound. With a full crowd it might change the room dynamic," I said.

"I thought the same thing," said Dutch. "I've never seen anything quite like this. What did you guys say that shit is?"

"Styrofoam!"

"Are you sure you guys thought this out? Styrofoam is porous – even if it's smooth. These things could be monstrous sound sponges."

Zany frowned, "Hell no! Have you felt this stuff? It's hard as a rock. The sound waves will bounce right off!"

I marveled at the effort that went into building our space age set. Finished, the stage looked like the interior of the space cruiser from *The Day the Earth Stood Still*. Plexiglas adornments of white, clear, black, and silver highlighted every line and curve. With our speaker cabinets tucked neatly out of sight except for the grill cloths, the set was magnificent. Eon's double set of clear Fibes, with the new gigantic X logo behind them, sat on top of the most beautiful drum riser I'd ever seen. Each mic stand held four clear Plexiglas rings, and our personal discs looked like beaming stations. Charlie Patton had set up two lasers to form a giant X that pierced the air above us. This was a first in the history of Rock 'n' roll — a theatrical, sci-fi fantasy come to life.

Wondering what our show might look like to the audience, I imagined Zany up there in his black and clear vinyl suit, warping space bass riffs that bounced off the stars. I'd be blasting out the laser leads on my Flying V, looking sharp in my orange and silver jumpsuit. Zory, decked out in his silver and turquoise spacesuit, would be zapping fans in the front row with his silver ray gun. High above the stage, from his flying saucer drum riser, Eon would be twirling his sticks and smiling brightly enough to break every teeny bopper's heart. I could see it clearly.

"Looks great doesn't it, Y?" said Zory. "Let's just hope the show goes off without any serious trouble, but I don't see any black cats."

"I hope so too," I replied, feeling just a tad nervous.

We went upstairs to wait and time crawled by slowly. This was our official showcase and much depended on its success. The butterflies in my stomach multiplied until I was sure they'd fly out of my ears. Everyone looked nervous.

Suddenly, after hours of boredom, roadie Slim stuck his head in the room. "Fifteen minutes to showtime! Good luck – the place is packed!"

The next fifteen minutes passed very quickly. Zory jumped up, eager to play. "Let's go deliver the future!" he said, animated and hyper.

We hit the stage, but I could tell from the first note that something was wrong. My guitar tone had no balls at all. Not only should I have been able to hear my guitar, but I should have been able to feel it. I knew it! The damn Styrofoam was soaking everything up, and our songs sounded weak and hollow. My worst fear was coming true. I hoped the soundman had turned up the PA because the sound onstage was total shit. Feeling hopeless, I played every note flawlessly and wailed on all the leads, but we played the whole set in a vacuum. We might have looked great, but we sounded terrible.

I exploded in the dressing room. "That was a disaster! I couldn't hear shit! There was a giant slab of foam in front of my speaker cabinet! Where was the foam with the holes cut in it? What did those motherfuckers do? Everything sounded fine at soundcheck! Fuck, I hope no record companies were out there. That was so embarrassing! I'm never getting on stage with that foam again! Talk about moronic!"

"What actually fucking happened down there?" asked Zory. "I couldn't hear myself or much of your guitar either! What the hell? From where I was standing, I couldn't even see your amp. You're saying they covered your fucking stack with a slab of foam? Which one of those monkey-faced pieces of shit did this? Let's find out quick."

I scratched my head. "Maybe somebody accidentally broke the slab with the holes in it and replaced it with a solid piece? But instead of moving my amp, they put a slab of Styrofoam in front of my speaker cabinets. Those stupid sons of bitches! A fucking chimpanzee could've done better! I came really close to kicking that shit off the stage. If looks could kill, those assholes would be dead right now!"

Charlie walked into the room. "Hey, guys! Did you like the lasers? The stage show was fantastic! Kind of sounded like you lost a little guitar volume though. You can't trust any of these amateur Starwood people with that. Hell, if I'd known this was your showcase, I'd have brought in some professionals to run the sound. Did you get any bites from the record companies?"

I frowned. "Not a single fucking one!"

KISS MY...

45

KISS MY...
HOLLYWOOD - FEBRUARY 1974

We put the botched showcase behind us and tried to move forward. In the end, it didn't really matter who had been responsible for the disaster. The damage was done. We still had more shows at the Starwood which would offer us the chance to recover.

Then Arthur told us about a New York band that wanted to meet us. "I just got off the phone with their manager Bill Aucoin," he said. "His band caught your show last week, so I invited them to visit us at the Starwood." He handed Zory a shiny new record. "This is your competition. They're on Casablanca Records."

"Lucky fuckers!"

"We must be their competition too if they're watching us," Zany commented astutely.

The band showed up at the Starwood with Bill Aucoin in a black limousine. Arthur made the introductions at the bar downstairs. As usual, we were decked out in our finery, but they wore blue jeans, cowboy boots, and velvet jackets. We didn't know anything about them at all, and they really didn't look like much. We hadn't even listened to their album. They could have been from the Valley as far as we were concerned.

Zory struck up a conversation with the band. Paul and Gene were cordial and gentlemanly, but they definitely had an air about them. Before long, they were asking Zory about our theatrical direction. He explained we were using science fiction and comic books as a source. "That's why we wear skin-tight, superhero looking suits!"

I listened to the words coming out of Zory's mouth and thought *We don't know these guys! Put a sock in it*!

The two drummers, Eon and Peter, were chatting, and I was talking to Ace, the guitarist. He told me they weren't allowed to be photographed without their makeup. That was a novel concept but I didn't want a picture of them anyway. Maybe I was a bit jealous.

One thing led to another, and within twenty-four hours, Arthur told us we'd been invited to see KISS on *Don Kirshner's Rock Concert* at the Aquarius Theater.

I had a word with my fellow Zolarians. "These dudes have a major head start on us. We've gotta go to warp speed!"

"I did white face in Shady Lady a year ago. It's nothing new! But I'm curious about their sound," said Zory.

"You'll be going in style tomorrow. They're sending a limousine and you'll get the whole rock star treatment," said Arthur.

The band was ready and waiting when the stretch limousine arrived. We had plenty of room and the world looked better through tinted windows. The limo also had a well-stocked bar.

"Help yourself to a cocktail," Arthur said, generously.

We had a mild buzz happening by the time we arrived at the Aquarius Theater. Bright searchlights cut the sky as we climbed from the limo in full Zolarian regalia. We weren't about to be shown up by these guys, but I was envious that they'd be on TV and we'd be sitting in the audience. Someday Zolar X would be where they were. Hopefully sooner rather than later.

Management ushered us backstage to the dressing rooms. Sitting in mirrored cubicles on a slightly raised platform, the KISS boys applied their makeup and got ready to play. The makeup was garish but original, like nothing we'd ever seen before. We made polite small talk with the guys and thanked them for inviting us before making our way to our seats. The emcee gave KISS a powerful introduction and they hit the stage in a dense cloud of smoke and flames. This was their national television debut, so they were doing it up big. They tore through three songs, during which Gene breathed fire and spat fake blood like a circus performer. They got a lot of applause, but Zory said the theatrical effects reminded him too much of the Shady Lady days. The stage show was too dark for him, and I had to agree.

KISS was unique. I had to give them that, but my brain couldn't wrap itself around their simple, three-chord bar progressions. There was nothing classical or progressive about the material—it was just basic Rock 'n' roll. But I was impressed with their stacks of Marshalls, and I had to admit that Paul and Gene harmonized nicely. Peter rose into the air with his drums at the climax of their performance, so I gave them two stars for that piece of showmanship. The crowd was more generous than we were. They loved it.

KISS MY...

After the show, we went back to the dressing room to congratulate them on their TV debut. Bill was very inquisitive about us. It kind of felt like he was picking our brains for information, but he was friendly. He wanted to know who made our costumes and asked how the Starwood was treating us. "What did you think of my band KISS?" he finally asked.

"Oh, they were good Rock 'n' roll," I said, somewhat begrudgingly. Not that we'd be stealing from them.

Gary and Arthur had nothing but positive things to say about KISS. "They represent the new wave of theater that will soon be upon us," Arthur said excitedly. "We wanted you guys to see them because their stage show is also highly theatrical, but on a larger scale."

"Fuck, give me the money they have, and I'll give you a stage show!" ranted Zory.

Arthur continued with his pep talk, but Zory and I weren't biting. KISS was too nasty for either of us to truly enjoy. The underlying message wasn't reaching us.

Other than KISS being theatrical, we didn't have anything else in common with them. If they were the competition, then it was light versus the dark – a Rock 'n' roll war.

L to R: Zany Zatovian, Zory Zenith
Photo credit: Zoann

Ygarr Ygarrist
Photo credit: Zoann

46

ASTRO TOTS
HOLLYWOOD - FEBRUARY 1974

After the Styrofoam fiasco, it was a blessing to have three more shows. They were packed and our sound was good again. My Hiwatt blasted enormously through the house PA system and I began to loosen up. I was having fun.

One morning we were having coffee on the terrace at Highland Bungalow. "Hey Zory," I said. "Do you think there were any A & R executives in the audience this week?"

"You mean did they recover from the nightmare and come back to give us another shot?"

"Yeah, if they're out there, why aren't we hearing about it?"

"Word is that a couple of the top guys from Electra Records and Warner Brothers were there at least one of the nights. But I'm not going to change my shorts until they say Atlantic or Capitol Records."

"Who said that? Shit, I hate being in the dark!"

"Arthur told me. He also said we need a demo. They want to hear what we sound like recorded. The next step will be to take us into the studio."

"That would be great if it happens."

Zany stuck his head out the door. "Charlie Patton is on the line. He's asking for Ygarr."

I took the phone but held it away from my ear as the voice coming through the receiver almost blew my head off. "Hey, how ya doin'? I think I can get you guys a deal with Doris Duke, the richest woman in the world! I met her when I had my art at the World's Fair in New York City. I have tons of contacts in music and movies! I worked on *After the Goldrush* with Neil Young and Dean Stockwell!" In one long-winded breath, he continued his spiel, "Those Starwood guys are crooks. You guys can stay with me. I have lots of room!"

"Okay, Charlie. We'll keep that in mind. We have two more shows next weekend. See you at the Starwood?"

We hung up and I looked at Zory. "With all the things coming out of his mouth, it's hard to tell what's true and what isn't. I don't think he's a liar, but he obviously drinks a lot."

"I like him!" said Zory. "I just hope he's not all hot air!"

The events at North Hollywood High and Beverly Hills High would be different because they would take place during the day. We were good at creating our own atmosphere but playing under fluorescent lights was sure to be a challenge. I knew it would be a bit weird, but we'd be the ones running around in space suits, tights, and pointed hair, so we could hardly complain. As far as we were concerned, being weird was the new black.

"These are the future fans of Zolar X, the next generation!" said Zory.

"We have to make these shows special! We should go to the toy store and pick up some sci-fi souvenirs for the kids!"

"Yeah, I wanna get a new ray gun!"

I grinned. "Eon and I have been playing with an idea. I wanna put one of those huge toy keys on my back and have Eon wind me up during my solo in 'Spacers.'"

"Have you seen those little UFO-shaped candies down at the market?" asked Eon. "We should get some of those!"

"Yeah, and let's douse the fans with a couple of bags of glitter!" said Zany.

"We'll make them forget all about David Cassidy!" Zory grinned.

"I was thinking more about the Beatles," I said. Cassidy was a bit light even for us.

The gymnasium at North Hollywood High's auditorium resonated with sound. The show was a noisy piece-of-cake and helped us put the Styrofoam incident firmly in the rear-view mirror. Afterward, we wandered the halls of the student union. I caught the principal gawking in shock as a frenzied mob of students engulfed us. We loved being chased by the little teenyboppers, all of them screaming and begging for autographs. Breaking free, Zory mimed his way through the corridors, in and out of classrooms, shouting "Eep Opp Ork Ah Ah" to the students in his robotic dialect. We'd promoted the band before, but this was a bit different because our target audience was so young. They were the perfect age to become new fans.

We finally navigated our way to the courtyard, where the students commonly gathered. We didn't bother to approach a group of jocks, but the stoners, with their long hair and bell-bottoms, all got stickers. The girls got stickers, of course, even the plain ones. All the nerds got stickers too. Who knew? There might've been a Steve Jobs in the bunch.

An hour and 300 Starwood stickers later, we worked our way to the exit. Zory gestured grandly from the top of the stairs and yelled to the students like the great orator he was. "Come to the Starwood for the all-ages matinee this Sunday at 2:00 p.m.! You're all invited to witness Zolar X, the greatest show on this or any other planet!"

We intended to have fun, no matter what the cost. Playing for a bunch of screaming Beverly Hills teenagers at the Starwood would be a hoot. Instead of our usual nighttime wardrobe of vinyl or stretch Lurex, we had opted for comfortable tights, space boots, and Capezio footwear. This would give us the freedom to be spontaneous and move unchoreographed. We also had our UFO candies, the astro gum, the glitter bombs, Zory's ray gun, and my giant toy wind-up key. This show would be for the kids, who were the same age we were when the Beatles appeared on *The Ed Sullivan Show* in 1964. We planned to bring our young fans aboard the Zolar X spaceship and whisk them away to another planet. They'd never forget this journey.

From our dressing room upstairs, we could hear the crowd chanting: "We want Zolar X! We want Zolar X!" We looked around the corner from the top of the stairs and saw swarms of kids fighting for position at the front of the stage. The club pulsed with Zolar-mania as we picked up our instruments and zoomed into our set like a spaceship taking off.

This was our sixth time playing the Starwood stage and we were having a great time. Members of the screaming crowd kept trying to touch us, reaching for our legs whenever we came near the edge of the stage. I liked to tease them by getting just within reach but pulling my foot away before they could grab me. Zory played up his robotic character by letting them touch his legs to make sure he was real. The robot disappeared for a quick costume change and reappeared with "ASTRO TOT" stamped across the butt of his red tights in bold white letters. Dancing pirouettes to our space age-beats, Zory shimmied his rear so the audience could get a first-hand view. He blasted the new fans with his ray gun, initiating them with UFO candies and bags of sticky glitter.

The kids must have been wondering about the giant key sticking out from my back. It had been there the whole set, affixed tightly to my skin with a big suction cup and a little spit. During the solo on "Spacers," I began to slow down like a toy running out of energy. I slumped forward inch by inch by inch, and the notes slowed down in syncopated rhythm with my movements until the only sound left was one sustained guitar note thin and lonely. By now, I was slumped over from my waist at a ninety-degree angle, the silver key on my back now clearly visible to everyone. My arms dangled at my sides, still bouncing slightly, and then I became completely still. Hopping up from behind his drums, Eon jumped off the flying saucer and sprinted over to wind me up, restoring the power supply to my circuits. As I recharged and my movements began to speed up, so did the notes on the guitar. By the time Eon was done, we were back to the original tempo of the song – fast. I finished the solo and Eon sprinted back to his drums. We wowed the kids by sharing a few crescendos between the Les Paul's high D note and Eon's bass drum accents. For our efforts, we got the loudest applause we'd ever received for that solo. The kids loved us.

The absence of alcohol changed the feel of the show. Instead of clowning around drunkenly, the kids absorbed all the details. From Zory's superhero antics to the new Zolarian phrases he created on the spot, they soaked it all up. "Nok voo!" said Zory, thanking them. "Vel artia voo, we love you!" Too bad no record companies were present that day.

L to R: Zany Zatovian, Zory Zenith
Photo credit: Zoann

47

LIES OF THE WOOD
HOLLYWOOD - FEBRUARY 1974

"You shuttle us to the Starwood every day," I said to Gary. "We rehearse there, we eat there, and then you shuttle us back to your bungalow at three in the morning, where we have to tip-toe around like mice. Wouldn't it be easier if we just *lived* at the Starwood?"

"And we're bored when we're stuck here with no transportation," Eon added.

"Let's see what Eddie says. Maybe we can get some mattresses and move you into the loft. But you know there's no shower, right?"

"Shit, I don't care. We'll figure something out!" I said enthusiastically. "At least we'll be where the action is."

"Uma goomba uma bay!" said Zany.

Things happened quickly, and soon we were living at the Starwood—the ultimate in Rock 'n' roll accommodations. The large, unused area just past the dressing rooms and offices was more like an attic than a loft, but so what? A "Do Not Enter" sign posted boldly on the door gave people the impression that maybe something dangerous or illegal was happening within, but mostly space was going to waste. We changed all that.

Large beams lining the floor supported the main bar and kitchen downstairs. More beams stretched from the floor to the ceiling overhead. There were all sorts of nooks and crannies, along with air conditioning units, smashed tables, chairs, and even a broken jukebox. The room was big enough to throw down three mattresses and still, give us some privacy. The loft smelled woody, like fresh-cut lumber. Not just that, but the absence of windows created an ambiance of mystery. A lone light bulb near the entrance illuminated roughly five square feet. Perfect.

Hollywood was a trip, and now we lived in the heart of it. We could walk onto Santa Monica Boulevard and find Winchell's Donuts right across the street. Hell, there was a liquor store, an art gallery, Theodore's Bistro, and a porno bookstore. We were living the life and soon learned that the Starwood was ours between 4:00 and 10:00 a.m. Eon figured out how to shimmy the beer cooler with a butter knife, providing us with an almost endless supply of long-necked Budweiser's. They didn't even bother to lock the huge walk-in cooler, so we helped ourselves to meats, cheeses, and whatever else was on the menu. I loved snooping around the club. We investigated every dressing room and bathroom. There was one room we called "The Red Couch Room." The massive curved couch made of red leather stretched twenty feet across the entire room. If a horny musician was lucky enough to score, that was the best place to take her.

March rolled around. One Saturday after closing, I walked over to examine the guitar setup for the headlining band, Stray Dog from England. I liked his sound and was curious about his gear. Inside a wooden box on wheels, I saw four sequenced Echoplexes he controlled with foot pedals that shot his crazy sound to an elevated speaker up by the sound booth. Very cool.

As great as it was after hours, the Starwood was even better when bands were playing. Sexually, the place was a revolving door. I'd put on my "look" and go downstairs to see the girls. I was small, thin, young, and probably very pretty for a man, or at least under nightclub lighting. There was something about the mystery of the tights and what was underneath them. I was a magnet and the girls were drawn to me. Multiple partners in one night were nothing new or strange for me. If a girl sent me sexual signals, I'd take her to the loft, do the deed, and go back on the prowl. That was nightlife at the Starwood.

ZORY ZENITH

With the band securely housed at the Starwood, I focused on design and fabrication. Life was easier at my parents' place until the Starwood followed through with their promise to get us a house. I think that would have happened by now if we'd been signed to a major label, but we'd only been in town a month and that ship had yet to sail.

Ve and I were getting along fairly well, so we set up an industrial sewing machine capable of sewing plastics and vinyl in the back room. I also turned a storage room into a workshop. I told my dad I wanted to make some props with resin, and he said, "That's fine but don't be smoking around that shit! I don't want the whole building goin' up." He might sound rough, but my parents were very supportive and cool.

I tried to be normal with Ve once in a while. We'd take in a movie or go out to dinner, but my mind would wander if the movie wasn't a sci-fi thriller. Our neighborhood, which was close to Paramount Studios, was a bit rough but was an extremely fertile scavenging ground. We'd find discarded plywood, plastic orbs, and scraps of Plexiglas on the sidewalks at night. I learned how to scavenge as a teenager in the '60s, when it was easier to build furniture with materials I found on the street than it was to spend money I didn't have. Ve and I never went out to a movie or dinner without cruising the streets looking for prop materials.

YGARR YGARRIST

Maybe it sounds like we were living the life, but it was starting to feel stagnant — like we weren't getting anywhere. Things had slowed to a crawl, and we had no new shows on the horizon. We weren't practicing at the Starwood anymore. Gary rented a studio in the Valley and moved our equipment out there. I think the Starwood cats realized they'd bitten off more than they could chew when they hooked their wagon to ours. Zory was about to blow a gasket.

ZORY ZENITH

I checked in at the Starwood every day to see if we were going to rehearse. One slow day, I popped my head into Dallas's office to ask what was next for us. Things had been slow lately, so it seemed like a fair question. Dallas seemed somewhat startled to see me, and then I noticed he had three well-dressed middle-aged men with styled hair in the room with him. They all turned around slowly to stare at me. I excused myself and apologized for busting in.

Gary said, "This is Zory, the lead singer for Zolar X, the band we're working with. They showcased here last month."

One of them, a slick-looking guy wearing sunglasses, nodded, and said, "Sure."

I spotted an expensive-looking hard-leather briefcase on the desk. The atmosphere in the little room was tense and I felt as if I'd interrupted something important. "I should go, Dallas," I said quickly. "I'll talk to you later."

I wasn't sure what I'd seen, but I had to find the boys and tell them about it. They were probably across the street at Winchell's having coffee and donuts. That damn little Ygarr could eat and drink anything he wanted and not gain an ounce. Meanwhile, I was doing crunches every night and popping pills just to stay trim. I was down to 130 pounds and wanted to stay there.

I approached Winchell's and saw the three little aliens through the window. They looked serious, and their looks matched my mood. I slid into the booth, but before I could utter a word, Ygarr shouted, "Those fuckers rented us a rehearsal studio in the Valley instead of a house in the Hollywood Hills! They're saying we need to rehearse more? We rehearse every fucking day! I don't fucking get it."

"The promises they made aren't happening," Zany said glumly.

"It feels like we're being betrayed," added Eon.

Wanting a donut I couldn't have, I said. "I should've known better, guys. My experience with these asshole manager types is that they'll promise you everything and give you jack shit!"

"They're not locked into a contract with us, so they can do whatever they want. They're gonna take us to the studio tomorrow around 1:00 p.m. for some sort of band meeting. Will you be there? Here's the address," said Ygarr, handing me a napkin.

I grabbed the napkin and annunciated each word carefully through clenched teeth. "Now I'm really getting irritated. Fucking amateurs! They can't pull their fucking fingers out of their asses long enough to do anything, because they don't know what they're doing in the first place!" I slammed my fist on the table and stormed out.

YGARR YGARRIST

We moved all our equipment, including the drum riser, into a 20' x 40' rehearsal space that was just a room off an alley in the Valley. It looked okay at first glance, but I noticed there was no PA system. Gary, Arthur, and two other men I'd never seen before stood in the middle of the room. "Where's Zory?" Gary asked.

"I think he's on his way," I said. "He has the address."

"We need a PA system," Eon said, frowning.

"We're renting one for you guys. It should arrive by 2:00 p.m. today," said Arthur.

"What was wrong with us rehearsing at the Starwood?" asked Zany.

"We'll get to that later," said Gary. "The reason we're having this meeting is to tell you about the feedback we've been getting from the record labels. They want to hear what you sound like recorded. They want a demo."

"They keep talking about the vocals. You need to get them tighter," said Arthur. "You need to practice, practice, practice. Zory in particular. That's what they're telling us."

I was thinking *where the hell is Zory?*

Arthur went on. "Rehearse here for about three months. Get the music *studio tight*, then we'll record you and showcase you again. Finally, look for a keyboard player – one that fits the band better."

The three of us nodded our heads. His suggestions sounded reasonable, but there was no mention of a place to live with showers and a kitchen.

"Okay, but if we're going to be rehearsing here, we'll need transportation," said Eon.

"If you rented us a house, we could live and rehearse there. It would make it a hell of a lot easier for Zory to practice the vocals!" I said.

Arthur ignored me. "Bottom line, the record companies want you guys *studio tight*." He liked that term for some reason. It irritated the fuck out of me.

We agreed that their proposal was reasonable. I mean, if they were footing the bill, we could handle staying at the Starwood a few more months.

ZORY ZENITH

By now, I was wary of going without answers, particularly where the boys' comfort was concerned. There was all this chatter about having to rehearse for recording, and our *managers* were getting comments from *unnamed* industry sources. They were telling us you can never rehearse enough. That might be true if your abilities are rudimentary, but Ygarr and Zany were phenomenal the moment they picked up and plugged in. Eon was snappy and tight, so I don't know what else they wanted from us. I was also singing better than ever, but it can take months or years for most vocalists to hit a higher octave. Sure you have to work, but you can also rehearse yourself to death. Once the spontaneous spirit is choked, you're dead in the water. There comes a time when you can only grow tighter from the challenge of the stage. How much more rehearsal time were we talking about here? And why in the hell were they moving us to the Valley instead of setting us up in a house? Why couldn't they have made us the house band for one night a week? That would have been a genius management move right there.

So yeah, I was pissed. We were ready to record, and we didn't need more rehearsal. With that mindset, I arrived at the rehearsal studio in the Valley.

YGARR YGARRIST

Like a perfectly orchestrated opera, the room became deadly silent when Zory kicked the door open with a well-placed blow of his space boot. In walked either the hero or the villain – I'm not sure which. Zory stood poised in the doorway, exuding brilliance and rage – a half-cocked space-age rooster ready to explode. In a black and clear vinyl space top, hair perfect, and black tights, he looked as if he'd just stepped offstage. Zany, Eon, and I were so terrified that we immediately dove behind the drum kit. I peeked around a cymbal and heard Zory say in a sharp edgy voice, "You guys have a lot of demands, but we have a few of our own!" From his hip, he pulled out a roll of toilet paper the same way a gunslinger would draw a Colt 45. With a snap of his wrist, he neatly flung it across the floor, and it unrolled like a scene from *The Good the Bad and the Ugly*. I saw hand-written words on the thin white paper—his meticulously penned list of demands.

The room was suspended in some surreal, frozen continuum of Zory space-time. Then the bomb exploded. "We want a house in the fucking Hollywood Hills!" shouted Zory, face red with anger. "We want to go to those meetings and meet the record label executives! We want every fucking Sunday to be Zolar X night at the Starwood! We want a fucking car and we want pocket money! You fucking want us to rehearse? Book us at the fucking Record Plant and give us a reason to rehearse! You guys call yourselves managers? Now, Brian Epstein, that's a manager!"

As I watched, I was amazed, shocked, scared, and proud all at the same time. I knew he had a temper, but I'd never seen this side of him before.

"The whole theme of this band is sci-fi and other-worldliness! I thought you guys got it but you fucking don't! You guys are so enamored with Bill Aucoin and KISS that you can't see what we're doing. We ARE NOT KISS – we're ZOLAR X! We're a sci-fi band from another planet! We're trying to bring hope to you, stupid humans!"

Zory's performance, although captivating, threw everyone into shock. It was like there was no air left in the room. I was rummaging through my brain trying to think of something to say, but I couldn't find the words. Blinking, I looked back to Zory but he was gone. Vanished – like he'd been teleported. Air rushed back into the room.

"I can't work with him! He's a maniac!" said Gary, throwing up his arms. "We'd like to continue working with you guys, but you'll have to get rid of him. You can stay at the Starwood a few days to figure things out but give us your decision as soon as possible."

Arthur shook his head. "He's a handful alright."

After Dallas and Arthur left, the three of us decided that Zory brought more to the band than he took away. I was 22 and still on top of the world. We knew what we had in our lead singer, even if he was a bit volatile. The band had to stick together.

48

CHARLIE PATTON
HOLLYWOOD - MARCH 1974

You'd think the situation would be stressful, but it wasn't. Within a few days, the whole band—including girlfriends, groupies, equipment, and clothes, were at Charlie's one-bedroom apartment situated conveniently between Melrose and Santa Monica. Café Figaro was down the street to the south, and the Troubadour was to the north. This was extreme West Hollywood, just at the edge of Beverly Hills. Cluttered with plexiglass, slides, Warhol prints, holograms, space-scape drawings, and Charlie's miniature 3D designs, the apartment became our refuge. We felt mobile and rugged like we were on a wild adventure. At last, there was a real comradery, and for the first time in a month, all four of us were together in the same space. Even though it was cramped, there was room for our mattresses and sleeping bags on the living room floor. The kitchen held nine drum cases, six speaker cabinets, two amplifier heads, all our guitars, and four trunks of miscellaneous gear. We kept our stage props in the milk truck. Believe it or not, we were fucking happy.

The Starwood was a distant memory and fading fast. We were ready to take this thing to the next level with lasers and holograms. We soaked up Charlie's knowledge and booze like the thirsty sponges we were.

Every night like clockwork, Charlie returned home from work with a case of beer and a bottle of scotch. His partner John Desko always had a bag of weed. The party never stopped. During the first few nights, Charlie sipped scotch and told us how he'd become the black sheep of the Serta mattress empire. We also learned that he was a designer and a fabricator who'd displayed his sculptures at the New York World's Fair in '64. A full-blown alcoholic, Charlie got up every day, went to work, and paid his rent. Luckily, our girlfriends brought us plenty of vittles, and I learned many exciting new recipes involving noodles and potatoes. Occasionally, we ate pizza at the Rainbow or went to Café Figaro for soup, salad, breadsticks, and icy pitchers of sangria. Life could have been worse.

"Charlie, what type of laser is this?"

"Oh!" said Charlie, pleased that we were so interested in things that most people didn't seem to care much about. "That's a Krypton coherent-beam laser! Let me show you how it works!"

We gathered around, and like a drunken schoolteacher, Charlie explained the intricacies of lasers and showed us how to operate them. "Don't look directly at them or you'll be blinded!" he warned, waving his drink.

"Let's shine it out the window!" said Zany. "Look at this, guys!"

Eon and Zany went to the window and soon they were laughing hysterically. I walked over and saw two people walking towards Café Figaro on the sidewalk below. Zany aimed the laser on a stop sign as they reached the corner and it immediately lit up as it had come alive with alien blood. STOP! the sign screamed.

The startled people ducked quickly and looked about in abject terror. Zany quickly turned off the laser and walked away. Good thing it never occurred to aim the laser at passing aircraft.

"Stop scaring the humans," said Zory in his robotic voice.

I popped a beer and addressed Charlie. "So, what do you guys want out of this?"

"Letting us stay here is great, but what's in it for you Earthlings?" asked Zany.

"For starters, I know we could do better than those Starwood people," grunted Desko, pulling on a joint. "We want to be your managers."

"A recording deal, guys!" shouted Charlie. "You know what you deserve! This is where everything happens—right here in Hollywood, the music capital of the world! All we have to do is find some deep pockets! We're out there talking you up, Zolar X!"

I looked at the pair and tried to wrap my head around the idea of them managing us. How could a sincere southern drunk with a fondness for lasers and a decrepit old hippie who smoked too much weed understand us better than everyone else in Hollywood? More importantly, should we trust them? The truth was, we didn't have any other options.

Charlie Patton, circa 1974
Photographer unknown

49

MY FAVORITE MARTIAN
HOLLYWOOD - MARCH 1974

The girls weren't around and it was Saturday night. Zory was in the bathroom using up all the hot water, and Eon paced the kitchen ready to go. We weren't leaving anytime soon, so I was still noodling around on my acoustic when John Desko walked in with a small brown cardboard box under his arm. One eye was looking at me and the other was on Zany. He tossed the box to me and said, "It fell off a truck. I don't know what's inside, but why don't you take a look?" The man was full of surprises.

I knew it wasn't a Hiwatt or a million bucks, but I looked inside the box and saw a bunch of little stick-like things pointing up at me. I pulled one out and said, "It looks like a little TV antenna." I put one on my head above my ear. "Hey look! *My Favorite Martian*!"

Zany decided to stay home, so Eon, Zory, and I walked over to the Rainbow for a few drinks. The place was loaded with pretty girls, as usual, so we hung around for a while. When we finally got home, Zany was wearing the silver-painted sticks on top of his head like antennas. He nodded his head and the antennas bobbed a little. "Do you guys see that? They wiggle!"

"Far out!" said Eon.

"Fucking cool!" said Zory. "We all need a set!"

ZORY'S GADGET

We were in the process of making jewelry out of the clear plastic tubing. You could never have enough spacey accessories.

"Hey Zory, check this out! I have six bracelets on this arm. Looks cool, huh?"

Out of the blue, Zory said, "You know I get sick and tired of not being able to hear myself when we're on stage."

"Can't you do something else besides sticking your finger in your ear?"

He picked up a piece of the tubing, put one end in his ear, brought the other end to his mouth, and said, "I'll be damned. Here it is, clear as day! My own monitor. Now all I have to do is engineer it!" Over the next hour, he fashioned a scrap of coat hanger wire, some Scotch tape, and a plastic earphone from a transistor radio into a functional, wraparound, in-ear monitor. This technology wouldn't be available commercially for many years, so he truly was ahead of his time. And it looked cool too.

ZORY ZENITH

To steal a little intimate time and get away from the crowded accommodations at Charlie's, Ve and I sometimes spent a few days with my parents, where we had the workshop and a bedroom. I was also trying to figure out what our next evolution in our stage wear would be. We needed four matching outfits, yet each one had to be a little different from the others.

I dug in my bedroom closet and found a small suitcase of trinkets that held six early '70s issues of Captain Marvel. One of the issues contained a startling image of Captain Marvel fighting a villain. The bad guy wore a purple bodysuit with a black outer layer that tapered down into a belt with a codpiece. Over that, he had a thin chest plate with subtle wings that flared upward and outwards from his shoulders. I wasn't impressed with the black because it implied villainy, but the garment itself was very intriguing. I showed it to Ve.

"Do you think you could make something like this?"

Ve studied the artwork for a minute and said, "The pattern is very simple. I don't see any problem. But we'll need fabric that is stiff enough to get the flare effect on the wings. Vinyl maybe."

"I'm thinking silver."

"We'll find something marvelous!"

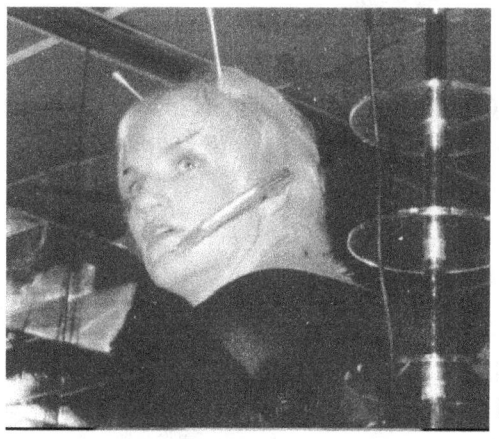

Zory Zenith
Photo credit: Suzan Carson

Ygarr Ygarrist
Photo credit: Syndee

50

TIGHTS, CAMERA, ACTION!
HOLLYWOOD - MARCH 1974

We talked to Rodney and Tom Ayers about booking a show. Just like that, and at warp speed, we had our first gig at Rodney's English Disco.

The drum riser, a small circular disc for Zory, and the Formica platforms to elevate Zany and I took up half the dance floor. Stacked against the mirrored walls, our amps looked twice as big. The setup was impressive—a sea of chrome and glass topped off with a disco ball that hung center stage over Zory's head. We did a soundcheck, and the music blasted loudly through the narrow disco and onto the street. Since there were no dressing rooms, we changed at Charlie's. We wore our antenna for the first time that night, and Zory had his new monitor gadget.

We figured Rodney's would be packed wall-to-wall, but it was a thrill to see a lineup that stretched down the block. Because it would be impossible to get through the crowd with our guitars, we entered through the parking lot at the rear of the building.

The kids were shouting for "Space Age Love". They knew our songs and we didn't even have an album out. Cool.

"You want it? You got it!" said Zory as we kicked into the song.

Cameras flashed everywhere, and I saw several people with 8mm movie cameras. We were surrounded by kids sitting on the floor, and Charlie was in the front row, near my left foot. People with cameras stood on chairs behind them, and beyond that, the room was packed. I could see over everyone's heads to the main entrance, and people outside were still peering around the door trying to get in. Even the VIP area was overflowing. Soon we were deep into our set and the crowd was digging it. With our iconic look and thundering wall of sound, we took glitter rock to the next shiny level.

Afterward, there was the usual swarm of fans and pats on the back. People were gawking and smiling and trying to touch our antenna. Groupies flirted, and musicians from other bands dropped by to drink up our free beer. "Groovy show," said Rodney, smiling at us in his humble sort of way. Tom Ayres was also a happy man. "Great stuff!" he said excitedly, probably thinking about all the tickets we sold. "We'll do this again!"

An older man toting a 35mm camera approached me and said, "Hi, I'm Michael Ochs and I loved your show. I think I got some great shots of you guys!"

"Thanks! Nice meeting you," I said, shaking hands. Fans were still pushing and reaching out to touch me, so I was unable to respond further.

Another man came over and said, "Fantastic music! Great songs! I think you have some hits there. My name is Brian Ross, and I work for Art Laboe at Original Sound. This is the second time I've seen you guys. The first time was at the Starwood. I'd like to talk some business with you guys about making a record. Here's my card. We'll set up a meeting and get down to some real business."

"Cool, Brian!" I said. "We'll be in contact real soon!" Those are the words every unsigned rock band wants to hear.

Zolar X at Rodney's English Disco, 1974
L to R: Zany Zatovian, Eon Flash, Zory Zenith, Ygarr Ygarrist
Photo of Zolar X Photo by Michael Ochs Archives/Getty Images

51

TO BE OR NOT TO BE!
HOLLYWOOD - APRIL 1974

Original Sound Studios, at 8510 Sunset Boulevard, wasn't Warner Brothers, but they made records, so we were happy to give them a chance. Brian impressed me immediately. He was a classically trained pianist with a 2600 Arp in his office. He was an engineer *and* a producer. Having seen us twice, he described to us in detail the structure of "Parallel Galaxy". "I love that song!" he said, with great enthusiasm, "but I feel it should be at the end of your set, not the beginning. And 'Space Age Love' could be a hit forty-five. It just needs to be recorded. 'Energize Me' is a great Rock 'n' roll ballad. Screw demos! Let's cut a record and put it out. I can get any sound you guys can imagine on this Arp and add it to the mix. We have a recording studio and a record pressing plant. Art definitely wants to expand his label."

Brian was a salesman. I liked him. He was thirty-something, balding, and fat, but he knew his shit. He played a synthesizer recording he'd put together himself, and it was just as good as anything Walter Carlos had done. I felt an immediate comradery with the roly-poly guy. We shook hands and told him we'd talk again soon. Thrilled with the possibilities, we headed home to discuss the offer. The four of us could hardly contain our excitement.

We sat around at Charlie's having drinks. "It's a great offer," I said, swallowing a large portion of wine. "Brian can play all the synthesizer parts we want: spaceships, strings, photons. Shit, it will be the spaciest album out there!"

Zory said, "Yeah but Original Sound does oldies but goodies. It's not the Record Plant."

"Yeah, but *Elvis* got his start at Sun Studios! That place was a hole in the wall compared to this!" I said, having given the offer some good thought already.

"I've never been in a sixteen-track studio before. Sounds cool to me!" said Zany.

"An album? That's pretty tempting," said Eon.

John Desko rubbed his chin and frowned a bit. "You know, to record and release an album, they'll want you to sign a contract."

I wasn't sure if he was concerned for us or himself. The guy mostly seemed paranoid about being cut out of the action. So far, Charlie was footing the bill, and all Desko did was sleep and smoke pot. I didn't want to backstab these guys, but they weren't our legal managers. We were still free agents and could do as we fucking pleased.

A week later, we were setting up at Original Sound Studio. Zory, Charlie, and John were in the control booth. After much preparation, we ran through Brian's favorite song "Parallel Galaxy" several times to set the levels. We were ready for our first take.

"Get that trill as clean as it can be," said Brian. We dropped into the song and worked on the first section for about ten minutes before nailing it well enough to move on. That dedicated attention to detail was Brian's classical background coming through, and we didn't mind that he was a perfectionist. We finished two-thirds of the song, and the session was going just the way I'd hoped. Eon's drums were massive in the headphones, and Zany's cello bass was phenomenal. When I thought about the instruments we'd add later—the twelve-string acoustic, the Moog or Arp, the synthesized strings, the double-tracked guitars, and the space age harpsichords—I just knew the final result would be incredible. We'd finally have a viable product we could hold in our hands and carry in our hearts. With this album doing the talking, surely some big fish would bite. Original Sound was merely a steppingstone.

Through the headphones, I heard Brian say, "Hey, Ygarr." I looked up at the sound booth and saw Art Laboe standing beside Brian with a small sheaf of papers in his hand. We went outside to the balcony where Brian gave us the lowdown. "This is sounding great, but for us to continue, you need to look over this contract and sign it."

I looked the thin contract over carefully. It was an agreement that would tie Zolar X up for a year at the most, giving Brian, Art, and Original Sound the opportunity to shop the album and get us signed to a major label worth at least a million dollars within a year. Otherwise, the contract would be null and void. It looked good to me.

We each had a contract and were looking over the terms. John Desko grabbed the contract from Zory's hands as if it was poisonous and quickly scanned the contents. "I can do better than this. Companies like Warner Brothers and Capitol Records can offer far more. I'll get you a better deal, and I'll get you in the studio by the end of the month." Then he pulled the pen from my hand just as I was about to sign. I felt conflicted, but for whatever reason, we leaned towards Desko and listened to what he was saying.

52

CRYSTAL STUDIOS
HOLLYWOOD - APRIL 1974

John Desko kept his word. By the end of the month we were at Crystal Studios on Vine Street recording demos for "Space Age Love" and "Energize Me" with engineer John Fischbach, the same guy who'd engineered Stevie Wonder and was currently recording Rick Springfield.

Fischbach's studio was much bigger than the room at Original Sound. After getting my Hiwatt set up, I looked over at Eon's kit. He was so far away that there were no worries about extraneous sound bleeding onto the drum tracks. Large sheets of baffling between Zany and I kept our sounds contained. We'd already decided to dub in the flying saucers, the Echoplex, and the sci-fi effects after we finished the instrumental tracks.

Fischbach had us run through "Space Age Love" while he adjusted the levels. Soon we were recording and the energy in the studio was incredible. We took the song through to the power chord climax, and Fischbach said, "You guys are one-take-wonders! Come on in, and let's give this a listen." We all went into the control booth as Fischbach played us a rough mix. Even at this early stage, it sounded great. Then Fischbach said, "Ygarr, I want you to go back in there and play the same riff so I can double-track the guitar. It'll make it very large and very thick." Three minutes and twenty-six seconds later, I was back in the booth listening to my take. The guitars sounded so full that I could hardly believe it was just me.

By the end of the week, we'd laid down the drums and bass for both songs and were ready for the lead guitar, the keyboards, and the vocals. Fischbach let us take the Arp home for a few nights to search for sounds of rocket ships, photon torpedoes, computer beeps – anything and everything we needed to make "Space Age Love" and "Energize Me" the first Rocket roll songs in history.

I twiddled a knob and looked at Desko. "Damn, this is great! We're recording in an excellent sixteen-track studio with a great engineer and we don't have to pay a damn penny."

"Fischbach is doing this on speculation," explained Desko. "He's betting we'll be able to sell the demos to a big record company. Once we do that, he wants to engineer the Zolar X album. He's in this for the long haul."

"Well, whatever the reason, it's still great!" said Zory.

"The only downfall is that we can't come in every day to record. We can only record after hours when Fischbach is free from other commitments."

Eon said, "Beggars can't be choosers."

"Hell, Ygarr, Fischbach gave you a key so you can go to Crystal and play anytime you want," said Desko.

"Yeah, that's true, as long as it's after hours," I said, trying not to sound ungrateful.

Charlie walked in with his usual packages of beer and scotch. He yelled as he came through the door, "Hey, guys! Are you ready to move? The landlord raised the rent, and I already got us a duplex on Holcomb Street just a mile away. Desko, call that hippie friend of yours with the flatbed truck. The rent will be $100 cheaper a month, and that puts more beer in the icebox."

After the move, we were back in the studio. John took us on a tour and showed us the room where he was going to cut our acetate.

"Hey John, what are those big metal tanks for?" I asked.

"Oh, the helium tanks? The helium keeps the stylus cool as it's cutting the acetate— but let me show you," John replied.

He put a blank on the machine and fired up a quarter-inch tape of "Space Age Love." The instrumental track came booming out of the speakers as the needle dug into the acetate. It was more complicated than that, but the details aren't important. "This will be more professional than handing out a cassette or a reel-to-reel," said John, as the machine did its work.

Zory smiled and said, "Elvis's first recording was an acetate."

As you might have guessed, Elvis loomed large in Zory's world.

"I'll be finishing Rick Springfield's *Mission Magic* the rest of this week, but I have you guys scheduled for vocals the week after that," said John.

We arrived at Beverly Boulevard just off Doheny. Zory and Ve wanted to meet us there for some sort of surprise. For a change of pace, they were staying with a friend of Ve's for a few days. I looked around at the nicely furnished apartment and commented, "Wow, nice pad. She must bring in some bucks!"

"The world's oldest profession," Zory said.

"What?" said Eon

"You know—call girl, hooker, prostitute!"

"Oh. Is she here?" I asked curiously.

"She's asleep. Her job starts at sundown."

"Anyway, we hope you like these!" said, Veonity quickly changing the subject.

"Like 'em?" said Zory. "Hell, they're gonna *love* 'em!"

With no further ado, Veonity pulled out an awesome silver superhero suit from a big black trunk. She looked at the fronts of the suits before handing them out. "Ygarr, this one is for you. Eon, here's yours. Zany, for you. And this one is for Zory."

Other than the geometric shapes cut in the front of each one, the four suits were identical. I had a pink circle at my belly button, and Zany had green ovals down the front of his suit. Eon had blue triangles, and Zory had a yellow circle at the front of his neck. The suits had no zippers or snaps, just Velcro. "And I thought the Lurex suits were cool."

We took a week off and came back without missing a beat. Soon we were finishing the leads and laying down the synthesizer effects to "Space Age Love". We also added acoustic guitar and piano to "Energize Me" before we did the vocals. I was disappointed that Fischbach wanted to edit the full-length version of the song. I wouldn't be adding the synthesized strings and French horns. It made sense though. Side B of a 45 RPM single couldn't be longer than three and a half minutes and "Energize Me" was more than five minutes long.

I'd known for some time what we had with those songs but laying down the vocal tracks sent me into orbit. Spacey, majestic, ethereal flight – they were like something from another dimension, and I was convinced that "Energize Me" was the ballad of the century. Zory and I recorded separate lead vocal verses and, like the Beatles, we harmonized into the same microphone for the chorus. We also double-tracked the harmony.

The spotlight was on Zory for "Space Age Love". I stood behind Fischbach in the control booth looking down at Zory's head through the ten-foot window. Headphones cupped his ears and a microphone suspended from a boom came to his nose. He seemed small in the large, open room, but his showmanship was felt by everyone. Zory definitely had the mindset of a robot lead vocalist. He was animated but not really singing – instead, he was talking with the *attitude* of singing. The concept that vocals didn't have to be pretty to be great was brand new in the days before punk rock.

I was up next to lay down a harmony track for Zory's lead. I'd sang the part so many times and the mix was so awesome that I knew why Zory was moving so much. I could feel the magical vibe of the music we were creating. By the time I got to the last line, I was disappointed that it was all over. I wanted to keep singing forever.

Fischbach's voice came through the headphones. "It sounded good up here. How was it for you guys? I don't think we'll need another take."

"It was cool," I said. "But talked it over with the guys, and we were wondering if you could move the helium tank in here so we can take a big breath of that shit before singing the stanza. It should give us a spacey, elven, alien sound."

Fischbach liked our idea and wheeled in a large green tank. He said, "This is the valve to turn it on. Just put your lips on this tube and breathe in the gas. Take a couple of test runs and I'll set the levels."

I turned the valve and the helium escaped in a long smooth hiss. We practiced our breathing a few times, giggling like school kids as we huffed the gas. Like a well-rehearsed alien quartet, we each took a big hit and held our breath until Fischbach told us to let it rip. With our high-pitched chemically enhanced voices, we sang "Why act prehistoric, don't be so square!"

Fischbach was at the board one night, mixing the songs and putting everything together. Charlie walked in the door sipping on a pint and was followed by a man toting a camera. "Hey, guy! Look who I found!" said Charlie in his loud southern slur.

A portly man with a wispy beard stepped forward and introduced himself as Buddy Rosenberg, Rock 'n' roll photographer. Fischbach had heard of Rosenberg and was thrilled to meet him in person. When Buddy saw that we weren't wearing bell-bottom Levis he realized we weren't your average rock band. He spoke to Desko and Fischbach, and they agreed to let Buddy take photos of us.

Back in those days, every time we met someone who could benefit Zolar X, we always turned on the Zolarian charm. Silly as it may be, it worked.

Zory got into his androidian character. "Bud-dee the human photo-bot, we are at your service. Welcome to our little slice of the galaxy. You know we are from outer space, light-years away. Compute?"

Buddy laughed and said, "This is going to be good."

Zany, Eon, and I moved towards the console and we played with the sliders, faders, and knobs.

"Will our alien family recognize us? Our lives here on planet Earth have been quite the experience," modulated Zory.

Buddy chuckled and said, "I'm sure we can get the photos to look very sci-fi."

Click, click, click. (Creem Magazine, 1974)

What were the chances of Charlie randomly bumping into this guy? Now we'd have photographs to go with our music. Things like that made me feel that this really *was* destiny; that these accidents were preordained, and success had to be around the corner.

Before long, we were looking at the photos Buddy had taken. "These are fabulous! I can't believe we just met Buddy a week ago!" I said.

"I love them all too but this one here—this is the shot!" said Zory. "This really looks like a spaceship. Look how Buddy captured the expressions on our faces. He caught just the right angle, and it looks as if all our eyes are on the viewscreen!"

With acetates in hand and the incredible prints from the Crystal Studios photoshoot, Desko and Fischbach made plans to deliver the Zolar X promo packs. Fischbach cut seven copies of "Space Age Love" on Side A and "Energize Me" on Side B. Five would go to record companies, one would go to Rodney Bingenheimer, and the last one was for the portfolio Zory was building.

In the midst of all this excitement, Buddy introduced us to the successful model Kay York. Zory had told me beforehand that she was the most beautiful woman he'd ever seen in his life. Kay brought a sample of her latest endeavor to the meeting — a Coca Cola serving tray embossed with an image of her wearing a tiny red-and-white polka dot bikini. I held the tray in my hands admiring it, but Zory whispered in my ear and pointed to an 8 x 10 glossy of a semi-naked Kay. "You can have the tray – I'll take one of those!" She was a very attractive young woman.

As it turned out, Kay wanted to shoot a demo—with Buddy's help—of Zolar X in the desert that she planned to pitch as a possible commercial to Love Cosmetics.

The morning of the shoot, Buddy, Kay, and a helper showed up at 4:00 a.m. in an RV. Wearing our antennas, wingsuits, and space boots, we jumped into the RV ready to go. En route, Buddy told us about his plans. "I'll be shooting the action scenes with the world's fastest lens—a 70mm Nikon capable of an incredible 125 frames-per-second. This will give the final product an extreme slow-motion effect."

We eventually arrived at the perimeter of Los Angeles, where the tall buildings gave way to a vast, arid tract of powdery sand dunes. The sun was just beginning to rise on the remote location. There were no telephone lines, no fences, and no trace of humans. Light beige in color, the landscape looked like something from a distant planet. Perfect.

After fooling around for a few minutes, Kay set up an antique vanity table covered with cosmetics. They wanted us to open the containers and play with the cosmetics, which wasn't very difficult. Buddy started shooting as we clowned around, looking at ourselves and each other in the mirror and messing with the cosmetics.

For the dune shots, they had us go to the top of a mound then run down as they shot us from different angles, focusing on the fine sand spraying up from our space boots. We did that sequence multiple times, taking direction from both Buddy and Kay. For another shot, they had us walk towards the camera from behind a dune. The first thing to appear was our antennas coming over the rise. I could imagine the glimmer of our wings as we came up over the dunes, each of us decked in our unique mono-colored garments.

Buddy yelled to us as we descended the dune. "Use force with your space boots as you walk." Sand blew up with each exaggerated step, making Buddy happy. "That's great! Keep doing that!" Buddy yelled excitedly.

The shoot took about ninety minutes, and we had the time of our lives feeling like movie stars. After the shoot, we went back to Crystal Studios. We were all damned tired, but Buddy insisted on getting one last shot documenting the event with a red-eyed photo of us. What a supersonic day.

53

PARTY POISON

HOLLYWOOD – MAY 1974

We were having so much fun recording, taking pictures, and shooting commercials. Having John Fischbach in our corner made me feel better about the people representing us. Our world seemed to be getting bigger. So shit, we decided to host a Rocket roll party.

It was party time. Charlie would get the booze, Desko would have the weed, and we'd invite groupies, fans, and friends from the Rainbow, Rodney's, and the Starwood. May was summer in LA, and we had a little front yard where people could have a good time. Ve would cut into Zory's action, and Syndee, the girl who loved her own voice, would definitely restrict my movements, but the party was sure to be a blast anyway

We finished the final preparations as the sun made its way to the other side of the sky. I was having a glass of wine when I heard a *ring-a-ling ding-a-ling* coming from outside. Looking through the window, I said to Zory, "Hey, it's our two little fans from the high school! How cute – they're on Schwinn bicycles!" We went outside to talk.

The curly redhead said, "Remember us? I'm Roxanne and this is Lisa. We were at Beverly Hills High, and we also saw you at the Starwood. You gave us your address at Rodney's, and I got an A on my English paper *Eep Opp Ork Ah Ah*, which was about the day I met Zolar X."

Lisa, the quiet brunette, handed me a foil tray. She could hardly look me in the eye. "Here's some brownies we baked for you."

"Looks like you guys are getting ready for a party!" Roxanne said.

I rubbed my chin. "You two are so sweet, but you're a bit young for our party."

"But you're the exact age of future Zolar X fan club leaders," said Zory.

Although the girls looked disappointed, they turned their bikes around and didn't raise objections. Roxanne batted her eyes. "I guess we'll go now, but we'll see you around, okay? When's your next show?"

"Three weeks from now at The Freak Ball. It's near LAX!" called Zory as they peddled away. When we were scoping out girls at Rodney's, we didn't know their age. We didn't think about it–but we knew for sure they were underage if we saw them in a high school. There were laws against that sort of thing, and it didn't matter how good they looked. Jailbait was trouble we didn't need.

Unfortunately, Syndee and I got into a big fight before the party even started. She wanted more than I could give her. I considered her a friend who bought me things and gave me money, but she wanted a relationship and a commitment. Things reached a boiling point when she hurled an empty wine bottle at me. I ducked just in time and the huge picture window took a hit. The bottle left a gaping hole the size of an LP.

We didn't have a party that night. Instead, the cops showed up and someone notified the landlord. Nobody was surprised when Charlie received an eviction notice giving us three days to move out. After reading it, Charlie let the paper fall to the coffee table and said in his loud, southern drawl, "Well everything happens for a reason, guy! Time to hit the pavement!"

We looked around and found something suitable almost immediately. I went with Charlie to look at the place and said, "This feels right. There's something about it that makes it seem like a Zolar X apartment." We brought our stuff over, but we didn't have to move our gear because it was still at Crystal Studios. Soon we were all moved in.

1055 La Jolla was great. There were plenty of liquor stores, restaurants, and markets within walking distance. We also had access to city transportation again, so we were only a short bus ride to Sunset or Hollywood Boulevard. The Starwood was just across the street, and there were tons of cheap clothing stores and pawn shops nearby. Not to mention the porno bookstore on the corner of Santa Monica and La Jolla.

Although the apartment was only one large room, a walk-in closet, hallway, kitchen, and bathroom, we were accustomed to tight spaces. One of the couches became a bed and another bed pulled out from the wall. A twin mattress fit perfectly in the closet, and that was the room we kept free in case one of us got lucky. A fuck pad, if you will. My leopard mattress went into the living room. It wasn't the Beverly Hills Hotel but it was home.

Our benefactor Charlie Patton got up every morning and walked to work. If you wanted a coherent conversation, it was best to catch him in the morning before he started tipping the bottle. From a rich family in Memphis, Tennessee, the wannabe architect did his best to involve himself in the art world, which included music. He always liked to have a nip of booze on hand, but he made it to work every day. Other than Zolar X and John Desko, Charlie didn't seem to have any friends. He had a lot of famous acquaintances, however. When he was deep in his cups, he'd throw out names like Elvis Presley, Andy Warhol, Mia Farrow, Jack Nicholson, Billy Gray, Lloyd Cross, Dean Stockwell, Neil Young, and Doris Duke — and that's only a partial list. Charlie had a knack for connecting with people. An educated man with street smarts, his drunken charm made him seem lost but knowledgeable. He talked a good game but didn't have a clue how to get where he was going. At least he was footing the bills.

L to R: Ygarr Ygarrist, Eon Flash at Crystal Studios, 1974
Photo credit: Buddy Rosenberg

L to R: Eon Flash, Ygarr Ygarrist, Zany Zatovian, Zory Zenith at Crystal Studios, 1974
Photo credit: Buddy Rosenberg

Charley Patton's Apartment where Zolar X stayed; 1055 La Jolla, #2
Photographer unknown

Ygarr Ygarrist at 1055 La Jolla, #2
Photographer unknown

54

TOM SNYDER
HOLLYWOOD - JULY 1974

We did the Freak Ball show out by the airport. Zory told us the show was all about being a freak. I suppose it was appropriate for us. Outside of Alice Cooper, we were definitely the freakiest band in town. We also played Rodney's again, which made it two shows in a month.

Zany, Eon, me, Charlie, and a couple of female friends were playing a little music, drinking beers, and clowning around when the door suddenly blew open. Our roadie Slim stood in the doorway, breathless and excited. The words tumbled from his mouth in a torrent. "You guys have to get down to Rodney's and fast! Tom Snyder and the crew from *The Tomorrow Show* are filming down there! I have a taxi out front waiting for you!"

Moving at supersonic speed, Zany and I planted ourselves in front of the mirror to draw on our eyebrows, groom our points, and put on our antenna. We were already in our tights, of course. Even at home, we were never completely out of costume.

In the cab on the way over, Zany and I discussed what we'd say. The show was a fairly big deal for us. *The Tomorrow Show* was national television and would be great publicity for Zolar X. Too bad Zory wasn't with us.

We jumped out of the taxi at Rodney's, but the TV crew seemed to be packing up already. A guy in a windbreaker with a curly wire behind his ear stopped us as we reached the entrance. "Who are you guys?" he asked, holding up his hand.

"We're the rock band Zolar X. We play space music," I said.

"We're recording right now at Crystal Studios," added Zany. Actually, we were finished, but he didn't need to know that.

"Cool," said Windbreaker. "You guys wanna be on TV?"

We both said, "Shit, yeah!"

The crew escorted us inside like we were the main attraction and introduced us to Tom. They hustled us into place under a blazing array of lights by the bar. Tom started with the questions as soon as we were rolling. "Who are you guys?"

"We're Zolar X," I said.

"Solar X?"

"No, Zolar X. With a Z," said Zany.

"What do you do?"

"We play Rocket roll music."

"Those are some pretty wild things on top of your heads," said Tom. "Where are you guys from?"

"We're from the future," I answered with a straight face.

Tom chuckled and rolled his eyes.

"Well, this is called *The Tomorrow Show*, isn't it?" I rejoined politely.

We shook Tom's hand. The interview had taken no more than a minute. They cut the lights and we hung out for a minute. With a lit cigarette in hand, Tom smiled and shook his head in disbelief. "Far out!" he said.

That was one way to put it.

"Tomorrow" TV host Tom Snyder interviews sci-fi band Solar-X at the party.

L to R: Ygarr Ygarrist, Zany Zatovian, 2 humans, Tom Snyder, 1974
Photo: Rock Scene Magazine

55

DEAD TIME
HOLLYWOOD - JULY 1974

Most days were filled with music, even if we were just goofing around. A typical scenario would involve Zory and Veonity stopping by to show us their latest costume designs. Zany might be sketching on the couch as Eon and I messed around on the acoustic guitar. Everyone was waiting for good news from Desko and Fischbach. Time crawled on broken legs.

Girls would start dropping by around noon with pot and beer. They dug hanging out with us and liked hearing Zolar X music. Syndee wove herself into my life more and more. When she came over it was for several days at a time, and usually on the weekend so she could keep an eye on me. She was the best looking out of all of the groupies and the funniest, so I tolerated her. Don't get me wrong—I cared for her, but who goes to a buffet and only samples one dish? I'll admit that the money and groceries she supplied were very helpful.

Friday night was an extreme cocktail hour when Charlie walked in with a bottle of booze and a mess of shrimp cocktails from Greenblatts. The groupies followed shortly and the night unfolded into the usual debauchery. People filled up the apartment and spilled into the hallway, otherwise known as the designated smoking area. Charlie was a serious dumpster diver, and our place was quickly turning into the neighborhood crash pad. He'd somehow found room for several chairs, mattresses, and a giant couch that folded into a bed. So what if the couch had to go in the kitchen.

Charlie tied one on every night and it was common for him to howl. He'd sit back after a great howl and sip his bottle contentedly—taking it all in like he was part of a screenplay involving the hedonistic nature of boys and the girls. He loved and understood the music and the concept of Zolar X. His intuition told him we would be huge and we'd be the greatest thing since Barbarella. All that was needed was the right backing and a bit of luck. I tried not to wonder if we'd tied our wagon to a drunk with major delusions. Charlie took another hit of brown liquor and yelled in his drunken southern slur, "Hey guy, did I ever tell you 'bout the time I played football with Elvis Presley? That's right, the King! Hey Y, take this $5 and pick up another twelve pack from the liquor store!"

I picked up the beer as requested. There were only two kinds of people in the world: those with beer money and those who walked to the liquor store. The party was on for real when I returned. Someone tried to pass me a joint, but I opened a beer instead. We were all taking Quaaludes, and everyone who mixed them with booze wanted to get laid. Syndee wasn't around so I was as free as a bird. I'd been making eyes with a young blonde who wasn't as hot as Syndee but was fresher and not as aggressive. With a bit of luck, I'd take her into the booty room for a bit of fun. The night was young.

The "booty room" was the only private room in the whole place. The space was just big enough for a twin mattress, a small black-and-white TV, and a couple of shelves sturdy enough to hold Eon's suitcase. The closet had two doors: one that opened into our apartment and another that opened into the hallway outside. Very odd, yet very cool and handy.

Eon and I often shared the booty room, depending on which of us got lucky. If a girl was in the mood, we'd slip away from the group. The closet was only five feet away from everyone in the living room, so they obviously knew what was going on. We'd emerge 20 or 30 minutes later and rejoin the party with smiles on our faces. Eon might even be standing there with his arm around a chick ready to claim the space. Sometimes he'd say, "I'll be in here a while," which meant he'd be in there all night with the girl.

Sometimes I slept in the closet. It was dark and quiet and I could watch the little TV. I'd fall asleep and have the most amazing musical dreams. Some nights I'd hear a knock on the outside door. "Who is it?" I'd ask. The voice on the other side would say something like, "It's me, Missy. I just had to see you again!" Then I wouldn't need the little TV.

There were nights when a girl would be coming in one door as another girl left through the other. The phrase "in-out in-out" took on a double meaning. Eon and I occasionally wanted the room at the same time, but it was strictly first come first served. Pun intended.

ZORY ZENITH

Going to Rodney's or the Rainbow as a band was always an adventure because we were inside the bubble. The bubble surrounded us wherever we went, particularly when all four of us were together. The bubble surrounded us, protected us. When Earth girls and other humanoids interacted with Zolar X, they realized there was something otherworldly about us. They were on the outside looking in. To them, we were either whacked-out crazy or mysterious superheroes from another planet—something invisible, unexplainable. Oddities.

The bubble drew humanoids hypnotically close to the edge, yet few ever penetrated the invisible shield. We saw their shock, fear, amazement, and admiration, but none of that really mattered. Our destiny was the stuff of mythos and legend.

YGARR YGARRIST

There was never a dull moment. Some days I taught guitar lessons to a couple of teenagers, Stan Lee and Kevin DuBrow. One afternoon, our roadie Slim dropped by with a new friend. Slim said, "Ygarr, this is Bobby. He works at Paramount Studios in the prop department. He saw you and Zany on *The Tomorrow Show*."

Bobby had platinum hair and pale blue eyes. He reminded me of a young Johnny Winter. He was naturally Zolarized.

Bobby said, "Yeah, I caught your show at Rodney's too. I loved it! I'd like to help out and be a roadie too."

"We can't pay you right now, but you're hired," I said. "What I can give you is a 'Z' to replace the 'B' in your name. What do you think, Zobbie?"

Zobbie said, "Cool! I have something for you too." He took an original 1966 *Star Trek* phaser from a little lunch pail he was carrying and presented it to me as a gift.

Nothing was happening with our acetate and we were frustrated. Were the record executives deaf? Part of me was beginning to question the people who were supposed to be our managers. They certainly weren't getting us any closer to a record deal. Stuck in the doldrums, we weren't rehearsing, we had no agent, and there were no prospects for a tour. What we did have was two hits that just needed to find their way into the right hands. With nothing else to do, we just partied and waited.

Thank God I had a key to Crystal Studios. It was easy to go there with my guitar and plug into my Hiwatt to play, create, and compose; and 3:00 a.m. was a good hour to head down with my little Panasonic recorder. I'd been working on an idea that came to me in a dream. I wasn't sure if it was an intro or an overture, but it definitely had balls. I had enough new ideas for several albums, but Zany just shrugged whenever I showed him a new one. I didn't understand.

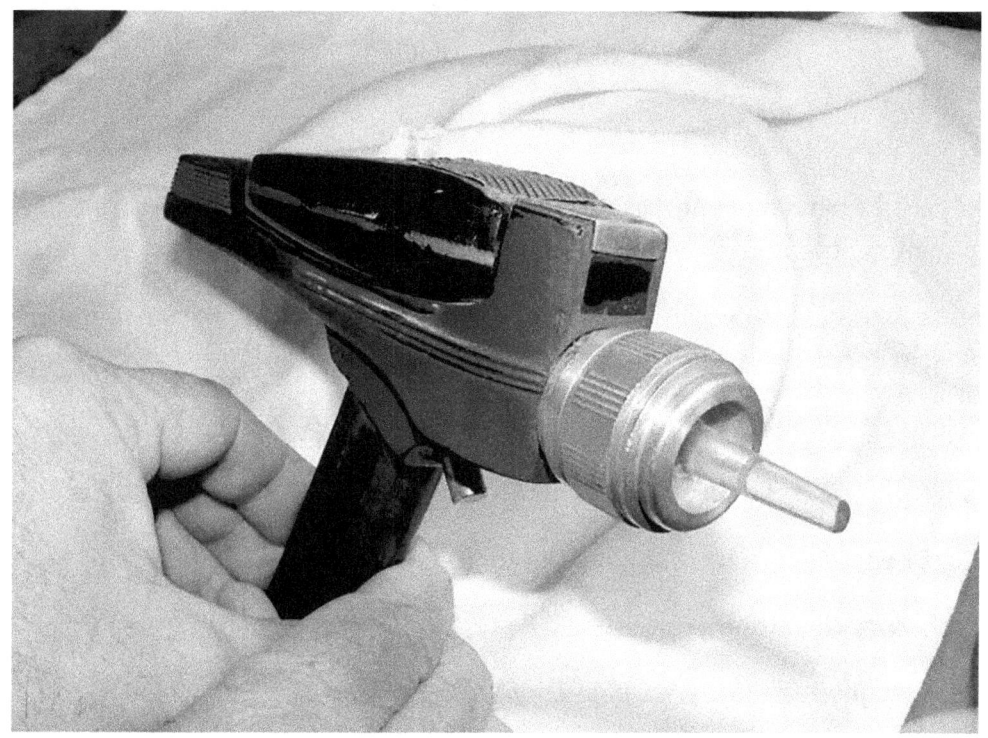
Ygarr Ygarrist holding the original 1966 Star Trek Phaser, 2002
Photo credit: Zoann

56

STEVE BINDER
BEVERLY HILLS - JULY 1974

Desko called a band meeting. He looked at us smugly and said, "Okay guys, we have an appointment tomorrow with Steve Binder, a television producer from Beverly Hills."

"Steve Binder? Beverly Hills? He's the guy who produced the Elvis comeback special in '68!" said Zory.

"Television? I wouldn't mind trying a little acting," I said.

Zany said, "We could do our own soundtrack!"

"Boys, behave yourselves," scolded Desko. "This could be a big meal ticket!"

"Yeah, Zory. No farting allowed!" said Eon.

We all laughed and looked over at Zory. We didn't trust him.

Zory stiffly held up two fingers and said in his robotic voice, "I will behave. Robot's honor."

We wanted to give Zory the benefit of the doubt, but he knew we didn't believe he wouldn't throw a monkey wrench in the works. This put him in the mood to speak his mind. "Listen," he said, looking around boldly. "The whole idea of grooming us to become the next Beatles is impossible. But if it were to be done, the stakes would have to be raised significantly. We have to be thinking about how we'd be remembered as writers and composers. With someone like Binder, we might be able to make the transition from the street all the way to the top. Doesn't it help that we're adorably cute?" He smiled blindingly.

"Just don't fuck this up," I said.

Our group arrived exactly on time at the small two-story building in Beverly Hills just off Rodeo Drive. Naturally, the band was in full Zolar X regalia, with winged suits, antennas, space boots, Spock eyebrows, and platinum hair with perfectly trimmed points. Binder's eyes popped open a bit when he saw us, exactly as we'd planned.

After the shock wore off a bit, Binder got down to business. He wanted to see if NBC would be interested in a TV series based around the fictional exploits of Zolar X. That sounded great until Binder said it could be like *The Monkees* TV show. I felt as if I'd bitten into a lemon when he said that. No respectable musician had ever taken the Monkees seriously. Then I thought that maybe we could take the concept in a whole new direction. We could make some money and reap tons of publicity. But would this be selling out? Would this typecast us forever?

I glanced over at the guys. Zory seemed excited at the prospect, but Zany rolled his eyes and looked disgusted.

"We want the Los Angeles Philharmonic to back us!" said Zany.

"Will we be playing ourselves?" asked Eon.

"Who's going to write the show?" I asked.

"This sounds very exciting!" said Zory.

The meeting was fairly short. Within thirty minutes we were shaking hands and walking out the door. "It was really great meeting you guys," said Steve. "We'll be in touch."

57

JAMMING WITH THUNDER
HOLLYWOOD - JULY 1974

I looked at my fellow bandmates and frowned. "I don't know if this is a good thing or a bad thing. I mean hell, we want to be the next Beatles, not the second coming of the Monkees."

"Yeah, and Binder probably didn't like us asking for the LA Philharmonic and wanting to write our own episodes!"

Zory and I sang the Monkees' theme song but changed it up a little, "Hey, hey we're the Zolars. People say we Zolar around. We're too busy singing to put planet Earth down… Nah!"

Desko opened his mouth and killed the whole thing. "Binder thought you guys were too far out for commercial television. So, we move on. Tomorrow night we have an appointment at Crystal Studios to meet with Doug Weston, the owner of the Troubadour. He needs an opening act for a newly signed band out of New York, Jobriath and the Creatures." He turned to Zory. "Is the Zolar X portfolio finished?"

"Shit, yeah. It's been done for a couple of weeks."

"Bring it."

"Finally, a chance to set it up!" said Zory.

"Far out!" said Zany. "Outer Limits!"

Crystal Studios had become central to the Zolar X enterprise. Everything that needed to be seen or heard was more impressive at Crystal. The studio was like a home away from home, and soon we would audition there.

Zory went upstairs to the conference room to set up the portfolio. None of us had seen it yet and we followed along excitedly. He spread the components of the portfolio across the ten-foot-long table and began assembling the 3-D display. Made from the same shimmery silver material as our wingsuits, the half-hexagon was four-feet wide and two-and-a-half feet tall. Buddy Rosenberg's shots of Zolar X formed the centerpiece of the display. There were two pockets: one for our acetate and the other for our one-page bio. Zolar X handbills artfully filled the other spaces. In front of the display were stand up cut-outs of each band member with placards underneath to identify them. It looked more like a presentation for a motion picture than a promo for a rock band. It wasn't something Desko, Fischbach, or Charlie could carry under their arm and leave with a record executive, but still something to behold.

Doug arrived with a couple of young men. We did the introductions and went up to the control room to listen to the music. Desko and Fischbach were talking business with Doug. A joint made its way around the room, and the wall of sound coming from the big speakers was impressive. The group made our way upstairs to check out the portfolio and discuss more business. "Alright, come in tomorrow and sign the contract," said Doug. "You guys have the gig for a week. Two sets a night starting on August 20th through the 25th."

The Troubadour was known for folk music. Acts like the Smothers Brothers, Jackson Brown, and Joni Mitchell had played here, so the heavy space rock of Zolar X would be a first for them. Surely this would finally bring us the attention we needed to get signed.

A few days later Eon asked, "How were the New York Dolls?"

"Very raw Rock 'n' roll with a bit of a blues twist. They had a youthful arrogance that was fun and energetic, but the songs didn't blow me away. They seemed like Rolling Stones cadets. What was really odd was that their bass player, Arthur stood onstage with his arm in a cast pretending to play while some other dude behind the amps actually played for him."

"You're shitting me!" said Zany. "He was just standing up there like a statue?"

"They have an album out?" asked Eon. "These guys make it look so easy!"

"I know, damn it!" I growled. "What do we have to do to get signed? Our appearance is unique and our sci-fi Rock 'n' roll breaks the sound barrier, but we're still looking! Fuck, this shit is getting old!" I said, swigging wine angrily.

It was after midnight and Syndee wasn't around, so I decided to check out the skirts down at the Starwood. Mingling in the smoky club, I ran into Gary Fontenot.

"Hey Ygarr, nice to see you!" he said, drink in hand. "What's Zolar X up to?"

"We'll be playing the Troubadour with Jobriath in August. I'll put you on the guest list. Any chance of a few free drinks?"

"Come with me," he said. We walked to the bar and he said to the barkeep, "George, put a couple of drinks on my tab for Ygarr."

The bands sucked and the skirts had wisely decided to stay away, but I had a few cocktails anyway. I started to make my way home at closing time when I ran into Johnny Thunders and his entourage in the parking lot. Johnny was carrying a guitar case and mentioned they'd been at SIR earlier. We stood around drinking and smoking until I invited them back to the apartment to jam. I knew it was late, but we didn't have to turn the amps to eleven. We'd just kick back with a little blues or some basic rock – simple stuff we didn't have to think about it. What could go wrong?

Back at the apartment, we walked past the main room where Zany was asleep. Zany didn't wake up, but Eon stuck his head from the closet and looked at us blankly.

"Johnny Thunders is here to jam. Wanna join us?" I asked.

"It's three in the morning!" said Eon.

Of course, he got up and we went to the kitchen to plug into my Hiwatt, which I'd just moved back from Crystal Studios. One of Johnny's friends brought out a saxophone and slung it around his neck. I wasn't prepared for that but was willing to give him a chance. We eased into a slow blues shuffle, but the sax easily overpowered our guitars. Tempting as it was, I couldn't turn up the Hiwatt at 3:00 a.m.

"Fuck, dude! Can't you blow that thing a little quieter?" I snapped, a bit drunk. I was trying to jam with Johnny Thunders and this chump was drowning us out.

Johnny looked at me blearily and jumped into an old Rock 'n' roll standard. He was a bit wasted but so was everyone else. We were all pretty smashed, and the horn was squawking at decibels nobody wanted to hear. My aggravation grew with each noisy honk until I finally lost my cool. I slammed the butt of my Les Paul down on the kitchen floor and said, "You guys gotta get the fuck outta here! Sorry Johnny, but I just can't take that motherfucking sax!"

Thunders and his pals muttered a few unkind words but slowly shuffled off. When they were gone, I sat down on the couch and gave my head a shake. I felt like a fool for throwing Johnny out, but why did that sax have to be so loud?

Syndee showed up on Sunday night, so we grabbed something to eat and went to Rodney's for a beer. We stayed for a few and were about to leave when Michael Des

OUT OF THIS WORLD: THE STORY OF ZOLAR X

Barres walked in with Johnny, Jerry, Arthur, and Nigel Harrison of Silverhead. Behind them, a couple of roadies hauled equipment into the club. I walked over to see if Johnny was upset about the previous night. "You guys gonna jam? I asked, giving myself 50/50 odds. He didn't seem very angry.

Johnny drawled, "Yeah. You wanna join us?"

"As long as that saxophone player isn't here," I said. "I'll be back in thirty minutes with my guitar and amp." Hopefully, Syndee would cover the cab fare.

Luckily, Syndee was at least as excited about the opportunity as I was. We hopped in the taxi and were back at the club with my gear before Thunders had even picked up his guitar. I guess he was busy with other stuff, but that was none of my business. I plugged into my Hiwatt half stack and looked around to see Nigel Harrison on bass, Jerry Nolan on drums, Johnny Thunders on guitar, and Michael Des Barres at the microphone. We jammed some old blues and rock standards, basically playing for ourselves because most of the kids had gone home. Syndee had a great time though and didn't complain about the cab fare. Too bad I left my little Panasonic recorder at home.

L to R: Ygarr Ygarrist, Syndee
Photo credit: Zoann

Ygarr Ygarrist at Rodney Bingenheimer's, 1974
Photo credit: Suzan Carson

58

THE TROUBADOUR SHOW
HOLLYWOOD - AUGUST 1974

I don't know how Desko did it, but he somehow pulled another small miracle out of his ass. Maybe he wasn't sleeping or smoking pot all the time because he hooked us up with a young entertainment lawyer who was interested in the band. His name was Ira, and we met the Armani-wearing lawyer in his ritzy eighth-floor, ocean-view office in West LA. Ira wanted to invest some greenbacks in us, which was always nice to hear. We set up a few rehearsals at SIR to prepare for the Troubadour show on his dime, and he took Zany shopping for a new SVT head. Most importantly, he wanted more demos so he could shop them to the record companies.

Opening night couldn't come quickly enough. The Troubadour had advertisements on the radio and in the newspapers, and we even heard a rumor that *NBC News* would be there to film opening night. Jobriath was the first openly gay musician signed to a major label, and it had the industry people talking. Of course, we planned to milk the publicity for all it was worth. Along with Jobriath's promotional stuff, the window of the Troubadour sported a color 11 x 14 Buddy Rosenberg shot of Zolar X in full regalia. We were excited.

Charlie came home with the Jobriath album *Creatures of the Street*. The album had a Broadway cabaret feel to it, but it was still rock and definitely not space music. I had to admit that Jobriath had a very futuristic look. He had his eyebrows up and wore a clear vinyl jacket over a designer leotard. The jacket was cool.

We listened to the Jobriath album a few times getting a feel for what his music was about. As far as competition went, we didn't stand a chance, one-on-one, against KISS. They had an album out and were touring the world while we were still trying to get signed. But we could definitely steal fans from Jobriath at the Troubadour. To see who'd be the last band standing; it was their sound and it was our sound, same stage, same PA system. Who would come out on top?

We arrived with our entourage around 4:00 p.m. for load-in and soundcheck. Eon's girl, Orley, was with us and so was Syndee, who had sort of managed to become my part-time girlfriend. This was a big chance for Zolar X to shine. We'd be doing two sets a night for six days straight, and surely the A&R guys would recognize our star potential when they saw us. There was no way we'd walk away from this gig without a recording contract.

Our silver wingsuits shimmered against the pale-yellow wall in the dressing room. Ve feverishly applied our make-up. Showtime was in forty minutes.

"We should all wear our wingsuits tonight so we look like the promo picture in the window out front!" I said as Ve worked on my face.

"I don't think I'll be able to drum in that suit. It'll get in my way."

"What's the big deal? I don't feel like wearing it tonight," Zany grumbled. Apparently, he'd already become jaded.

"I can't wear my wingsuit tonight. I'm gonna wear the black and clear vinyl top because it has a holster for my ray gun," said Zory.

"Okay," I said, defeated. "I'm gonna wear my wingsuit tonight. Let's at least all wear our antennas!"

"I'd look pretty silly if they fell off while I'm drumming so I won't be wearing any."

"Zany, what's up with the eyebrows? Why aren't yours drawn up?"

"I want to look kind of different tonight. I have my point and my antennas on. I'm tired of looking the same."

Rebellion was clearly in the air so I wisely decided to let it go. We'd been waiting so long to get signed that they were starting to lose hope. They could play in Levi bell-bottoms and T-shirts on opening night at the Troubadour for all I cared, but I was going to look awesome. I wasn't about to let them bring me down.

The dressing room was a revolving door of friends, industry acquaintances, and well-wishers. We even received several Western Union telegrams wishing us luck for our show. Doug Weston, John Fischbach, our lawyer Ira, and even Jobriath peeked their heads in the door to wish us luck. Jobriath was a soft-spoken, reserved little guy, but I was guessing he wouldn't come across that way onstage. The stage is not for the timid.

The stage manager fetched us five minutes to showtime. I looked down at the stage as we walked out of the dressing room and saw the lights glowing soft pastels that would change when we hit the stage. A low buzz roared from the red-carpet audience. Standing onstage looking out at the packed house, I saw plenty of recognizable faces. Ringo Starr, Roger McGuinn, Mickey Dolenz of the Monkees, and of course, KISS and their manager Bill Aucoin, to name but a few. To the left, I saw the NBC cameraman panning his shots. Anticipation was high and so were the guests.

The organizers hadn't told us who the emcee would be, so we were surprised when Mickey Dolenz jumped onstage and grabbed the microphone. "How are you all doing, Earthlings?" he shouted. "Our first band tonight is from outer space, but they're not here to invade us. Instead, this lovable bunch of aliens are here to entertain! Klaatu barada nikto – Zolar X!"

We dropped into "Space Age Love," and the sound system was great. For a change, I could hear everything. We had enough props to provide atmosphere, and our huge silver and black X towered behind us on the stage. The audience was giving us a lot of love, and the time flew past because we were having so much fun. Soon we were nearing the end of our first set. I thanked my lucky stars I was a musician and not a ditch digger.

After the encore, a young man came up to the stage and presented the band with an original piece of art. We invited him to the dressing room to talk more. His name was Armando Norte, and I was really impressed with his art. The futuristic, brightly colored drawing of the band on an alien world had the look and feel of a comic book cover. Each bandmember was represented in stunning detail, with the gigantic X suspended in space behind us. We exchanged numbers and set up a meeting. Armando started the drawing after seeing us at Rodney's in July and had finished it from memory.

I went downstairs to see who I could see. Ace was hovering about somewhere, and I wanted to find out what KISS thought of our show. I was talking to some fans when Bill and Ace motioned for me to come over to their table. The first thing Bill said was, "Why didn't you guys wear the suits you were wearing in *Creem* magazine tonight? We came to see you guys in those amazing costumes!"

I shrugged. "I don't know. They wanted something else."

Ace didn't seem completely disappointed "That was still a hell of a picture. You guys really looked like you were on the bridge of a spaceship!"

They congratulated us on our set. After five minutes of polite conversation, I moved back into the crowd to mingle some more.

OUT OF THIS WORLD: THE STORY OF ZOLAR X

ZORY ZENITH

For once, I wasn't disappointed with our sound. The band was tight, and we won the crowd's hearts, but I was a little jealous and resentful of Jobriath at first. I was even a bit itchy around my butt cheeks when I saw he had his eyebrows drawn up like us, and I was freaked that somebody had come as close to our "look" as he had. He was already signed and had beaten us to the punch. Then I realized he didn't represent any real sort of threat to us. We had our thing and he had his—totally different. For the first night, Jobriath wore a pink space suit that looked a bit like leotards, but custom tailored and not off the rack. He also had a round, clear helmet with a small pin on the top. When he reached up and pulled out the pin, the pieces of his helmet slowly came down around his neck to create a collar that looked like rose petals. His band members all wore black and were very tight musically. The set was a weird, eclectic collection of music that seemed to be about planetoidal, fantastical, strange things. I didn't quite get it.

YGARR YGARRIST

Jobriath and his Creatures were solid and sounded just like their album. Visually, Jobriath was also a tiny dynamo. I enjoyed the way he made it look like he was making out with someone in the corner of a cabaret but he was totally alone. His piano playing showed signs of classical training, but the songs weren't really to my taste. It just wasn't for me.

The next night, Jobriath dropped most of his space theme in lieu of cabaret. He later told Zory we had the space thing "all sewn up." Our band was tight by the end of the week, and we were feeling comfortable on stage. Two sets a night for six nights will do that, and we took "Parallel Galaxy" to the extreme on closing night. Bot's vocals and enunciation, and especially his talking vocals, were absolutely stellar. We brought down the house.

But still, nobody came up to the dressing room. Nothing at all during the whole Troubadour experience. I was bewildered, disillusioned, and disappointed. My mind tried to make sense of it but couldn't. Maybe the band was cursed.

59

SWAN SONG

HOLLYWOOD - SEPTEMBER 1974

Zany always had an ego, but now he also had an air of superiority about him. He told me our songs were bubble gum. Instead of hanging out with the band, he was driving around in a van designed to look like the shuttlecraft Galileo from *Star Trek* with makeup artist Steve Neill. The band unity seemed damaged or gone.

With nothing better to do, Eon and I decided to visit our families and drive back in the van Eon had been storing with his parents. That went okay, but when we got back, we learned that Ira wanted to meet, which seemed a bit strange. My stomach fluttered uneasily.

Ira got straight to the point. He told us he'd already had an informal meeting with Zory and Zany with the intention of getting Zolar X back into the studio to record "Parallel Galaxy" and "Spacers". Perhaps those songs would find traction where the earlier tracks had failed. However, Zory and Zany had insisted they didn't need to record more songs and had acted like prima-donnas. I'd been feeling hopefully optimistic, but then Ira delivered the coup de grâce: "I'm going to have to stop working with you," he said, looking at us with grave seriousness. He looked like a cat that had eaten a bug.

I could hardly believe what I was hearing. No recording? I lived to record. "What the fuck!" I exploded. "Give us some time to straighten those assholes out!"

"Let us go back and talk to them. We wanna record!" begged Eon.

But I could tell by the look in Ira's eyes there was no way to redeem this situation. Whatever had taken place between the three of them had been catastrophic. Because of Ira's connection with John Fischbach, Crystal Studios was also gone. We were finished.

I was aggravated, confused, and angry. Talk about a low blow. I thought we were a family—members of the same team. Zany and Zory had destroyed our relationship with Ira, and Ira had thrown us to wolves. I was mad at all of them. But the moment of anger soon faded. I loved the artistic creativity of Zolar X, and divorce was out of the question. I'd rather suffer this bullshit than be in a long-haired band that wore Levis. Tomorrow was another day.

We spent most of September partying, drinking, chasing skirts, and hanging out with new wannabe manager on the block Nik Pascal and his girlfriend Gypsy. Nik was an artsy, musically inclined character with a studio down the street from Rodney's. An older guy with a distinct accent, his insight into the underbelly of the music business was insightful. He had released a few albums of sound effects on his own label, Narco. We'd seen them in record stores. Did I mention that he also loved Zolar X?

His girlfriend Gypsy arranged for us to stay at her parents' vacant house in the Hollywood Hills for two weeks. Eon and I loaded his drums and my Hiwatt into the van and headed for Coldwater Canyon. I was disappointed that Zany didn't want to join us. As we were loading up our equipment he mumbled, "Bass guitars are just too human." Whatever that meant. I guess he preferred to stay in that little apartment and dream about synthesizers.

Zory came up several times, bringing lots of party supplies. The living area was amazing, with floor-to-ceiling windows that ran the length of the twenty-foot room. Below us, the rolling hills and twinkling lights of Hollywood stretched as far as the eye could see. With a view like that, it was easy to pretend we were rock stars living the life. I spent much of my time recording science fiction effects on my Panasonic and playing guitar through the Echoplex with a bottleneck. Very spacey.

We wanted to go out in style on the final weekend, so we scored a bottle of Quaaludes and invited a boatload of skirts. This would be our swan song in the Hollywood Hills, and we planned to cut loose like there's no tomorrow. The girls started to arrive and the party commenced. We gobbled the Rorer 714s, and soon we were higher than kites and laughing our asses off. Quaaludes were a euphoric pleasure pill that enhanced sex. On the right dosage, you could keep a hard-on for hours. The night was looking up, pun intended.

Everyone was having a good time but something was missing. Eon disappeared into the kitchen for a mug and returned holding a bottle of cooking oil. "Look what I found! Anybody game?" he grinned. Nobody was sure what Eon was actually suggesting, but they didn't seem to care either. The girls smiled ear to ear and soon they were completely naked. Not wanting to injure important bits they'd be needing later, the guys peeled down to their shorts. We didn't want to look at each other's junk anyway. "Hey, Ygarr!" shouted Eon. "Get the tarp from my van!" The party was definitely on.

I woke up the next day and it was all a blur. All I could remember was boobs flopping, oil spraying, and naked girls sliding down the big blue tarp screaming for more. Gypsy didn't appreciate the slippery mess we left for her parents, but that's Rock 'n' roll for you.

L to R: Zory Zenith, Zany Zatovian, Eon Flash (back), Ygarr Ygarrist: The Troubadour, 1974

Photo credit: Syndee

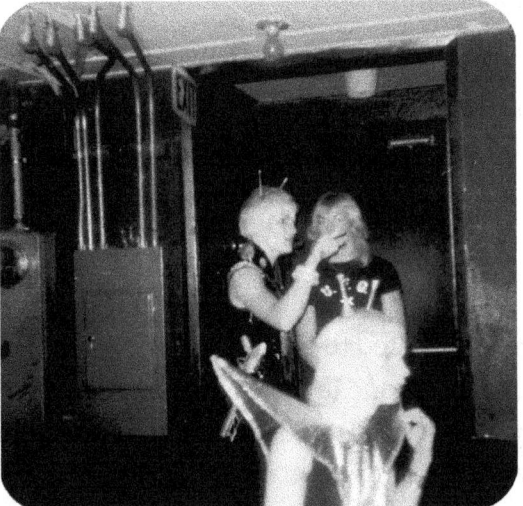

L to R: Zory Zenith, Eon Flash, Ygarr Ygarrist (front) Back stage at the Troubadour, 1974

Photo credit: Syndee

L to R: Eon Flash, Ygarr Ygarrist, Zory Zenith: The Troubadour, 1974

Photo credit: Syndee

L to R: Zany Zatovian, Eon Flash, Zory Zenith, Ygarr Ygarrist - The Troubadour, 1974
Photo credit: Jerry DeWilde

Armando Norte, 1974
Photographer unknown

60

SIXTH FINGER
LOS ANGELES - OCTOBER 1974

In late September, we got a call from Pacific Presentations asking if we wanted to play with the New York Dolls, Iggy Pop, GTO's, Flo & Eddie, The Hollywood Stars, Kim Fowley, and Michael Des Barres at the Hollywood Palladium. Only fools would turn down an offer like that, so we jumped at the chance to play Trash Dance at the Palladium on October 11, 1974. Importantly, we had the 11:00 time slot directly before the Dolls. This was a big opportunity to step onto the concert stage.

We'd asked makeup artist Steve Neill if he would make us some pointed ears for next week's show. "Sure!" he said. "Come on over and we'll have a party and watch *Outer Limits*. 'The Sixth Finger' episode is going to be on."

A few days later we showed up at Steve's place. "The Sixth Finger," which I'd seen a few years earlier, was about an angry man who'd volunteered for an experiment that would evolve him by 20,000 years. Not only did the procedure work, but it transformed him into a frightening entity with an extreme dislike for his fellow townsfolk. To evolve beyond hatred and vengeance, he enlisted the help of his girlfriend to propel himself even further into the future. Instead, she betrayed him by reversing the process and returning him to his former self. What I found interesting was that the "evolved" human looked more alien than human—very similar to the aliens in the pilot episode of *Star Trek*.

After the show, Steve explained he could only make ears for one of us due to the short notice. Being the "elf," I was the winning candidate. We hung out for a while, but then Steve agreed to teach Zany the art of prosthetic makeup, so we left him there and drove back to Hollywood in the van. Being in a band meant meeting interesting people.

I'd been playing guitar every day for the past two weeks, but we hadn't rehearsed as a group since before the Troubadour shows. "We should book Dress Review and run through the set a few times. What do you think, Zory?"

Our singer didn't seem concerned. "I'm really busy working on my robot suit from *Earth vs. the Flying Saucers*. Ve and I have been trying to figure out what type of material to use for the elbow and knee joints, but it's looking really cool, even though the helmet weighs a ton. The suit is purple metal flake!"

"Well, think about it 'Bot. This is the Palladium. We'll talk to you tomorrow."

"Nah, I'll be in my workshop. I know the songs, but I wanna finish the suit."

Zany showed up the next day with his head shaved – no more pointed haircut. I couldn't believe what I was seeing, and I even felt a bit sick to my stomach. "I had to shave my head so I could be fitted with my big brain!" Zany explained. "We sculpted the brain in clay and Steve made a mold of it. The plaster is setting up right now, and we'll attach it tomorrow."

"I'm sure it's going to look outrageous, but couldn't it have waited till after the gig?"

"I'm tired of being Zany Zatovian. Call me QB311X."

"Zany, I know you're a fucking genius but you're selfish. This will wreck our image!"

"You're crazy, this will enhance it."

"So, I suppose you won't have time for band rehearsal?"

"I don't need it, but you guys go ahead and rehearse without me. The songs are easy. I'm going back to Steve's. I'll be home tomorrow night."

Of course, we knew the songs, but the band still needed to practice and Zory needed to sing. He thought a robot suit was more important than rehearsal.

We had a new member in the house, aka QB311X the "Big Brain". He looked just like the character from the TV show we'd watched a week earlier, and I was amazed by the detail of the prosthetic head. The outfit made him look like he'd stepped off a soundstage at Warner Brothers, and Zany had even procured a black T-shirt with his new name on it. Unfortunately, the head wasn't even slightly practical. He showered in it, slept in it, and walked to the store in it, stopping frequently to re-apply makeup and glue parts that were falling off. Steve had loaned him a makeup kit that he carried at all times. Imagine walking past Zany sleeping and seeing his big brain sticking out from under the covers. He'd taken it too far.

We were hyped with the 11:00 time slot and couldn't have asked for more. Eon and I had trimmed our points and fixed our eyebrows, and we'd even started shaving our legs so the hair didn't show through our tights. We felt more Zolarized to look down at our feet and legs and not see all that hairy man stuff. Zory was still working on his robot suit, Zany was in his big brain from *Outer Limits*, and little Eon looked like a mild-mannered Zolar cadet. I'd decided to go as the green elf; green hair, face, and torso decked in green greasepaint with purple accents of lipstick and eye shadow. Zory hadn't resolved the problems with the joints of his robot suit, but I told him to bring it along–it would look great on stage as a prop, and meet us at the Palladium at 5:00.

We were very excited about the show. There would be parties afterward, and I didn't give a shit that Zany was wearing the big brain or that Zory was working on a robot suit that none of us had seen. Rodney Bingenheimer would be hosting the event, and it would be fantastic to play with acts that had released albums. The exposure would be great.

We finished up last-minute details with the roadies. People were dropping by to ask for backstage passes, and the phone kept ringing with friends and fans asking to be put on the guest list. "Shit it's only $5.50!" I told them. "Surely you can afford that for so many bands!"

I was about to do my hair green when the phone rang again. Charlie picked it up and yelled, "Hey Y, it's for you. It's the stage manager from the Palladium."

I grabbed the phone, thinking they were probably just making sure we'd be there. I listened in disbelief and then slammed down the receiver. "Fuck! You're not going to believe this!" I shouted.

"What's all the noise about?" said Zany, walking into the room with Eon.

"Those assholes bumped us! We go on at fucking 8:30! Those fucking cutthroats are also squeezing our set to thirty minutes! Shit, nobody in Hollywood will be there at 8:30! We should just cancel!"

"They're scared of you guys Y. They're scared of ya!" yelled Charlie.

"8:30 is way too early!" said Eon. "Whose idea was that?"

"Probably the Dolls' managers. They don't want us going on right before them," Zany guessed, his big brain bulging obscenely.

"We'll have to finish up our makeup at the show. I'll call Zory, but I don't want to tell him we got bumped. He'll blow a gasket." I told Zory anyway and he wasn't impressed.

"FUCK!" said Zory in a way that only he could.

OUT OF THIS WORLD: THE STORY OF ZOLAR X

ZORY ZENITH

I was flattered when they asked us to do the show, but then suddenly we were just filler. It was my impression that we were going on just before the Dolls, and that was enough of a fucking insult already, but I could live with it because they had an album out. I went from being totally thrilled to being completely crestfallen on the day of the show. But we decided to knock ourselves out and give it everything we had anyway. Maybe we'd win over a few new fans. Maybe people would talk about the amazing opening band for years.

YGARR YGARRIST

What should have been a smooth process for me turned into rampant chaos. Before the phone call, I was about to put on my makeup and color my hair green— an undertaking that would easily take an hour. Now I'd have to do all that at the Palladium, which meant bringing extra towels, a blow dryer, my makeup, and my outfit. That's where it got hectic. I used the bathroom sink to do my hair green and dripped all the way back to the dressing rooms where the electrical outlet was. I didn't have any help with makeup, but I sure could have used some. Then I was getting very hot while trying to put on the greasepaint, sweating and dripping green all over the place. I finally got a stagehand to bring in a fan, which helped keep me dry and eased the stress a little. Zory was cussing everybody out, and it didn't help matters that his robot suit wasn't finished. Zany paced back and forth with his big brain, giving me a little comic relief. Little E was out in the hall practicing twirling his sticks.

The Palladium held over 3,000 people, but we would have been lucky if 500 arrived early enough to see us play. This was Hollywood and people didn't start coming out till at least 10:00. "Hey Zory," I said. "Let's take a peek–see if anybody's here yet."

"Shit, I told everybody that we were going on at 11:00! I didn't get a chance to tell them our new set time," said Zory.

"This is fucked. We should just walk out of here, but I know we can't do that."

"Damn, it's 8:00 and look out there! Can't be more than 100 people!"

I looked at the band. "We only have a 30-minute set tonight, so let's play 'Space Age Love', 'Energize Me', 'Spacers', and 'Parallel Galaxy.'"

Five minutes before showtime, I took a deep breath, let go of everything negative, took a shot of bourbon, and made my way to the stage with the band. There were probably only 200-300 people in attendance, but I made up my mind to have some fun. After all, this was the Palladium, with a nice sound system and great lighting. I saw some crazy shit going on in the audience. A bunch of people were carrying a coffin around and yelling "Death to Glitter"! That was cool with me because we weren't glitter.

"Space Age Love" went off without a hitch, but "Energize Me" was another story. I knew Zory was going to do a costume change during my solo, but I never dreamt he would get close enough to the edge of the stage for the crowd to pull him in. One second he was there and the next second he was gone. I looked into the small but dense knot of people and waited for Zory to reappear. I was prepared to play a lead from thirty seconds to two minutes, but ten? To solo that long, you needed to smoke a joint and be in a fine mood to jam.

But the "Energize Me" solo was a precise pattern. There were variables, but not enough to last ten minutes. I was so pissed that I was probably bright red underneath the green greasepaint. *Where the fuck was Zory?*

Like magic, our singer finally reappeared, smiling like he'd just got a blowjob. He'd certainly been gone long enough, and his absence had cost us two songs. The stage manager yelled, "You have time for one more – a short one!"

We closed with "In Command", but obviously our set could have been better. Unless, of course, Zory actually did get a blowjob.

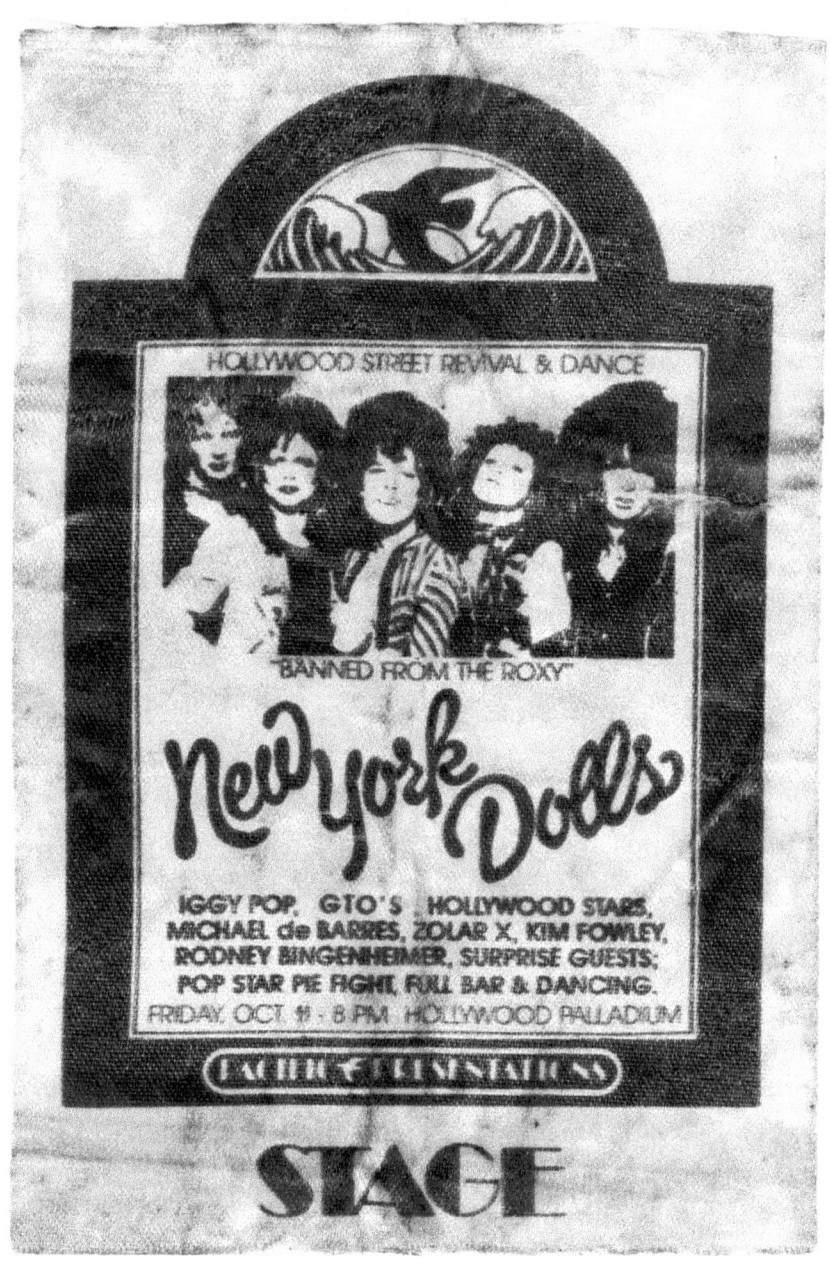

61

FILLING THE VOID
HOLLYWOOD - OCTOBER 1974

Armando Norte had been coming over with his sketch pad and colored pens more frequently since the Troubadour show. It was such a pleasure having him around. One day I was doodling around to see if I could find his space name. In the end, I simply reversed his last name and came up with Etron. He loved it. With Etron, all I'd have to do was sing a song, recite lyrics, or tell him about a character, and within twenty minutes he'd show me a sketch and say, "You mean like this?" Nothing was ever planned; there was no schedule, just total creativity, and spontaneity. Void of the Pointed People and Zoomen came to life. I told him about Galaxy girls and his drawings looked like they could step off the page. Very sexy. Sometimes he brought drawings that inspired me to create a character or write a new song. With both sides giving and taking, we assembled a story that grew into something we called Alien Visions. Zany was no longer my creative partner, so developing Alien Visions with Etron was a breath of fresh air.

Our individual talents were like gifts from the cosmos—two halves of a highly ordered structure. I channeled the music and poetry, while Etron harnessed the visual, artistic side. Our two halves merged to create the perfect crystal.

Art with Etron filled the void during the day, and escapades of sex and partying helped fill the other part at Nik's place some nights. His pad was a little portal to get away. He'd given Zory, Eon, and I keys to the place so we could come and go as we pleased. Located conveniently down the street from Rodney's, it definitely came in handy. Zany and Nik didn't seem to like each other. They were always arguing about music, art, or business. Nik called Zany lazy and Zany fired back, "You're just an amateur!" No wonder Nik didn't give him a key.

Zany and I hadn't written anything together for more than a year. A fork in the road had developed between us. We were like kindred spirits when we began, but now he was pitting his music against mine. He criticized riffs like "Art of Robotics", "Orbiting Cosmic Ovals", and the intro to my new untitled song I was calling "Horizon Suite". He complained constantly, calling the music "bubble gum" and fantasizing about synthesizers. The most important thing in his world was the upcoming 20th Century

Fox Costume Contest. He wasn't acting like part of the Zolar X team and with his shaved head and missing eyebrows, he didn't look like one either.

Zolar X had been in LA for almost a year. We'd had multiple managers that got us nowhere. We'd played showcases at both the Starwood and the Troubadour that didn't get us a record deal. We recorded a demo that failed to get us a contract. We'd been living in a small apartment with little or no money and were dependent upon either Charlie or our girlfriends. Rejection was hard to take. We'd see other bands getting signed, yet there we were, probably the most original band on the planet, and we weren't getting any offers. I understood why Zany was frustrated. If I was feeling those things, he must have been too. One day bled to another, but they all seemed the same.

Then it was October 31, Zany's big night. The 20th Century Fox Costume Contest was scheduled to take place directly before the premiere of *Phantom of the Paradise*, which added an extra air of excitement to the proceedings. The whole crew showed up in force: Charlie, Desko, the band, the girls, Nik, and Gypsy. Everyone was Zolarized except for Zany, who was wearing a robe he rented from Western Costumes that was used in the "Sixth Finger" *Outer Limits* episode. There were around thirty contestants, but looking around at them, we felt that Zany just had to win. With his silver robe and boots and that big brain, nobody else even came close. The emcee asked each contestant to pick a number that would be his or her identifier. When the emcees called each contestant's number, the crowd would either clap a little or even boo. In the end, it was between Zany and a bushy-haired ghoul with a Tarzan build. Zany won the contest and came home with $250 bucks. We never heard the end of it, and he slept in that moldering costume for another week or so. I think he finally had to bury it.

Zany Zatovian as 6th Finger, 1974
Photographer unknown

62

BILL AUCOIN
HOLLYWOOD - NOVEMBER 1974

Out of the clear blue sky, I received a call from Gary Fontenot, who told me that Bill Aucoin, KISS's manager, was interested in signing Zolar X. Bill wanted to meet the band at the Starwood for a 6:00 p.m. meeting. Of course, I was extremely excited.

It made sense that Bill would call Gary at the Starwood because that's where he first met the band when the Starwood was managing us. That was eight months ago, and a lot of things had changed since then. This could finally be a real opportunity. I remembered how friendly Bill Aucoin had been towards us at the Troubadour. He'd shown genuine interest. Did he want to be the manager of KISS *and* Zolar X? Maybe his intentions were good, or maybe he just wanted to shelf us, but we were already shelved and had nothing to lose.

Zory was supposed to arrive at La Jolla no later than 5:00 p.m. to prepare for the important meeting. Then we planned to walk over to the Starwood together. Wouldn't you know it, Eon and Zany had taken a few days off to visit family and friends in the Bay area. I kept waiting for Zory, but he was two hours late. Syndee watched me pace the floor as I became more nervous by the second. Where the fuck was he? As a last resort, I thought I might have to go there alone if he didn't show up. I'd called his house and he wasn't answering. Every minute that went by was sheer torture. My stress level was maxed out, so I drank a beer and popped two yellow Valiums to keep it in check.

At 5:59, I finally bit the bullet and went over by myself. I walked through the parking lot. There was no limousine, and Bill always traveled by limo. I arrived ten minutes late, but people in show business always ran a little behind. Up the back stairs I went, the same stairs I'd climbed a hundred times when I lived there. I knocked on Gary's office and opened the door.

The room was empty and there was a chemical odor like angel dust in the air. Not a soul in sight. I went back down the stairs and home to La Jolla. My brain was going crazy trying to figure things out. Was Bill pissed because Zolar X was a no show? Shit, if that's how it was, the Starwood could have called. They had our number, and I could've been there quickly. I don't think I'll ever know what happened.

Zory Zenith, Rodney's English Disco, 1974
Photo credit: Suzan Carson

L to R: Zany Zatovian, Eon Flash, Ygarr Ygarrist - Rodney's English Disco, 1974
Photo credit: Suzan Carson

63

BULLET WITH NO NAME
HOLLYWOOD - NOVEMBER 1974

It was a beautiful Sunday afternoon in November. I was hanging out at La Jolla with Janet Planet, sipping sangria, and playing acoustic guitar with Eon. It was a small get-together, the windows were open, and a slight breeze blew through the house.

An incredibly loud bang startled us as Zory kicked the door open and strutted into the house. He was standing in that cocky rooster pose we knew so well, a snub-nose .38 revolver in his hand. We were all very frightened. I couldn't believe Zory had a gun—a potential murder weapon. He wasn't saying anything, just glancing madly about the room. Holding the gun up in the air, he continued to glare at everyone. I was sitting on an ottoman maybe eighteen inches off the floor, and he was directly in front of me. This was not a good day to die.

I babbled mindlessly to Zory, wondering what the hell was going on. I was trying to make sense out of this, but there wasn't any. I had the gut feeling that he was there for me. At that moment, Zory pointed the motherfucking pistol right between my eyes. Thinking my heart was about to stop, I bent forward just as he fired. I heard the loud bang of the gun, but I was still alive. The crazy fucker had fired through the open window. The bullet could have hit someone outside, but it didn't hit me. Then he was gone with no explanation. Strange days were upon us.

Zory Zenith, 1974
Photo credit: Jeff Austin

64

REFLECTIONS
HOLLYWOOD - JANUARY 1975

The Zolar X spaceship dropped out of warp over the next few months and traveled at sublight, space-normal speed, which is very slow. Some of the few highlights included our fifth show at Rodney's. I met Ian Anderson, of Jethro Tull, who told me I was one of the best guitarists he'd ever heard. At Christmas, Charlie kept the Hollywood apartment but went back to Memphis to visit his family. He did some smooth networking while he was gone and managed to set up a show for us at the Cotton Carnival in May. We got the red-carpet treatment when Nik rented a white limousine for the premiere of *Stardust* with David Essex, a real Rock'n'roll movie. As we got out of the limo, we heard over the speakers, "Oh, and here is ZOLAR X!" We were the most famous unsigned band around.

Meanwhile, Zory and Ve broke up. Zory said it was a full-blown catfight. He was with one of his other girlfriends Clorinda, but when Ve caught them smooching in front of Nik's pad on Sunset, he popped her in the mouth, loosening her front teeth. Devasted, Ve sped to Zory's parents' house and cleared out the closet. Looking back, 1974 was the year that lasted a lifetime.

We vacated Hollywood and headed north for a change of scenery. Almost immediately, Zory hooked up with my old friend Karen and moved into her place in Santa Clara. Syndee and I stayed in Newark with Zoann and Dave, Zoann's fiancé. Eon stayed with his parents and Zany with his. We'd been there for about a month. Zory and Zany were building props, and we'd get together for rehearsals at Yesterday and Todays' studio to practice for a show at Weeks Park. Everything about us felt different. Zany was still shaving his head and thinking about the big brain and the fact that Zory had toted a .38 was still too fresh to forget. It was hard to capture the same passion we had in Laurel Canyon putting the band together. We had a show to play, and I was going to try to have fun, but something was missing.

OUT OF THIS WORLD: THE STORY OF ZOLAR X

Ygarr Ygarrist, 1975
Photo credit: Jeff Austin

Zory Zenith, 1975
Photo credit: Jeff Austin

Zany Zatovian, 1975
Photo credit: Jeff Austin

65

HUNG OUT TO DRY
HOLLYWOOD - FEBRUARY 1975

"Hey Zory, it's been a week since the accident. How's your head?"

"It hurts! What started as a quiet night drinking a little wine and playing music with you guys ended up like something out of the *Twilight Zone*!"

"It's a good thing we weren't buckled up!" he said. "That's the type of accident where *not* wearing seatbelts probably saved our lives. From the looks of the car, we could have been decapitated if we hadn't been thrown out. We're fortunate. A few broken ribs and minor concussions are better than the alternative."

"I guess it wasn't your time," I added.

"Talk about spooky!" said Zory. "I guess I must have passed out, but I'd say the accident qualified as an out-of-body experience. I was lying there on the highway, and I could see a pinpoint of light coming down out of the darkness that turned into a funnel. The funnel grew as it moved towards me. As it got closer, I could see what looked like waves of wheat under a pool of light. The waves moved back and forth in a sweeping motion, and the closer they got, the more scared I became. I remember thinking, *I'm not ready. I'm not ready!* I was so terrified that I woke up as the wave began to wash over me. I pushed myself up and looked back at the car. It was probably fifty feet away, upside down with the roof scrunched to the seats, one wheel still turning and smoke coming out of the engine. Then a plump, middle-aged woman, almost motherly-like, leaned over me. She said, "You'll be alright. Help is on the way!" And I was thinking, *It's nighttime, with no houses around—no gas stations, pay phones or nothing!* This woman just appeared out of nowhere. And then she was gone. Vanished. I'll remember it for the rest of my life."

"Crazy," I agreed.

"Ygarr, I'm going to ask Karen to marry me," Zory continued. "After the accident, I feel like I've been given a second chance and I don't wanna lose her."

"Speaking of weddings," I said, changing the subject. "Zoann and Dave are getting married, and I'm the entertainment. I'll be playing the wedding march! I'm thinking about wearing my pink and green spacesuit."

Zory doubled over clutching his chest. "Oh Y, don't make me laugh! My ribs can't take it. That's an endearing, comedic visual: Ygarr Ygarrist amongst the humans."

Home sweet home. Charlie would have his shoes in the oven and his socks drying on the oven door. Almost every day he washed his shoes and his only pair of socks. It was a hoot watching him—like he was slow roasting peanuts, only instead it was rubber and cloth. For all his faults and eccentricities, Charlie was always good to us.

We'd known for about a week that we had the show in Memphis. We'd even decided to play some gigs in New York at CBGBs and Max's Kansas City after. These would be our first shows outside of California, and we'd be flying out of LAX at 8:00 a.m. on Thursday, May 1. Who knew, maybe we'd finally meet Andy Warhol! This gig was a breath of fresh air.

Charlie turned a shoe and paused like he was reading my mind. "Guy, it's a ten-day, ten-night event, one of the city's great traditions – like the Mardi Gras," he said. "From there, we'll head to New York. I have a friend with a loft in Soho we can stay with. By the way, thanks for letting me set up the laser for Led Zeppelin. I wouldn't have done it if you told me not to."

"It's cool, Charlie. I wish it could have been for Zolar X, but at least you got to set up a $25,000 laser and beam splitter for Zeppelin! But where are we staying when we get to Memphis?"

"Rooms for everybody at the Holiday Inn! All expenses paid! We'll pick up our tickets at the airport, including Zory's new bride. What's her name, Sharon?"

"No, her name's Karen," I grumbled. There was a time and a place for everything, and this was not a good time for a honeymoon. Although it was none of my business that Zory had married her, it pissed me off that he'd conned Charlie into getting her a ticket without asking us. I liked Karen—she was my friend too, but something was bordering on stupid about this.

Charlie took his mostly dry shoes from the oven. "I think it's cool that Pepsi Cola is bringing you guys to Memphis. The Zolar X logo is gonna be on Pepsi bottles! They've been saying your name on the radio for two months now."

Eon came in the door loaded down with sacks of stuff from Guitar Center. "I think I got everything – strings, picks, sticks, and a new head for my snare! I dropped the drums off at the airport earlier. They're being shipped tonight. I'm ready to go!"

"Me too. I've packed our wingsuits, makeup, and antennas. Did you hear that Zory will be bringing Karen?"

"Yeah, I know. Too much, huh?"

"Hey Charlie, what's the name of the place supplying our amplifiers?"

"Strings n'Things – one of the biggest music stores in the South! Thanks to Pepsi Cola and WHBQ, you're the talk of the town."

We made it to LAX and boarded with no real difficulty. I was bringing both my guitars. The Flying V would ride in the belly with the rest of the luggage, but my '59 'Burst would stay with me. The stewardess told me I could put it in a mini closet up by the cockpit where I could keep an eye on it. I wasn't taking any chances with my Les Paul.

Lunch was served and I had several champagne cocktails. The atmosphere on board was very jovial. We were still flirting with the stewardesses when the captain announced, "We're on final approach to Memphis, Tennessee. The skies are clear and the temperature is a balmy seventy-nine degrees. On behalf of American Airlines, we're doing what we do best. Thank you for flying with us. Have a great day!"

The outstanding thing about Memphis was the oxygen. You could practically see it from the plane window, and after living in the LA smog, it was fantastic. The extreme greenness of the trees and foliage was almost too much. Zory took a deep breath. "Wow!" he exclaimed. I knew what he meant, and no explanation was necessary.

We were very excited to be in Memphis. I carried my Les Paul to the baggage claim, but they didn't have the Flying V. The representatives were very apologetic about losing my guitar and promised to deliver the instrument as soon as it returned from New York. Good thing I'd kept the Les Paul in the cabin with me.

From out of the crowd, I saw a couple of guys and two cute cowgirls walking towards us smiling. We were the only people dressed differently, so I thought they were just locals getting a kick out of us. Then Charlie elbowed me and said, "Hey guy, it's your sponsors, Pepsi Cola and WHBQ!" We were getting the star treatment.

After the introductions, we piled into a black limo and headed to the radio station for an interview. Our hosts kindly offered us cocaine, drinks, and joints. They were loose Southern Rock 'n' rollers in checkered shirts—not surfers or longhairs, but somewhere in between. So far, we were enjoying the southern hospitality.

Upon arrival, we posed for a few promotional pictures with the girls and Ricky D, the main DJ. When that was done, we headed upstairs for the interview. The guys broke out some more nice-sized lines and we all did a toot. I'd reconsidered my position on cocaine and had decided a line or two was okay once in a while. "So, how do you like planet Earth?" asked Ricky D, wiping white powder from his nostrils.

Zory, being the ham he was, replied, "Humans are fun!" His comment sent a wave of laughter throughout the booth.

I was more serious. "We're still adjusting to your way of life. Your females are the only ones who wear makeup." More laughter.

"Do you ever get snide remarks?"

"All the time in the metropolis of Los Angeles. Some call us fags and some call us freaks, but we're not. I can't say were superheroes either. We're Zolarians – a whole different ball game!"

The booth roared with laughter and it wasn't even canned. This went on a bit longer, but they eventually wrapped it up by promoting the carnival, urging listeners to come down and see us on May 2nd to May 10th.

We got back into the limo. "Time to head over to Strings n' Things," said Ricky. "They're waiting for you."

"Who's waiting for us?"

"Your fans! We've been promoting your show for two months now."

"This is so cool!"

There was a good-sized crowd at the music store. Everyone turned to gawk as we stepped inside. I heard someone say, "It's Ygarr Ygarrist!" Then someone else said, "Ooh look, it's Zory!" We were surrounded, and I could barely see little Eon for all the cuties around him. I heard a fan say, "Where's Zany?"

"He's right here," said Zory. "He just looks a little different."

The reception was somewhat mind boggling, and it was clear that the station had done a good job with the promotion. People were excited to see us. Maybe it was the pointed hair and space tights. I didn't care why or try to figure it out, it sure felt great. After the past year and all its disappointments, we were finally getting our due and were being treated like rock stars. We were a big deal in Memphis, Tennessee.

One of the guitar techs edged through the crowd toward me. "You want to go back and see where we make our custom guitars?"

"Of course, I'd love to! I'll be needing a futuristic guitar soon. Something that sounds as good as my Les Paul but looks cooler."

The tech led me to a large workshop, where many guitars lay in various states of assembly. He picked up a fine piece of mahogany with strings and showed it to me. "This is a guitar we're making for Todd Rundgren. We can do anything you'd like."

"You'll have to call it a guitron," I suggested off the top of my head.

"Perfect!"

Charlie walked in and told me the car was ready to take us to the hotel. In short order, we all climbed back into the limo for the ride downtown. We might have had another drink and line on the way.

We arrived at the hotel and split off to our various rooms. When you share a one-room apartment with six people, having your own room at the Holiday Inn was the height of luxury. I threw myself down on the bed and looked up at the stippled ceiling. With any luck, I'd find someone to share the bed with me later.

The radio people came up to my room and partied with me for a bit, and then I went down to hang with Zory and Karen. They weren't in the mood for company, and Zory seemed more interested in his wife than he was with the band. I guess it was fair because they'd just married, but still. Feeling like a third wheel, I went back to my room to get Zolarized. Soundcheck was at 5:00.

People milled about the auditorium during soundcheck. This was the first day of the carnival and they were checking us out. We ran through a couple of songs testing the Ampeg amplification. It sounded alright, but I missed my Hiwatt. The tone on my amp was super clean, so I was adjusting knobs on the fly. Maybe I could maneuver a Marshall or a Hiwatt from the music store. At the very least, I'd need a distortion box to make things a little more spacey. The Ampeg was fine for bass, but no guitarist in his right mind wants to play out of an Ampeg.

We headed back to the hotel to freshen up for dinner. It had already been a long day and we needed some food. Downstairs, we found a large buffet-style dinner waiting for us. It was quite the spread, and I hadn't eaten so well in a long, long time. It was just so cool to be there. We were having a blast. Laughing, we sampled every southern dish from crawdads to grits. Zory and Karen arrived a bit late, and I looked around at my bandmates thinking *it can't get any better than this*. We were all giddy thinking about the possibilities that might arise because of this gig. Suddenly, we had hope again.

We finished up the meal with an after-dinner drink and conversation. The maître d' came to our table and asked, "Is there a Mr. Ygarrist here? There's a delivery waiting for you out front."

"Thanks. That must be my Flying V."

Everyone followed me. The American Airlines employee was very proper in his sparkling white uniform. I gave him the luggage stub and signed for the guitar before he handed me the case. Luckily, the instrument wasn't damaged. I took it as a good omen.

We invited two groupie girls to come back after dinner, but Zory and Karen retired to their room. After downing a few more drinks and tootin' more lines, the five of us talked about music. I fantasized about adding synthesizers and the Philharmonic Orchestra to create an incredible audio-visual experience. Eon and Zany said they were getting tired and headed to their rooms, leaving me with the two girls. That was nice of them.

The next morning, I went next door to see if Zany wanted to go for breakfast, but there was no answer. I figured he must already be downstairs at the buffet, but he wasn't. I went back to the rooms to see if he was with Eon. "Have you seen Zany this morning?" I asked. This was getting kind of weird.

"No, haven't seen him."

Eon and I went to Zory and Karen's room. Too frustrated to pay attention to the Do Not Disturb sign hanging from the doorknob, I pounded loudly.

No answer. I pounded again more fervently.

Zory looked agitated when he finally opened the door as I blurted, "Have you seen Zany?"

"Fuck Ygarr, I'm on my honeymoon! I haven't talked to Zany since last night."

"I'll go ask the concierge if he's seen him. We think Zany's AWOL."

Eon and I went to the front desk. "Good morning, gentlemen," said the concierge. "May I help you with something?"

"We're looking for our bandmate in 403. Have you seen him? He's dressed like us."

"Ah yes, room 403? He turned in his key at 6:00 a.m., and I think he caught a cab to the airport."

Eon and I looked at each other in disbelief. "Gone?" We were flabbergasted.

"He seemed fine last night," I said, dumbstruck. "Did he say anything to you when you guys left my room?"

"He was fine! I can't believe it! What are we going to do? The carnival starts today!"

"What *can* we do? We'll have to cancel! We gotta call Charlie and tell him the bad news!"

"First we need to tell Zory."

"Shit, this is bad!"

So many things went through my head. Inside my world of sickness, I felt as if I'd been kicked in the gut. What in the hell had provoked Zany? Why did he sneak out without telling anyone? This was the guy I'd started the band with. I wrote music with him, even though we hadn't collaborated in a while. The bad taste in my mouth wouldn't go away. This was a betrayal of the lowest kind. Zany had slithered away like a snake.

We broke the news to Zory. "What? Are you fucking kidding me? Are you sure?"

"Absolutely. Now that we've told you, we have to call Charlie."

Charlie said he'd be over in a half an hour, that he'd get it all figured out. I hung up the phone, knowing it was much worse than that. We were in Zory's room trying to calculate our next move. Could we get another bass player? Would we have to cancel? What was Zany thinking? I heard Charlie walking down the hall towards us. He had a six-pack under his arm and had already popped the top on one. I glanced at the clock. It was 9:00 a.m.

"Hey, guy! You sure 'bout all this—that he ain't hidin' out with some cute gal?"

"We're sure. The guy at the desk said he split, way before any of us were even out of bed. He saw him get in a taxi heading for the airport! Fuck!"

Charlie took a long sip of beer and looked out the window while grinding his teeth. After another gulp, he said, "Asshole! I put my name on the line for this show. Do you really need him to do this? This is Zolar X right here. Just go on without him!"

If things weren't bad enough, the room suddenly filled up with a load of Memphisonians. Along with Ricky D and his entourage, there were several promoters and a Pepsi big-wig I recognized from the day before. The scene was chaotic. Somewhere in the distance, I heard Charlie's words dropping in and out, "He left… no… I don't know." Then I was hearing things like, "We have a lot of musicians here in Memphis. I'm sure we could find a studio musician bass player who could fill in."

"Maybe if we were a simple Rock 'n' roll band playing three-bar progressions and blues riffs," I said, shaking my head at the impossibility of such a thing.

"But we're not," added Zory.

"We're nine hours away from showtime, and that's just not enough time to teach someone these songs! It's impossible. Maybe if we had a week, but we don't," I said, wearily. I picked up my guitar and played a few bass riffs from "Parallel Galaxy" just to show them what I meant. "This is just a glimpse of what happens in the bass section of our melodies. These are 64th notes, and it goes on like this. It took us over a year to get to the point we're at right now. I'd love to play the shows, but this is our reality."

I could see it in their eyes. They got it. Suddenly the promoters were graciously shaking our hands. "Sorry it didn't work out," said an important-looking gentleman. "This is very disappointing for everyone. I guess we'll have to find another act for the Carnival. Talk to *you* later, Charlie."

The room almost felt empty when they left. Charlie seemed lost for words. He stood there grinding his teeth, his face getting redder and redder from embarrassment and anger. Zory and Karen quietly sipped white wine. What was there to say?

At length, Charlie rubbed his chin. "Hey guy, let's just move on to New York City! I have friends in Manhattan, and some of them have lofts. We can make the rounds, look at the clubs, and talk to Steve Paul about getting you boys booked at the Scene. Then we'll just bring everybody back to New Yawk and play more shows." He looked at Zory. "What else would you wanna be doing on your honeymoon?"

I responded first. "No way! I'm not mentally prepared to take on that city without the whole band. You guys can go, but Eon and I will be heading back to California," I said, speaking for our drummer as well. I turned to Eon. "Let's get your drums shipped back and check out of these rooms before we head for the airport. I guess we're going back to Hollywood." It was the hardest decision of my musical career, and all because Zany had screwed us, the selfish bastard.

"You guys can go back to LA if you want," said Zory, "but Karen and I are on our honeymoon. We're not ready to go home just yet."

We said goodbye to Zory, Karen, and Charlie. "See you in Hollywood," I said, solemnly. "Good luck in New York."

As we turned to leave, I took a mental snapshot of Zory in his black Klaatu space suit and Karen in her sleek Ralph Lauren dress, with the crisp, white carnation corsage pinned over her heart. What an odd-looking couple.

Eon and I took a cab to the airport with our luggage and gear. The ride was quiet and both of us were lost in our thoughts. I felt so humiliated and ashamed by Zany's betrayal that I didn't know how to process my feelings. I'd been doing my best to sever my emotional and mental ties with the bass player, but it was still a shock to accept that I'd never step on stage with him again. We'd hung out in California for more than a year, but now he was running away just as exciting new opportunities had finally arrived. What a coward.

I felt bad for Charlie. He'd used his connections to get us this show, but now those doors had slammed shut. I felt deflated. Empty. No Cotton Carnival. No backers. No New York.

The night sky had turned from beautiful hues of pink and orange to dark blue by the time we lifted off. There couldn't have been more than twenty people on board, so we sat where we pleased. We got a lot of TLC from the stewardesses, who kept the drinks coming. That helped boost our spirits, even as we flew near a heavy thunderstorm. The captain's reassuring voice came over the intercom. "Good evening, this is Captain James Kern, and I just wanted to let you know that what you're seeing from both sides of the aircraft are two separate thunderstorms. We're in no real danger because those storms are more than thirty miles away, so just sit back and enjoy the show. Thank you for choosing American Air Lines, where you get the best of everything."

"We'll just find another bass player!" I said, copping a little buzz.

"I dunno, Ygarr. I just dunno. He's always been strange, but I didn't see that coming!"

I had mixed feelings as we landed. It was good to be back on the ground, but the hole in my gut still felt raw. I'd made arrangements before we left Memphis for Syndee to pick us up, and she was waiting when we landed. The ride home was fairly quiet and solemn.

We got back to La Jolla, and I expected to walk into an empty apartment. Instead, the first thing I saw was Zany. He was in tights, shuffling along with dirty white socks that looked too big for his feet. My anger almost boiled over but I controlled myself. Although there was so much I wanted to say to him, I somehow kept my mouth shut. I couldn't bear to be around Zany or even look at him. He was acting as if nothing had happened.

L to R: Eon Flash, Zory Zenith, Ygarr Ygarrist, 1974
Photo credit: Buddy Rosenberg

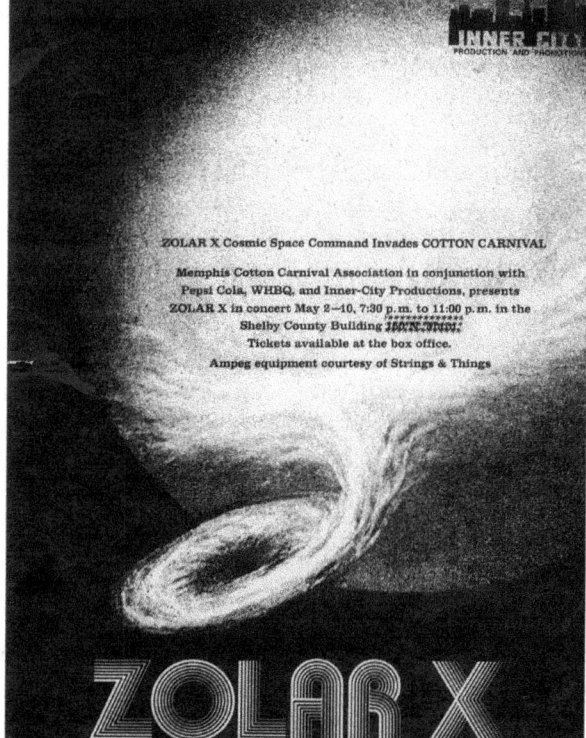

Cotton Carnival Flyer, 1975

66

NEW YORK NEW YORK

MAY 1975

ZORY ZENITH

Flying to New York with Charlie and my new bride helped ease the shock of Zany leaving us in Memphis. Maybe he didn't realize how important the Cotton Carnival could have been. We'd all been waiting for something to happen, and everyone would have been back on board if it had. Instead, Charlie, Karen, and I traded our return plane tickets for a chance to promote the band out east. I was thinking Charlie would be in his element in New York City. With his connections, surely something would come our way. I was almost excited.

Charlie worked overtime trying to make a bad situation good. The stewardess came around again, and he was somewhere between loud and charming. He waved at her and said, "Get us all another round, would ya darlin'?" Turning to Karen, he said. "We just might see Andy Warhol and get invited to the Factory while we're there!"

We only seemed to have been in the air for a few minutes before I saw the glow of the massive city beyond the wing of the plane. Flying into Kennedy International Airport at night was beautiful. The vast city lay spread out below us like jewels on black velvet.

We collected our luggage and Charlie called his friend in Manhattan from a payphone.

He stepped out of the booth, grinding his teeth back and forth and mumbling. He'd received some bad news.

"So, what's up Charlie?" I asked, worried.

"A couple of gal pals of his came up from Jamaica and he rented the loft to them!" he said, almost yelling. "Don't worry—it'll work out. We'll hop a cab to the city and get a cheap hotel tonight. I'll wire Memphis and get some more money tomorrow."

Skyscrapers reached for the moon on every street. We walked and walked until we came to a run-down area teeming with scary-looking people. A poster peeling from a brick storefront featured a nasty skull and crossbones and the message "Welcome to

Fear City." I'd never seen so much trash. Between the graffiti, pimps, and junkies, I was starting to feel that my world was crashing in around me. Why was I taking a beautiful young woman into this dangerous hellhole? New York was supposed to be this artsy-fartsy place where we could make the nightlife for a week or two and check out Steve Paul's Scene and CBGBs. But moneywise, we were running on fumes.

"We're in Greenwich Village," said Charlie. "Just a little further and we'll be at the Albert Hotel."

"Shit, Charlie. This looks like skid row! Some honeymoon this is turning out to be!" I said, glancing around nervously. A gnarly hobo with a black eye glared back.

"Oh hell, guy! At least we got a hotel!" said Charlie. "See that dumpster in the alley over there? We could be sleeping in it! I used to do that all the time when I lived here before. Sometimes you just do what you gotta do. The Albert will be a walk in the park. It's a happenin' place! Jim Morrison, the Byrds, and Cream – they all stayed there! The Mamas & the Papas even wrote California Dreamin' there!"

"That's exactly what I'm doing – California dreaming!"

We stopped walking at the corner of East 11th and University Place. "Here we are!" said Charlie. "I don't know about you two, but I'm ready to buy a bottle and get off my feet!"

"Let's get checked in first, then we'll find a liquor store and some food."

The hotel was a full-on disaster. Our door had been kicked in so many times that it was beyond repair, and even the chain was split in two. I went into full panic mode. The walls were splattered with what looked like dried blood that had been there since the beginning of time. I guessed that was better than fresh bloodstains, but Karen and I just wanted the night to be over. We were terrified. This wasn't Hollywood.

We propped a chair in front of the door to create a false sense of security. Karen and I slept on the bed while Charlie passed out on the floor, bottle still in hand. I drifted in and out of a very light sleep. Karen had a death grip on me, and I knew I hadn't given her any sort of honeymoon at all. We were out of that lumpy bed as soon as the first rays of light poked through the cracked and dirty window.

"Let's go to Western fucking Union," I said to Karen. "I'll phone my dad and have him send us money to get home. I've had enough of this shit!"

"Where you goin'?" asked Charlie, tipping the bottle.

"We're going back to Los Angeles. You coming?"

"No, guy. I have friends I can hook up with. Who knows? I might run into Andy again. You sure you don't want to stay and get Zolar booked?"

"No. We'll see you in Hollywood."

The Western Union was a little over a mile south of the Albert Hotel. We cabbed it with our last few dollars and I made a collect call to my dad. He wasn't very happy, but he sent us enough money for bus tickets and a little extra for food. I thought about the last twenty-four hours while we waited for the money to arrive. My first thoughts were about Zany leaving. Why had he done that? What was going through his big brain when he decided to leave?

And then there was the trip to New York. Charlie had dropped the ball on that one. He was perfectly capable of handling his duties as manager, and he did a great job getting us the Memphis gig, so I was shocked when he failed to secure our accommodations in New York. It didn't occur to him to call his friend before dragging us into this vast kingdom of darkness — this huge, gothic, horrifying place! I just couldn't deal with his drunken incompetency any longer. This had been one of the worst experiences of my life, and wouldn't ever want to return unless I was sheltered safely in the arms of angels.

Within the hour, we boarded a Greyhound bus for the long trip west across the United States. I was still in my black Klaatu spacesuit, and Karen was in the same dress she'd been wearing since Memphis, the sad little corsage still pinned on.

We rode for days, sniffing diesel fumes with no air conditioning to ease our discomfort. We rolled through Hells Canyon South, Hells Canyon Midwest, and Hells Canyon Southwest. With only a few dollars left from the money my dad sent, we ate shitty mashed potatoes and gravy at every truck stop. Stepping off the bus in Albuquerque, New Mexico, I spewed my guts all over the asphalt. My stomach could only take so much. We still had 790 miles to go, and the bus was scorching hot. Sweaty, sticky, and sleep deprived, the only way we could clean ourselves was to splash water on our faces and armpits in filthy gas station restrooms. Karen was a trooper though.

The bus finally lurched to a stop at the Hollywood and Vine station. I helped Karen off the bus, feeling like death warmed over. We were still in the same clothes we'd been wearing in New York. Karen's corsage was barely recognizable after the cross-country fiasco—just a sorry nest of wilted, brown petals. The bus driver stood there smirking as I got down on my hands and knees and kissed the pavement. I said out loud, "Never fucking again! No more half-assed unpredictable bullshit when it comes to travel!"

Photo credit
iStock.com/M. Kaercher

67

BROKEN
HOLLYWOOD - MAY 1975

Zory was still weak from the five-day, hell-on-wheels road trip when he walked into the La Jolla apartment to check on the band. More than angry, he seemed bewildered by the chain of events that had led to our current predicament. Nobody had much to say when he came in, but Zany was sitting on the couch acting as if everything was fine. The atmosphere was colder than ice. To break the silence, Zory finally said, "Zany! Come on man! What the hell? You just hop on a fucking airplane with no discussion? What the fuck were you thinking?"

Zany just shrugged and didn't say a word. I don't know how we restrained ourselves from beating the hell out of him. He deserved all that and more.

I could see Zory was doing his best not to completely explode, and we must have all been wondering if he still had that snub-nosed .38. Walking over, I put my hand on his shoulder. "Zory, this band isn't just broken, it's irreparable! I can't play with that asshole anymore," I said as if Zany wasn't sitting right there on the couch. "He might be a genius, but we all know that bass players are replaceable."

Zory was beyond being exasperated. "But that jerk won't even tell us why he did this!"

"I love ya Bot, but I'm going up north. I'm not quitting or giving up on Zolar X. I'm gonna find us another fucking bass player! Wanna walk with me to the corner store?"

Outside, Zory strained to enunciate, hissing through clenched teeth. "That selfish bastard! He didn't even have the guts to tell us to our faces!"

Negative feelings caught in my throat as I struggled to respond. "Shit, we could have worked it out if he'd said something to us! We could have made some sort of deal with him at least until the Carnival was over. He could have waited 'til we got back!"

"He probably got tired of you and me being the dynamic duo," Zory said, morosely.

We stopped walking on Santa Monica Boulevard, directly across the street from the Starwood. Ironically, this was where we would say our goodbyes. The afternoon sun exaggerated the weariness on 'Bot's face as he squinted at me, searching for answers that didn't exist.

"It's not over 'til it's over," I said, leaning in for a hug.

Zory smiled thinly "I see no fat lady," he whispered in a monotone voice.

We both chuckled as we wiped away our tears.

I'd been back at my mom's for a couple of days, recuperating from Zany and the nightmare of Memphis. The very first morning, when I woke up and didn't have to see or hear Zany made it feel like a brand-new day. He'd been in a whole other world for the last eight months of Zolar X anyway, but I'd tolerated it for the sake of the band. I'd put up with him laughing at my new songs and acting like a superior dork. He was very easy to love for one second and hate for the other fifty-nine. His final decision to walk out on the band was the final straw.

I turned my thoughts to finding a bass player, but I couldn't quite get the electrons in my brain to focus on the new evolution of Zolar X. Putting up a flyer looking for a drummer had been different because the whole band was involved, and now it was only me. It wasn't my nature to post a flyer at the local music store. I'd been in a band that was full of art, but I wasn't an artist. I couldn't design a bitchin' flyer like Zory could. Eon, meanwhile, could probably make one phone call in Hayward and get fifty phone calls back the same day. But due to my shy streak, my unorthodox style, and an inconsiderable ego, I couldn't join just any old band—they would have to join me.

I'd learned as much about songwriting from Zany as he had from me, so I hadn't walked away with nothing. But what could I do now? So I asked myself, *What are the odds of finding a bass player that I can mold, right here, right now?* Very slim if any.

The phone rang. It was Pete Angeles. "Hey, what's going on?" he asked. "Word on the street is you're looking for a new bass player and drummer."

"Yeah, Zolar X kind of hit a wall," I confessed.

"That's too bad," continued Pete. "But I was wondering if you wanted to jam?"

PART 2

engineering x-o-planets

1975 TO 1982

68

THE SPACERZ
BAY AREA - JUNE 1975

Later that week I hooked up with Tom Lee and Ron Eiseman. Even though I wasn't looking for a drummer, I figured jamming with a rhythm section would be the best way to break in a new bass player. On the way to the studio in Fremont, California, I tried to prepare myself. I was fairly certain I wasn't going to walk in and see two spacemen. Still, I decided to remain open-minded about the possibility of working with them.

The two musicians were definitely human and I recognized Pete from my old party days. He started with, "Hey Stev—"

"I don't go by that name," I said, cutting him off coldly. "Call me Ygarr."

Tom and Ron shook their heads and grinned. "I saw you on *The Tomorrow Show*!" said Ron, looking a bit awestruck.

"This is like meeting one of those far-off, out-of-reach heroes!" said Tom. "You're my guitar hero."

"So what happened with Zolar X?" asked Pete, effectively changing the subject.

"Oh, our damn bass player went into the outer limits and quit the band." I gave them a level look to let them know the subject was closed. "Are you boys ready to elevate your style both musically and visually?"

"Yeah!" said Tom.

"We're tired of playing covers," added Ron.

Their attitude was encouraging, even though I probably looked as odd to them as they did to me. Dressed in casual space wear, I still had my point and my up eyebrows. They were short like me, which was a plus. Some of the other details weren't as good. They both wore Levis and flannel shirts, and Tom even had a mustache. My first visual impression of them wasn't good, but Tom's chops were damn fine for an Earther. I figured I'd have to look past what I saw and use my ears to see the future. Could they play? Were they teachable? Were they malleable?

Coming off a disaster, I was hoping for a new opportunity. These two guys had shown up out of thin air and they seemed willing. I felt my perspective shifting as the night progressed. All these guys needed were different clothes.

Over the next two weeks, we jammed acoustically at Pete's apartment. I showed them some of my new songs including "The Horizon Suite." What had started as a quest to find a bass player was turning into a new band. I felt rejuvenated.

Between rehearsals, I worked feverishly on new material. Melodies that had been floating around in my head since the early days began to pour forth. For the last year, I'd been recording new ideas for songs on cassette, jotting down song titles, and lyrics on scraps of paper. Now those songs were beginning to take shape. I loved writing with Zory and Zany, but these new guys were blank canvasses and I was the conductor. Because the new songs were all mine, I could teach them the music the way I heard in my mind. It was, as they say, a brand-new day.

We rehearsed anywhere and everywhere we could. I taught Tom some Zolar X-style bass patterns, and the 21-year-old was a quick study. When he didn't pick something up right away, he practiced until he did. Ronnie was a decent drummer, although he was better with his snare than his kicks. One night in the spring of '75 we hung around after rehearsal to watch the lunar eclipse. We figured it was a sign and named the band Eclipse. I realized it wasn't good enough within seconds, but then it dawned on me. The Spacerz.

The guys were like sponges soaking up my music. I was controlling my musical destiny and the music flowed from my heart. I soon finished "Horizon Suite", "Take Me to Your Leader", "Zolar Eclipsing", and "The Plutonian Elf Story". I gave the guys space names. Tom Lee became Ufoian Ufar (Ufo) and Ron Eiseman was dubbed Eclipse. Our first show was a block party and we hammered the large crowd with our spacey thunder. Before long, the Spacerz were starting to get noticed around Northern California.

But Rock 'n' roll is never drama free, and Syndee phoned one day to confess she'd been unfaithful with Zany, that dreaded quitter. Between sobs, she attempted to fit 200 words into a span of thirty seconds. "You know how much I love you! I can't live without you! Come on, baby! Just let me explain! I got all twisted up in the moment. He means nothing to me!" On and on she went. My first reaction was anger, but how could I be mad when I too had been unfaithful? I had to let it go.

Syndee and I were married in June of '75. I'm still not sure what I was thinking. What I didn't know back then, but can see now, is that her dad was steering our lives. The powerful, judicial mogul was known for saying, "Don't put all your eggs in one basket." In essence, I'd done just that.

Music wasn't paying the bills, so I went along with the program just to survive. Syndee's dad got me a normal job at a record store in Marin County, north of San Francisco. Then he found Syndee a job at a clothing shop in San Francisco. He footed the bill for a new car, a Minimoog, and an Echoplex. He even paid six months' advance on our cozy apartment in San Rafael. We lived five minutes from my job, but now the rest of the band was fifty miles away across the bay. Ufo and Eclipse continued to practice, and we rehearsed on my days off. Job or no job, music was still my life.

At Warehouse Records, I unpacked new albums when they arrived and rang up sales at the counter. It wasn't a hard job but everything about it killed me inside. Why wasn't I worthy enough to have a few albums in those racks? The only good thing about the job was the financial stability and a bitching record collection that included everything from Walter Carlos to Tomita. For a while, life was kind of normal. But I hated normal.

After three months of that shit, I told Syndee, "I have to get the guys over to this side of the bay. I need to be playing music more often!"

I found a motel that rented by the week and moved them over. Then I used some of my savings to rent a rehearsal studio. Now we could finally get to work. Syndee wasn't happy because I'd be spending more time away from her, but that wasn't my problem.

The boys told me about a great singer from Boise, Idaho who sounded like the lead singer from Yes. They wanted to bring him in for a test drive. They argued that if he made the cut, my job would be easier because I wouldn't have to sing everything. In the end, I decided to go along with it because my new bandmates were so keen on the idea. It was worth a shot.

I was in for a shock when the Idahoan arrived for his audition. Ufo, Eclipse, and I stood roughly 5'6 in height, but this pot smoking hippie with hair down to his knees was more than six feet tall. I could have worked with that, but his voice was like fingernails on a chalkboard. He only got through a few bars of "The Plutonian Elf Story" before I mumbled, "He's wrecking my opera!" Then the beanstalk hippie pinched my wife's ass!

"Really?" I said, shocked by his audacity. "NO FUCKING WAY! This sour singer ain't gonna be in my band!" And because I was drunk and maybe a little belligerent, I told him, "GET LOST!"

Like Johnny Thunders, he left without a fuss, but I'd never regretted kicking him out.

The band was driving a wedge between me and Syndee. I could feel her animosity, her jealousy. Even though she loved my music, she wanted all my attention and my attention went to the band. During a heated argument one night, it came as no great surprise when she shouted, "It's either them or me!"

I just looked at her. She was giving me an out.

"And I'm taking the Mr. Coffee!" she added.

I was relieved. Being married and working a day job wasn't for me. Syndee left and I moved the boys into the apartment. The savings account came in handy. With the rent paid up and an efficient public transportation system, we were set for six more weeks.

Free from normalcy, we rehearsed with a passion. Progressive songs like "Zolar Eclipsing" and "Take Me to Your Leader" required extreme dedication and gave the word rehearsal a whole new meaning. We practiced ten hours a day, seven days a week until the rent dried up. Then we moved to plan B.

Plan B meant moving back to my mom's in Newark, and the boys lived with Pete in Fremont, just a bicycle ride away. Always wanting to add to my equipment, I skimmed the want ads hoping to score a deal on a '63 Fender Stratocaster or a Les Paul Jr. Instead, I saw a Danelectro Longhorn bass just like Zany's. Pete coughed up the $350 bucks, and Ufoian had the Zolar X bass tone. "This instrument has twenty-four frets instead of twenty-one!" I said, excitedly. "There's no way you could play Parallel Galaxy on your Rickenbacker."

To look the part of being Spacerz, I groomed them with a little space-mod style. Although I was still a firm believer in the quote "Never look like your audience", this band was going to be more about the music.

L to R: The Spacerz: Ufoian Ufar, Ygarr Ygarrist, Eclipse, 1975
Photo credit: Jeff Austin

69

SOMETHING'S MISSING
CALIFORNIA - 1975

ZORY ZENITH

Karen and I moved in with my parents in Hollywood, where we fucked like rabbits several times every day. We felt a bit awkward at first, but then we realized we were newly married and that's what you do. So we did.

I was still traumatized about Zany leaving the band, and from the cross-country trip back from New York City. Slowly, it dawned on me that Zolar X was done. Ygarr was in Northern California, I had a brand-new bride, and I didn't know how to do anything but play music. I was adrift on the high seas of reality, untethered by anything familiar. A change had arrived.

My look also had to change. I went to a hairdresser, who listened with the same wise understanding as a bartender. "You have great fashion sense," he said, lopping off my point. "You know hairstyles from being a musician, so why don't you become a hairstylist? $750 bucks and a year later, you'll have your license!"

And so it was. Beauty school during the day and married life at night. But I couldn't shake that restless feeling. After the excitement of Zolar X, being a normal civilian wasn't enough. I enjoyed beauty school but it wasn't music. It wasn't what I was born to do.

Then one day I got a bright idea. I still had some white pancake makeup, so I drew on a mime face. Then I rummaged through the closet and found a striped T-shirt, black jumper, and white gloves. Looking like a British waif from the fifteenth century, I went down to the boulevard and started clowning around, doing little routines leftover from my time with the band. I moved up and down the boulevard, waving through the window at the beauty school to my fellow students. They had no clue it was me, and I had a great time.

Ironically, Shady Lady bass player Gerhard Helmut was working at a pop art clothing store on Hollywood Blvd called Ants n' Pants. Gerhard, who had no idea that I would or could do street mime, called me into the store. "Hey, I have an idea," he said, amused. "Let me ask my boss if you can do some promotions for the store."

I spent the rest of the year attending beauty school during the day, practicing street mime, and handing out flyers at the store afterward. It wasn't entirely unpleasant.

Zory Zenith, 1975
Photo credit: S. Stopek

70

FREEDOM

JUNE 1976

It was the Summer of '76 and America was about to celebrate her 200th year. I wrote a song titled "Bicentennial Rock" and planned to debut it at our July 3rd show at the Center Theater. The gig was the talk of East Bay. This was our biggest show yet, and the bill read Y & T, The Spacerz, and Legs Diamond. Craig Rinehart, former drummer of Zolar X, was in Legs Diamond on guitar so I was curious. Backstage, all the musicians were mingling. I saw some familiar faces and then spotted Craig.

"Hey, buddy! What should I call you, Craig or Eon?" I said, swigging beer.

Eon gave me his famous bear hug, lifting me off the ground. "I'm playing guitar for Legs Diamond again, so I'm going by Craig these days. Have you heard from Zory?"

"Not for well over a year," I said, shaking my head. "It feels weird to be on the same bill as you, but not in the same band. Zolar X was so great." There wasn't much else to say, so I went off to tune my guitar. I took about ten steps before turning to yell, "You gotta catch 'Horizon Suite.' It's up second!" It was good seeing Eon again and I missed that hug, that smile. I'd been tempted to ask him to join the Spacerz on second guitar. But I didn't.

The rest of July, we played a few small shows and a couple of outdoor parties. At one of those gigs, Zany showed up. "Zany!" I said, shaking his hand. "How are you doing? Are you working on any new music?"

"I'm working on synthesized music and a song called 'Black Hole.' I see you're still doing the space thing too?"

"Yeah, it's in my alien blood," I said, introducing Zany to my bandmates. "This is Ufo and Eclipse." They'd heard me talking about Zany before, but never in a positive way. We'd been very tight once, and as hard it was to throw that away, I felt the familiar resentment rising in the pit of my stomach. Saying goodbye, I walked away with Ufo and Eclipse. It was time to get ready for our set.

So many things went through my head. Ufoian had studied old Zolar X tapes to get a feel for Zany's style, but Zany had been responsible for the death of Zolar X. He'd never even apologized for leaving us high and dry in Memphis. Zany acted as if we had no history together at all. Never mind that we'd lived together in Los Angeles for eighteen months and had created beautiful, glorious music with our highly original band. I guess it meant nothing to him. The Spacerz were received well that night but seeing Zany had shaken me a bit.

A couple of weeks later, we decided to record ourselves live at the Center Theater with Pete's reel-to-reel tape recorder. No audience or fancy equipment—just us and the reel-to-reel. "The Horizon Suite", "The Plutonian Elf Story", "Orbiting Cosmic Ovals", "Take Me to Your Leader", "Zolar Eclipsing", and "Bicentennial Rock" were all recorded for posterity. Hearing the songs in an empty theater with the band firing on all cylinders filled me with joy. We sounded massive and epic—a great band doing great things. But as cool as this was, I still found myself thinking about Zory in LA.

ZORY ZENITH

What started as miming to ease the boredom had turned into a decent money-making endeavor. I donned a tuxedo and tails, slicked my hair down, put on flesh-tone makeup, and started refining my mechanical man moves. Generous "Valley-ites" and tourists showered me with bills and coins. I was pulling in $25 an hour, which was good money in '76.

One day, a limo pulled up in front of the store. A "suit" hopped out and gave me a card that read American International Pictures. "We're releasing the sequel to *West World* called *Future World*," he said. "Would you like to do promotion for the movie?"

"Well, yeah!" I said. Within the week I'd negotiated a $150-a-day deal plus expenses.

YGARR YGARRIST

Out of the clear blue, I got a phone call from Charlie Patton. "Hey, Ygarr, I found an investor/manager out east named Ben Cotton who wants to hear your music," said Charlie, shouting so loudly that I had to hold the receiver away from my ear. "He has big plans to bring you to Memphis to record! Guy, you hear what I'm sayin'? This is your shot!"

We quickly assembled a package of Spacerz music we'd just recorded and mailed it to Ben. Within a week I was back on the phone with Charlie.

"Ygarr, they'll fly you to Memphis and put you up in a mansion. You'll be recording at Ardent Studios with ZZ Top engineer Terry Manning and producer Jim Dickinson.

FREEDOM

The only catch, guy, is that they want you to record as Zolar X with Zory Zenith!"

If that was the price I had to pay to record in a professional studio with professional producers, then I was all in. "When do we leave?" I asked.

ZORY ZENITH

When I got the call from Charlie about going to Memphis, I realized instantly that it could be a phenomenal opportunity. I didn't even think about turning it down. *Future World*, Karen, and miming on Hollywood Blvd grew dim as I contemplated the past and future. I thought, *Zenith and Ygarrist, again? Hmmmm*. If the call had lasted another 30 seconds and I had thought about it, I probably would have said, "Uh, I don't know."

YGARR YGARRIST

My first professional band, Zolar X, was always in my mind and heart. As hard as it was to give up that dream, the new band Spacerz provided me with a fresh independence—a wild creativity that had previously been denied. This new chapter in my life was exhilarating.

Then, like that, everything changed again. I had to tell the boys a little more about Zory, his personality, and what it meant to be Zolarized. I could see they were nervous wrecks with the idea of becoming Zolar X. After all, these dudes were from Boise, Idaho. It had taken a lot of effort to groom them into mild-mannered little space cadets—to be clean shaven and Rock 'n' roll-sexy. Becoming Zolar X would be like stepping away from everything they had known.

I was selling the idea and soothing them at the same time. "I guarantee this will be a whole new experience. We'll record an album with a famous engineer and producer! The last deal Charlie put together for us could have been a life-changer."

They were in.

I made one last phone call to Charlie. "Send us four tickets. We're bringing our roadie, Pete. And we'll need to ship our equipment."

"Done," said Charlie. The future doesn't tell you what's going to happen. You have to find out for yourself.

L to R: Ufoian Ufar, Ygarr Ygarrist, Eclipse, 1975
Photo credit: Syndee

Spacerz logo, 1975
Art credit: Garrett Moore

71

MEMPHIS – ROUND TWO
AUGUST 1976

Ben was a gigantic stretch of a man, weighing in at more than 250 pounds. We walked through the front door of his mansion and he waved his massive arms as if shooing small animals away. "Plenty of room for ya'll, but the ex-wife cleaned me out of just about everything except two beds, the icebox, and my guns."

I imagine everyone thought the same thing as we stepped inside. *Guns? Shit, what guns? And where are we going to sleep?* But we had more pressing matters. We were here to record an album, and all I could think about was working Zory into the songs.

"Hey, Ben, where do we set up our equipment?" I asked, glancing around the spacious interior. There was plenty of room at least.

Ben nodded towards the back of the house. "You boys okay with settin' up out on the screened-in porch? Just be careful not to trip on the dead bodies." The big man made a low throaty noise like a laugh, but there was something off about him. First impressions were important, and this felt like a scene from *Psycho*.

We fucked around for a bit and night had fallen by the time we set up our gear on the back porch. The Memphis night was like nothing I'd ever seen. Twinkling dots of lights sparkled like stars just above the grass. I turned to the boys and said, "Well, this is a first! We'll be playing to the fireflies tonight!"

We had a nice little PA system: two mics, a separate head for the speakers, a double kick drum set, two Echoplexes, a Minimoog, the Hiwatt, and the SVT. There was plenty of room for Zory to mime, even with all our speaker cabinets. We were ready to rip.

But first, Ben rolled out the red carpet. He took us out for dinner and drinks, making sure to bring a bevy of party girls along for the ride. This sort of rock star treatment was brand new to my boys, but they lapped it up eagerly. We tried not to indulge too heavily, but Zory didn't seem to be holding back.

Later that night, we jammed the songs for Zory, showing him what we'd been working on for the last year. Stuff like "The Horizon Suite", "The Plutonian Elf Story", and "Nativity" was all brand new to him.

We played well, but I couldn't help but notice that Zory seemed a little intimidated and even agitated. He kept making comments like, "What's my fucking part?" or "Tell me again: why am I here?" The situation was escalating; maybe it was the booze talking. "I could be back in LA making money!" he said, a bit drunkenly.

Charlie tipped his bottle to the corner of his mouth and tried to laugh it off. The boys didn't know what to think. Ben, however, was fed up with Zory's antics. "I'll take ya to the airport right fucking now if you don't wanna be here!" he growled. "These guys can be Zolar X without you. Make up your mind!"

Trying to smooth things out, I said, "Shit Zory, you know me. I'm like a mad scientist in a laboratory when it comes to writing songs, but we'll change whatever we need to make things work. I *know* we can do this!"

If anyone can read Zory, it's me. Although he didn't say anything, he knew he was out of line. The band continued to jam as he sat on the floor against the wall with his yellow notepad, his head down. The song ended and I shouted over to him. "Wanna write some lyrics? I'm working on a new song, 'Rocket Roll'!" Zory started scribbling words, and that was the end of any half-cocked notion of him going anywhere. It was like having my brother back.

By now, it was 2:00 a.m., and we weren't getting any quieter. Even the fireflies took off and left us. The Echoplex sounded like a flying saucer, but probably a bit louder. "I think we should move the gear indoors," mumbled Ben, worrying about distant neighbors. We hauled the equipment inside, and I worked with Zory on "The Horizon Suite", "Nativity", and the "The Plutonian Elf Story". Slowly, he started to get the hang of the new songs.

We paused for a break and Zory pulled out his notepad. "I scribbled these alien words on the plane. What do you think? It starts with *Nop trea vu-duraz, varitrexon*."

"This would be great for the album. You should read this in your mechanical mediator voice!" I said, pleased.

Zory tilted his head. "*Olio-ey, navitri, doutra, dootra,*" he recited in a nasal, monotone robotic tone. Shit, that's some crazy Zolarian language! Who gives a crap if humans can't understand it?

The next week went something like this: rehearse, girls, party, sex, rehearse, repeat. One day we met with producers Terry Manning and Jim Dickenson for a tour of the studio where we would be recording. Everything was fine until we decided to go out on our own. "Hey Ben, we'll see you later. We're going out tonight."

MEMPHIS - ROUND TWO

Ben wasn't having it. "I don't want ya'll going anywhere!" he replied gruffly. "Your recording session is tomorrow and I want you in good shape!"

So the five of us snuck out the back door and piled into the blue 1965 Chevy pickup that Pete had bought at a used car lot in Memphis a couple of days earlier. Ben wasn't the boss of us and we deserved to have some fun.

Sadly, we didn't get very far before two cop cars pulled us over. We were summarily handcuffed and thrown into a drunk tank. That might have been understandable but we weren't even drunk yet. Our cell wasn't much bigger than the jail on *The Andy Griffith Show*.

We couldn't see Ben when he walked in, but we could hear him calling the officers by their first names. "Nice seeing you, Joe. I guess I'll take my boys off your hands, 'less they broke some laws, that is." Then he chuckled maliciously and said in a low voice, "Did you find 'em where I said they'd be? This'll show 'em who's boss!"

Ben had the run of the town, and we were his prisoners. Somehow, the knowledge that we would be recording an album the next day made that tolerable. We were on a mission.

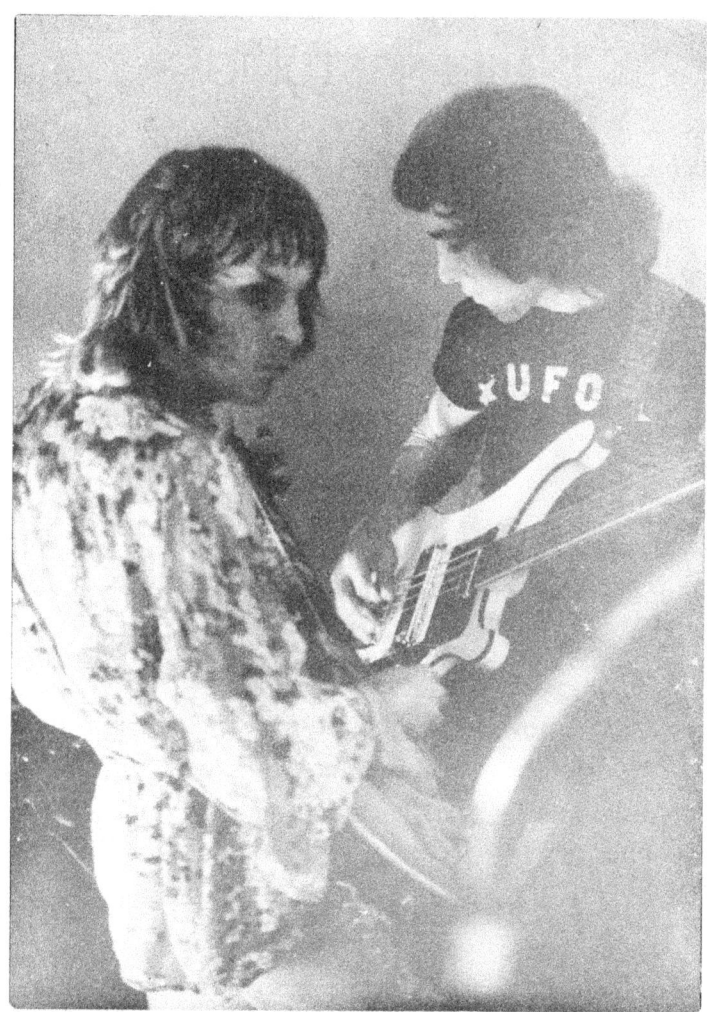

L to R: Ygarr Ygarrist, Ufoian Ufar, 1975
Photo credit: Syndee

ARDENT STUDIOS

72

ARDENT STUDIOS
1976

YGARR YGARRIST

"You want me to use a Fender Twin Reverb instead of my Hiwatt? Shit!" I cursed, feeling ambushed. "What about my guitar tone?"

"If you use the Hiwatt, it will bleed into the drum tracks," Terry explained.

ZORY ZENITH

Ygarr, Tommy, and Ron furiously laid down the bed tracks. The staples of Zolar X, "Space Age Love" and "Energize Me" were up first. Everything was going like clockwork.

YGARR YGARRIST

We finished "Nativity", and moved into the prog-rock of "Horizon Suite" and "The Plutonian Elf Story". "You finished the rhythm tracks in two hours!" Jim exclaimed. "That's a new record! No splicing or editing!" We still had six hours booked and it was all me for the rest of the day.

ZORY ZENITH

Ygarr was in and out of the control booth, laying down synthesizers and guitar. He was like a frenzied space-age genius from another planet. Zolar X had fucking landed.

YGARR YGARRIST

I double-tracked the electric rhythms, added the acoustic guitar, and moved into the leads. The Echoplex and the Moog blasted from the house speakers like photon torpedoes. Now the album was starting to sound special.

The humbucker pickups on my Les Paul got every inch out of that Twin Reverb and I had it cranked to ten. We were nearing the end of the lead in "Energize Me" when the amplifier blew and smoke snaked from the back. But this was Ardent Studios, so they just brought in another Twin. We still couldn't get over the fact that we were recording with an engineer who'd been around the block and the professional producer, Jim Dickenson. Where would the Stones have been without Andrew Oldham? But the adrenaline slowly began to fade and I realized I was exhausted. So was everyone else. "Let's call it a day," Jim said wearily.

ZORY ZENITH

To be honest, I was scared shitless. We got back from the first day and the fuckers didn't even give us a rough mix of what we'd done. The unknowns weighed heavily upon us. How did we sound? I was freaked out because the songs weren't your average three-minute standards. Hell, "The Plutonian Elf Story" was a nineteen-minute space opera. Upset and worried, I slipped out the back and tried to stretch my dried-up vocal cords. I walked around in the woods screaming and doing all kinds of weird shit. I even got down on my knees and prayed. Thinking about how the project might turn out scared me to death.

YGARR YGARRIST

On the second day, Zory recited his Zolarian, alien poem in one take. Then we were ready for "Space Age Love" and "Energize Me". I leaned towards Zory. "This is easy, Bot. You know these songs and they'll loosen your vocals cords. I'll sing 'Nativity', 'Horizon Suite', and 'The Plutonian Elf Story'. But I'd like you to sing 'Forever More'."

We added harmonies and Zory's falsetto. One by one, we worked through the songs at a pace that began to feel rushed. We soldiered on and did "The Plutonian Elf Story" in one take. All nineteen minutes of it!

Terry opened his mic channel. "One hour remaining of the session, guys."

Zory whispered, "Another one of those quick fucking blocks of time!"

To get the rest of the harmonies done, Zory and I sang from the same microphone. No more synthesizer tracks, no fixes, and no second takes. We left not knowing what was going to happen. There was a buzz going around that Ben hadn't paid the studio yet.

Back at the house, I called the guys together. "Let's have a band meeting while Ben's away. Shit is going down and we have to decide when to beam out of here."

"There is some sort of scam going on. I can feel it!" said Zory.

"He's a pervert too!" I added. "That fucker was spying on us when I was screwing that pretty blonde."

"Weird," said Eclipse, shaking his head.

"I wanna go home," said Ufo, a little uneasily.

Pete stood up. "Let's load the truck and get the fuck…"

ZORY ZENITH

The door busted open and Ben stumbled in stoned out of his mind. This freak of an ex-Marine Corp captain was flying high. At last, we were getting a glimpse of who he was. He bounced around in his underwear waving a fucking .45 Magnum. "You're gonna do what I say or else!" he yelled. Then just like that, he was gone.

YGARR YGARRIST

"What in the fuck was that?" I said, still in shock.

Ufo's voice was barely audible. "I *really* wanna go home."

"Charlie has a duplex with a swimming pool. We could go there to get away from this nut!"

"Let's do it then," said Pete. "Let's load up the truck and head over to Charlie's."

Zory wasn't impressed. "Once again, here we are in a strange land—bent over the table with no Vaseline."

"What are you thinking, Bot? You have that mischievous look going on," said Pete.

ZORY ZENITH

I went to the fridge and found a bag of carrots in the crisper. Making sure the coast was clear, I took one out and jammed it up my ass. I keep myself clean, so the carrot came out looking much the same as it went in, except maybe with a little "juice." Then I stuck it back in the bag for our fine and beautiful host. Hopefully, he'd eat it raw.

Ardent Studios interior, Circa 1976
Photo credit: By Katie from Memphis, TN, USA - IMG_1200Uploaded by clusternote, CC BY-SA 2.0, https://commons.wikimedia.org/w/index.php?curid=27479621

Jim Dickenson, 1976
Photographer unknown

73

REDEMPTION
1976

I stumbled around in a suspended, surreal fog. There was the usual booze and chaos at Charlie's bungalow, but at least he wasn't a psycho and a crook.

"Shit Charlie, where'd you meet that fucker?" chortled Zory. "What a freak!"

Charlie laughed his drunken belly laugh. "I met Ben in ROTC, when I was in college, guy. He turned out to be a fuckin' lunatic, didn't he?" He tilted his head back and howled.

Zory smirked at Ronnie and Ufo. "You guys have never been down Disaster Road before. Now you know what it's like to be members of Zolar X. You just got educated!"

Once again, Charlie had led us down a promising road that ended with another horrendous crash. As weird as it was, what we'd accomplished in the studio was nothing short of a miracle. I knew what we'd laid down was pure gold. Unfortunately, we weren't sure if anyone would pay the studio bill, or if we'd ever hear the recording. Maybe it was time to think about getting the hell out of Dodge? Escape to California?

The jangling phone tore through my thoughts. Charlie picked it up and I heard him shout, "Why yeah, guy! They're here. I'll let 'em know. Tonight at eight!" He turned to us. "Hey, Zolars! Jim and Terry want us to come by the studio tonight to hear the tape. They've been up all night mixing!"

"That's fucking great news, Charlie!" I said. "That's only two hours from now."

The listening room looked different at night and I savored every detail. We made ourselves comfortable on the leather couch and matching love seat. "Drinks for everyone!" said Jim, who was clearly in a celebratory mood.

Excitement, apprehension, and curiosity swirled through my brain. I wondered if it was possible to record an album in two days and mix it in one night. Were Jim and Terry magicians? Were we? I was a bit scared to find out.

Zory and I settled into the middle of the couch. "Are you ready?" said Jim, passing us a joint. He hit "play" and I held my breath.

OUT OF THIS WORLD: THE STORY OF ZOLAR X

ZORY ZENITH

I hauled on the joint as the sound came booming out of the mammoth overhead speakers and the 18" floor cabinets. What I heard was shear euphoria! It shook me down to my bones. What this pit crew did with the dialogue I jotted down on the plane blew my mind! Eerie. Mysterious. Otherworldly. Shit!

YGARR YGARRIST

It was a total sci-fi horror show and the volume made me numb. When the tape stopped after the first fifty-one seconds, there was a great whooshing noise as everybody finally remembered to breathe. Jim had done a brilliant job. Then the sound of a flying saucer taking off engulfed the room and "Space Age Love" began. Everyone was mesmerized.

We began to realize that our team had created this masterpiece in only two days. I could only wonder what we could have done if we'd had more time. Many famous Rock 'n' roll bands spent months or even years on albums. We must have set some kind of record.

The last notes of "The Plutonian Elf Story" faded away, but my fingers and toes were still vibrating. I could already imagine the songs pressed into vinyl. "Wow!" I said, stunned. "This is what I've always wanted! We did it!"

Jim and Terry looked at each of us, one by one, square in the eye. Then Jim spoke. "Okay guys, your sound is magnificent and the songs almost mixed themselves, but Ben didn't pay the $3,500 bill, and if the studio doesn't get paid, me and Terry don't get paid either. However, the studio doesn't know about this tape, so we'll trade you for the Moog and the Rickenbacker bass. That way, we'll get something for our work, and you'll get your songs."

My mind was completely focused on acquiring the tape. Nothing else mattered. "Jim, I have no problem trading you the Moog." Then I looked at Ufo and Pete. "What do you think, guys? Are you willing to surrender the Rickenbacker?"

Ufo looked at Pete. "Can you go back to Charlie's and grab it for us?"

Pete jumped up, eager to help. "You got it, buddy! I'll be back in thirty!"

Time never stretched so slowly. We chain-smoked cigarettes and filled the gap with awkward small talk and general bullshit. Then Pete finally returned, Rickenbacker and Moog in hand. Jim handed me the tape and I sat there clutching the small cardboard box as if it were the most important thing I'd ever held. My years of dedication had finally paid off, and my goal of standing shoulder-to-shoulder with Beethoven, John Lennon, David Bowie, Led Zeppelin, and Jimi Hendrix almost seemed within reach. It was all there in my sweaty little hands.

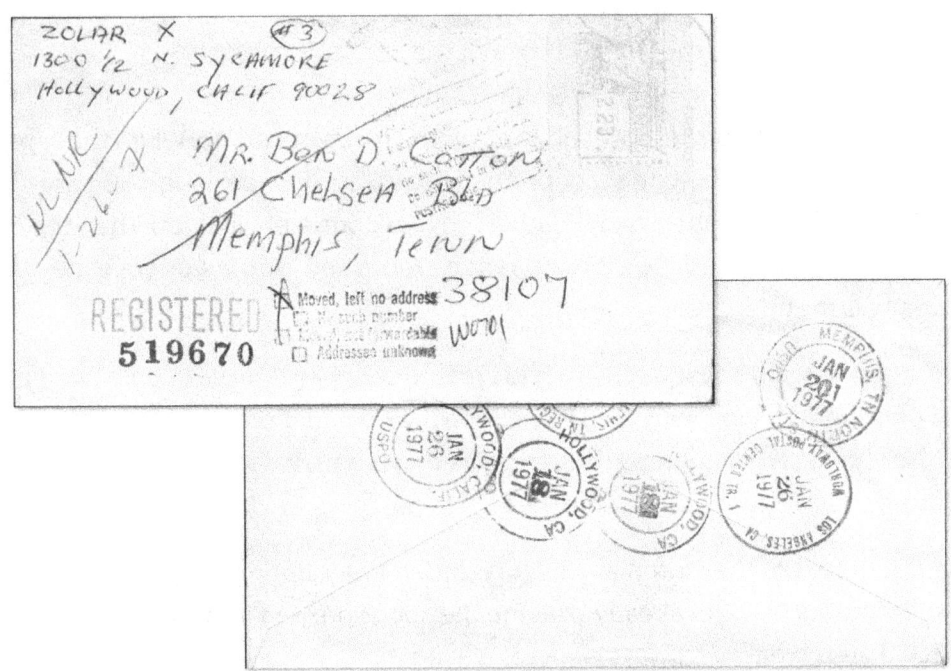

L to R: Ygarr Ygarrist, Ufoian Ufar, Zory Zenith, Eclipse, 1976
Photo credit: S. Stopek

Ygarr Ygarrist holding the Memphis tape from 1976.
Photo credit: Raidii, X photographed in 2020

The Memphis tape, from 1976.
Photo credit: Raidii X, photographed in 2020

74

BACK IN HOLLYWOOD
SEPTEMBER 1976

It was great to be back in Hollywood. Standing on the roof of Zory and Karen's apartment, now dubbed "Elf Manor", I glanced over at the Bot. He was quiet too. The hum of traffic drifted up from the streets below. Even six stories up, we could hear the occasional honk of a horn—one of the iconic sounds of Los Angeles. We were home.

Looking across the rooftops of old Hollywood, my gaze instinctually came to rest on the nine huge white letters of the Hollywood sign. Finally, my eyes focused on the Capitol Records Building at Hollywood and Vine, the West Coast's first record company.

Zory popped open a Schlitz, rupturing the silence. "Shit, it's so cool being back in Hollywood. I've really missed it! Living in suburbia at my mom's house was so dull compared to this. Let's face it, Hollywood has an addictive personality."

"It's really great being back together with you, Ygarr. I've been idle for an entire year, and I was starting to lose my mind. I'd put our new songs up against any fucking songs in the entire fucking world! Queen, ELO, or fucking KISS—I mean we just shit all over them! As tight and brilliant as some of that music is, your licks are something beyond that. They're coming from outer space!"

"Yeah, Bot," I said, soberly popping a can of beer. "Inside my soul, I know how good our music is, but we've been down this road before. Doing the same thing again, in the same town with the same name, is the definition of insanity. Punk rock and new wave is the next big thing. How about that UK band, the Sex Pistols? That's gotta be one of the greatest names ever!"

Zory wasn't impressed. "Yeah, but it sounds like they just learned how to play. Three chords and they're a band? Oh, please!"

"Yeah, well it isn't Mozart, but it's really aggressive with a hell of a lot of energy!"

"But we have something this time that we didn't have last time. This time we have an album recorded!"

I chose not to engage Zory on that subject. "These last few weeks have been such a whirlwind. Besides the recording session, how did we find time for three shows in Memphis and a sci-fi convention in Kansas City? Good thing Girlfriend #737 paid for my flight back. We'd earned some money on those shows, but I still had to sell my Flying V to cover the cost of shipping our equipment back to California. I had enough left to copy the master tape and stash it under the bed at my mom's place."

"What would we do without the girls?" grinned Zory, pouring Schlitz down his throat. "I'm sure we would have died long ago without them."

"Charlie helped us a lot too. Can you believe he just got another apartment? It's in the same building on La Jolla where we lived before! I can't stay with you and Karen forever, so I'll be floating around. Pete got a place on Willoughby, and the boys will be staying with him. This time we're gonna rehearse a lot more. I found a rehearsal studio that rents for $10 an hour and we're gonna get tight. I also made five cassettes of our new recording, so let's get those suckers mailed. Do you have the addresses?"

"Yeah, I got Capitol, Warner Bros, Columbia, RCA, and A&M."

"I think we need to put a new photo of the band with the packages." I was also wondering about our hair and stagewear. With Veonity out of the picture, who would do that for us? Not only were we without makeup artists, but we had no real management either. Charlie meant well, but we'd had too many disasters with him, even if they weren't all his fault.

Zory's mind was obviously wandering. "If we start getting a few shows, I won't have to do perms for little old ladies on Saturday mornings any more."

"I hope so too," I said, squinting across the rooftops at the giant Hollywood sign. "The Starwood is across the street from Charlie's, so I'll walk over and try to get us a gig."

Zory looked down at his beer. "I know I pissed Dallas off the last time we spoke. He probably fucking hates me!"

I'd been trying to bury that memory. "I don't think that matters, Bot. He loves Zolar X!"

"How are your two munchkin bandmates doing?" Zory chuckled. "Are they adjusting to life in the big city? Think they'll be ready for a photoshoot?"

"I think Ufo is adapting somewhat, but Ronnie seems like he might have a problem with gay people, so he'll have to get over that. They'll have to work hard if they want to be in this band. They're not in Idaho anymore."

75

RHINESTONES FOR SAFETY PINS
1976-1977

People had always told us we were ahead of our time, but in reality, we'd stepped through time while the machine marched on, over, and around us.

"Do you believe it, Zory? Our last Hollywood show with the original Zolar X was in December 1974, and here we are, December of '76. We just had our first show of the resurrected Zolar X with Van Halen. Crazy!"

"Yeah, it's bizarre and impressive," said Zory. "Although we aren't fighting to create a movement like we were last time, we can still be great science-fiction theater. Maybe this time we'll slow down enough to make better plans and get out there. On another note, I guess Van Halen has some radio-worthy stuff. I mean, they just got signed to Warner Bros."

"I'll tell you one thing: Eddie is one hell of a guitar player! I talked with him after our set and he told me I was damn good on guitar and knew my way around the Echoplex."

"Our show went without a hitch and being well-rehearsed didn't hurt either." The highlights had included opening with the nineteen minute "Plutonian Elf Story", and Zory popping out of the trunk.

Zory laughed. "Did you like my circus mime character Pim, with the black teardrops on my white face? Veonity helped me paint the trunk and put the letters on the front. We even drilled air holes so I'd be able to breathe. Shit, that was a life time ago!"

"I loved it when you popped out at the crescendo of 'Forever More' and started doing mime. It was like you said: part circus and part theater on a Rock 'n' roll stage. Our look was less extreme than the original band, but the music was more advanced."

"It was fun, that's for sure."

One day, KROQ called to offer us the opportunity to play a series of shows at the Cabaret Club, nicknamed the Cave. While setting up for soundcheck the first night, a man came over and introduced himself as George Clayton Johnson. We knew the name well.

Zory immediately got into character. "Nop trea, or greetings, sir!" he modulated in his robot monotone. "We loved *Logan's Run*, and I've recalibrated my chip to include the *Twilight Zone*."

George seemed impressed. "You guys are extremely far out, and I love your sci-fi style! I caught you at the Troubadour in '74, and I'd like to introduce you tonight. Would that be cool?"

"Hell, yeah! You wrote 'Man Trap', the first episode of *Star Trek*. You're like a founding father of that show. It would be an honor!"

That night we played with the Quick, Berlin Brats, the Dogs, Smokey, and The Motels. The crowds were starting to look more punk, but we didn't look punk by any means. In just two years glam had faded into punk rock. In that Hollywood era, everything was a rivalry. And because Zolar X had been part of the glam scene of Rodney Bingenheimer's English Disco, everyone identified us with that. As far as I could see, the ex-glam rockers had simply traded their rhinestones for safety pins. I could tell they didn't think we were cool. Punk rock was against the establishment and Zolar X was established.

Show by show, punks were beginning to outnumber the "normals". When we played with the Nerves at the Punk Palace, the whole crowd was punk. Green, blue, and purple hair, loads of safety pins, and tons of eye makeup - Punk had landed.

It was March 1977. We no longer wore our spacesuits to the market or the laundromat, saving it instead for the stage. Tom was living with Rose, who was pregnant. Ronnie was living with a girlfriend, and Pete had moved back north. Since we didn't have a full-time hairdresser, and asking Zory was out of the question, I let my hair revert to its natural color. I still had my tights and space boots, and my pointed hair and eyebrows, but I missed putting party colors in my hair. With Charlie, my new girlfriend Nancy, and other girls helping, I ate maybe once a day.

ZORY ZENITH

When I wasn't cutting hair, I was doing mime for Ants n' Pants on Hollywood Boulevard. I came across several large pieces of wood in a room upstairs and made a deal with the owner to acquire them in exchange for some of my time. With Ufo's help, I built two massive, fake amplifier cabinets eight feet tall. We beveled the sides and cut holes for the lights and speakers before we dusted the towers silver. Lastly, we added the grill cloth, but couldn't finish them until we had enough money for the lighting.

76

SMILE AND SAY MOON CHEESE
FEBRUARY 1977

The last time we had professional photos taken was with the original band. Photographers were thicker than fleas on a stray dog in West Hollywood, but photographers with professional studios were another story. Then one of my girlfriends took me to a gay bar for happy hour. I was Zolarized, and a man approached our table and introduced himself as a photographer. He was curious about my look and outfit. "Are you in show business, darling?" he asked, smiling.

I explained Zolar X, Rocket roll, and space theater to him. As it turned out, his studio was just down the street. We went to check it out, and his work looked good, so we set up a shoot.

Neither of the munchkins had any fashion sense. They had no idea how to dress glam or space, and punk frightened them. Back in '74, if one of us went into the bathroom to shower, we'd come out Zolarized, no matter what day. These boys didn't know how or when to dress unless we told them. We hoped the photoshoot would inspire them to step out.

We packed every outfit into the trunk, including four sets of antennae, makeup, and gigantic elf ears. Zory brought his space helmet, and I brought my original 1966 *Star Trek* phaser. We arrived with a small entourage, but the photographer immediately kicked out everyone but the band. The photographer and his helper were gay, but I saw men holding hands all the time in West Hollywood so it was no big deal. Whenever I was approached, I'd simply tell them I liked girls. They'd typically reply with something like, "Too bad, honey. You don't know what you're missing." Those encounters never became violent or ugly. It was a very free time.

We must have taken over a hundred shots. Constantly pulling different ideas from the trunk, we took some with pointed ears and some with antennas. We also did group shots, singular shots, semi-nude shots, and full-on nudes. It was quite an experience.

Ufo and Ronnie were paranoid. Ronnie half gulped, half-shouted, "What if they put these in gay magazines!"

"Are you gay?" I asked.

"No."

"Then don't worry about it!"

The cover of our *Timeless* reissue came from this photoshoot.

L to R: Ygarr Ygarrist, Zory Zenith, Ufoian Ufar, Eclipse, 1976
Photo credit: S. Stopek

77

SPACE SOAP
MAY 1977

Nik Pascal, one of our wannabe managers, got us a week-long engagement at a new club called Changes on Pico Blvd in May of 1977. We used the new fake amplifier props for the shows. To give the stage more of a sci-fi look, Nik brought along a silver mannequin and a gigantic, six-foot silver tube that looked like something from *2001: A Space Odyssey*. The tube looked like it could have housed alien or human life forms. You could climb inside, and believe me, Zory did. We drew an average-sized crowd on the weekend but smaller crowds during the week. We got even tighter. It was like getting paid to rehearse.

After the last set of our engagement, we approached the club manager. "Jim, could we store our props here for a while?" I asked. "Just until we find a place for them."

"No problem. Do you guys mind if we leave them on the stage for décor?"

"They do look kinda supersonic up there," answered Zory. "Like intergalactic robots."

We played a few more shows in the Valley. To my surprise, Eon Flash showed up at one of them. "Hey, Eon! What the hell are you doing here?" I asked, happy to see him.

"When I heard you were playing, I just had to come by and say hello. I'm in between bands at the moment and had nothing better to do."

Like a light bulb switching on, I said, "Hey, do you want to play second guitar with us?" I looked at my bandmates. "It's alright with you guys, right? It'll make us better, more versatile."

Zory and Ufo nodded in agreement, but I noticed Ronnie staring at Eon rather coldly. I was caught up in the moment and let it go. Maybe he thought Eon was gay?

Eon's face lit up, "Of course, you bet Ygarr! When do I start?"

"I'm still at La Jolla, but in number three. Come over tomorrow and I'll show you the new songs."

Eon beamed happily. "Zolar X, a five-piece band!"

OUT OF THIS WORLD: THE STORY OF ZOLAR X

We re-read our 1974 contract with Doug Weston's Troubadour and discovered that he was legally obligated to give us a few shows. "Zolar X is back together, and we've recorded a new album," I told Doug.

"I'll give you a show next Sunday night. Does that work for you?"

"Nok voo and thank you. We'll be here!"

For the first time in the history of Zolar X, the rhythm didn't drop out when I played lead because Eon was there. The sound was tighter, bigger, and for me, much easier.

However, tension was brewing by August. One night at rehearsal, things got ugly. "Hey, Ronnie," I said. "You know that lead passage in 'Space Age Love'?"

"Yeah, what about it?"

"I want to try something that'll make it a little more distinct. Eon, if you don't mind, show him how you used to play it."

"You mean like this?" said Eon, playing the passage flawlessly.

"Yeah, exactly."

For whatever reason, Ronnie didn't like Eon. He stood there in the classic angry man stance, drumsticks folded across his chest. "I'm the drummer on the recording, and I'm getting sick of you Zolar X guys!" he said, voice rising.

"Ronnie, we're just trying to make the song better. Heavier on the accents," Eon offered.

"Calm down!" said Ufo. "We're all on the same team."

"Take a chill pill, bud. Hell, take *any* kind of pill!" smirked Zory.

Ronnie remained unmoved, his face like stone.

We had a problem, and there was also the girlfriend factor that we'd never openly discussed. I didn't know if Ronnie had chosen to ignore the fact that his girlfriend had slept with all of us before they got together, or if he was just naïve. In my opinion, a band was like a family and should share things: riffs, drugs, ideas, booze, and, of course, women. Whatever the case, it wasn't a total surprise when I got the news from Ufo that Ronnie had quit. Unlike Zany, at least Ronnie told someone.

But if that weren't bad enough, Zory dropped another bomb. "Karen and I are moving to the Bay area. She wants to be closer to her parents with the new baby."

SPACE SOAP

I'd almost forgotten that Zory was a dad. If I wanted to keep the band together, I'd have to accept his situation. "I'm ready for a change. Not just a move but a change," I told him. "We can probably book some shows in the Bay area, and what about that new club Mabuhay Gardens that features new wave and punk?"

"I'll be up there, so I'll call the Mabuhay Gardens and get us some gigs. I'll contact Ed. Maybe he'll help."

Now there were only three of us in LA. We had a new recording, photos that had instantly become obsolete, and a depleted line up. There was an air of sadness to it all. It felt the same as before, except now—even worse—the band was splintered. Zory was gone, and Ufo was about to become a father. Kids don't mix with Rock 'n' roll.

We should have been rehearsing and playing, even without Zory. But gigs were hard to find with no real manager or booking agent. Once again, Zolar X felt like a hobby rather than a career. It had been months since we'd mailed out those cassettes, and even though I'd followed up, we hadn't heard a fucking word. What were they, deaf? At least we had several shows booked in the Bay area. Until that time, the band was at a standstill.

Patience, in the Rock 'n' roll business, is not a virtue. A typical day went something like this: get money from a girlfriend, buy some beer, play acoustic guitar, maybe write a song, drink some more, and fuck the girl I was with. It was boring but I had no idea how to change it or do anything else. On a rare day, we'd get together and rehearse.

Changes had been storing our props for more than two months and now they were holding them for ransom. We weren't about to pay to get our property back, so we came up with a plan that required both precision and strategy—a clandestine operation if you will.

The opportunity to infiltrate Changes bumped into high gear when Zory called me. "Hey bud, I have a contact for you. His name is Lenny and he drives for Viking Trucking."

"Gimme his digits."

Zory rattled off the number and hung up.

Truck driver Lenny was up for a bit of counterespionage at a Zolarian discount. We made careful arrangements with him and put the plan into motion. In those savage days without internet or cell phone, we still managed to synch our operation with utmost precision down to the last second. At exactly 1400 hours, our driver pulled up in front of the club. His instructions were to keep the truck idling, open the trailer doors, and lower the lift. Like a crack team of secret agents, Ufo, Eon, Charlie, and I made our entry through the large but unlocked double doors. We hurried through the dimly lit interior and there they were, our majestic silver cabinets standing watch from the stage. We grabbed our property and headed for the door, doing our best not to get rolled up by enemy forces. The air hummed with energy and tension.

We were almost at the door when a rival operative disguised as a janitor emerged from the toilet. Rather than stop to chat, we rushed past him with the humongous but empty cabinets. "Hey, you goons!" yelled the startled agent, trying to look inconspicuous with mop in hand. "What the hell are you doing? Get back here!"

"Fuck that!" we shouted. "This is our shit and we're outta here!"

L to R: Ufoian Ufar, Zory Zenith, Ygarr Ygarrist, Eclipse - at Changes 1977
Photo credit: Nancy Allen

78

MABUHAY GARDENS
AUGUST 1977

We moved back to the San Francisco Bay area in August of 1977. I soon called my friend Jeff Austin, who had a house in Hayward. His basement was the bomb. There was a massive stereo system at one end, a dark room for his photography at the other, and plenty of room for us to crash and rehearse. One night, I brought the Ardent master tape from my mom's and played it for Eon and Jeff.

"Fuck, listening to this on your system is almost overwhelming!" Eon exclaimed, beaming. "Sure, we've listened to the songs on cassette, but this is THE tape. First-generation, master mix!"

Ufo looked at Eon. "I think the two of us can make this even better."

"Yeah, Ronnie always wanted to follow the guitar instead of the bass. Ufo, you've learned the counter-point theory I've been teaching you these last two years. You guys are great musicians. Once you start playing as one, this will go down in Rock 'n' roll history as one of the best damn rhythm sections ever!"

One of Jeff's friends invited us to play a party at a mansion in the Oakland Hills. It turned out to be a private, small gathering filled with horny women and more cocaine than you could snort in a year. I was attacked. These women wanted me and there was no way I could escape, not that I tried.

The next morning, I noticed that my bandmates weren't there.

"I'll give you a lift back to your friends," said Gary, the owner of the mansion. "By the way, I want to manage your band."

Still, in a cocaine fog, I did another line and said, "Sure, why not?"

We did a couple shows in the East Bay and began getting ready for three more at Mabuhay Gardens in San Francisco. In September, we decided to go check it out. Devo was playing. As the set unfolded, I shouted in Zory's ear. "They sound more new wave than punk!"

"They have some robotic moves and they're dressed alike in matching jumpsuits.

They got the unit thing going."

"Haven't we seen something like this somewhere before? Maybe in a mirror?"

"I'm not impressed," griped Zory. He rarely was.

I was impressed with the club, though. Just because a club is known for promoting punk shows didn't mean it was exclusively punk. If Zolar X had green hair and dressed in punk clothes and shot piss from water pistols instead of strapping Flash Gordon ray guns to our skinny hips, we would have blended in quite well. Our songs were more complex musically, but that came from playing guitar and writing songs for more than a decade.

To us, playing the Mabuhay was playing San Francisco. It was a happening spot. The bands that played there were either trying to make it, were on their way to making it, or had already made it. They didn't care if they were playing Winterland the next night—it was that kind of place. Although the sound was raunchy and the place was kind of dirty, it was fun. The dressing rooms were nothing to write home about, but like Rodney's, the bands still played and people still went. Whatever "it" was, the Mabuhay had it.

Of the three shows, the October show was the most notable. We rented a big ass U-Haul truck on the night of the show and had to double park on Broadway to unload the monolithic props. Luckily, our entourage included my sister Zoann, Charlie, Nancy, several photographers, roadies, wannabe managers, and tag-along girlfriends.

As we were setting up, Eon yelled across the stage, "Let's make sure we have enough electrical outlets for all the equipment and the laser light props."

"Yeah, let's test the circuitry and make sure it won't blow."

"Where's the soundman?" asked Zory. "I wanna make sure he knows to put echo on my voice for that *Forbidden Planet* sci-fi feel."

"We'll make sure he knows, Zory. Here he comes now," said Ufo.

One last soundcheck and we were ready.

Club owner Dirk Dirksen introduced us, "AND NOW, FROM OUTER SPACE – ZOLAR X!" he shouted exuberantly. The man should have been a carnival barker. In a way, I suppose he was.

Our sound bounced loudly off the bricks. Our rehearsals were paying off, and we looked intergalactic. The crowd was charged. Although our recording wasn't available as a record yet, I felt we were reaching them with our music and the mood we created. With our cool props, and our space suits and helmets, we were riding the crest of *Star Wars*, which had recently begun showing in theaters. Although it would be tough to win over the punk rockers, we brought *Star Wars* to the Rock 'n' roll stage. The force was with us.

We finished in true Zolarian form—Eon and I were dripping with sweat. Dirk jumped up on the stage to send us off in style. "Let's really hear it for Zolar X! They'll be back in January with their fantastic sets and special effects. It's nice, every once in awhile, to be able to present something slightly out of the ordinary."

L to R: Zory Zenith, Ufoian Ufar, Ygarr Ygarrist, Eon Flash, Mabuhay Gardens, 1977
Photo credit: John Tremblay

L to R: Ygarr Ygarrist, Zory Zenith, Eon Flash, Ufoian Ufar (front), Mabuhay Gardens, 1977
Photo credit: John Tremblay

79

HIATUS
1978

After our last show at Mabuhay Gardens in '78, Zory informed us that he would be taking a break from the band. He wanted to stay in San Jose and try to make his marriage work. "I have to stick around for the kids," he said revealingly. The relationship was a bit rocky.

Zolar X had been on hiatus before, so it wasn't the end of the world. The Spacerz had morphed into Zolar X, and now we were headed back to LA again. All these songs could be performed without Zory, so this was merely an improved Spacerz with a better drummer. I wasn't angry but I was disappointed.

The three of us loaded up Eon's van and headed back to Hollywood. Ufo was back with Rose, Eon had enrolled in sound engineering school, and I went back to Charlie's place not knowing what would happen next. He welcomed me back with open arms. Home sweet home.

With Zolar X scattered, I felt as if I were on an extended vacation. Although I didn't consider myself an alcoholic, I preferred to be a little tipsy rather than straight. This attitude led me to the Tropicana Motel, where I hooked up with a sweet little thing. I loved that place, and every rock star that went through LA had stayed there. With a little cocaine, a joint or two, plenty of booze, and a stained king-size bed, you could get lost for a weekend, and I did exactly that. If idle hands are the devil's workshop, then alcohol is the elixir.

Returning to Charlie's, I found a note taped to the apartment door that said, "Come up to Apt. 6, Y." I wondered what the hell was going on. My head hurt and I needed to lie down.

I went up, and to my surprise, Charlie had moved the entire place from downstairs to upstairs, including my Hiwatt, my guitars, and my much-used leopard skin mattress.

"This is great Charlie! Shit, you carried my speaker cabinets all the way upstairs by yourself?"

Charlie acted like it was no big deal. "Look at that view, Ygarr!" he said excitedly.

"We're directly above the porno bookstore!" He was almost shouting. "What do you think? Huh, guy? You ready for a beer?"

I looked around. All I saw were two beds, two broken chairs, and a wilted palm tree in the corner, but it was home. There was something special about the freedom of living with an alcoholic who treated me like a little brother and inside of that, a rock star. "Sure!"

We drank into the night celebrating the new place. He was genuinely excited to have his roommate back. I'd been gone for months.

"Zolar X is on a break again, Charlie. Zory's staying in San Jose. The other guys are down here, but Tom, Rose, and the baby? Who knows?"

"Just find some other musicians and put a new band together, Ygarr. Hell, this is the music capital of the world! You gotta get out there and prove you're a new-age Mozart!"

"Easier said than done, Charlie!"

We raised our bottles.

80

ROCK BOTTOM

JANUARY 1978

A horribly familiar smell hung in the air as I opened my eyes, hungover again. "Charlie, have you forgotten your shoes and socks in the oven?" I yelled. "I think they've been in there long enough—I smell burnt rubber!" Charlie had purchased an additional pair of socks, so now he could go two days without washing his footwear in the kitchen sink. For all his faults, he was very meticulous about his personal hygiene.

"I'm on it, guy!" shouted Charlie, rushing from the washroom to the kitchen. Sometimes he forgot to pay close attention, and his shoes came out well-done instead of medium-rare. Another day in the life of Charlie!

I yawned widely and rolled out of bed. If I had any plans for the day, they would probably involve cleaning up a bit before switching on the Hiwatt to serenade the neighbors. Plans seemed to present themselves in ways I hadn't always anticipated when I first woke up. Sometimes you are offered an alternate road.

I headed down to the dumpster with a load of empties. As I turned the corner, I saw a James Dean-looking cat decked out in black leather opening the lid. He was nice enough to hold it open as I tossed in my crap. I had to ask, "Are you a musician?"

"I'd like to think so," he said, and I caught a glimmer in his eye.

"Shit, I live upstairs. Do you live here too?"

"Nah, I'm visiting the girls in apartment two, the Plunger Pit."

"Apartment two? That's where my band Zolar X lived for over a year!"

"That's rad! You guys had the same crib as the girls!"

I noticed something on his jacket. "Where'd you get that Johnny Rotten button?"

He shook his head and smiled. "I just got back from seeing the Sex Pistols at Winterland! They were fucking great!"

"Cool! I was just up in the City. My band played the Fab Mab and I was thinking about catching that show but couldn't find a ride. I can't help but wonder what the

Sex Pistols sound like. What a name!" I stretched out my hand. "I'm Ygarr Ygarrist. You can call me Y."

"Cool!" said the stranger. "I'm Rock Bottom."

"Come on up to #6 later. We'll jam." I didn't know if I would see him again, but I felt like I'd just met a real punk rocker.

A few hours later there was a knock at the door. It was Rock with a friend, Elias Morales. I invited them in and told them to sit where they could. The apartment was still woefully unfurnished.

We talked about music, who we liked, and who we didn't like. "The first punk rock band that caught my ear was the Ramones," I said.

The Pistols get my vote!" offered Rock.

"You can't really call the New York Dolls punk, but I like them. They sound punk but look glam," said Elias.

The one band that all three of us liked the most was the Beatles. Within minutes, I had my acoustic guitar in hand. I was thinking, Okay, here I am, a spaceman with these two punk rockers. Should I play simple three-chord songs? Jam a little punk style? Or should I just forgo the damn acoustic altogether and plug in the electric? I knew that eventually my ego would win out and I'd have to show off. Even with the acoustic I soon had them digging every note. It was nice to have new company.

Rock nodded his head. "The girls in the Plunger Pit told me about you and Zolar X. But I gotta know man, what's up with the tights?"

"Two things, Rock: they come in every color and they're very fucking comfortable. That's all I wear." I popped open my trunk and waved absently towards the heap of spandex.

Rock stood up and pointed. "How loud is your amp?"

"Well, I could tell you, but let me show you instead." After I got everything plugged in, I broke out the 'Paul, flipped the switches, and hammered home some sweet power chords.

I stopped before too long. The night was young after all. I had some money in my boot and was feeling really good. "I think it's Miller time. You guys wanna beer? I'll make a run to the corner store."

ROCK BOTTOM

"Sure," said Rock. "Here's a fiver. Get me a six-pack of Micky's."

The walk to the corner store took all of two minutes—just long enough for me to play out the possibilities in my mind. I didn't even know those guys and I'd left them with my Les Paul, my Hiwatt, and my Echoplex; basically, everything I owned. Somehow I wasn't worried. Instead, I was excited and thirsty. Sometimes fate doesn't nudge, it shoves.

I went up the stairs, still partly wondering if I was out of my mind. With a turn of the doorknob, there they were, playing and singing "In My Life" by the Beatles. Elias was strumming my acoustic guitar left-handed and reversed, with the high E on top.

"The last time I saw someone play a guitar that way," I said, a bit surprised, "was when Jimi Hendrix played Albert King's Flying V at Winterland!"

"Yeah, I'm 'bi', grinned Elias. "Most guitars are right-handed, but I learned both ways."

I played a couple of my original ballads and they started harmonizing with me. Then I handed the guitar to Rock. Before he started, he made a point of telling me that he too was left-handed, but had taught himself to play right-handed. Then he jammed the fuck out of "Heroes" by Bowie, which totally changed my view of them. Those guys looked and acted punk, but they weren't your average beginners.

A day that began with the smell of burnt rubber and dumpsters had transitioned into something beautiful and creative. As the afternoon shadows moved across the apartment, the beer, weed, and vibe resurrected something within me that had been missing lately. Fun. The unique comradery I shared with these punks filled the vacancy left by Zolar X.

"Charlie will be home from work at any time. There's no preparing you for him. You'll just have to meet him when he gets here. He's a loveable but wild man."

Within a couple of minutes, a sober Charlie came through the door with a bag of take out food under one arm, and a twelve-pack and pint of scotch wrapped in brown paper under the other. His usual.

He unloaded the packages on the table. Without putting anything away, he cracked open the scotch. As usual, he didn't eat but settled on the bed to drink. The first sip was always to kill the jitters. "Anybody hungry?" he roared. If he was surprised to see my punk guests, he didn't let it show. "Greenblatts make the best jumbo shrimp in Hollywood! There's breadsticks too."

"Let's smoke this joint first and get a nice buzz. Maybe later we'll get the munchies and dig in," said Rock. There wasn't enough for all of us anyway. Charlie was just being generous.

"By the way, Charlie, this is Rock and Elias," I said, making the introductions. "I just met 'em. We've been jamming all day."

Charlie was a man of the moment and saw potential in anything I was connected to musically. In between sips, he asked, "You guys from the Masque?"

"What? No. I've been to the Masque, but I'm not from it. We know the girls from the Plunger Pit. That's how we met Ygarr," said Rock.

"You've heard of the Jimi Hendrix Experience? Well, this is the Charlie Patton experience," I said, exchanging smiles with Rock and Elias. Charlie was already halfway through his bottle and my comment went over his head. Holding the pint in his left hand, Charlie tilted it to the side of his mouth as he rambled on about all the ideas that had flown into his head. His eyes glazed over and he looked right through me into space. "You guys gonna make a punk band?" he slurred. Even when he became loud and boisterous, he somehow always managed to maintain his teddy bear charm.

I picked up my beer and took a good swig. "Yeah, we're thinking about it. These guys aren't in a band and I guess I'm not either."

I didn't surrender to punk rock or give up on Zolar X that night. Instead, I let go of my ego and admitted that sometimes it was nice just to rock out on a three-chord song. Maybe simple songs were the ticket. I had plenty of progressive, symphonic space music, but maybe to move forward I needed to take a step back. But what I never changed, in any band, was the way I played guitar.

As the night wore on, everything flowed. More pot, more booze, and more music. I picked up the guitar. "Fuck, punk rock is easy!" I ranted. "The songs still have the basic elements: an intro, a verse, a chorus, a second verse, the lead to the last chorus, and the end. It's a formula that works. These three chords are fast," I said, chopping my guitar aggressively. This is probably a 180 tempo. If we want to take it a step further, we could add a counterpoint on bass." Their jaws dropped when they heard the riff. The song became "Rich Girl".

"And there's this one," I said, firing off a violent 210 tempo. "And every song has a chorus, so you back it up, throw in a lead, and you're done!" That one became "No Good".

"And if you want to go augmented, you'd do this," I fired off three gnarly sounding chords that became the intro to "Death Trap". Within a span of ten minutes, I played ten melodies. The other songs written that night went on to become "Mouth is Quicker", "I Don't Like You", "Spy Theme", "1055 La Jolla", and "I'm No Surfer", which we eventually changed to "Slab Lab". The songs just floated in. It was so simple.

"Oh, shit!" yelled Rock and Elias. "But will we remember them?"

"We should be able to." I grabbed my cassette player and hit record.

I moved them in that night.

Charlie Patton, circa 1970
Photographer unknown

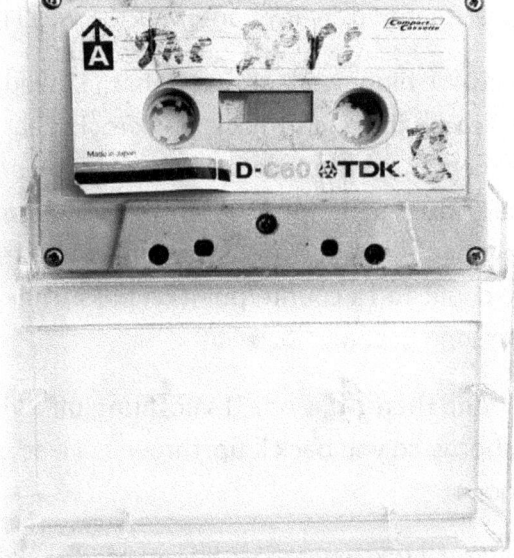

L to R: Rock Bottom, Elias Morales, 1978
Photobooth

Blank Frank, 1978
Photo credit: Charlie Patton

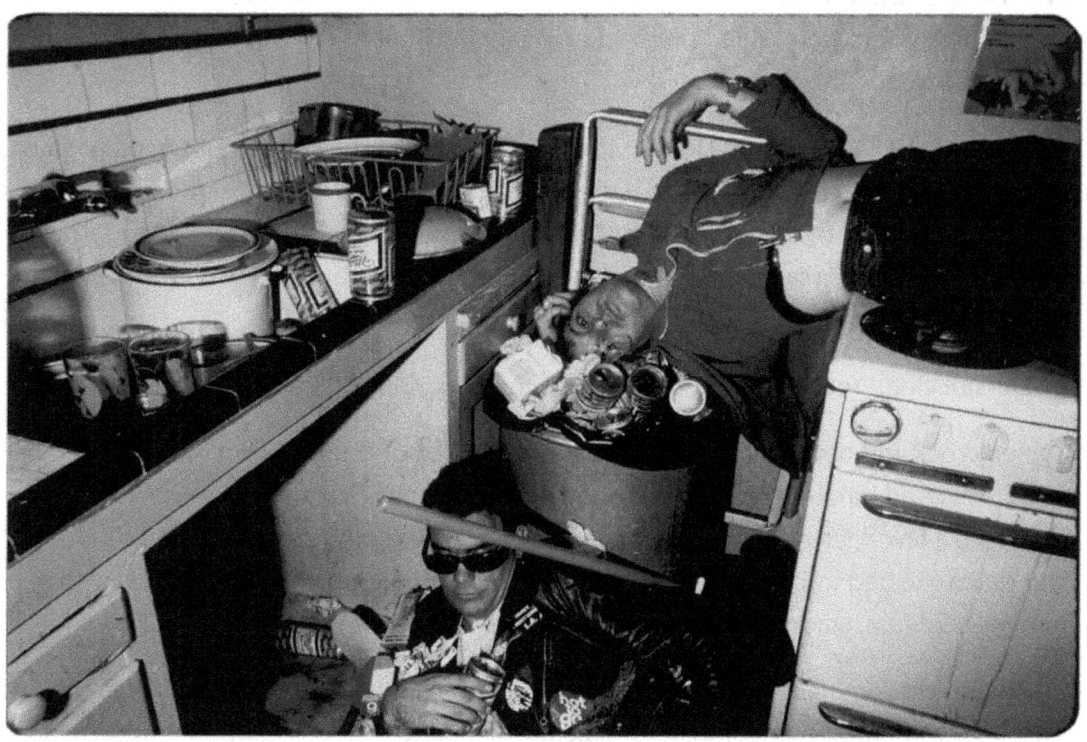

L to R: Rock Bottom, Ygarr Ygarrist at 1055 LaJolla, 1978
Photo credit: Stefen Shady

81

THE AURORA PUSHUPS
1978

ZORY ZENITH

There I was in a strange city, married, and with two babies. Thinking back a few months, I found myself getting pissed. I'd accepted an apprentice position at one of the oldest, established styling salons, a respected place that catered to movie stars. I should have put my foot down and said, "Fuck no, I'm not moving to San Jose! Are you out of your mind? We'll have to figure out something else. I just got offered a job in Beverly Hills! You know? Zolar X will play whenever shows come up. If I have to take a day job, at least I'd be working in the right fucking neighborhood!"

But there I sat in fucking San Jose. To keep from going insane, I started teaching myself guitar on my Mosrite 12-string and began writing a science fiction novella. The book was set in the future at Aurora, Colorado, with the usual themes of good versus evil and aliens. In the story, an elite squadron, the Aurora High School Angels, and their superpowers were called upon to save the day. That flurry of creativity also gave birth to my song "Angels on Runway 1."

Once in awhile, I'd visit Ed Dorn in the City. We'd shoot the shit about the early days of Zolar X and talk about music. I ran my new song by him and mentioned that I had the idea for a band to be named the Aurora Pushups. "We could put a band together and record a demo," I said. "Shit, maybe we could get some backing from the ice cream company. You know?"

Ed chuckled. "You're always scamming something, Billy McCartney!"

Punk rock and new wave were in full swing. Ed had nothing to do. I had nothing to do. I showed him my song and he showed me his song "Victims of Terrorism." We practiced a few days, and the next thing I knew we were in the studio. Ed quickly laid down the bed tracks. He did all the instrumentation, including the drums, with a minimum of fuss. I didn't know he could do that, so I was impressed.

Ed pressed some 45s and handed them out to a couple of contacts he had in the business. Somehow, miraculously, the record started to get some airplay. Within a few weeks, both songs on the 45 went into rotation.

At this time, we still didn't have a band. It was just me and Ed. He was still trying to talk me down from the sci-fi theme, but he liked the music.

Ed made his sales pitch. "We're going to have to put a band together now because the record is getting airplay. We can play clubs in the City to start with. I think it will be worthwhile to go out and back this single. Even though I'm not into punk, these new songs will fit right into my new wave formula."

"Okay."

He called me a few days later. "I put together a lineup. Rehearsals start this week."

I was thinking, *this is cool. There might be some semblance of redemption here.*

At the second rehearsal, I showed up drunk and didn't even try to participate. Listening to the band play, I was thinking, *this is your ordinary, typical, run-of-the-mill shit. It's not Zolar X*. I finally blurted out, "My song, 'Angels on Runway 1' had a sci-fi theme! It had HEAVY spiritual overtones! We're talking apocalyptic! And *then* you come in the back door with sci-fi! Get it? Obviously, you don't!"

"Fuck, Zory!" Ed shouted. "You're drunk and it's my band now! You're going off on another one of your Zolar X, sci-fi tangents, talking about the sky opening up and all that shit. Nobody wants to hear it. And by the way, I'm dropping Aurora from the name."

"That's cool. You know I'm not going to be crushed by that, but if I'm going to write *my* song, and I did, it's going to be fucking played the way I want it to be! That's just the way it goes when you're sittin' in that seat!"

So that's how that came and went.

L to R: Ed Dorn, Al Leis, Tony Reainer, Ricky Swanson
Photographer unknown

82

ROOFTOP POETRY

1978

The guys were still sleeping, and I was watching the second hand on the clock waiting for the corner store to open at 6:00 a.m. This was my routine roughly three days a week. It was always the same. Then, with alcoholic beverages procured, I'd head to the parking lot behind the apartment with my sixteen-ounce Bud and a pack of smokes. There was a lot to think about this particular morning, as I contemplated what had happened the previous night.

A punk rock band? I could hardly imagine such a thing, but I was writing music for the joy of writing music again and was having fun doing it. It was clear to me that Rock would be the lead vocalist and Elias would play bass. We'd still have to find a rhythm guitarist and a drummer, but who would write the lyrics? Somehow, the weight of the world had lifted from my shoulders. There was a new sense of freedom.

I hadn't realized how difficult Zolar X had become. There were some incredible times and putting the band together in '73 had been a lot of fun. And we played some great shows. We were on TV and in magazines, but without a record deal, we were just a blip. With this new band, I didn't feel the pressure of trying to get record companies to listen to us. I didn't have to think about the fact that Zory was up north, and I didn't have the stress of trying to keep Zolar X together. I didn't have to think about the lack of representation or management. Zolar X wanted to change the world, but punk rock wanted to destroy it. While I wasn't on board with that, the creative freedom was exhilarating.

Charlie shouted from across the street. He was on his way to work. "Hey Y, the guys are still crashed on the floor. You sounded good last night!"

"I'll see you when you get back, Charlie!" I called back.

At home, the first thing I did was sound off like a bugle horn. I grabbed the acoustic and wailed on one of the melodies from the previous night. That woke them.

"It's beer for breakfast and time to write a song! Who's gonna write the lyrics?"

After a cigarette and a beer, they were finally awake. "Get me something to write on and play that for me again," said Rock.

I did as he asked, strumming my acoustic fairly vigorously for the early hour. "This song can be about a girl who will give me money and keep me happy!"

"Go for it!" I said, handing him the notepad.

In a frenzied ruckus, pen to paper, Rock scribbled across the notepad. "What do you guys think?" he said, handing me the lyrics.

I don't wanna be
like the rest I see
Looking from my window
I'm here on the street
Wish I'd meet a rich girl

"Let's try it with music," I said, excited. The lyrics were raw, avant-garde, and cool.

"I've messed around with lyrics before, but this is the first time I've had a partner," Rock explained. "Do you mind if I go up on the roof and finish this puzzle?"

I was thinking, *the roof? What roof?*

"A friend of mine has an acoustic guitar. I'll be back with it and some good dope soon," said Elias, getting up.

An hour later, the door opened. Rock had finished the lyrics for "Rich Girl." Our first song together and it was only day two. I'd write the music, he'd write the lyrics, and we were moving fast. Within days, our ideas had become songs. Rock understood how I worked, and I was beginning to understand how he worked. He liked to be alone when he wrote; the rooftop or the bathroom—sometimes he'd leave for hours and come back with a complete song. Rock took pleasure in the isolation, and that privacy allowed him to tap the creative zone. Then he'd spring new songs on me, his face bright with pleasure. He wasn't seeking total approval, but he didn't hate my endorsement either.

I knew I could write the music, but I was also going to switch gears visually and enter the world of punk rock with these guys as my escorts. I was a rookie at punk and this was a brand new age. In a word, it was exciting.

83
INITIATION
1978

Elias blasted in toting a six-pack and an acoustic guitar. "Hey, there's a punk rock show tonight! Have you ever been to a punk rock show, Ygarr?"

"I played the Mabuhay Gardens. Does that count?"

Elias smiled. "Let's go! Everybody's gonna be there!"

"Who's playing?" asked Rock.

"The Weirdos and the Bags! Doors open at 8:00, but that's too early. Let's get there after 10:00. That's when everybody shows up to get wasted."

"Hey Charlie, you wanna go?"

"Sure Y! Sounds like a hell-of-a-bah-bah-bop happenin'!" said Charlie, lifting his pint.

"Maybe we can find a drummer and a rhythm guitarist!"

"Going to be a hell of a lot of chicks there!" said Rock.

"Rich girls?" I said jovially. "I'm getting dressed, guys!"

Rock looked at me and squinted. "Ygarr, we're going to have to figure something out with your threads, man. Time to join the club."

I piled through a lot of junk before I got to the bottom of my trunk. I finally uncovered a pair of Levis with holes in them and a T-shirt that looked like a Japanese comic book. What I didn't find was my 1966 original Star Trek phaser. Such a cool thing to show off and now it was MIA. I was sure it was that girl from last week.

Rock's voice pulled me back into the moment. "Bring 'em on, and let's get this party going!"

For five years, everywhere I went I was Zolarized: the market, the stage, to court, to the bank. Now blue jeans were staring me in the face, but I'd had a good run in my tights.

My newfound sense of freedom was intense. I hadn't been in Levis for ages and they felt tight around my crotch, but this was all for a good cause, right?

"Come here, Ygarr," said Elias. "We gotta punk that shirt up!"

I knew I would have to find my own look, one that reflected the truly spacey person I was and the modern punk rocker I was about to become. I could do punk the Zolar X way.

Elias poked a hole in the neck of my shirt and ripped it down the front. I didn't like them ripping my quasi cool shirt. But okay, whatever.

Rock started pinning up the rip with safety pins. Nothing was more punk rock than safety pins. Rock looked at Elias and said, "Now he's ready."

"Well, you guys can rip my shirt, you can get me into Levis, but I'm still having my eyebrows up and I'm not trading in my pointed hair for a mohawk. I'm keeping my style."

We set off for the show and soon we were there. The venue entrance was like something from an old Hollywood movie—elegant, regale, and majestic. Then we stepped into the club and were swept into the sea of punk rockers talking, drinking, and smoking. A wave of noise and smoke washed over me, and that earlier sense of elegance gave way to a full-on party scene. The place had a twenty-foot wide staircase with handrails on both sides that led up to the action above. I'd never seen anything like it.

"Hey guy!" shouted Charlie. "This is like the Elvis mansion back in Memphis!"

They've been having punk shows here for the last six months," said Elias, our punk rock tour guide.

Upstairs was packed, standing room only. Glancing around I saw the usual mini mob by the stage with the music pounding extreme decibels. A real anti-social event! Chicks were everywhere. Getting laid was going to be a piece of cake. Rock seemed to read my mind and said, "We're such pussy mongrels!"

Changing subjects, he nudged me and said, "Hey Ygarr, this is Blank Frank, the ex-rhythm guitarist of the Plugz."

Frank nodded. "What's up?"

"We're looking for a rhythm player. You any good?"

INITIATION

Like a statue, he stood there draped in black, black, and more black. Short, curly brown hair framed an albino face accentuated with black-rimmed sunglasses. "I play rhythm, killer harmonica, and keyboards. I'm available," said Frank in a monotone but very Velvet Undergroundy voice. He looked cool.

"Come by our place tomorrow, 1055 La Jolla, Apartment 6. We'll have a meeting."

From across the room, I saw three Latino guys smiling and walking our way. One of them nodded towards me and said in a foreign accent, "Zolar X? We saw you at the Starwood and the Troubadour. You guys are great!"

"Thanks. I'm Ygarr. This is Rock Bottom, Elias, and Blank Frank. You are?"

"I'm Nelson," said one of the Latinos. The other guy stuck out his hand and introduced himself as Mario. "You can call me G," said the third guy.

"Are you guys musicians?"

"Yes, we are."

"We're putting a band together," I said. "What instruments do you play?"

"I play guitar," said G. "Nelson plays drums, and Mario is on bass."

"Gimme your numbers and we'll be in touch."

We went out to catch the show and were immediately swallowed up by the sweaty ball of noise and energy. I still wasn't overwhelmed by the musicianship, but this was something different. Something primal. It was all so crazy that I barely remember the two girls I took back to the apartment and fucked later.

OUT OF THIS WORLD: THE STORY OF ZOLAR X

84

FORTRESS

1978

"No Good" was fine on the acoustic guitar when we were rehearsing or having fun but we needed to amplify our hardcore punk band. I knew what I could do sonically, but those guys? I guess we'll find out. "When will you be getting your equipment, Elias? We can't wait forever. Punk is on the move and we want in!"

"I've got this quack doctor, and he'll write prescriptions for whatever we want for fifty bucks," said Elias. "I'm talking Quaaludes, Tuinal, Codeine, and Dexedrine! We can make some money and buy my equipment. I've already made appointments for us using fake names."

I was thinking, *you want me to go to a doctor's office with a fake name, pay fifty bucks, and get a bunch of drugs? Shit, I could go to prison!*

"Well, Elias, in the meantime, I wanna hear Frank play. And what was that drummer's name? Oh yeah, Nelson. Let's see what his chops are like. Rock and I set up a rehearsal at the Fortress."

Frank showed up at rehearsal with his SG, Fender Twin Reverb, and an electronic keyboard. Nelson brought his kit and Mario was there with his amplifier and bass.

I turned up the Hiwatt to three in the apartment, but it went full throttle in that little studio room. I played the first three notes of "No Good" and Frank's eyes bugged out. "Wow. Holy shit, Ygarr!" he mumbled. "Talk about a power structure!"

The door cracked open and a guy popped his head around the corner. "Do you guys mind if I listen?" said the stranger.

"Sure, come on in," said Rock. "We're putting a new band together."

"I'm Don Bolles, drummer for the Germs. I was upstairs hanging out with some friends at their recording session when I heard the riffs. Thought I'd come to check it out."

We were just doing our thing and getting a feel for the room when Don said, "I'll bet you a case of beer that a Les Paul Jr. is louder than your Les Paul."

"What do you mean? You don't have a guitar."

Don said, "Hold on, I'll be right back."

A few minutes later, Don returned with a Les Paul Jr. "Don, you don't want to make this bet," I told him. "I've had Les Paul Jrs. before and there's no comparison. This '59 is the king of the fucking jungle. But to be fair, let's both play out of my Hiwatt."

But Don stood tall, and it was the easiest case of beer I ever won.

After rehearsal, Rock and I were outside having a smoke while the guys were packing up their gear. "I think we've got a band, Rock. These guys seem willing and able. But as much as I love the idea of a left-handed bass player, I don't think Elias will use the money for a bass, let alone an amplifier if we get those pharmaceuticals."

"We'll figure it out," said Rock. "This is my first real band, and I see potential here. Who knows, we could be at the Whisky next month. I know the guys who do the booking."

"I'd love to play there! Well, this is our band, so let's give our new guys the news."

We could see the nervous faces as we went back in and looked around the room. Rock didn't keep them in suspense for long. "No sweat, guys. You passed the audition. Let's schedule more rehearsals and get a gig!"

85
WHAT'S IN A NAME?
1978

With Zolar X, we had a doctrine before we had the name. We decided we would be from outer space and our message was space-age love. We genuinely believed in the existence of extraterrestrial life and we were sure that flying cars and space colonization would become a reality within our lifetime. Inside that philosophy, we searched for the name that would perfectly convey our message. We knew Zolar X was the right name as soon as we heard it. The band was a lifetime commitment within multiple facets.

Entering the threshold of punk, it was time to step down from the lofty confines of my previous existence. This newfound society wanted to fuck the establishment, and that sounded good to me. Why waste time worrying about tomorrow? It was much more fun to turn up our amps and ridicule the world with noisy punk rock.

Now it was time to name the band. When we think of the Who, the Rolling Stones, or The Beatles, do we see those names as being great on their own, or did the bands make the names great? I thought back to my first meeting with Rock and the mystique around him. When Elias showed up at my door, he could have been a member of the cartel. Blank Frank completed the dark visual that had been swirling in my brain. Then it dawned on me. We were secret agents hiding in plain sight. We could see the world, but the world couldn't see us.

"Alright guys, we could all pick a name, put them in a hat, and draw and get stuck down the road with something we hate."

Blank Frank dryly said, "Smog?"

We all laughed.

"Or we could just agree on a name we all liked," I said, leading them gently.

Rock caught on fast. "Do you have an idea, Y?"

"Yeah, I do. It's simple and it just feels right. I think we should call our band the Spys." To be punk, we didn't even bother to spell it right.

Concept: Ygarr Ygarrist,
Graphic Design: Christian Lunch

86

THE EARTHLINGS
1978

ZORY ZENITH

First I was up north and Ygarr was down south. Then Ygarr was up north and I was down south. Now I was stuck up north again. The responsibilities of having a wife and kids and bills to pay had limited my options, but the Aurora Pushups were done and I was looking for another band. I'd keep the sci-fi thing but interweave it with prophetic events and apocalyptic themes that spoke on the judgement of man. I was tied down to this human existence, so why not call it The Earthlings?

I clicked on the television and *Rollerball* was on. I was fascinated with the idea that global conflict in some distant future could be settled by a competitive game. Thoughts of intergalactic travel, corporate espionage, political corruption, and spiritual theories merged with astrophysics and poetry in my head. The next thing I knew, I had my twelve-string in hand and was writing a new song, "Jet Star 19".

There was a shitload of musicians in the Bay area so I didn't think it would be hard to find a couple. I was working in San Jose when this chick came in to get her hair done. She was a local, and I learned that her boyfriend was a Southern California boy who'd grown up in the surf scene. His name was Joel and he played bass. She brought him in and we talked a bit. Within a couple of days, I went over to their place to jam.

"God I've done everything: from Jan and Dean to the Yardbirds, and everything in between!" said Joel, plunking away on his bass.

I broke out my guitar and plugged in. I started running down "Jet Star 19", and I played the mini-opera "Judgement of Man" for him. When he jumped in on bass, I told him to make it as "McCartney" as he could. The guy was a virtual fucking encyclopedia of Rock 'n' roll and could play anything.

We found a drummer in Fremont named Dennis. We moved the operation to his house and started rehearsing in one of the empty bedrooms. The three of us carved away at this for about six months, rehearsing two to three nights a week. It was easy to put together because the stuff I was writing wasn't rocket science. Just straight-ahead pop.

Staying inside the "grounded on Earth" theme, I had some uniforms made to go with my idea of the Jet Star 19 spaceball team.

By this time, Ed's band was playing around the City. They were getting a following. Even though me and Ed were on the outs, he contacted me. "My band, The Pushups, and a bunch of new wave and punk bands have rented a hall. You want to come play this thing?"

"Sure," I said. "Thanks!"

The show was wild. Ten bands, one after another. A member of one of the punk bands came out on stage playing his guitar on roller skates. It was one of the first wireless guitar rigs I'd seen. There was a lot of other craziness as well.

Before our set, I met this young kid Tommi Carrera. He was a drummer who wanted to move to guitar, but he was willing to stay behind the drums if he could join our band. He came up afterward and said, "Your drummer's good, but I could outplay him. I know you don't have a lead guitar or keys, but I can see what your bass player is doing and my drum riffs would beef up your sound."

So we sacked our drummer and moved the band to Tommi's garage in Santa Clara. We didn't regret our decision because Tommi brought a lot more snap to our game. But Tommi wasn't getting my spot if he wanted to play guitar.

Aside from music, I also loved women and they always seemed to be around. I returned home from rehearsal one day to learn that Karen had thrown away my novella, my lyrics, and my drawings after discovering that she wasn't my only lover. After four years, this was a fork in the road. I moved in with my girlfriend Mary.

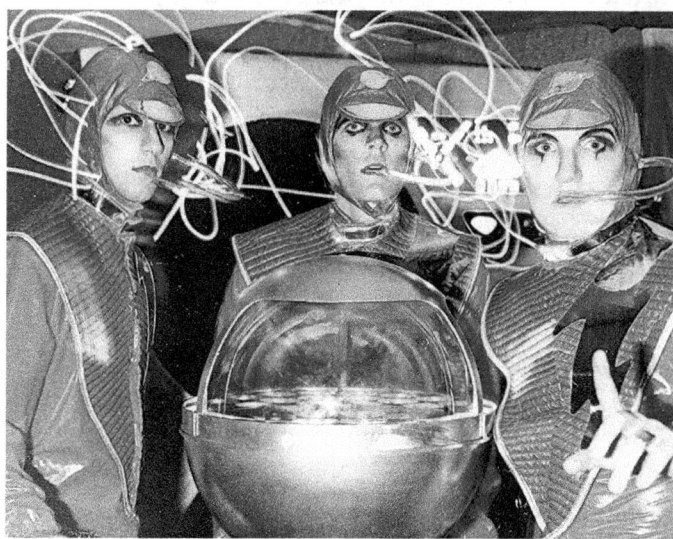

The Earthlings
L to R: Tommi Carrera, Joel, Zory Zenith, Bay Area, circa 1978
Photo credit: Unknown

87

THE WRITING'S ON THE WALL
1978

The job of writing music, working on the conception of the logo, and hitting as many thrift stores as possible to look for a new wardrobe fell on my shoulders. I also seemed to be responsible for organizing rehearsals, which could be difficult unless everybody was alert and ready to go. I was trying to get this punk band going but life always seemed to get in the way.

I never asked a girl to go to work and bring me money. It just happened. Did I ever think about it not being fair? Not back then. It seemed natural. I was a guitar player, singer, songwriter with a girlfriend. Nancy had a job and was quite content to spend her money to help me survive. From time to time, I'd pawn my Echoplex for a few extra bucks. The band occasionally got work as movie extras. One was *Hardcore* with George C. Scott, but our scene must have been lost on the cutting room floor. At least I wasn't homeless or hustling.

We were the Spys: Rock Bottom/lead vocals, Blank Frank/rhythm guitar, Nelson/drums, Mario/bass, and me on lead guitar. Our first gig was a pool party, where we got paid $100 and all the booze and food we could consume. Nobody booed, so we must have been okay.

Elias showed up at rehearsal with a bag of pills. He informed me that my appointment with the quack doctor was set. "Your name is Jack Smith. Here's fifty bucks for the appointment. Tell him that you're having trouble sleeping and you hurt your back. Works every time."

Elias was the teacher in this circumstance—the expert pill pusher. This was his world and I was about to enter it. From that point on, the three of us, Rock, Elias, or I had an appointment with the quack every week. The plan was to use the money for rehearsals, an occasional movie, booze, nice clothes, or equipment. We wouldn't have to stand on corners or make deliveries. They would come to us. That was the plan.

The reality was something else entirely. Most of the profit went down our throats. Pushing and taking pills was becoming more important than the band. I couldn't seem to get past the daily fatigue. I was with musicians, but we weren't rehearsing, cranking it up, or getting our message out on the street. Instead, we were nothing more than a cavalcade of alcoholics and dopeheads with musical gear. And reputations travel.

I'm no quitter, so I was willing to stick around to see if things would change. To break out of the boredom, I'd take the codeine and Quaaludes and watch the world go past. Our rehearsals were dropping off and the band was more about sexual conquests and staying high. It was becoming monotonous.

Passing out, blacking out, and living in the moment were the common factors of our existence. Sometimes it was tough to get up and get off the mattress. We'd take our pills, have our morning light beer, then we would switch to Mickey's Big Mouth for lunch. And for dinner, it would be the hard stuff plus whatever pills we got from the doctor. There would be about three days every month where I wouldn't eat very much. The rest of the time it was one meal a day. When we had money, we'd walk to the market and buy fixings for an Italian goulash that could feed twenty. Other times Nancy would come by and drag me from the apartment, and we'd go to Theodore's for dinner.

One night I was getting ready to go out and Charlie began making threats, "Ygarr, you're taking too many pills from that doctor! I'm worried you're going to pass out and not wake up."

I was in the bathroom drying my hair and yelled, "Charlie, you're pissing me off. I know what I'm doing. I like being stoned. I like the damn euphoria!"

Charlie came to the doorway. "Nancy told me she's worried too!"

By now I was mad, "Fuck Charlie, leave her out of it," I shouted. "I can handle it. What are you doing talking to her anyway?"

Charlie screamed at me and his face turned red. "I'm gonna put a stop to this shit. I'm calling the doctor's office right now to report you! Jack Smith isn't your real name!"

Without a thought, blow dryer in hand, I whacked Charlie in the side of his head. His eyes glazed over from shock. Then, dead silence. Immediately, I was overwhelmed with guilt and remorse. "Shit Charlie! I could have killed you! I'm sorry. Are you alright?"

"Hey, guy, you got me damn good."

It's never been my nature to be violent. It's not in my DNA. Drunken arguments are strange though. Things escalate and then they're over. Most of the time you wake up the next day and can't remember much. The incident blew over as fast as it happened, but I remembered that one and always felt bad about it.

THE WRITING'S ON THE WALL

There was some rejuvenation after we played the pool party. With this band's talent, the promise remained high, but the strategy and execution were evaporating. You bet your bottom dollar we made it to every appointment with the quack, but if it was a rehearsal, a meeting with potential management, or a club promoter, somebody would forget. It was maddening.

After three months of that shit, Charlie stayed true to his word. He called the doctor and reported us, which brought an end to that saga. Looking back, it was an act that probably saved my life and restored my sanity.

Ygarr Ygarrist
Photographer unknown

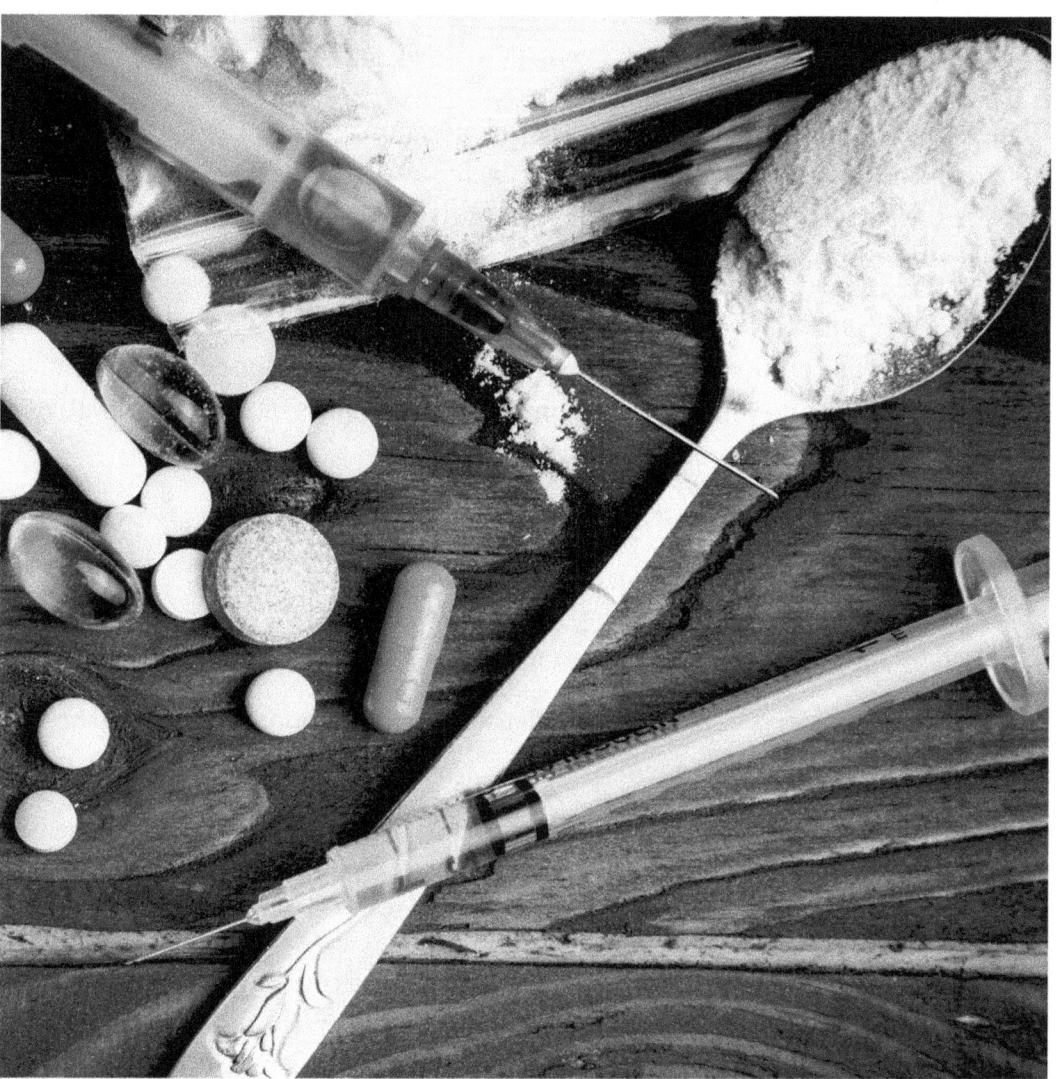

Photo credit
iStock.com/Stas_V

88

THE CANTERBURY
SEPTEMBER 1978

What seemed like an ordinary Saturday took an odd turn. *Rock and Elias* weren't around and I wondered where they were. I concluded they must have partied the night before and were shacked up someplace. Although I was enjoying the quiet, I found myself missing the pandemonium that had become normal day-to-day life at La Jolla.

All that changed abruptly when Charlie stormed through the door. "Hey Y, I got us a new apartment" he yelled. "You're gonna love it. It's only $150 bucks a month off Hollywood Boulevard! Everybody's moving there."

"Does the place have a name? Who's everybody?"

"All the punk rockers. It's called the Canterbury!"

"When do we move?"

"Right now! My friend from work has a flatbed truck. He's gonna honk when he's outside!"

"Well, I guess we'd better start packin'! We should pin a note to the door so Rock and Elias will know where we're at!"

What a ride. It was just me, Charlie, his friend, and the truck. Charlie rode upfront and I rode in the back to keep an eye on things. The move could only be described as insane, but I loved knowing that a new adventure was just around the corner. I grasped the little deck railing firmly with one hand and clutched my Les Paul with the other, bracing the amplifier head with my foot to keep it from sliding around. Charlie howled from inside the cab as the truck lurched forward. We didn't have much to move—just a twin mattress, my famous leopard mattress, a trunk, a suitcase, a box of pots and pans, and a few miscellaneous items that belonged to Rock and Elias. Still, it would have been nice if they were around to help us move.

The trip over reminded me of riding one of those old wooden roller coasters, being jerked every which way. The box of pots and pans bounced and clanked, and everything slid around wildly. I did my best not to fly off the back, but Charlie's buddy was driving like the cops were chasing us. The fucker was taking corners on two wheels, or at least that's how it felt.

The drive was only ten minutes long but seemed like an eternity. Finally, the truck came to an abrupt stop just outside the front gate. I was surprised that the only thing that got damaged was Charlie's Salvador Dali hologram. That and my nerves.

"Hey Charlie, what's our apartment number?"

"We're on the fourth floor Y. Just across from Blank Frank's apartment."

I looked down the sidewalk and across the courtyard at the double doors of the lobby and then back at the truck. Even though we didn't have a lot of stuff, moving would be a lot of work without a dolly or a hand truck. "I hope this place has an elevator!"

I still wasn't thinking of myself as a punk rocker. I was just this guy playing punk music in a punk rock band, and now I was living in a punk house—a stranger in a strange land. Every band in town seemed to have a few people at the Canterbury, and at least one member of the Germs, Screamers, the Plugz, Go Gos, Weirdos, and the Bags had lived there at one point. We were a block from Hollywood Boulevard, with all the movie theaters, liquor stores, pawnshops, and everything else we needed. The Masque was just down the street.

I called dibs on the closet for my bedroom. My mattress, trunk, and equipment fit the four by eight-foot space perfectly. It even had a small shelf and a clasp on the door for a padlock.

When Rock finally showed up, he had his new Beverly Hills girlfriend Penny in tow. I whispered in his ear. "You found your rich girl. Be careful." Then I spoke at a normal volume. "Where have you been staying?"

"We've been renting a motel by the week."

"So you're serious?"

"I think I am."

The first couple of months were cool, and it was like living in a commune. We had an open-door policy with Blank Frank and another neighbor. There was Mary Criss, who fucked everybody and hung out everywhere. There was the straight dude next door who did drugs and was studying to be a truck driver. One day, I ran into

Don Bolles in the lobby and he invited me down to the basement to catch a Germs rehearsal. They were working on "Steppin' Stone" by the Monkees, playing it over and over again. There were parties every night and lots of drugs to go around. Some people knew I was from Zolar X, but I wasn't advertising it.

One night, I needed to shower and Rock and Penny were in the bathroom. They'd been in there for a long time. I knocked on the door and waited some more. Were they having sex in there? When the door finally opened, I immediately realized they'd been shooting heroin. I watched them stumble out in slow motion, gently scratching at themselves, unaware of anything but the euphoric world that held them prisoner.

The Spys hadn't had a real, electric rehearsal since we moved in. I knew the songs front and backward. Frank and Elias would come over, or I would go over to Frank's place and we'd jam on our acoustics. Mario and Nelson showed up a couple of times a week, but Rock, every time I saw him, he was arguing with Penny over drugs – totally unavailable.

On one rare occasion, they stopped by. "I've got some news, guys!" Rock announced happily. "Penny and I are getting married, and I got us a show at the Whisky opening for the Weirdos! Ygarr, I want you to be my best man."

"Unbelievable!" I managed to utter.

This would be my first time playing the Whisky, and the Spy's first real show. For the last two months, I'd been in disguise as a performing musician. Getting high and being under the influence took the edge off that dull existence, but the Whisky show brought purpose to the day. This could be the domino that got the ball rolling. In 1978, major labels were still looking to sign punk bands. They didn't realize that punk wouldn't become mainstream until the early '90s. We just wanted to make a record, and we didn't need management to help us get a deal. This was the age of DIY. We could do it ourselves.

A week before the show, the whole band actually showed up. We rehearsed at the Masque, which provided a room and electricity. I met Brendan Mullen and the Go Gos. Then we moved out to the Valley for two more rehearsals. It was great to hear Rock pound out "No Good" and "Rich Girl." He was a natural frontman.

On the afternoon of the gig, I gathered in the apartment with Rock, Blank Frank, Elias, Charlie, and Penny. We were having a few beers when there was a knock at the door. I was shocked to see Syndee and her sister Trudy standing there.

"We heard you were playing with your new band," chirped Syndee. "We just had to see you guys! You remember my sister Trudy, right?"

"How did you hear about this show?" I asked as they spilled into the apartment without being invited. "Do you have a radar implant?"

Syndee rattled like a machine gun. "You know I have connections! I was at the Whisky the other night and the owner Elmer Valentine told me that a band the Spys were playing. I just knew it had to be you! Then I asked my friend who lived here in the Canterbury where the Spys were living and she told me you were here. So here we are!"

I looked at her, still amazed that she could say so much in one breath. "Some things never change! By the way, are we still married?"

"Oh, my Dad got our marriage annulled over two years ago!"

"Fantastic! I'm so glad I haven't been committing adultery."

Syndee acted as if she didn't hear me and motioned to her sister. "You guys wanna get high?" Trudy began emptying her handbag onto Charlie's bed. There was an assortment of pill bottles in various sizes. "We have uppers, downers, opiates—anything you want! Go on, help yourself!" Syndee babbled. It was quite the smorgasbord of treats, so I decided to grab some uppers for the show and a few Quaaludes for afterward. I also grabbed the opiates so nobody would fall asleep onstage. "These are for after the show, guys!"

In Hollywood, it's better late than never and the crowd doesn't arrive until later. There were a few heads bobbing up and down during our set, but nobody was going mental. We sounded good. Nelson was steady and Mario was accurate. Blank Frank was there. Rock was dead-on-magnificent, and I was me. No fuckups onstage, but our roadie managed to lose one of my Echoplexes. Our first *real* show was a success.

The next month was one of the low points of my musical career. Looking back, I'd say it was a disaster, but at the time it was just my life. We were taking handfuls of pills non-stop and washing them down with booze. I'd make a shopping list and Trudy would show up with the items. Whether I sold them or traded them, the demand was high. I was the supplier, and someone was always knocking on the door.

One day, Frank and one of my old girlfriends came to the door. The girl was holding something that looked very familiar. "So you're the one who stole my Star Trek original phaser! I knew it!"

"Frank told me you wouldn't sell me some Diluadids unless I confessed," she said sheepishly.

"You're right!" I was happy to get my phaser back, but Blank Frank could have bought them for her and made a few bucks on the side. He'd done me a solid favor.

I began to long for the Zolar X days when my only crutch was a beer or a glass or two of wine. When I picked up the guitar, I'd think about 1973 and Zolar X. I had many fine memories of Rodney's and the Starwood. I thought about the magic that formed the band and the joy of hearing the songs come to life. We'd been so dedicated to the goal of playing and recording that nothing else mattered. We were like a family but closer. Canterbury was so far away from Zolar X musically, visually, and ideologically that my mind had to take trips to the stars just to survive. I was twenty-six now and writing punk songs with Rock was fun. I had money in my pocket for cigarettes and booze, and I had pills in my bag. Elias or Trudy would show up with some dope and Charlie would be home later with booze. Nancy would stop by with some food, and I always had what I needed to get through the day. But we weren't rehearsing. Rock was shooting junk with Penny somewhere, and without him, there wasn't much point with the Spys.

I wrote, "Timeless", "Mirrors", and "Earth Dreams" trying to figure out what band would play them. They definitely could go either way. I had the music and the melody for another song, but couldn't decide what it would be about. Then, like a scene from a sci-fi movie, Charlie came in the door waving a science magazine. "Hey Y, listen to this!" he said, reading excitedly the headline. "World's First Test-Tube Baby Born!"

"Wow, Charlie! Test Tube Baby! That's the title I've been searching for!" He read the article aloud and I furiously began jotting down lyrics. When I got to the end, I needed a word that rhymed with fate. Charlie thought about it as he opened a pint of scotch. "Well, there's this stuff they put in a test tube called Adenosine Triphosphate."

Not only did Adenosine Triphosphate rhyme with fate, but it also had six syllables— the exact mathematical count I needed to finish the verse.

Considering everything else going on around me, these latest songs were an achievement. They were definitely more Zolar X style than Spys, but I just couldn't give up the dream.

Debauchery comes to mind when I think back on those days. The elevators smelled like piss. Going down, we'd take the stairs to avoid the stench. Then the rancid smell of piss started creeping into the hallways. Fear was becoming commonplace and the women didn't feel safe. Rape was whispered everywhere. And if that weren't bad enough, fires became an everyday occurrence. The place was dangerous.

One particular day, I smelled smoke and stepped into the hallway to check it out. Geza X was in the hallway doing the same thing. We made our way to the back of the building, where we saw smoke coming from under a door. Taking deep breaths, we entered the apartment and found a crumpled pile of newspapers smoldering in the corner. The fire was small enough that we were able to stomp it out, but we were wondering who started it and why.

A bit later, two guys told me the owners had paid them to create an atmosphere of terror by starting small fires around the building. Development plans were in the works and the punks had to go. What had been a vibrant community became a ghost town within weeks.

But Charlie always had his ear to the ground and quickly found us a new home across from the Chateau Marmont at 8228 Sunset Boulevard.

L to R: Ygarr Ygarrist, Nelson, Rock, Mario, Blank Frank - The Whisky 1978
Photo credit: Nancy Allen

A Punk Rock Wedding
Photo credit: Nancy Allen

89

THE SPYS RECORD
1978

Nancy, who was also Ufo's wife's best friend, kept me in the loop of little U's world. I didn't see much of him and his girlfriend Rose these days, but we were still on good terms. "Ufo and Rose are going out of town," said Nancy. "Will you stay over for a few days to keep an eye on things?

"Sure," I said.

Because Ufo's apartment was in a shadowy area of town, I pawned my Hiwatt and Echoplex and had Nancy take my Les Paul home with her. I was always in danger of losing my most prized possessions based on my experiences with scorned women, shady characters, and the nature of Hollywood but I needed the money and security that pawnshops provided. I settled in with a couple of beers, happy for a little solitude and a reprieve from Charlie's snoring.

Later that night I heard a knock at the door. I figured it had to be someone looking for Ufo or Rose but was surprised when I opened the door to see Blank Frank and Ian Icon. I wasn't hard to find, even when I was staying elsewhere.

"Hey Ygarr, we need you on lead guitar," said Frank.

"We're recording the Spys with Rock Bottom!" added Ian.

I was shocked and pissed. I mean I hadn't heard from any of the Spys for quite a while. "I guess you thought you could do it without me but realized you couldn't?" I said, almost amused.

"Yeah," mumbled Frank.

"I don't have my equipment with me."

"We have an amp and a Gibson SG for you at the studio," said Ian.

"Let me lock up the place and let's get the hell out of here."

I soon learned they'd started recording earlier that night, and everyone was very high when we arrived. Somehow, we still managed to lay down some rhythm tracks.

The rest of the night was heroin and cases of beer. We finished the six songs on the second night: "Rich Girl", "No Good", "Deathtrap", "Spy Theme", "Mouth is Quicker", and "Determination".

Rock ran out of money so we only mixed three songs. And that's the story of the recording session that became a rare, almost impossible-to-find EP. The 7-inch has been reissued twice. It never had a formal name but most people call it Rock Bottom and the Spys. But to this day I'll never call it that. Hell, I started the band and wrote all the music! We were the Spys.

90
QUICKSAND
1979

Old Lang Syne and then it was 1979. I'd lost touch with Zory, Ufo, and Eon, so Zolar X was floating somewhere in the cosmos. Rock had disappeared into holy matrimony and heroin addiction. Would a brand-new band be playing my music in the New Year? I was living in Hollywood on Sunset Boulevard, so surely the music gods would cooperate. But the months rolled by, and the first half of the year was a continuation of the usual sex, drugs, and no Rock 'n' roll. Elias, Dave, G, and I were the "wannabe" Spys. At this point, the real Spys didn't technically exist, so why not?

G belonged to a group of South American dealers hanging out in LA. They were huge fans of Zolar X, and since I was the songwriter and guitarist, I was like a hero and a guitar teacher to them. They were helpful to me because G had a garage rehearsal studio full of equipment he'd bought with drug money. We'd get high and jam and these guys could pretend they were in a band. There was never a shortage of booze and drugs.

The wannabe Spys were never a gigging band. Nothing about the wannabe Spys ever felt serious. We never played any shows—we just jammed. I didn't bother to write new songs, so we mostly played Spy songs. Every so often, we'd record a few of G's tracks on his little Teac four-track. G thought he was a songwriter, and I went along for the ride. On one recording, I composed the keyboard parts but didn't play guitar. I was indifferent when he showed up with an acetate. I figured I had a choice; I could either label it for him which he would take as a sign of approval or refuse which would have made him resentful. And since I enjoyed his cocaine, I signed it.

As '79 waxed and waned, I continued to descend into the world of addiction, cocaine, heroin, booze, and a variety of pills that would lead the casual observer to think I was trying to kill myself. But one small, purple, kick-your-ass-down a steep flight of stairs pill was far worse than the others and had a crippling effect on me–Lotus A's. I began having monthly seizures that created a variety of problems such as a dislocated shoulder that still bothers me, rides in ambulances, ER visits, and scars on my face from falling. Although I only took the purple pills for a month, the chemicals took six months to work their way out of my system. I didn't clean up completely, but I did stop taking some of the pharmaceuticals.

Rock, Elias, and Blank Frank lived for the next fix. I liked smack, and I did it with them, but I was satisfied with beer. I needed alcohol the moment I woke up. It calmed the shakes and steadied the nerves. Those guys lived for the needle. I'm not saying I was any better than they were, but my alcohol habit was legal.

One night, Rock was looking to score some heroin. After an exhausting search, I remembered Girlfriend #737. I'd met her at the sci-fi convention a few years back and we'd lived together for a few months. She dealt on the side and I still had her phone number, so I gave her a call. Rock and I hopped in the first cab we saw, but I'd forgotten how things had ended with her. Let's just say I was pretty sure she felt scorned. She wanted me, I didn't want her and broke it off a year ago only to receive a bill in the mail for $1,000 from small claims court. Never underestimate an angry woman.

Rock was happy, but we both got sick as dogs after we shot up. The high was totally different from a smooth euphoric mellow scratch-your-face buzz that good heroin always provides. We got through the night, but our lips were covered in nasty sores the next morning. I was a recluse for two weeks waiting for my lips to heal. The only person I allowed to visit me was Nancy. We figured it had been cut with rat poison or something of an equally toxic nature. We were lucky to be alive.

91

JET STAR 19

1979

I picked up the phone and heard Zory's familiar, endearing monotone. "What are you doing, bud? I'm back in LA, bud. Are you ready to do Zolar X again, bud? I have another manager, Mark Quincy, who owns a clothing store, the Hollywood Boutique, on the boulevard."

I set my beer carefully on the coffee table. "A boutique owner? How did you talk him into managing a rock band?"

"That was his idea after he heard my new songs with The Earthlings and the Zolar X tape on cassette."

"Shit let's get together! I know where Ufo is, but Eon could be anywhere."

"That's okay. Remember Tommi Carrera, the drummer from The Earthlings? He's down here with me!"

"This is good news. I've been stagnant for the last year. Too many drugs and not enough music!" I said, telling Zory more than he needed to know.

"Mark wants to meet you tomorrow. Let's meet at the Chinese Theater and walk to the boutique."

"Cool. I'll see you then. I'll contact Ufo and see if he's ready for another run at Zolar X."

"Oh, I'm sure he will be. Hell, he's probably going stir crazy!"

"Let's do this! Third time's a charm!"

The third re-birth of Zolar X was the answer to a prayer I didn't even make. One moment I was in the gutter wondering how I was going to eat and drink the next day, and then the antennas were back. Never question fate.

Mark seemed like a nice guy. He was a store owner and a businessman and offered something I hadn't felt for a while: stability. Even as a first-time manager, he was aware that this was going to cost him some money. In his late thirties with thinning red hair,

Mark stood six feet tall and dressed like a mod ready to step onto the disco dance floor. His wife was gorgeous and he had three young daughters. The guy was smart and successful, unlike Charlie who was drinking himself to death even faster than I was. Optimism hung in the air. Brian Epstein had started in a store too.

Mark assembled the new band in his head. "Where's our bass player? I want to get this thing moving as soon as possible."

"He's ready for lift-off. I could get him here right now," I said, hoping this wasn't too good to be true. We'd been down this path before.

"What's his name?"

"Ufoian Ufar, bass guitar from a star."

Mark digested the news quickly. "You guys need to get it together because you have a gig at Filthy McNasty's this Friday!"

"That's what I'm talking about!" yelled Zory.

I was all in.

We ran into one of our previous managers Nik Pascal when we arrived at the club.

"Hey, Nik. Good to see you! What are you doing here?"

"Hey, Zolar X! You're early!"

"Yeah, we thought we'd try to get some rehearsal in. It's been a year since we've played."

"Just so you know, I got you this gig! I was talking to Mark at his boutique last week and one thing led to another. I do the booking at Nasty's, so here we are!" Nik motioned towards the stage. "Go ahead and set up, guys. The stage is yours and we'll get you some drink tokes."

We started with "Rocket Roll" and the 'Bot sounded like a world-class lead vocalist in a league of his own. Nobody sounded like him. The attitude he projected, his flirtation with the microphone, his inflections, and whispers—he had it all.

But I felt bad for Tommi. I didn't know if he'd ever heard "Rocket Roll," but he managed to keep up. Now we had to find out if he could really cut it.

"Hey Ufo, Zory, let's do 'Horizon Suite'. Tommi, try to keep up."

From the first notes, Tommi was struggling. I knew he'd been in The Earthlings with the Bot, but these songs were a universe apart from anything he knew. Halfway through, he stopped abruptly and began packing up his drums, "I can't do Zolar X. This is too much," he muttered, entirely defeated. What can you say to that?

Miraculously, Eon walked in the door with his drums just as Tommi was leaving. They didn't even look at each other. More fate.

We ran through the old material and it sounded just like Zolar X. After a while, I looked at Zory and said, "Show me your new songs and I'll show you mine."

Zory broke out his Mosrite twelve-string. "I'll play 'Jet Star 19' and 'Science' for you. Eddy and me put them together."

I was impressed. "You guys have really captured the new wave energy that I want to play."

"I could hear those punked up, with new rhythm attacks and tempos. I guess playing in a punk band for a year wasn't a total waste." Then I showed them "Timeless," "Mirrors," and "Test Tube Baby," which were relatively simple riffs with straightforward structures. Reforming Zolar X was like riding a bike.

Mark nodded his head happily. He seemed giddy. "This is great! I want to get you guys into a recording studio as soon as possible!"

Who were we to argue?

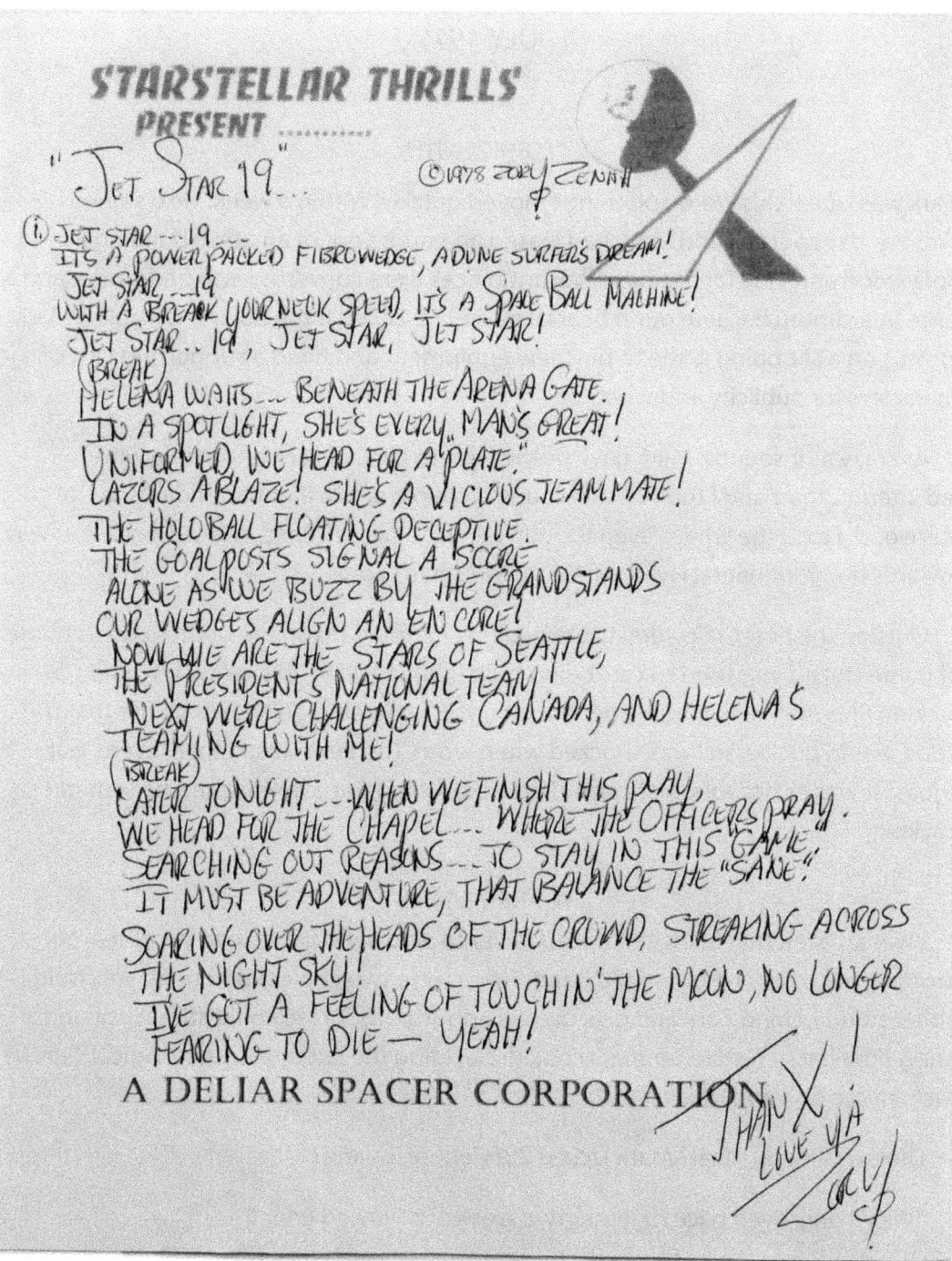

92

THE CADILLAC IS BUCKLING
JULY 1979

ZORY ZENITH

Mark was true to his word and things moved quickly. Within a week, we'd signed a ninety-day contract and Mark had leased an entire floor of an office building at Hollywood and Vine for the band. Vacant offices were converted into bedrooms, and a large boardroom became our rehearsal space. We called it the Zolar X Complex. Mark took us on a shopping spree to buy new equipment and hired a supporting cast of characters for publicity and whatnot.

As crazy as it sounds, Mark gave us the keys to his Cadillac convertible with red interior. Ygarr and I took off and found a couple of hot flight attendants at the Starwood. I took the wheel, even though I didn't have a license, and we made our way towards the Continental Hyatt where the girls had rooms.

Outside the hotel, I decided to show off by jumping up on the hood to do a couple of mime steps. I was used to cars being built in the fucking '50s, okay? It would take a fucking Sherman tank to put a dent in one, you know? It didn't dawn on me that the hood would buckle, so I was shocked when it did. The dent wasn't that severe, but I guess it was noticeable. Mark and I had a big falling out over that and he sent me packing.

YGARR YGARRIST

I was amazed that Mark had the audacity to actually kick our lead vocalist—our droogie, our brother—out of the band. There were two choices before us: we could either stand behind Zory and give up this opportunity, or we could stick it out and bring Zory back in when tempers cooled. Deciding the latter was more logical, I broke the news to Eon and Ufo.

Ufo exclaimed, "What? Mark kicked Zory out of Zolar X?"

"We've only been back together two weeks!" bellowed Eon.

"It depends on what you guys want to do. We have a ninety-day contract, we have new equipment, a place to sleep, and rehearse, so let's take advantage of this shit.

We'll work on our new songs, get them tight as hell, and record. I met this cat named Clem Fisher who wants to release a Zolar X album. I know we have the Memphis recording, but we need more music—shorter songs, faster tempos, and more aggression."

Eon asked, "Are we really going to do Zolar X without Zory, I mean 'Space Age Love' and 'Energize Me'?"

"It's temporary. We'll get him back. He's just up north."

They both agreed.

I have to admit, Zolar X without Zory was like being naked. But we went on anyway. We'd lost our stage wear designer and our look suffered. Zory had sold most of the outfits in the Bay area, so we had to start from scratch. I missed the comradery between the four of us— the Bot-antics and practical jokes. But the music grew and lived on with just the three of us. We focused on the sound. What we lacked in the visual, we made up for in the technical execution.

It was very cool being able to wake up, walk out to the Boulevard for coffee, then go back upstairs to rehearse. There were so many rooms to get lost in. Mark moved in a couple guys as roadies. He even brought in a music teacher to teach us how to read and write music.

Mark booked a recording session in a studio in Redondo Beach, where we recorded "Science", "Test Tube Baby", "FE1142", "GT3", "Silver Shapes", and "Blues on Blue". After we finished mixing, Mark took the tape and locked it in the store safe. The safe was open during store hours, so I swiped the tape and had it duplicated. Then I put the copy in the safe and kept the master. That would teach Mark for firing our lead singer.

PREAMBLE TO A NIGHTMARE
FEBRUARY 1980

The first show for Zolar X in a year and Zory was MIA. But I knew exactly where he was. Theatrically, we were underdressed, decked out in make-shift stage wear straight off the racks from the local department store. The days of antennae and colored hair had melted into Zolar X history.

The music was tight as shit though, thanks to the recent Redondo Beach recording session. We slammed them with "Test Tube Baby" and "Science" – songs born from the punk rock subculture. Although the new songs were fun, they didn't fill the bitter void. I was missing my frontman. Now I was the sole vocalist and we had no backing harmonies. To counteract that additional pressure, I drank more. Sometimes I'd get a bit sloppy, and those closest to me began to worry about my drinking.

In Zory's absence, I was also keenly aware of my habit of closing my eyes when I sang. It was easier when I didn't have to look at people, and the noise of the crowd helped to keep me grounded. That historic night as I opened my eyes for a split second and glanced at my band mates then out into the audience. It felt diluted. The energy was missing, and our sound bounced around weakly in the half-filled room. I saw Nancy and Rose over to the side, but they didn't count. Our loyal fans seemed to be dropping away. I kept playing.

Then I looked to the right and saw Girlfriends #737 and Double D. They were whispering intently while looking at me. Something about the picture wasn't adding up and a shiver ran up my spine. I had a bad feeling.

Back at the Zolar X Complex, we had a little gathering after the show. Eon, Ufo, our roadies, Mark, Rose, and my trustworthy girlfriend Nancy were all there. We were having a few drinks and feeling fine when Double D and Girlfriend #737 slithered in. I didn't have a problem with Double D. She was a good lay and I'd crashed at her nice apartment a few times. Nancy didn't need to know about that. But Girlfriend #737 was downright evil, and I could see #737 pumping animosity and resentment into Double D's ear. Double D glared at me and I could see she was taking it hook, line, and sinker. My paranoia doubled then tripled.

"Let's get out of here for a bit," I told Nancy. We headed up to the roof for a nice little fuck, but there were even more nasty looks and hostile vibes when we got back. By then, I was starting to get drunk and no longer gave a shit. I stormed towards Mark. "What in the fuck are those two doing here? They have nothing to do with Zolar X. Especially that one!" I shouted, pointing at Girlfriend #737.

Mark laughed. "Well, she's your new publicist."

"What the fuck? You have no idea what you've done! She's no publicist. That chick tried to fucking kill me! A publicist should be getting the band stadium shows, but she's just a plastic jewelry maker! And, she hates me!"

"Calm down, Ygarr," said Mark, raising his hands defensively. "You're getting drunk, but I'll find a way to get her out of here."

"You better make it quick or I'm gonna blow up!" I said, chugging my beer. I got through the night, but I knew bad shit was coming down the road. I could feel it in my bones.

I'd cleaned up quite a bit since the Canterbury. I'd stopped taking pills and hadn't had a seizure in six months. I was eating better and had stopped waiting for the liquor store to open at 6:00 a.m. Instead, I sat at Denny's and drank pots of coffee with the band till they booted us out and we went home to rehearse There were alcoholics in my family, and I knew I was susceptible to overdoing it, but I was twenty seven and invincible. No rock stars died at age 27. Well, maybe a couple…

Those who were closest to me looked on judgementally. "Ygarr drinks too much," they might whisper behind my back, raised eyebrows turning to looks of scorn. I had to deal with comments like, "You know you're an alcoholic" or "I just want you to get better." When I would pop open a beer, everyone in the room would turn towards me and look pointedly looking at the clock "It's pretty early," they might say. The constant harassment masked as concern was starting to piss me off.

I wasn't surprised when Mark and the guys ganged up on me. "I'll pay for a 28-day rehab program," said Mark. "We found a real nice hospital in Santa Monica."

"We don't want you getting sick," Ufo said.

"We need you, buddy" added Eon.

Mark had an ace up his sleeve. "Come back from this a new man and we'll get you a record deal," he promised.

PREAMBLE TO A NIGHTMARE

I was sick of this bullshit and lost my temper. "Fuck sakes! You want me to get sober and to go onstage straight? Okay, I'll do it to just shut you guys up!"

Ygarr Ygarrist and
The "59 Sunburst
Photo credit: Nancy

27 DAYS
MARCH 1980

I would be locked up for 28 days, so I decided to stay at Double D's place on my last night of freedom. Nancy still lived with her parents and Double D had her own apartment, which made my decision that much easier. We partied and fucked all night as if I'd never do it again. When morning arrived, I was reluctant to go but willing to give it a shot.

We got ready to leave. Glancing at my 12-string acoustic and the Les Paul, I knew I had to make a decision. Since I was going into a hospital with all sorts of drunks and dope fiends, I decided to take the twelve string with me and leave the Les Paul with Double D. This was probably not the wisest decision I'd ever made.

"I'm leaving the 'Paul with you," I said, trusting her implicitly. "You have a secure apartment with all the locks and such on your door. This 12-string doesn't need an amp."

"I'm going back to New York to visit my folks so, yeah, it'll be fine."

After a 40-minute drive, we arrived at the hospital. The tangy salt spray that had drifted in from the ocean was a sharp contrast to the antiseptic surroundings that lay in front of me. After I survived a gruelling indoctrination, I was shown to the room I would share with another male. The first few days were kind of rough, but I soon fell into a routine of blood tests, group meetings, doctors, and more food than I'd eaten in years. I might even have put on a pound or two.

Once I was there, I decided to follow the rules. I would take advantage of this opportunity to bust through my chemical dependency of alcohol. Instead of nodding out at the end of the day, I might learn how to sleep again and wake up without a hangover.

My freedom, however, was limited. No phone calls and no coming and going. Within the closed-off walls and corridors of the hospital, I met doctors, ministers, priests, and even a guru. At least my roommate was also a guitarist, so we got to talk about music.

"When we get out of here, you'll have to stop by and see my '59 Les Paul Sunburst," I said, proud of my guitar.

Sam's jaw dropped open. "You have a '59 Les Paul? I've heard those are the best."

"Yeah, it's my Stradivarius."

I met other patients set against the backdrop of Twelve Step meetings. With this new way of navigating life, things seemed possible. My thinking became clearer, more alert. Coffee and cigarettes were my new best friends. During the evening meetings, everyone shared the most gut-wrenching stories that had brought them there. I admired everyone that had chosen to get help and stop the nasty habits that could end in death. I became a good listener and the serenity prayer seemed to offer hope. But as willing as I was to try and make this work, another part of me kept asking, *why am I here?*

Finally, after two long weeks, I was allowed phone calls and visitors. Nancy came twice that week, which was a four-hour round-trip bus ride from Glendale.

I was glad to see Nancy and grateful for contact with the outside world. On her second visit I asked, "Okay, give me the scoop. What's going on out there? What are the boys doing?"

"Well, Rose told me that Tom and Eon are playing with Lance Romance, and Mark moved them into the Complex.

I was dumbfounded. "Fuck, talk about being stabbed in the back! I'm in here doing what they wanted me to do, and Mark has the balls to fuck me like that? Why would he move that shitty band into our place? That's betrayal."

Nancy had no answers.

Double D called several times from New York. "What's it like in there?" she asked. "How much longer do you have?"

"A couple more weeks and I'll be done. I'm feeling better than I have in years."

Day by day, minute at a time, the clock was winding down. On day 27 out of 28, a nurse came into my room. "Stephen, you have a phone call at the nurses' station."

I picked up the receiver and Charlie started in frantically before I could even say hello. "Y, those girls stole your guitar! They fucking stole it!"

Everything went silent as the life I'd known came to a crashing halt. That Les Paul was everything to me. "Charlie, I have to go. I've gotta get it back."

I grabbed my suitcase and my twelve string and headed for Double D's apartment, where I knew she'd eventually show up. I didn't check out, I just left.

The bus ride back to her apartment was a blur. Her car wasn't there, but I tried the door anyway. After banging away unsuccessfully for five minutes, I decided to wait downstairs. I was half insane with anger, sorrow, rage, and betrayal. Time passed slowly, but Double D eventually returned. She turned beet red when she saw the look on my face.

"Why? What did I do to you?" I implored, trying to make sense of it.

"You cheated on me!"

"Where is it?" I yelled. "Is it upstairs? Is it in your trunk? I just want it back!" In that second, I thought about doing something unthinkable. Somehow, I restrained myself.

Double D began to sob hysterically. "It's gone. I don't know where it is!"

"What do you mean you don't know where it is? Is she part of this? Your new best friend? The evil bitch? Give me your fucking keys. I wanna check your trunk!"

"Just leave me alone! Get out of here!" screamed Double D. By now, she was bawling so hard she couldn't catch her breath and crumpled to the ground.

People walking by looked our way. This futile situation was getting me nowhere. "I'm going to the police station to report this crime," I said, furious beyond words.

Back at the Complex, I grabbed an 8 x 10 photo of me onstage with the 'Paul in 1974. I frantically scribbled on the back, all the pertinent info that tied me to the guitar, including the serial number, my stage name, my real name, and my current phone number. Time was not on my side and four hours had already passed since Charlie's fateful call. Every fucking second counted.

I busted through the door of the police station and watched men in uniforms milling about in slow motion. Breathless because I'd been running, and frantic to get my guitar back, I slammed the photo down in front of the desk sergeant. "I'm reporting a crime. My guitar's been stolen!"

The officer held up his hand. "Slow down, sir! That would be the Stolen Property Division. Have a seat over there and a detective will come and get you."

Caught somewhere between a bad dream and my worst nightmare, I lost track of time. I eventually found myself sitting at another desk. "Let's get some paperwork started. How much is the guitar worth?" said the detective.

"It's priceless!"

He looked up. "Let's try this again. How much is it worth?"

"Twenty-five," I grumbled.

Even though the form was upside down, I could see him writing –$25.

"Thousand," I added. Now I had his attention. Some people just thought it was a guitar. I knew what it was. It was the Stradivarius of electric guitars. Even if I found another '59, this one dealt me "Space Age Love", "Spacers", "The Horizon Suite". Shit, it had been writing Zolar X for almost a decade. Today, the 1959 Les Paul is one of the most highly sought-after guitars in the world and regularly fetch six-figure sums.

Looking up again briefly, the cop filled in the zeros. Not that the value of my guitar made any difference. The process dragged along at a glacial pace and made me feel invisible. Eventually, the details on the back of the photo were on the police report. The cop didn't give a shit.

"Can you send some officers over to the girl's house where I left it? I'm sure she knows where it is!" I said, desperate.

"We'll get around to that."

"But you've got to do it now! It'll be gone forever if you don't act fast!"

"Look, we have a lot of other things that take precedence over your guitar! You're not in Led Zeppelin so just cool your jets. We'll do our best to check the pawn shops, but here in Hollywood, we don't recover many stolen guitars. I'll be in touch."

I left with zero confidence, unsure as to whether they would investigate at all. I was beat down, exhausted, and destroyed. Heading back to the Complex, all I wanted was a beer and a Quaalude. I felt dead inside.

95

CLIMBING OUT OF THE SHITHOLE
1980

I had no electric guitar in the spring of 1980. Other than the acoustic twelve string, the rest of my equipment was in the possession of G, who was holding it as collateral for the cocaine I'd hoovered up my nose. Eon and Ufoian were sympathetic to my plight.

Eon patted me on the back. "We have my Les Paul so we can still play."

"It's not the guitar that made you great, it's your playing," added Ufo.

"I'll buy you another guitar, Ygarr," said Mark.

All I could muster was a sarcastic laugh. "Mark, I don't think you understand the importance of that guitar, but maybe you could hire a private investigator?"

But Mark didn't buy me a new guitar or hire a private investigator. I was drinking every day again, from morning to night. Paranoid, I thought about some of the people who'd been in my life these last few months and found them guilty of conspiring against me.

Mark was also getting on my tits. When the three of us were alone, I held an impromptu meeting with my bandmates. "We've gotta get the hell out of here. Think about it: Mark hooked you up with Lance Romance while I was in the hospital, and he was ready to dump me if given a chance. Do you want to play with Lance's band or with me?"

"Shit Ygarr, we'll follow you anywhere," said Ufo.

"We were just killing time. We had nothing else to do," added Eon.

"Then we should prepare to head north as soon as possible and get Zory back in the band. But for the time being, I'm going back to Charlie's. I can't stand this place!"

"I can stay at my girlfriend's," said Eon.

Ufo said he would move back in with Rose.

Discussing our exit plan, we knew the equipment Mark bought us was there for the plundering. He wouldn't miss one of the amplifiers or the Martin acoustic, but we unanimously agreed to leave the bad karma behind. With only our personal belongings and the clothes on our backs, we walked out the door.

Back at 8228 Sunset, my mattress was exactly where I'd left it. "Hell, Charlie. I still can't believe my 'Paul is gone," I said, popping a can of beer despondently. "I'm in shock."

I could smell wires burning as Charlie clamped his jaw and ground his teeth. "Word on the street is they sold your guitar to some rock star for $4,000 and then got busted for possession of heroin. The cops confiscated the money and drugs."

"That makes me feel a little better, but I still need an electric guitar," I said, lifting the can to my lips. At least Charlie never had a problem with my drinking.

To my surprise, Nancy stopped by the next day with a '64 Silvertone guitar she'd picked up from a pawnshop for 50 bucks.

I was flabbergasted. "Wow, Nancy. Thank you! I never thought I'd find myself saying this, but any electric guitar is better than no electric guitar. This means so much to me!" The little Silvertone wouldn't give me a Zolar X tone, but it was a fine guitar to rehearse with. It was the first step in climbing out of a very deep shithole.

"I'll be heading north in about a month. I already made contact with that "wanna-be" manager Gary in Oakland and we'll be staying with him." I said to Charlie. "We're putting Zolar X back together." We'd escaped from Mark, and now I had to make contact with Clem Fisher. Then I had to get my Hiwatt and Echoplex back from G. Once we were settled in northern Cal, I'd bring Zory up to date. Things were beginning to look up.

"Well guy, do whatever you got to do! I'm in the same boat," Charlie yelled. There was an edge of frustration to his voice and I knew why. For someone who came from money, he always seemed to have his back against the wall. "This apartment's costing me too much," he explained. "Come on, I gotta show you something."

We took the elevator down to the basement. The doors opened to cement walls, cement floors, and cement ceilings. The only color I could make out in the dim light was grey, but it was clean and the electricity worked. Although there was no kitchen, there was a bathroom with a shower and toilet, and the plumbing worked.

"Hey!" I yelled, and the sound echoed and bounced off the walls. "This would make a great rehearsal space."

Charlie smiled. "I'm gonna call it the Slab Lab. It'll be real artsy, like Andy Warhol's Factory, only in LA. We move down here next week."

Over the next two weeks, Charlie transformed the place with stuff he pulled from dumpsters. Broken lamps draped with silk scarves, mannequins with amputated arms, and an odd assortment of broken ceramics and mirrors suddenly appeared. His most prized find was a rusted machete that he placed in a corner. Almost everything in the place had been discarded, only to be brought home by Charlie and repurposed. Waste not, want not, or some shit like that.

It seemed like he was adding another mattress every other day. "Charlie, where do you find this stuff! We have five mattresses now. It looks like a looney bin with all those dirty things lined up against the wall."

"Those are for the band, guy! You never know how things will work out. I mean we're in prime real estate in the music capital of the world!"

"Okay, Charlie. And what's with the spray paint?"

Charlie picked up a can from a broken table propped against the wall. Giving it a good shake, he proceeded to write "The Slab Lab" on the cement wall in large squiggly letters. "It's art, guy! Whoever comes over can grab some paint and have at it!"

"That's great, Charlie. Say, do you still have your laser?"

"Why yeah, guy. That's what the mirrors are for. I'll rig it so the laser bounces off the mirrors and it'll create a web of light on the ceiling."

"Sounds good, Charlie." It was another brilliant idea that would probably never materialize.

Band stickers plastered the walls and a salvaged boom box with one speaker blown completed the Rock 'n' roll vibe. Restaurants and liquor stores lined the street outside and we were eight blocks from the Whisky. The Slab Lab was a punk rock hotel in the making.

8228 Sunset
Photo credit: Raidii X, pulled from video footage 2008

96

BUYER'S REMORSE

1980

ZORY ZENITH

Was I surprised when Ygarr called? Pleasantly surprised, maybe, but not shocked. Ygarr seemed to call every other year with some new opportunity for the band. This time he had difficult news.

"Shit, remember the bitch who bought my plane ticket from Kansas City? She got together with some other miserable losers and ripped off my Les Paul."

"Those little fuckers! You want me to come down there and smack 'em silly? Did you file a police report?"

"Yeah, but they didn't find it yet. I feel completely lost without my 'Paul. And that fucking Mark, and even Ufo, talked me into going to rehab. Fuck! I had no desire to play it straight, but I went along with the program just to get them off my back."

"Being a '60s kid, I would have told them to fuck off and stay out of my business."

"I tried, but they had me backed in a corner," said, Ygarr.

"You have to volunteer for that," I said. "Nobody can force you."

"Exactly. I wasn't ready."

"So what happened then?" I asked, lifting my own can of beer.

"I had to get out of there. There was all kinds of crazy shit going on. Mark hired some clowns that thought they knew the music business."

"Yeah, and what about that cute salesgirl Mark was trying to keep for himself? He was married but got all warped whenever I went near her. The whole thing started out pretty cool and we got those spandex pants, but then..."

"He kicked you out of the band."

"Yeah, jumping on the hood kind of ended that!"

Then Ygarr changed the subject. "I'm at Charlie's right now, but me and the boys are ready to head your way. We need to book some gigs, save some money, and record again. I have a killer version of your song 'Jet Star 19' and a new one called 'Timeless'. I've been talking to Clem Fisher, who wants to do an album with us. One more recording session should give us plenty to pick from."

The plan sounded good to me. "I'll contact Army Street, the studio where the Aurora Pushups recorded. Let me know when you beam in."

"Roger that."

Hanging up, I couldn't help but notice the parallel between Ygarr's drinking and my own. There was an odd, interdimensional thing that went on between us. Songwriters who work closely together sometimes pick up the same habits. John and Paul and Mick and Keith to name but a few. Success didn't seem to be part of the equation for us though.

I'd been wondering what to do about The Earthlings these last few months. All I'd been doing was running around getting drunk, and I felt as if I'd wasted another fucking year of my life. I was feeling a great deal of angst about my life and looking for the relevance at that juncture. I was hearing a lot of stuff over Christian television at the time on the subject of feeling apropos in a fast-changing world. I realized, at that moment, that was me and it was a frustrating place to be. I had the flash thought–*I didn't even have a scene anymore.*

Before Ygarr called, I'd been thinking about Zolar X. From almost any perspective, the band had come and gone. The whole thing seemed hopeless, and I always felt as if our failure to get signed was somehow partly my fault. It was such a destructive place to be that I was surprised I hadn't overdosed on alcohol. Although I never was a druggie, I think Jim Morrison and I could have sat at the same table. We would have had some discussions.

Something seemed to have passed us by. Punk, of course, and the ridiculous onslaught of horrible disco thumping on the radio every fucking day, it had rendered us irrelevant. If that weren't bad enough, the cities were saturated with dance clubs. But as embittered as I was, Zolar X was family I couldn't abandon. We'd put too much into it to back out now.

97

PONG
1980

Being back at Gary's Oakland Hills mansion was like déjà vu. We'd only been there once before at the invite of our friend Jeff, and now Gary had invited us to live and rehearse there. The place was all cocaine, horny chicks, and dysfunctional people trying to operate a band. I'd been down this road so many times it was beginning to feel like home.

Gary was a man of money who'd inherited a successful tractor-trailer business. He had a wife, Mattie, and two sons, Gary Jr., and Karl. On the side, Gary dealt drugs, mainly cocaine. The sprawling two-acre plot showcased a white, elegant, nineteenth-century mansion with white pillars, a circular driveway in front, and a decent-sized pool in the back. The interior had a spacious lived-in feel, with lots of cool features such as the solarium adjacent to the living room through the glass double doors. Tucked inside the sunroom was a comfy chair, a twin bed, and a state-of-the-art Pong video game. Ufo and I stood at the gargantuan eight-foot by twenty-foot picture window and peered down at the urban sprawl below.

"Would you look at that!" I said, wondering how we always seemed to find such generous benefactors. "You can see all the bridges: The San Mateo, the Bay Bridge, and the Golden Gate!"

"And you can see San Francisco too," said Ufo.

Instead of flipping a coin, I said, "Go ahead and choose where you want to sleep, Ufo. There's the solarium or the living room."

"Oh, I'll take the living room. It has a television with the couch."

"I know you don't like it here as much as I do, but once we start playing and you get a little coin in your pocket, your mood will improve."

After a week and a few rehearsals, Ufo still seemed disgruntled. "Why can't we ever end up in a place where I'm comfortable? This house has a weird, creepy vibe."

"You mean the loose women, the porn, the cocaine, and yet another rich guy who wants to be our manager? You mean that kind of stuff?"

"Yeah, that stuff. It never seems to end well."

"Rock 'n' roll's a crazy life and I love it," I said dismissively.

But I knew what Ufo meant. Within the first week of being there, Mattie made it clear that I had something that she wanted. Mattie must have known that Gary preferred his porn star girlfriends to her. They had a child together, so it hadn't always been this way, but Mattie found her way to my bed most nights instead of the room she referred to as "Gary's room." Gary even ate his meals there. He'd go downstairs, fix a plate, and take it back upstairs. He and Mattie lived separate lives.

One day Mattie and I were alone in the kitchen. "His room is always locked when he's out, but here's a key. He doesn't know I have it and I want to keep it that way," she said, pressing it into my hand. "And as far as the sex goes, we have an understanding."

They were swingers. Gary left the bedroom door open late at night, and I'd often see him in there with a silicone-enhanced young woman. He'd be in there fucking his catch of the day, lines of blow on a mirror, and porn playing in the background. It was a bit kinky, but I was thankful for a place to stay. I just needed to weather the storm.

We rehearsed five nights a week in a garage that had been converted to a rehearsal space. Being re-united with Zory brought back the energy that had been missing. A new dedication to the future had been established, and I was no longer wallowing in self-pity. Mattie often assembled a handful of girlfriends and their presence gave rehearsals a little extra spunk. Some songs were nearly two years old, but we'd never played them as a band before. We were playing "Space Age Love" at a blistering tempo. Short, fast, simple to play, and lyrically outrageous, newer anthems like "Timeless" and "Jet Star 19" were relevant to the times.

At one rehearsal, I plugged a Flanger I wasn't using into Ufo's bass rig. None of us were prepared for the sonic mayhem that boomed from his cabinet. Photon torpedoes screamed through the air, ripping alien worlds asunder with feedback and distortion. Our jaws dropped. This became the intro to the song "Timeless".

Within six weeks, we found ourselves at Army Street recording studio. Our engineers were Jim Keylor and Jimmy Alcivar of Ronnie Montrose and Gamma. We had a $250 budget, so as always, we had to be fast and precise. We had two days to record and one day to mix. How long did it take Axl Rose to record his last album?

On game day, we recorded "Space Age Love", followed by "Timeless", "Jet Star 19",

"Rocket Roll", "Mirrors", "I Pulled My Helmet Off", "Torrack", and finally "Parallel Galaxy". "Parallel" was a bit of a challenge, and the lead took me several tries to perfect.

We had been in high-end studios and low-end studios. We recorded at Crystal in 1974; two days, two songs. We recorded at Ardent Studios; two days, eight songs. And at the Redondo Beach garage/studio it was two days, seven songs. And now we found ourselves in San Francisco at a garage converted to a studio; three days, eight songs. I was beginning to wonder, *did everyone record this way*? After the mixing, it was playback time. Although it wasn't as loud as Ardent, Zory said what I was thinking. "Shit, this is Zolar X's greatest hits!"

Money well spent.

"I'm so proud of us," said Eon. "After all the hell we've been through, we did it. This is red hot!"

"The 'Timeless' intro is far out. I'm glad we have some shows booked," said Eon. It was nice to see him so happy about the band.

I knew we only needed four songs from this session to complete our album. "You guys sounded great," I said when the tape had stopped playing. Songs like "Timeless" and "Jet Star 19" came from a place only visited in dreams.

Photographer unknown

OUT OF THIS WORLD: THE STORY OF ZOLAR X

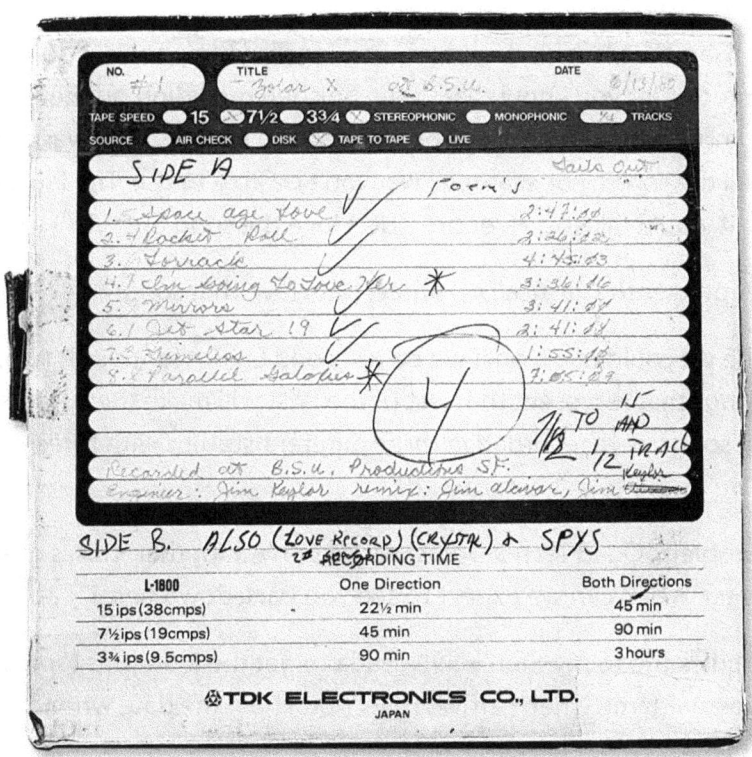

98

THE POWER OF THREE
1980

I stared at the suitcase that held everything I'd brought from LA. Packed fairly tightly, the battered valise contained random space clothes, my antennas, the recording we did in Redondo Beach, and a variety of other cassettes. I had two of the three master tapes and several copies on cassette from every major Zolar X recording session over the last three-and-a-half years. The tapes represented my life; my guarantee that Zolar X would not die with me.

My task now was to call Clem Fisher, but I had to be discreet. One phone was upstairs in Gary's room and the other was downstairs in the kitchen where there was always a lot of foot traffic. Then Gary announced he was going to the shop, so I knew he'd be gone half the day. Taking the key from the same leather pouch that held my X ring and necklace, I nervously made my way upstairs. I let myself into the room quietly and shut the door.

"Hey Clem, Ygarr here," I said, almost whispering into the phone. "I don't have much time, but I wanted to let you know that we've finished recording our newest tracks and they're killer. I know I've been putting you off for quite a while, but I wasn't completely satisfied with all the songs. For example, we won't be able to use 'The Plutonian Elf Story' because it would take up an entire side. I love the song but…"

Clem interrupted enthusiastically. "I agree, but I love that song."

"Well, maybe we could put it on if we do a second LP. But for this LP, two, three or four-minute songs that represent the best of the best will make the cut this time. And remember, the songs were recorded in three different studios with three different engineers, so we'll have to get it mastered."

"Yeah, no problem. Quad Tech Studios will be perfect for that. This is great news, Ygarr. I'll tell Peter. When can we expect to see you back down here?"

"I'll make a quick trip to my mom's in Nevada to get the Memphis tape. Then I'll have all the tapes with me when I arrive. I'll let you know the date when it gets closer."

"Can't wait, Ygarr. This is important. Zolar X's music should be out there."

OUT OF THIS WORLD: THE STORY OF ZOLAR X

99

SERMON AT THE FAB MAB
1980

ZORY ZENITH

We were amidst the punk rock, new wave movement. There was a lot of controversy going on within the DIY movement, record industry, and society in general. To me, most of punk rock was extremely shocking. I was spending my downtime watching religious shows and had turned back to the bible. I decided it was time to take the bible to the stage for our next show at the Fab Mab. I didn't think it was important to tell the boys. Why did I take a bible onstage with me? The punks would certainly wonder.

I did it for three reasons: the first was my faith, which was weak at times but strong at others. The second was the duty I felt to bring an element of truth and reality to the seemingly crazed and out of control punk scene. Thirdly, I felt that Earthers periodically needed to be brought into some sort of perspective about what was outside of this planet and its surrounding territories in space, a vast area beyond the ceiling. If I could convince even two people that the ceiling of outer space was actually the floor of heaven, or even raise their consciousness to that way of thinking, I'd be satisfied that I'd had contributed to my faith.

In keeping with that, I wanted to introduce something that wasn't completely crazy. Nothing could be more shocking to a bunch of humans who didn't believe in anything except eating, drinking, and fucking at any given moment. With that in mind, I figured I'd blow their minds by opening the bible during our new song "Millennium" at the show.

YGARR YGARRIST

The Mabuhay show was a bit of a disaster. I've known Zory long enough to know you cannot approach him when he's in that zone. He's the alpha male when it comes to winning disagreements, and at his insistence, we'd opened with "Millennium" — a lyrically optimistic song about the future with religious overtones we'd written together in '79. With a fast tempo, an aggressive power chord structure, and kick-ass accents, we were off to a dynamic start. The crowd was digging it, and Zory's vocals were about to come in. Then I glanced his way and caught the light reflecting off the gilded lettering of the Holy Bible in his hand. I thought, *oh no*.

The song sounded great, but the fact that he was holding the bible open like he was reading from it while he was singing was strange and, in my opinion, extremely out of place. We were on a rock stage, not in a church. Trying to convert supposed sinners who had come to the show anticipating good music and fun was not cool. Those close enough to notice that it was a bible were pointing at Zory and withdrawing in horror. What had begun as a real cool time had withered to a frozen group of statues looking back at us with blank faces. As the song ended, any anticipated applause had dropped off to a few weak claps. The dance floor looked and felt like a ghost town. Zory's plan to pull the audience in by shocking them had failed. Appalled and stunned, the punks backed off.

DESERTION

100

DESERTION
AUGUST 1980

"We have six more shows booked," I told Ufo. "It will be cool to be a part of the *Jerry Lewis Labor Day Telethon*, and we have the Starwood industry showcase in December."

Ufo acted like he hadn't heard me. "Rose is complaining about money," he grumbled. "I'm not making enough to support my kid, and I'm tired of sleeping on the couch and not getting enough to eat. Do you know I'm down to 110 pounds?"

I tried to add some humor to deflect the barrage of negativity coming my way. "Hell, I love weighing 110 pounds, Ufo."

"Well, that's alright for you. You get all the extra attention, the preferential treatment, and the girls, while I'm stuck here watching *Johnny Carson*!"

"Come on, U-ie! We just recorded the songs and they sound fantastic! I talked with my friend Clem and he wants to do a Zolar X album. It's going to be mastered—the whole enchilada."

"Yeah, don't get me wrong Ygarr, I love the music but… I…"

Mattie's voice rang out from the kitchen. "Ygarr, phone call—it's Zory."

I spoke briefly to Zory then hung up, hoping the news would make Ufo a bit happier. "Hey Ufo, we're invited to a barbecue at Ed Dorn's brother's house. There will be lots of food and you'll be able to fill up your tummy."

"I don't feel like it. I'm going to stay here."

I could see there was no convincing him, but wanted to try one last time. "Are you sure?"

"Yeah."

Mary and Zory picked me up for the short trip down the hill to Berkeley. The party was at a rustic, two-story house with plenty of yard space on a half-acre. The 100-strong crowd milled about drinking, smoking, and talking loudly. There was a barbecue pit, a large metal tub loaded with iced beers, and a stage with a PA system.

The Pushups were about to release a new video, and we were there to celebrate with them.

Spotting Ed and his bandmates by the stage, I went over to say hello.

"Hey, Ed."

Ed seemed happy to see me. "Hi, Steve! How'd you like Army Street? Pretty nice, huh? We recorded our 45 there."

"Yeah, it's a great little studio. I've been in worse, that's for sure," I said. "I'm gonna grab a beer and a burger."

"Cool. We gotta finish setting up. Stick around and catch our show, and thanks for coming Steve."

"Great to see you, Ed." I wasn't going to fight it. He'd been calling me Steve since 1965.

I spotted Zory munching a burger by the beer trough. As I got within earshot, he yelled in his James Brown voice, "Ow, I feel good! I see you were talking to the man."

"I had to say hello. Hell, I formed my first band with him."

"How long are we going to stay?" Mary said, glancing at Zory.

"Let's stick around for a couple of songs. I dunno how much pop music I can take," said Zory.

"That sounds good. Yeah, before we head back up the hill, I wanna grab a couple of burgers for Ufo. He's been complaining about his belly—about not getting enough to eat."

Zory swallowed another bite of burger. "He's always such a worrywart."

Ed's band was alright. They knew how to play, but they weren't punk and they weren't space rock either. We quietly departed after a few songs. Back at the mansion, Zory and Mary decided to come in and say hi to Ufo.

Mattie was bent over the kitchen counter doing a line as we walked in. "Where's Ufo? We brought him some burgers." Unable to look me in the eye and in a tone that was barely audible, she said, "I took him to the bus depot. He said he had to go home."

"Home? Back to Rose in LA?"

"No, back to Boise."

Zory and I looked at each other. "Fuck!" cursed Zory. "That little weasel! This can't be happening again?"

"Shit, his amplifier is gone, and that takes money to ship," I said. "He must have been planning this for a while."

We had shows booked and needed a bass player immediately. Within minutes I was on the phone. "Hey Eon, you're not going to believe it. Ufo took a bus back to Boise. Did you know anything about this?"

"Shit no! But I know a bass player off the top of my head. Dennis has an SVT, a Fender Precision bass, and a truck."

Eon gave me the info I needed and we said goodbye. I hung up the phone and thought about Ufo. I wish he'd been able to tell me what was going on with him. We're all just shells unless we talk.

L to R: Ufoian Ufar, Zory Zenith, Ygarr Ygarrist, Eon Flash
Photo credit: John Tremblay

L to R: Ygarr Ygarrist, Zory Zenith, Eon Flash, Ufoian Ufar
Photo credit: John Tremblay

COMMITMENT

101

COMMITMENT
1980–1981

Soon we were rehearsing hard—four to five days a week. We had to find out what Dennis could and couldn't do, *and* prepare for shows at the same time. It would be cruel to throw somebody in the fire and expect them to learn "Parallel Galaxy" or "Horizon Suite" in a couple of days. But Dennis had chops, and I could tell he would develop nicely given time. With the *Jerry Lewis Telethon* coming up, we would concentrate on what we had just recorded adding in Mirrors and the short songs. We shrank the set. We gave Dennis the music on cassette tapes which he took home to supplement his training. There were conversations about appearance, and I had to find out how far he was willing to go.

"Hey Dennis, did Eon brief you about becoming Zolarized?"

"I saw you guys at Weeks Park so I figured you would want me to do something about my haircut and eyebrows. But it can't be too extreme because of my day job."

As Zory sized him up, he added "I'll give you a little cut and trim your point. We could probably just give your eyebrows a little slant upwards."

I wanted to be clear, "We not only need to sound like Zolar X but we need to look like Zolar X too. Zory, have you been working on our new stage wear?"

"Yeah, I found these blue bodysuits and orange motorcycle jumpsuits. I just need to get the patches sewn on and they'll be ready to step into."

Dennis asked, "What about shoes?"

"You look like you're the same size as us. We found some space slippers that we've attached silver lurex to. They'll work fine." My thoughts turned to the trunk that had held all the wonderful winged suits, tights in every color, and three sets of antennas that had been lost years ago. It sure would have been nice to have still had the trunk but we were moving on somewhere? So I had to accept it. These spacesuits were mild compared to where Zolar X had been in the visual realm but Zory did his best with what he had to work with. Time went on. The Telethon was memorable and put a little money in our pockets. It was for a good cause and we helped in raising money for

Muscular Dystrophy.

Rehearsals continued and we steadily got tighter. The possibilities lying ahead were something to think about. The Starwood show was around the corner and with the industry changing, there were a lot of Indie labels that had popped up. We played a couple of small shows in the Bay Area. I couldn't escape noticing the flyers though. We were now pulling from artwork that had been created years ago. The approach to playing a gig, that spark, the enormous effort that was required; on our end, the club's end, even the wanna-be managers end had dried up. We were filling time and finally found ourselves in December, packing for the trip to LA for the Starwood show.

Gary always watched Monday-night football. He was a sports fan. As I walked past his room he said, "Ygarr come here. I've got a couple of lines for you. You into football?"

"Well, I've always been a fan of the 49ers but they don't win. They're never in contention for the Superbowl. But I'll watch a little with you. Who's playing?"

"It's the Dolphins vs the Patriots."

As we watched the hustle on the field, Howard Cosell's voice narrated. "Time out is called, three seconds remaining, and we have to say it's just a football game no matter who wins or loses. An unspeakable tragedy, confirmed to us by ABC News in New York City, John Lennon, outside of his apartment building on the west side of New York City – the most famous, perhaps, of all the Beatles, shot twice in the back! Rushed to Roosevelt Hospital. Dead on arrival."

All the anticipation for our upcoming shows was completely drained out of me. My favorite Beatle, songwriter – gone – assassinated – absolutely crazy! I called Zory immediately.

"Did you hear? John Lennon was murdered?"

"Yeah, I just heard. To lose John is such a huge loss no matter how you spin it. The whole world is going to be mourning. This is profound! And he's so young, just 40 years old."

"Let's dedicate our set when we play the Starwood, to John Lennon. Shit, I can't believe he's dead!"

The cluster of shows we had booked I could only describe as lack-luster. Sure, we ended up with a little coin in our pockets, the music sounded good, but we looked like four guys with instruments that were ready to dance ballet. Maybe it was me, maybe it was the fact that the 'Paul was gone but it felt like we were trying to fix something that was unrepairable. The days of having options for stage clothes were gone. The babbles and accessories had evaporated. Instead of saying, "What color tights are you going to wear under that wing?" Now it was more like, "Are we wearing the navy blue or orange paratrooper suits?" I've never, never liked navy blue. But instead of creating a ripple, I let the Captain–Zory Zenith–call the shots.

I was at Zory and Mary's apartment. Having another place to go, a change of scenery was nice. We were rehearsing vocals for our show in San Rafael that night and the phone rang.

Mary looked at me and said, "There's some guy named Rock Bottom for you." I was stunned.

"Hey Rocky. How are you doing? How'd you find me?"

"Charlie gave me your number."

"Where are you?"

"I'm at San Francisco International. Give me your address. I'm catching a cab. And I want you to play a Spy show tomorrow night in L.A."

"Shit Rock, I'm playing tonight in San Rafael with Zolar X. You can catch our show."

"Cool Ygarr! Yeah! I've always wanted to see your other band. I don't know how long it'll take this cab to get to your apartment, but I'll buzz when I'm there."

As I hung up the phone, I turned to Zory and Mary, "Is it okay if Rock sleeps here tonight? It'll just be for one night. He wants me to fly down to LA with him for a Spy show at the Hong Kong Café tomorrow night."

Zory looked at Mary, "Sure! Let's drive down. We can stay at my parent's place."

I think it is important to mention that there was no competition between the two bands. I would have gladly continued along that path with the Spys a few years ago but that path deteriorated. And Zolar X was never a "fallback" plan–ever. I don't know if I would call Zolar X a flower or a weed but when you think it's dried up or dead, it sprouted anew.

I was looking at two shows, back to back, two different nights, with two different bands–"my bands"; one night in northern California and the second night in southern California. The analogy of the word parallel comes to mind when I think back to those shows. It was a historic moment for me. Both of my frontmen were in the same house and it flipped each night. I was on stage with Zory one night and we looked out into the audience and saw Rock. He was enjoying the show, smiling and clapping. Zory was at his best. The Spys show in LA was just as rare. There were no rehearsals, just straight out of the gate going from memory. We played the songs that we had recorded two years previously. It was great seeing Frank and Ian again. The Spys show was not better by any means but it was different. To think that Rock had flown to San Francisco with a round-trip ticket and a ticket for me for one Spys show. I felt honored and it was like he was saying "we need you Ygarr." And to look out into the crowd and see Zory, the whole thing was a surprise, a happening, an event. It loosened up the doldrums.

When I got back, I felt spunky. There was something about being a musician and a performer – things we needed and craved; an audience, the applause, and the sensuality of rubbing shoulders with groupies. Those things had been missing. But probably just as important was the realization of the isolation of where and what I had been doing. I had been on an island – the Oakland Hills mansion – and I was shipwrecked. It was time to change that.

Over the phone, I submitted my game plan, "Hey Nancy, I need to get back to Hollywood. I'm going nuts up here. These people treat me good, but I need to get back into the loop, the action."

Without hesitation, she said, "I can get an apartment and you could live with me."

"That would be terrific! Let me know when you're ready and I can start shipping you my new equipment that I've accumulated here in Oakland."

Two more shows were coming up in Sacramento–Friday and Saturday night. We were headlining and got $250 per night. The crowd was awesome. We were playing Zolar X's greatest hits and were pounding home what the world was craving – a fast, loud, intense, short, and melodic set. What ensued over that weekend was a debacle of pleasure. I took advantage of the aggressive, loose women that approached me afterward. Sex, drugs, and Rock 'n' roll was the pinnacle of my escapades. There was a silent wave of trouble in the air – Angel Dust, police, and friction. And then reality slapped me in the face. It was time to get a grip.

None of us exchanged words like, "I'm done", "I'm quitting", or "I give up". It never came as a concrete decision to hang up our guitars, microphone, or drumsticks. Instead, it was more like allowing the unspoken idea to emerge, of letting things dissolve into memories of the past. There was something zapped from me. In becoming a Zolarian, it's a commitment to that life. It's much more than cutting your hair into a point or drawing your eyebrows up – it's an attitude, it's believing, it's feeling the desires and passions and it takes a while, if ever, to achieve that. Little did I know going into that weekend that it would be the last two times that Zolar X would play in the 20th Century.

L to R: (Top) Zory Zenith, Eon Flash, (Bottom) Dennis Souza, Ygarr Ygarrist 1980

Photo credit: Jeff Austin

L to R: Dennis Souza, Eon Flash 1980

Photo credit: Mikey Souza

STARWOOD
DEC. 14TH, 1980

Zory Zenith 1980
Photo credit: Mikey Souza

Ygarr Ygarrist 1980
Photo credit: Mikey Souza

102

LEAP OF CONVICTION
OCTOBER 1981

I flew to Los Angeles in October of 1981. In many ways, this was a monumental leap of faith. Nancy and I married, and I had a new job, putting together a Zolar X LP. Over the next few months, Clem and I listened to every song in the Zolar X catalog. I listened with a fervent ear. Anything that was slightly off–a note, a beat, a word went on the "doesn't make the cut" list. I selected. "Space Age Love", "Energize Me", and the "Horizon Suite" from the Memphis tape and without a doubt, the Zolarian poem now dubbed "Recitation". From the Redondo Beach recording, I chose "Science" and "Test Tube Baby". I liked "Blues on Blue" and it was on the alternate list–a maybe. And the pièces de résistance from the Army Street sessions – "Timeless", "Jet Star 19", "Mirrors", and "Rocket Roll". As I calculated the length of each song, I realized "The Horizon Suite" would have to be broke apart to give more flexibility in arranging the songs for airplay.

Nancy worked graveyard so I had a lot of time on my hands and word had spread that I was back in town. Elias stopped by frequently and one night he said, "Hey, Charlie's having a party at his Slab Lab. You wanna go?"

"Shit yeah! I haven't been over there since I left LA in 1980."

"The place is getting pretty crusty."

"I figured that. So much for it being an 'Andy Warhol Factory-West.' Let's head down to the Boulevard and catch the 91W."

The basement at 8228 was wall-to-wall people. Most of them I had never, ever seen. An indistinct roar blended from fifty different conversations going at once and was punctuated by a scream here and there, someone yelling in a drunken blitz, and blasts of distorted music coming from a boom box. It was almost deafening.

I leaned into Elias and yelled, "Who are these fucking losers?"

Elias leaned towards me and directed his words towards my ear and yelled, "Oh Charlie lets anybody in, drunks that follow him home and ladies of the night come in to piss then they go back out."

"Shit!" I looked across the room and saw a guy pissing on the floor and the people standing around him were either laughing or were so wasted they didn't notice. "Where the hell is Charlie? I can't believe it. He lives here, this is his apartment and it's a damn crash pad!"

The wall that Charlie had declared as the place to make spontaneous art now had primitively drawn illustrations of people having sex, sexual parts, and cuss words scrawled across the cement.

I went into the bathroom to pee and the stench was overpowering almost knocking me on my ass. The toilet no longer worked and people had been taking shits in the toilet with no way of flushing it. It was like walking into an outhouse in a modern bathroom. I found Elias and said "This is a song waiting to be written. Let's get the hell out of here."

"But we haven't seen Charlie yet."

"I'll catch up with him later."

Slab Lab
8228 through the alley's broken gate
You enter at your own risk into the cement abyss
Broken bottles, empty beers, lost souls, wasted years
Hookers with stiletto heels, junky bangers popping pills

Sirens wailing, cops with cuffs, Fire marshal's, acting tough
Void of humanity, kick in the door that was the key
Crash pad promenade, blood spilt, trash bouquet
Music faded, art cried, overdoses, many died

Not for the faint of heart, across from Chateau Marmont
A haven for punk refuges, dirty mattress, new disease
Needle, spoon, dope and cotton, cocaine plans, names forgot
On Sunset in tinsel town, LA's underground?

DESTINATIONS
1982

There was a new drug in town called Loads and of course, my connection with Elias made it available. This drug was in demand – the partiers, the druggies of the underbelly of Hollywood, a big chunk of society- they were at every party and every get-together. People were either on them, selling them, or buying them. Hollywood doctors and pharmacies made a fortune. If you had them you were King Shit and here's the thing – if you got a prescription with your name on them, it was legal! Obviously, in my return to Hollywood, my bad habits again rose to the surface but even that could not deter me from my quest.

Over the next few months, Clem and I got together regularly. He told me about his friend Peter who wanted to back the project.

"Okay Clem, my vision for the album is I want it to be clear vinyl. It just sounds like Zolar X–futuristic, spacey. You'll pull out this clear LP and see the silver Zolar X logo on a black label. We can have the song titles on each side, very professional. It'll be special with Armando Norte artwork on the cover. He's an incredible artist! I've already been in contact with him and it's almost finished."

Clem listened and said, "That sounds great Ygarr. What about the song "Blues on Blue"? Didn't you want that on a 45?"

"Yeah, that would be a good promotional tool. The 45 would be the only way anyone could get it. And I think it would be the perfect little song to hit the AM radio stations. "Science" and "Blues on Blue" on one side and "Mirrors" on the other side."

"First things first, I'll run all your ideas past Peter since he's footing the bill. We've scheduled the mastering for next week."

"Damn, this is exciting Clem. I've been wanting to get Zolar X's music on vinyl for almost a decade. I've got to thank you for believing in the same thing that I believe in – that the music is great."

"I'll see you next week at Quad Tech Studios."

Phone calls with Zory became spaced further and further apart but there was one particularly odd call, even for Zory.

"Hey, Bot!"

"Hey, Ygarr. What are you up to?"

"I'm working on our album, you know the DIY that I told you about a couple of months ago."

"Oh yeah. That again. The solo project?"

I sharply replied, "No, it's our music, the music we wrote together!"

Changing the subject he said, "I have a proposition for you. I need an Elvis Presley, Rockabilly-type vintage microphone. I've been looking for one up here and haven't had any luck. I'm sure you could find one down there and I'll trade you for my Mosrite 12-string."

"I just saw one of those. I think it was a 1960 Shure – you know the big, wide silver kind. It sounds like I'm getting the better end of the bargain but hell, I'd love your 12-string."

"Well, I'll be down in a couple of weeks to visit my parents, so we'll make the trade then."

As I hung up the phone I was running it through my brain. *The Mosrite? He loves that guitar. Why was he willing to trade a $300 instrument for a $60 mic? It sounded suspicious but I was willing to do it.*

ZORY ZENITH

I guess you could say I've always been a media shark. Always feeding that innate part of myself with information, trends, and tracing shit back to their roots then creating something new from it. Over the past few years, several things had happened and began to collide. When I was stationed at one of the hair salons – my day job, the owner had a collection of tapes that he liked to play throughout the day. One of them was Robert Gordon who was on RCA. Robert had become an iconic, underground musician after leaving a new wave band he was in. He took the classic style of country tunes and bumped them up a bit – like what Ygarr did with "Jet Star 19". Robert's stuff was junked up and Ricco crazy. Also, I had been affected deeply by the deaths of Elvis Presley in '77 and Keith Moon in '78.

When Elvis passed away, it was like a sucker-punch to the gut. It was tragic. I mean the dude was 42 years old. After I read more about all the shit surrounding his death and the revelations started to surface that it was self-inflicted, I realized, *oh this guy was fucked up!* You know? Those were hard details to swallow. There had been deaths in the Rock 'n' roll community all through the 60s and 70s but Elvis? Come on! Elvis had started as a rock 'n rebel that all the grownups shook and quaked over and preachers preached against from the pulpit. Then he went into the army and ended up becoming the boy next door–America's male sweetheart. Elvis dying affected me personally and profoundly. I don't know why. I mean I wasn't a rabid fan but felt like I had lost a family member for some reason. Maybe it took me back to my childhood, the long-ago days of living in West Virginia. In '76, when I first saw the place where Elvis had recorded at Sun Records, it looked stripped down and bare-bones. There were a couple of the old broadcaster mics sitting in the corner and maybe a few wires hanging on the wall. It struck me how small the recording booth was. I thought wow! We'd already been to Crystal and Ardent Studios and Sun Records just didn't look like anything but after Elvis passed away, I guess you could say I got bit by the Rockabilly bug and started researching Sun Records, started collecting his LPs- catching up and just kind of got into that whole scene. I thought, somebody has to do a good tribute to him but I didn't want to do the tried and true stuff that a 50's band would do, it would have to be the obscure stuff. Once again, there was a break in Zolar X so why not.

OUT OF THIS WORLD: THE STORY OF ZOLAR X

104
LEAKING SECRETS
1982

It was like radar – the word had spread that I had the place to myself after 9:00 pm. I'd walk Nancy to the bus stop to go to work and when I got back to the apartment, people started arriving. Like a cavalcade, here they came–a barrage of visitors, anywhere from people just wanting to hang out, to see if I had any dope for sale, or invitations to parties. I was back in the apartment and was just settling in and heard a tap on the window then heard a call from the other side of the glass, "Ygarr, Rock Bottom. I got something for you."

I hadn't seen him since our gig a year ago. He had a guitar case with him.

"New guitar? It looks like a Fender."

"It's a Telecaster. Wait till you see the color! It's orange with a maple neck. I've got a new song I want to show you."

As he was pulling it out of the case I exclaimed, "Hell, I'd call that shocking orange. That's a beauty. I've got a new electric too."

"Before I play the new song this is what I really wanted to give you. You helped make it happen." A notebook was lying at the bottom of the case. In one smooth motion, he scooped up the notebook letting the pages fall open exposing a 7-inch vinyl in a white sleeve. He handed the package to me.

As I pulled the black vinyl out the first thing that struck me was seeing my name alongside Rock's. "It looks official," and I read aloud the printed text, *"Written by Rock Halsey and Stephen Della Bosca."*

"Yeah, I wasn't going to put you on it but my mom said I'd better do the right thing. She gave me the money to press them."

I was thinking, *why would Rock want to leave me off the record?* I finally said, "Shit Rock, I wrote, recorded, and formed a damn band with you! That's fucked up. Thank God your mother was thinking and persuaded you to be honorable."

"I don't know what I was thinking. I guess I was mad at you for choosing Zolar X over us."

As I turned the 45 over to Side B I asked, "How many copies did you have made?"

He grinned and said smugly, "Enough."

"And you're giving me just one?"

"That's all I brought with me. I bounce around all over the place. I gotta show you this song. It's called Leaking Secrets."

"Let me grab my cassette recorder and I'll record it for you. Here, you can play it on my acoustic."

My first impression was it sounded more like a David Bowie influence than punk rock. I liked it and was very intrigued by the texture of his voice and the lyrics. When it got to the chorus, I found myself wondering as he sang, "Gee I thought it nice you write to me. But what was it that made you think of me." Where were these lyrics coming from? This was a different character than I had written music with a few years ago. It was also a mystery of how it made me feel when I listened to it. It hung heavy in the air for me.

"That's definitely different Rock. That's a ballad. It's like a premonition or a message in a bottle."

We talked a little longer, got a buzz-on and then he left. It would be the last time I saw him.

105
LEGACY
1982

All systems go! Ready for liftoff, Quad Tech Studios mastering – Day 1: I was beyond excited for this opportunity. I met Clem outside the small storefront. I had a leather briefcase that Nancy had given me which held the tapes and the typed tracklist we would be working with. We made our way inside and were greeted by Hank Waring who was the owner of the place and he was also the mastering engineer. It's kind of amazing looking back; with all the times I had recorded over the years I had never been involved with mastering. I found out very quickly that a mastering studio was a lot different from a recording studio. At Quad Tech, the room was small, 10' x 20'. Machines and multiple tape decks lined both walls and there were elevated speakers everywhere. There was no place for anything else except us and my briefcase. After introductions, I jumped right in with letting Hank know there were three tapes we would be working with. "And there's one song, 'The Horizon Suite', that's 10 minutes long that I want to cut into three sections. It'll give it a better chance for airplay." I pulled out my paperwork that had the songs from each tape I had typed weeks before and stacked the three boxes on the counter in front of the tape machines.

Hank didn't seem to be concerned and I could tell he was a seasoned mastering engineer. "Yeah, sure. We can do that. Let's see what you got here. The first thing we'll do is take a listen to all the cuts that will be the album. I want to make sure the quality of your recordings is top-notch. Which tape do you want to start with?"

"Let's start with the 16-track Memphis tape. The first one up is 'Recitation.'" Hank mounted the tape onto the spindle and threaded it onto the take-up reel. He pushed the play button and the sound boomed into the small space taking us to another orbit. *NOP TREA VU-DURAZ...*

"Holy shit!" Hank yelled. "Sounds like something from Star Wars. It's the force! What's he saying?"

"That's the Zolarian language. It's a greeting to planet Earth."

Clem yelled over the sound, "Isn't it cool?"

"I want this track to open up the album and get their attention!"

Clem said, "That's Zory!"

"Yeah, the Zor-bot. We worked on our own language which we called Zolarian throughout the early years. It made its way into the songs, was a lot of fun but I haven't spoken it in years."

This was a really big deal. And I couldn't help but think, there I was a songwriter with an ego, and I was having to become a producer, on the fly, without the ability to remix anything. What was on those tapes is what we had to work with. I knew what we'd end up with was a representation of Zolar X. This would be what planet Earth would come to know as the Zolar X sound so things like the quality of the mix, the vocals, and instrumentation was what was guiding me. Hank was busy taking notes on the selection of the tracks. He asked, "What's the name of that one? I really like it."

"That's 'Moonbeam'. I wrote it in 1971 and recorded it in '76."

"You don't think it's good enough for the album?"

"Oh, I think it's good enough. I just don't want people to think that I was ripping off the song 'Cat Scratch Fever.'" I looked at Clem, "Are we still going to release that promotional 7 inch?"

"Oh yeah, Peter loves that song 'Blues on Blue'. It's a mover, very Rock 'n' roll."

Hank said, "I'll add it to my list."

We spent six hours that first day just listening.

Day 2: We transferred the tracks from the three tapes onto a brand-new tape, the Quad Tech master tape. We spent the remainder of the day working on the full-length "Horizon Suite". Two cuts, three tracks, and each was recorded onto another new tape. The three sections of "The Horizon Suite" were then manually cut and spliced back onto the master Quad Tech Studio tape. Hank said, "Now we know what songs are going to be on the album. It's going to be a dynamite record. All that work we did on "The Horizon Suite" will be worth it. Thirteen tracks Ygarr, now all you have to do is arrange the order."

Day 3: I returned with a typed sheet of credits, the Zolar X logo artwork that would be on the album label, and the kick-ass album cover art created by Armando Norte. It was a full day of mastering. Hank squeezed out every inch of sound, brought out every buried note through all his mechanical knowhow in the world of frequencies, dials, and buttons. If he wanted to make the vocal a little louder, he could. If he wanted to soften a pounding cymbal or pull more out of the recordings, he did. Every track was pushed to the edge of extreme Rocket roll with decibels as the perfect balance of treble and bass emerged. The experience of being in it and watching it unfold landed somewhere between wizardry and surrealism.

I turned to Clem, "How long does this process take? When will I have them in my hand?"

"Oh, maybe three weeks."

"How many are you having pressed?"

"A thousand of the clear LPs and a hundred of the promotional 45s."

"Fantastic! I can't wait. You've got everything you need Clem. You have the master, the artwork, and the tracklisting and credits. Let me know."

Within days I got a call from Clem.

"Hey, Clem."

"Ygarr, the printshop called and said they're finished with the artwork. Can you pick it up for me? I'm really busy."

"Sure. I'll go this afternoon."

"Cool. It's in North Hollywood on Cahuenga Blvd and Barham Blvd."

"Oh yeah, I know the place."

It was easy enough to find, exactly where I thought it would be in a little strip mall. Walking up to the desk, I told the man, "I'm here to pick up the artwork for Zolar X and Clem Fisher." He said, "I'll be right back" and disappeared through a door into the back room. He was gone for about five minutes and came back empty-handed.

I started to feel uneasy not seeing anything in his hands. He shrugged his shoulders and said very matter-of-factly, "It looks like someone already picked it up."

I needed to know and prompted him, "What do you mean someone picked it up! Who?"

"Don't know. They didn't say. There's nothing here under that name."

I could see there was no point in trying to pull answers from a dude that didn't care and had no clue what this was about. I was pissed and headed for Clem's who was ten minutes away.

"What the fuck Clem. They told me somebody picked up the artwork, that it wasn't there."

He was half-whacked out on speed and said, "It wasn't me!"

"Hell Clem, who else besides you and Peter knew it was there?"

"I don't know what to tell you. I thought they were finished with it and you were picking up the prints."

"What the fuck are you talking about! There's no way 1,000 album covers would fit into my little car. You told me to pick up the artwork. The artwork Clem! Is there even going to be an album?" I searched his face looking for something, some sign, that would tell me this was going to end differently than the direction it was heading but I got nothing. "This is futile," I said as I stormed out feeling extremely pissed off. Mentally kicking myself in the ass I thought, *I could have very easily had a couple prints of Armando's artwork made just so I had a copy of it but didn't*. It was another endeavor unraveling before my eyes and lost to time.

That night Peter called me. "Hey Ygarr, I just wanted to let you know the albums are being pressed as we speak. We should have them within a week. Can you come up with a Zolar X insert that we can place in the clear plastic sleeve?"

"Fuck, all my Zolar X pictures are at my Mom's house in Nevada."

"Don't you have something, anything – pictures – that would work?"

"I do have a few prints on copy paper from a photograph of me on stage."

"That'll work. And hey, we can only afford to press ten of the 7-inch promos."

I was pissed alright, pissed at Clem and Peter for conning me, for losing shit, or stealing shit and changing shit. It was all changing behind my back – I just didn't know the full extent of it yet.

A month later there was a knock at the door. As I swung the door open, I could see it was Clem. He said, "Better late than never. I have a box of 25 for you."

We went down to the car and he opened the trunk. The box was open and half full. At first, all I saw was pink–the insert showing through the clear sleeve. They had taken the photo I gave them and had black and white prints made on cheap pink paper. I reached in and pulled one out. As I turned the insert over, I could see the songs were in the order that I wanted. It was sinking in. I was holding a Zolar X album in my hand and it was clear. Clear vinyl. There was the Zolar X logo and the name of the album underneath, …"*TIMELESS*"… It was the music that we had started in 1973 and I was staring at it, holding it in my hand. What I didn't get was my dream record. The label on the vinyl was red and I had typed out 'From 1973, To 1982' to be the text on Side A. Now it said 'From_____ To_____'. The credits that I had typed had been changed. Things were added to the text that I had no idea where they came from. My name wasn't even spelled correctly – all the things that weren't – the Armando Norte album cover art, the sealed package, the slick look of a professionally-done package. But no matter how pissed, no matter how cheated I felt, the days, weeks, and months before that day, now it was in my hand.

I wanted the album to be called *Timeless*…I wanted the music of Zolar X to be preserved and not be lost to oblivion. I knew there were photos of us floating around the planet that painted a picture of four spaced-out weirdos but there was no music until now. I had changed that!

TIMELESS
SIDE 1
Recitation (0:51)
Timeless (2:00)
Science (1:25)
Test Tube Baby (1:42)
Mirrors (3:50)
Overture on Air (2:40) [Horizon Suite]
Space Age Love (3:20)
SIDE 2
Tomorrow's Sunrise (3:30) [Horizon Suite]
Rocket Roll (2:33)
Energize Me (4:32)
Jet Star 19 (2:38)
Inside the Outside (2:47) [Horizon Suite]
Sound Barrier (1:30) [Horizon Suite]

OUT OF THIS WORLD: THE STORY OF ZOLAR X

The music industry had shut the door. There were the friends that dropped away and some bandmates that dissolved into the frays of society. There were the lies and the betrayals, the ups and downs, the near misses. But these songs, they couldn't be stolen. A guitar is a guitar and words are words but music – it's like breathing and to survive you just keep going. Don't ever quit. Don't ever jump ship.

CONTINUING MISSION: 1983 - ?

EPILOGUE

CONTINUING MISSION: 1983 - ?

YGARR YGARRIST

In '83 I found myself hooking up again with Eon and Ufo putting a new band together. It fizzled before it got started. Ufo headed back to Boise, ID *again*. Eon vanished to northern California.

I did some recording in an 8-track studio. Two of those songs; *Children of Darkness* and *Now You See It Now You Don't*, are on the Zap! You're Zolarized CD.

I got together with my old bandmate from the Spys, Ian Icon. We recorded a couple of punk tunes that he was planning to release as Deep Six. We smoked a hell of a lot of pot and drank beer like there was no tomorrow.

Money was a necessity, so I got a job delivering packages but still managed to have music in my life. I got together with Blank Frank and Rick Wilder spiraling deeper into my alcohol addiction. Blank Frank and I played a Halloween show with Rick Wilder's band, the Mau Mau's where I ran into a lot of old acquaintances from the Canterbury. Loads were still wiping people out in numerous fatal overdoses.

In '86 my addiction finally forced Nancy out of my life and I ended up with a bunch of assholes in my apartment to help pay rent.

When I was straight it seemed like life was a world of pipe dreams. I tried to escape it but every way I went it continued to backfire. In a rare moment of lucidity, I called my mom in Reno. "I'm going to die if I stay here in LA. Can you come pick me up?" I asked, sober but not for long. She was there the next day. This was the beginning of a very long road to recovery.

I got a real job in 1988. It was my apprenticeship in learning how to live like an Earther. I got sober in 1989 and have been sober since. I'd be dead if I hadn't made that call.

In the late '90s, I sold my Spys 45 to a man in Hollywood who put me in contact with Ryan Richardson, who reissued it. Ryan also gave me the news that Rock Bottom was serving time in federal prison. I began corresponding with Rock and still have twelve letters from him.

Chuck Nolan, a fan who saw a photo of Zolar X in *Creem* magazine, contacted me in 2002 and put me in touch with Zory Zenith. We hadn't spoken since 1982.

Chuck also hooked me up with Jello Biafra of Alternative Tentacles Records. I found out that he'd purchased the clear album from a San Francisco record store and loved it. He proceeded to buy as many of the albums as he could find and sent them to friends all over the world. Those friends made cassettes and shared them with other friends. Unbeknownst to me, Zolar X music had been making its way around the world. Jello wanted to take things to the next level and put out a Zolar X album on his Alternative Tentacles label.

I talked to Zory on the phone a handful of times to relay the exciting news. Although I thought he'd be excited, I could tell he was mostly intoxicated. I remember him saying, "Zolar X is your baby, and my baby is Billy Bo Day." Although Bot's voice was the same, his tone was different. We'd trekked up Laurel Canyon in our space boots together and had been through so much, but now there was a major disconnect between us.

ZORY ZENITH

I launched my band Billy Bo Day and the Howlers in the early '80s. It was a good gig, and we made decent money playing five nights a week in Las Vegas. This went off and on, back and forth, for about three years.

In 1991, I moved to Oregon. Even though I was a functional alcoholic who spent most evenings drinking beer, I got a job and went to work. I almost wanted to blow my brains out when Kitty, or Ve Neill, won an Oscar for her makeup work on *Mrs. Doubtfire*, but I was happy that somebody from our team had made it.

I was incapacitated as far as music went. My whole life at that point was about getting up, putting on a pot of coffee, hopping into my VW van, and working to make money for booze. That went on for quite a while.

By the time Ygarr and I reconnected in 2002, I was trying to resurrect Billy Bo Day again. I wasn't looking for anything to happen with Zolar X. Although I wanted to help Zolar X achieve the recognition it deserved, I couldn't imagine another resurrection of the band. I just couldn't see it, couldn't get a vision of it.

People in my neighborhood liked to party, and one of those people became my drinking buddy, Bob. Our "friendship" was just a big swirl of crap, and we both functioned in a state of semi-oblivion for months on end. Bob and I eventually got into a conflict when I confronted him for physically abusing his kids, his friends, and me as well. He attacked me several times and I let it go, but there was also the question of whether he and my wife were having an affair. Bob assaulted me again one night, and I cracked him over the head with a two-liter bottle of wine that was nearly empty. I knocked the living shit out of him and that's what he deserved. Bob didn't die and even testified on my behalf at the trial, but Oregon had some bullshit minimum sentencing policy and I got ten years.

YGARR YGARRIST

I remember getting the news that Zory was going to prison. Both my frontmen were doing long stretches in the slammer. I couldn't believe it, or maybe I could.

My life was much better since I'd gotten sober. I'd safeguarded Zolar X music and pictures all those years, and by 2003 it was starting to pay off. The *Timeless* reissue was released in August, 2004. I reconnected with Eon and Ufo and we jammed a few songs. "We should put the band together to promote the album," I suggested.

We separated with that on our minds, but Ufo decided to get married instead of reforming the band. "She's a really good cook," he told me, as if that was a good reason not to play Rock 'n' roll. Jello Biafra put me in contact with the Canadian bass player Jett Black. Jett became Jett Starsystems, and I also reconnected with artist Armando Norte. With the reissue came some attention from magazines and newspapers. We also appeared on radio shows such as *Jonesy's Jukebox* and *Rodney on the Rock*.

I began getting letters from Zory. He wrote lyrics from prison and those lyrics became "Sci-fi Head", "Saucers on Sunset", and "Eternity" to name a few.

So many things were moving at light speed. I began to daydream about future possibilities. I had several proposals to make a Zolar X documentary and a movie. The best offer came from Chuck Nolan and an Illinois company. Filming began at the Knitting Factory – our first live show in Los Angeles in 25 years. Needless to say, it was sardines that night. With the filming of the show, the documentary was officially underway.

Chuck was the project director, and I met the producer Rhaine Heissinger, who was also a videographer, graphic designer, writer, and musician. It didn't take me long to realize I wanted her to be part of my life. I told myself we would marry, and all I had to do was talk her into going along with the plan. Rhaine became Raidia Visual-X, aka Raidii X, my mate for life. There was something about her that grabbed me from the inside.

To date, the documentary Starmen on Sunset has not seen the finish line. We moved on from that project and once the decision was made, we decided to write this book to bring the Zolar X story to planet Earth.

In October of 2005, I got the shocking news that Rock had been murdered in prison. Through his letters and my contact with Ryan Richardson, I found out that Blank Frank, Ian Icon, Joel Martinez, Jesus Elias Moralez – all the original Spy members that recorded the classic Spy single had died under a variety of circumstances; even Rock's wife Penny, overdosed on heroin. And I was the last man standing. There are some feelings in life that no words can describe.

Zolar X reformed in 2005, with me on lead guitar and vocals, Eon Flash drumming, and Jett Starsystems on bass. We did some touring and played 36 shows, including the Alternative Tentacles Showcase at SXSW. Zolar X recorded "X Marks the Spot." I moved to Illinois and Raidii and I became engaged.

We also visited Zory in prison, twice. The first and most vivid visit was in 2006. It was the first time Zory and I had seen each other since 1981. Only seeing prison life from my living room TV, this was a definite reality check. I mean this was prison; restricted movement, restricted diet, restricted everything! There was a long laundry list of dos and don'ts that were expected of all visitors, or we wouldn't get in. After an extensive check in we found ourselves being escorted along a corridor outside which ran between two buildings. The sides and top were lined with barbed wire. We eventually came to the visitor's arena in another building - a noisy crowded room that was like a large mess hall. Tables were randomly scattered across the room where inmates and visitors got caught up with exchanging the brief moments and recounts of outside life. The officers that ushered us in said, "They'll be bringing him out in couple of minutes."

From across the room I spotted Zory. What a surreal moment. He appeared at the doorway and then mechanically bobbed his head from side to side like he was looking for us. He was making an entrance in prison fatigues! He began robotically miming, gliding around the perimeter of the room and then making his way towards us slipping in and out between the tables. What should have taken 30 seconds to get to us took three minutes. I couldn't believe it. He was acting like it was a stage. As he came closer, I got a clearer look. His hair was natural dark brown, and I noticed his cheeks were red. I figured he had been preparing for our visit and with no makeup available, had been pinching his cheeks to give himself some color.

One of the guards leaned in and said, "You can hug one time then that's it. No more touching."

There was some reminiscing, some small talk, questions about his safety.

"Are you okay Bot?" "Yeah, I'm okay."

CONTINUING MISSION: 1983 - ?

We missed an hour of visitation time as we were traveling between shows during the Thor tour, so the time went quickly. He looked around and quickly bent over pulling out a small torn piece of paper from his sock. It was a list of items he desired, how to deposit money into his account and there were a couple names of people he was trying to locate.

So many things flashed through my brain all at once. In a weird way, I wasn't surprised that Zory ended up there. I had seen his anger. Remember, I'm the guy he pointed a gun at and then pulled the trigger. At the same time, hell, it was also great to see him, but in those surroundings, it was heartbreaking. His timing was lousy at best, I mean just when Zolar X was going to release the reissue with Jello he got put away. I couldn't help thinking, *you should be on stage with me. Zolar X is finally getting our "due" but it's without you.* That October I had already heard that Rock was killed in prison so the fear factor that some red neck might pop Zory was real. I made it a point to keep that to myself and finally told him when he got out many years later. Those nightmarish flashes of thoughts and worries that zipped across my brain were what Bot had to endure every day. It's a damn shame when murderers get parole in seven years and Bot got a 10-year, no-chance-of-parole, sentence for assault.

Jett was let go and Quasar was brought in as bassist in 2007. That lineup appeared on *America's Greatest Band*, but we didn't win. As always, Zolar X was just a bit too "out there" for mainstream consumption. We released the 7" vinyl from the Crystal Studios recording session, complete with amazing artwork from Armando Norte (aka X-Etron) and Stephen Banes (aka Vion Beemz.)

Later that year, *X Marks the Spot* was released. The band also self-released *Zap! You're Zolarized*. Quasar quit and Eon said he couldn't do it anymore.

With nothing to hold us back, Raidii and I headed for the bright lights of Hollywood in 2008. Of all people, we moved in with Charlie Patton. Although he was still the same old Charlie, he'd inherited some money and was now a millionaire. Raidii and I began playing select LA clubs as a duo, which was enormously fulfilling. We were married on August 8, 2008 in Las Vegas. My efforts had finally paid off.

A bass player Rick Swanson contacted me one day and said, "I'm your new bass player." Rick, who'd been in the Pushups with Ed Dorn, became Moto Bass Unit. We contacted Ron Eiseman (aka Eclipse) to see if he wanted to play drums, and we soon had a new lineup: me on lead guitar and vocals, Raidii X on keyboards and vocals, Moto Bass Unit on bass guitar and vocals, and Eclipse as the drummer. Zolar X was back.

OUT OF THIS WORLD: THE STORY OF ZOLAR X

The band needed more equipment, so I decided to sell my original 1966 *Star Trek* phaser. In an attempt to have it authenticated, Zoann had sent close-up photos of me holding it in 2002 to Sotheby's auction house. They weren't convinced, and their reply read something like this: "Mr. Della Bosca, we cannot authenticate your collectible from the attached photographs, but we'd be more than happy to work with you if you can get it authenticated from a verified source." Sadly, we had no idea how to do that.

One night, Raidii was looking on the Internet for ways to authenticate the phaser. She eventually found a picture of a phaser on a *Star Trek* fan website and called me over. "Hey, that looks like my hand!" I said, leaning into the computer screen. "I have a small scar by my thumb just like that." Then it hit me, it *was* my hand, holding *my* Star Trek phaser. It was the picture Zoann had sent Sotheby's six years ago, and the caption stated that it was authentic. We put a promo video on YouTube the next day, and a collector bought the phaser before we could even offer it on eBay. The collector's item fetched several thousand dollars.

In 2010 we had four shows booked and played two before Ron quit - Home 157 (Los Angeles) and The Blank Club (San Jose). Talk about DeJa'Vu? Same old Eclipse. He started talking about bringing in someone he knew to be the lead vocalist and was resistant to getting Zolarized but faked it. Somewhere way in the back of my brain that little voice was saying *but Ronnie's not a Zolarian*. I'm not sure where the tipping point was but maybe it was shortly after a rehearsal where I suggested he play the tom toms like Eon did in Retro Rockets. We played three of the remaining of shows with a drum machine; 924 Gilman Street in Berkeley, opening for Jello Biafra and the Guantanamo School of Medicine at Great American Music Hall in San Francisco and opening for Death (legendary punk band from Detroit) at Slim's in San Francisco. We played Pershing Square in Los Angeles with The Tubes, and Don Bolles of Germs fame sat in on drums for us.

Being a touring band wasn't in the cards at that moment, so Raidii and I took a break and moved to Reno, NV after the Death show. We looked forward to Zory's release from prison in 2012 with hopes of reforming Zolar X one last time. I dreamed of having Zory next to me onstage and feeling his powerful presence as we performed songs we'd written almost forty years ago. You can imagine how disappointing it was to learn that he would be on parole for three more years. He couldn't tour. Zory visited several times over the next few years. We recorded music, wrote some new songs, took pictures, filmed a few little things, and began writing this book in 2013. Zory officially retired in 2016.

For me the thought of retirement from music is prehistoric. In 2020 planet Earth shut down under quarantine. As we observed earth from our living room we could see the chaos, violence, and collapse of systems we had known our entire lives. The world was devolving before our eyes. But our creative energies were alive and four single tracks with a dystopian theme were recorded. We designed costumes, built sets, and were creating art even as the world turned upside down.

In 2022 Drew Dempsey from the infamous Sunset Sound Studios in Hollywood and Brian Kehew, musician, engineer, record producer, and author, contacted me and invited us to be guests on the Sunset Sound Roundtable podcast. It was an in-depth 90-minute conversation covering 50 years of Zolar X/Rock 'n' roll history.

Nobody can tell what will happen tomorrow, but we've put words to paper, and the Zolar X legacy is intact. We will live long, and—who knows—maybe even prosper.

Nok voo.

DISCOGRAPHY

Zolar X Pressed Acetate Crystal Studios 1974

Billy McCartney/Aurora Push Ups, Angels on Runway One and Victims of Terrorism, 7" Vinyl 1979

Ygarr Ygarrist/Rock Bottom and the Spys, Rich Girl, No Good, Death Trap, Bottoms Up Records, 7" Vinyl EP 1981

- 7" Spys Vinyl reissued in 2005, Break My Face, Ryan Richardson, 200
- 7" Spys Vinyl reissued in 2013, Jessie Edelman

Zolar X/Timeless, Clear Vinyl , Pyramid Records 1982

Zolar X/Timeless reissue, Alternative Tentacles Records 2004

Zolar X/7" Space Age Love and Energize Me, 500 2006

Zolar X/X Marks the Spot, Alternative Tentacles Records 2007

Zolar X/Zap! You're Zolarized, CD, Zolar X 2007

Zolar X Live at Pershing Square, Los Angeles, DVD, Zolar X 2011

Zolar X/Life Signs from the Stars, CD, , Zolar X 2012

Zolar X/Urban Myths, CD, Zolar X 2012

Zolar X/00X: When Worlds Collide, Zolar X/The Spys 2018

Zolar X/50-Year Edition Digital Album

SINGLE TRACKS--

- ZX Spirit Mistletoe Fever, Zolar X 2017
- Condition Chaos, Zolar X 2021
- Point of View, Zolar X 2021
- Ultra Violent Vector, Zolar X 2021
- Dark World, Zolar X 2021

*To date, there are approximately 500 songs in the Ygarrist catalog of music ranging from genres of Rock, Punk, Sound Track, and New World. To date the Zory Zenith catalog of music is comprised of approximately 50-100 original songs and covers.

Billy Bo Day and the Howlers, Circa 1986
Photographer unknown

CONTINUING MISSION: 1983 - ?

L to R: Jett Starsystems, Ygarr Ygarrist, Eon Flash 2006
Photo credit: Gale Rinehart

L to R: Eon Flash, Ygarr Ygarrist, 2006
Photo credit: Raidii X, pulled from video footage

L to R: Ygarr Ygarrist, Jett Starsystems 2006
Photographer unknown

L to R: Eon Flash, Ygarr Ygarrist, Quasar 2007
Digital art credit: Raidii X

Charlie Patton 2008
Photo credit: Raidii X, pulled from video footage

L to R: Charlie Patton, Ygarr Ygarrist 2008
Photo credit: Raidii X, pulled from video footage

L to R: Moto Bass Unit, Raidii X, Ygarr Ygarrist 2010
Photo credit: Raidii X

Ygarr Ygarrist at Charlie Patton's house 2008
Photo credit: Raidii X, pulled from video footage

CONTINUING MISSION: 1983 - ?

L to R: Raidii X, Zory Zenith, Ygarr Ygarrist 2012
Photo credit: Raidii X

L to R: Ygarr Ygarrist, Zory Zenith, Raidii X 2012
Photo credit: Raidii X

OUT OF THIS WORLD: THE STORY OF ZOLAR X

The Dystopian Singles Series 2021
Photo credit: Raidii X

CONVERSATIONAL ZOLARIAN FOR COSMIC TRAVELERS

OUT OF THIS WORLD: THE STORY OF ZOLAR X

THE LANGUAGE OF ZOLAR X

ZOLAR X began experimenting with and creating Zolarian words in 1973 shortly after experiencing the 'Boomerang Incident' – witnessing a UFO. These bits and pieces that would become the language began making their way into the lyrics of the early ZOLAR X music such as Silver Shapes, Recitation and Spacers and in some of the more recent delarts (songs) such as Message Transmitting and Oveon Triopp.

The Zolarian language is a form of communication that involves words, hand gestures and telepathy. It's fun and is probably easiest to use in a broken style where Zolarian words are used within the native-spoken language. However, it is possible to communicate in full Zolarian and we will cover some of the basics here.

ENGLISH	ZOLARIAN
A	Ix (ick)
Admire or love it	Ameez
And	Oo
Are, is, was	Aakk
Asshole!	Poenvorta!
At	Vy
Can	Vuso
Cool (very)	Wooteeta
Do	Ceva
Drink	Zervo
Drive, transport	Laitu
Everywhere	In-tu-te to
Feel	Waka
Friend(s)	Xemi(z)
For	Daro
From	Darmo
Future	Triopp
Get	Xom (Zome)
Good	Ove´
Goodbye	Avolta
Got	Xomm
Guitar	Guitron
Have	Inta
Here	Nube
House, home	Danu´
In	Zo
It, this, that, they, them	Bök
Later	Avoon
Leave	Relot
Little	Tee-ot
Look	Strata
Meet	Tee-dou
Monster	Eeddoo
New	Xeos
No or stop	Dătt
Of	Okk
Old	Voma
On	Zuk
Past	Nalu´
Pick	Yatta
Planet	Varka
Please	Valmok
Present	Natoo´
Say	Ropa
See	Tok

CONVERSATIONAL ZOLARIAN FOR COSMIC TRAVELERS

THE LANGUAGE OF ZOLAR X

Sex	Dekta	There	Tota
Sexy	Voomin	Tonight	Ta-ooma
Show, gig, event, band	Bangta	Very much	Ou-sa
Sleep	Sovin	Sweetheart	Vudaytay
Song	Delart	Work	Hytoo
Stage	Muta	Yes or okay	Vota
Star	Komata	Zolar X fashion	Zolarize
Talk	Ropo		
Text me	Kamia ve		

NUMBERS

One	Ou	Thirteen	Tri-vo
Two	Tay	Fourteen	Dar-vo
Three	Tri	Fifteen	Vot-vo
Four	Dar	Sixteen	Rel-vo
Five	Vot	Seventeen	Covon-vo
Six	Rel	Eighteen	Drey-vo
Eight	Drey	Nineteen	Vey-vo
Nine	Vey	20	Taeo
Ten	Zay	Meet me at the 7-Eleven.	
Eleven	Ou-lon	Tee-dou ve vy bop Couvon Ou-lon.	
Twelve	Tayz		

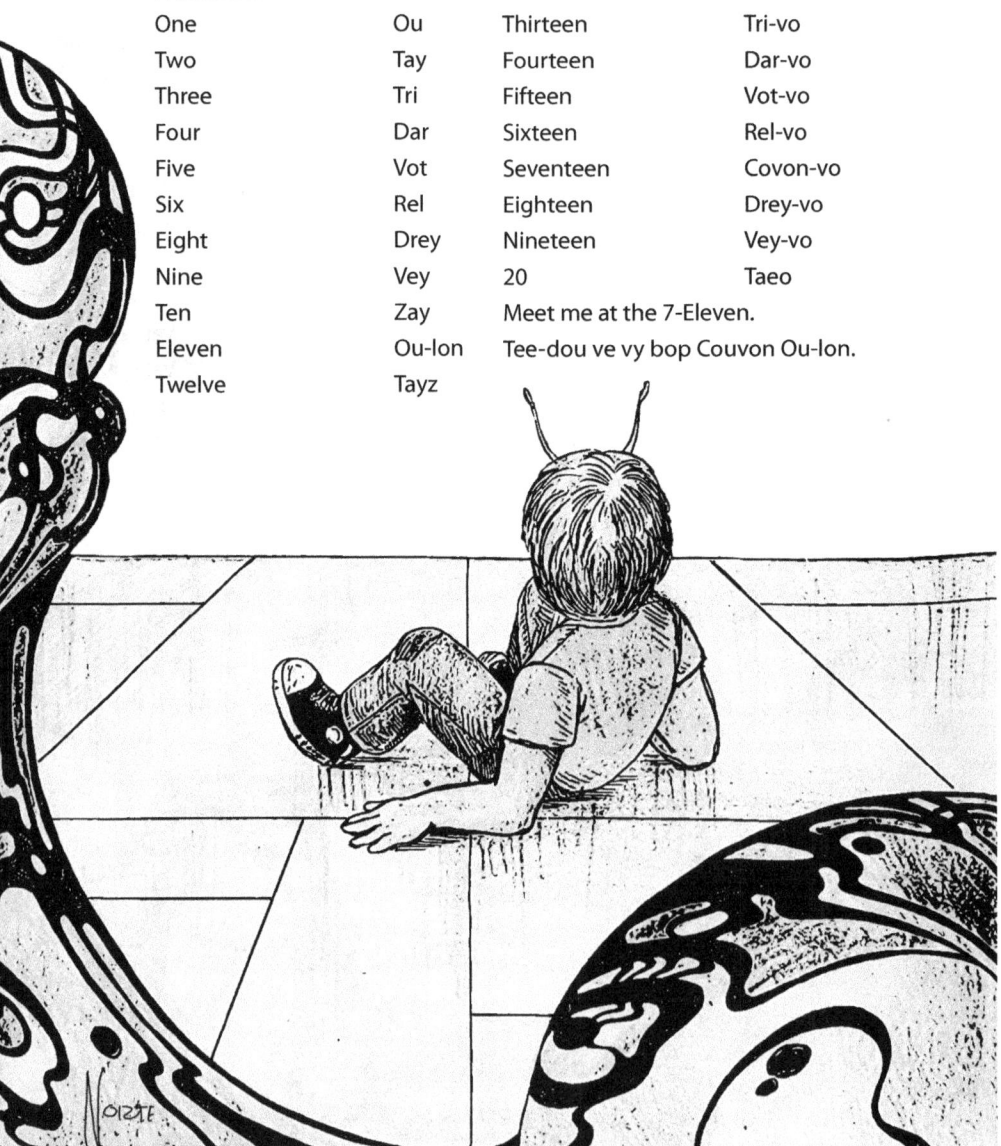

OUT OF THIS WORLD: THE STORY OF ZOLAR X

GREETINGS AND EVERY-DAY TALK

Greetings or hi. *Nop trea.*

Thank you. *Nok voo.*

Goodbye. *Avolta.*

Greetings human(s)! *Nop trea vu-dura(z)!*

How are you? *<Quo aakk voo>*

I am good. And you? *Ve aakk ove! <Oo voo>*

Are you ready? *<Aakk voo doo´ta>*

Good morning. *Ove mera.*

Meet me for coffee? *<Tedo daro zakoo>*

Pick me up at 3. *Yatta ve mok vy tri.*

You bet. *Voo rok.*

It was a lot of fun! *Bök aakkt ke-ôtu ou-sa.*

I love Zolar X. *Ve ameez Zolar X.*

I'm glad you love the band. *Sontoo voo ameez bop bangta.*

How can I get Zolarized? *<Quo vuso ve xom Zolarized>*

I want a space name. *Ve qia ix crellasch zooda.*

We are from the planet Plutonia. *Vel aakk darmo bop varka Plutonia.*

Humans are fun! *Vu-duraz aakk ke-ôtu*

To dislike or no f@* way! *Odätt´ (+ hand gesture)*

I want a drink. *Ve qia ix zervo.*

What is your name? *<Joppo aakk vool zooda>*

<JOPPO HONTOO REMTOR>
(WHAT DO YOU THINK CAPTAIN?)

CONVERSATIONAL ZOLARIAN FOR COSMIC TRAVELERS

My name is Ygarr. What's yours? *Ve zooda aakk Ygarr. <Joppo aakk vool>*

I am Raidii X. *Ve aakk Raidii X.*

Text me! *Kamia ve!*

Okay, I'll text you. *Vota, ve kamiat voo.*

Romance is here. *Zova aakk nube.*

Good night. *Ove ooma.*

Look at the stars. *Strata vy bop komataz.*

Message transmitting *Qia-en-lon*

I know what you mean. I agree. *Odedaku*

Meet me at the 7-Eleven. *Tedo vy bop Covon-Oulon.*

It's a good day. *Bok ix ove darou´.*

What do you think? *<Joppo voo hontoo>*

No worries. *Datt oogla!*

I am working on it. *Ve aakk hytoo zuk bok.*

We are from the future. *Vel aakk darmo triopp.*

Sweet dreams. *Sontoo oomiaz.*

You are a great friend! *Voo aakk ix yavolla xemi.*

Thank you, same to you. *Nok voo, zemos tay voo.*

(THE CAPTAIN IS MEDITATING.)

www.ingramcontent.com/pod-product-compliance
Lightning Source LLC
Chambersburg PA
CBHW080329170426
43194CB00014B/2503